KNIGHT'S MICROSOFT® SQL SERVER® 2012 INTEGRATION SERVICES 24-HOUR TRAINER

Continues

KNIGHT'S

Microsoft® SQL Server® 2012
Integration Services

24-HOUR TRAINER

Brian Knight
Devin Knight
Mike Davis
Wayne Snyder

WILEY

John Wiley & Sons, Inc.

Knight's Microsoft® SQL Server® 2012 Integration 24-Hour Trainer

Published by John Wiley & Sons, Inc.
10475 Crosspoint Boulevard
Indianapolis, IN 46256
www.wiley.com

Copyright © 2013 by John Wiley & Sons, Inc., Indianapolis, Indiana

Published simultaneously in Canada

ISBN: 978-1-118-47958-2
ISBN: 978-1-118-47960-5 (ebk)
ISBN: 978-1-118-53914-9 (ebk)
ISBN: 978-1-118-53915-6 (ebk)

Manufactured in the United States of America

10 9 8 7 6 5 4 3 2 1

For general information on our other products and services please contact our Customer Care Department within the United States at (877) 762-2974, outside the United States at (317) 572-3993 or fax (317) 572-4002.

Wiley publishes in a variety of print and electronic formats and by print-on-demand. Some material included with standard print versions of this book may not be included in e-books or in print-on-demand. If this book refers to media such as a CD or DVD that is not included in the version you purchased, you may download this material at http://booksupport.wiley.com. For more information about Wiley products, visit www.wiley.com.

Library of Congress Control Number: 2012948658

CREDITS

ABOUT THE AUTHORS

 BRIAN KNIGHT, SQL Server MVP, MCITP, is the owner and founder of Pragmatic Works. He is the cofounder of BIDN.com, SQLServerCentral.com, and SQLShare.com. He runs the local SQL Server users group in Jacksonville (JSSUG). He is a contributing columnist at several technical magazines. He is the author of 15 SQL Server books. Brian has spoken at conferences like PASS, SQL Connections and TechEd, SQL Saturdays, Code Camps, and many pyramid scheme motivational sessions. His blog can be found at http://www.bidn.com, which covers many BI topics and miniature donkey training tips. Brian lives in Jacksonville, Florida, where he enjoys his kids and running marathons.

 DEVIN KNIGHT is a Senior BI consultant at Pragmatic Works Consulting. Previously, he has tech edited the book Professional Microsoft SQL Server 2008 Integration Services and was an author on the books *Knight's 24-Hour Trainer: Microsoft SQL Server 2008 Integration Services, Knight's Microsoft Business Intelligence 24-Hour Trainer,* and *SharePoint 2010 Business Intelligence 24-Hour Trainer.* Devin has spoken at past conferences like PASS, SQL Saturdays, and Code Camps and is a contributing member to the PASS Business Intelligence Virtual Chapter. Making his home in Jacksonville, Florida, Devin is the Vice President of the local users' group (JSSUG).

 MIKE DAVIS, MCTS, MCITP, is the Managing Project Lead at Pragmatic Works. This book is his fourth on the subject of business intelligence and specifically Integration Services. He has worked with SQL Server for almost a decade and has led many successful business intelligence projects with his clients. Mike is an experienced speaker and has presented at many events such as several SQL Server User Groups, Code Camps, SQL Saturday events, and the PASS Summit. Mike is an active member at his local user group (JSSUG) in Jacksonville, Florida. In his spare time, he likes to play darts and guitar. You can also find him on twitter @MikeDavisSQL, and his blog on MikeDavisSQL.com and BIDN.com.

 WAYNE SNYDER has worked as a DBA for about 20 years, learning about databases and the data which they contain. For the past 8 years, he has been entirely focused on business intelligence, using the Microsoft BI Stack for Mariner (www.mariner-usa.com). His role at Mariner is Distinguished Architect, and in that role he spends a lot of time with Integration Services, Analysis Services, Reporting Services, and PowerPivot. There are hundreds of packages in production right now that he had a hand in making. He is a SQL Server MVP and a former President of PASS (Professional Association for SQL Server). When he is not working or writing, he plays the keyboard in a regional cover band, Soundbarrier (www.soundbarrierband.com).

ABOUT THE TECHNICAL EDITORS

CHRIS ALBREKTSON is an experienced BI Consultant and Trainer currently at Pragmatic Works in Jacksonville, Florida. During his tenure at Pragmatic Works, he has designed and developed business intelligence solutions using the Microsoft Business Intelligence stack for a wide variety of customers across multiple industries. Previously, he has been a technical editor for the book *Professional Microsoft SQL Server 2012 Reporting Services*. Chris is an experienced speaker and has presented at many SQL Saturdays and Code Camps events across the United States. He's also an active member of the Jacksonville SQL Server User Group (JSSUG), and is a regular blogger on BIDN.com.

CHRIS PRICE is a Senior Business Intelligence Consultant with Pragmatic Works based out of Lakeland, Florida. He has a B.S. degree in Management Information Systems and a Master's of Business Administration, both from the University of South Florida. He began his career 12 years ago as a developer and has extensive experience across a wide range of Microsoft technologies. His current interests include ETL and Data Integration, Data Quality and Master Data Management, Analysis Services, SharePoint, and Big Data. Chris has spoken at 24 Hours of PASS and regularly presents at SQL Saturdays, Code Camps, and other community events. You can follow Chris on his blog at `http://bidn.com/blogs/cprice1979/` or on Twitter at @BluewaterSQL.

ANTHONY COLEMAN is an experienced BI Consultant and Trainer for Pragmatic Works. Currently he designs, develops, and implements business intelligence solutions using the Microsoft BI stack. Anthony blogs at BIDN and contributes to the local SQL Server Users Group (JSSUG) in Jacksonville, Florida. In his free time, Anthony enjoys playing chess and poker.

ACKNOWLEDGMENTS

THANKS TO EVERYONE who made this book possible. As always, I owe a huge debt to my wife Jenn for putting up with my late nights and my children, Colton, Liam, Camille, and John for being so patience with their tired dad who has always overextended. Thanks to Kevin Kent and my tech editors Chris Albrektson, Chris Price, and Anthony Coleman for keeping me in my place. Thanks also to the makers of Guinness for providing my special juice that helped me power through the book. Thanks for all the user group leaders out there who work so hard to help others become proficient in technology. You make a huge difference! Finally, thanks to my professional yodeling coach, Helga Felenstein, for getting me ready for my debut this fall.

—BRIAN KNIGHT

I MUST GIVE THANKS TO GOD, who without in my life, I would not have such blessings. Thanks to my wife Erin who has had amazing patience during the late nights of writing, editing, and video recording. To our three children, Collin, Justin, and Lana, who have sacrificed time away from daddy. Thanks to the group of writers Brian, Mike, and Wayne, who all worked very hard while missing time with their families, too. Finally, I would like to thank my jousting mentor, Shane Adams, for showing me the way to become a real knight. Competitive jousting has always been a dream of mine, and I look forward to competing at the Liverpool Renaissance Fair.

—DEVIN KNIGHT

THANKS TO MY PRAGMATIC WORKS TEAM for their support in this book. Thank you to Brian Knight for giving me the opportunity of a lifetime. Thank you to Adam Jorgensen for growing me. Thank you to the Wiley team, especially Kevin and Bob. Thank you to the technical editors for their help in making this book great. Thank you to my mother for raising me to be the man I am today. Thank you to my wife and kids for being by my side. And finally, thank you to the Flying Spaghetti Monster for his noodlely blessings, ramen.

—MIKE DAVIS

THIS BOOK IS THE CULMINATION OF THE WORK of many people, smart people, all who have worked very hard. To Kevin Kent, the senior project editor — you have been great to work with. Kim Cofer, the copy editor, who has taken my sloppy, southern version of English and made my chapters sound intelligent. And to Chris Albrektson, Chris Price, and Anthony Coleman, whose eagle eyes have enabled the work to actually be intelligent and technically accurate. Thank you all so much. Working with you all on this book has been a great pleasure!

To the reader — Do not be afraid of SSIS. You can learn this and be successful. This book will help you get started. Do not simply download the completed packages and look through them. Go through each Try It yourself. Do not let your brain go into auto-pilot mode. Engage your brain and think about each step. As you develop your skills, you will become very comfortable with the tool. You will be able to solve difficult ETL problems using SSIS. With the combination of Integration Services and your hard work, great things can happen for you, your company, and your customers.

—WAYNE SNYDER

CONTENTS

PREFACE

IF YOU'VE PICKED UP THIS BOOK, *Knight's Microsoft SQL Server 2012 Integration Services 24-Hour Trainer*, you've decided to learn one of SQL Server's most exciting applications, SQL Server Integration Services (SSIS). SSIS is a platform to move data from nearly any data source to nearly any destination and helps you by orchestrating a workflow to organize and control the execution of all these events. Most who dive into SSIS use it weekly, if not daily, to move data between partners, departments, or customers. It's also a highly in-demand skill—even in the worst of economic environments, jobs are still posted for SSIS developers. This is because no matter what happens in an economy, people still must move and transform data.

This book, then, is your chance to start delving into this powerful and marketable application. And what's more, this is not just a book you're holding right now. It's a video learning tool, as well. We became passionate about video training a number of years ago when we realized that in our own learning we required exposure to multiple teaching techniques to truly understand a topic— a fact that is especially true with tutorial books like this one. So, you'll find hours of videos on the DVD in this book to help you learn SSIS better than reading about the topic alone could and to help demonstrate the various tutorials in the book.

WHO THIS BOOK IS FOR

This is a beginner book and assumes only that you know SQL Server 2012 to run queries against the database engine (T-SQL skills are assumed and used throughout this book). Because this book is structured for a beginner, providing many tutorials and teaching you only what you'll likely use at work, it is not a reference book filled with a description of every property in a given task. It instead focuses on only the essential components for you to complete your project at work or school.

WHAT THIS BOOK COVERS

This book covers SQL Server 2012 and assumes no knowledge of previous versions of SQL Server. The differences between SQL Server 2005/2008 and SQL Server 2012 mostly exist around the administration of SSIS, and there are a few new components. By the time you've completed this book, you'll know how to load and synchronize database systems using SSIS by using some of the new SQL Server 2012 features. You'll also know how to load data warehouses, which is a very hot and specialized skill. Even in warehousing, you'll find features in the new SQL Server 2012 release that you'll wonder how you lived without, like Change Data Capture (CDC)!

HOW THIS BOOK IS STRUCTURED

Our main principle in this book is to teach you only what we think you need to perform your job task. Because of that, it's not a comprehensive reference book. You won't find a description of every feature of SSIS in here. Instead the book blends small amounts of description, a tutorial, and videos to enhance your experience. Each lesson walks you through how to use components of SSIS and contains a tutorial. In this tutorial, called "Try It," you can choose to read the requirements to complete the lesson, the hints of how to go about it, and begin coding, or you can read the step-by-step instructions if you learn better that way. Either way if you get stuck or want to see how one of us does the solution, watch the video on the DVD to receive further instruction.

WHAT THIS BOOK COVERS

This book contains 62 lessons, which are broken into 11 sections. The lessons are usually only a few pages long and focus on the smallest unit of work in SSIS that we could work on. Each section has a large theme around a given section in SSIS:

➤ **Section 1: Installation and Getting Started**—This section covers why you would use SSIS and the basic installation of SSIS and the sample databases that you'll use throughout this book. If you already have SSIS and the sample databases installed, you can review this section quickly.

➤ **Section 2: Control Flow**—This section explains how to use tasks in the Control Flow of SSIS.

➤ **Section 3: Data Flow**—Seventy-five percent of your time as an SSIS developer is spent in the Data Flow tab. This section focuses on the configuration of the core sources, transforms, and destinations.

➤ **Section 4: Making Packages Dynamic**—Now that you've created your first package, you must make it dynamic. This section covers how you can use variables, parameters, and expressions to make your package change at run time.

➤ **Section 5: Common ETL Scenarios**—In an effort to show you some real-world business scenarios, this section covers some of the common ETL scenarios like performing incremental loads and using SQL Server's newest component, Data Quality Services (DQS), with SSIS.

➤ **Section 6: Containers**—This section covers one of the key Control Flow items, containers, which control how SSIS does looping and grouping.

➤ **Section 7: Configuring Packages**—Here you learn how to configure your packages externally through configuration files, tables, and other ways.

➤ **Section 8: Troubleshooting SSIS**—No sooner do you have an SSIS package developed than you start experiencing problems. This section shows you how to troubleshoot these problems.

➤ **Section 9: Administering SSIS**—Now that your package is developed, here you learn how to deploy and configure the service.

➤ **Section 10: Loading a Warehouse**—A little more on the advanced side, this section teaches you how to load a data warehouse using SSIS.

➤ **Section 11: Wrap Up and Review**—This section was one of our favorites to write. It contains a lesson to bring everything together and also Appendices A and B, which contain crib notes for quick reference. As trainers and consultants, we are constantly asked to leave behind a quick page of crib notes of common code. In these appendices, you find guides on when to use which SSIS components and useful solutions and code snippets that address common situations you might face.

INSTRUCTIONAL VIDEOS ON DVD

As mentioned earlier in this preface, because we believe strongly in the value of video training, this book has an accompanying DVD containing hours of instructional video. At the end of each lesson in the book, you will find a reference to an instructional video on the DVD that accompanies that lesson. In that video, one of us will walk you through the content and examples contained in that lesson. So, if seeing something done and hearing it explained helps you understand a subject better than just reading about it does, this book and DVD combination is just the thing for you to get started with SSIS. You can also find the instructional videos available for viewing online at `www.wrox.com/go/ssis2012video`.

CONVENTIONS

To help you get the most from the text and keep track of what's happening, we've used a number of conventions throughout the book.

> **WARNING** *Boxes like this one hold important, not-to-be forgotten information that is directly relevant to the surrounding text.*

> **NOTE** *Notes, tips, hints, tricks, and asides to the current discussion are offset and placed in italics like this.*

> *References like this one point you to the DVD to watch the instructional video that accompanies a given lesson.*

As for styles in the text:

➤ We *highlight* new terms and important words when we introduce them.

➤ We show URLs and code within the text like so: `persistence.properties`.

➤ We present code in the following way:

```
We use a monofont type for code examples.
```

SUPPORTING PACKAGES AND CODE

As you work through the lessons in this book, you may choose either to type in all the code and create all the packages manually or to use the supporting packages and code files that accompany the book. All the packages, code, and other support files used in this book are available for download at `www.wrox.com`. Once at the site, simply locate the book's title (either by using the Search box or by using one of the title lists) and click the Download Code link on the book's detail page to obtain all the source code for the book.

> **NOTE** *Because many books have similar titles, you may find it easiest to search by ISBN; this book's ISBN is 978-1-118-47958-2.*

Once you download the code, just decompress it with your favorite compression tool. Alternatively, you can go to the main Wrox code download page at `www.wrox.com/dynamic/books/download.aspx` to see the code available for this book and all other Wrox books.

You will need two sample databases for the tutorial, both provided by Microsoft for use with SQL Server: AdventureWorks2012 and AdventureWorksDW2012. The two sample databases are not installed by default with SQL Server 2012. You can download versions of the sample databases used for this book at the Wrox website at `www.wrox.com/go/SQLSever2012DataSets`. Lesson 3 also covers how to install and configure the databases.

ERRATA

We make every effort to ensure that there are no errors in the text or in the code. However, no one is perfect, and mistakes do occur. If you find an error in one of our books, like a spelling mistake or faulty piece of code, we would be very grateful for your feedback. By sending in errata, you may save another reader hours of frustration and at the same time you will be helping us provide even higher quality information.

To find the errata page for this book, go to `www.wrox.com` and locate the title using the Search box or one of the title lists. Then, on the Book Search Results page, click the Errata link. On this page you can view all errata that has been submitted for this book and posted by Wrox editors.

> **NOTE** *A complete book list including links to errata is also available at* www.wrox.com/misc-pages/booklist.shtml.

If you don't spot "your" error on the Errata page, click the Errata Form link and complete the form to send us the error you have found. We'll check the information and, if appropriate, post a message to the book's errata page and fix the problem in subsequent editions of the book.

P2P.WROX.COM

For author and peer discussion, join the P2P forums at p2p.wrox.com. The forums are a Web-based system for you to post messages relating to Wrox books and related technologies and interact with other readers and technology users. The forums offer a subscription feature to e-mail you topics of interest of your choosing when new posts are made to the forums. Wrox authors, editors, other industry experts, and your fellow readers are present on these forums.

At http://p2p.wrox.com you will find a number of different forums that will help you not only as you read this book, but also as you develop your own applications. To join the forums, just follow these steps:

1. Go to p2p.wrox.com and click the Register link.

2. Read the terms of use and click Agree.

3. Complete the required information to join as well as any optional information you wish to provide and click Submit.

4. You will receive an e-mail with information describing how to verify your account and complete the joining process.

> **NOTE** *You can read messages in the forums without joining P2P but in order to post your own messages, you must join.*

Once you join, you can post new messages and respond to messages other users post. You can read messages at any time on the Web. If you would like to have new messages from a particular forum e-mailed to you, click the Subscribe to this Forum icon by the forum name in the forum listing.

For more information about how to use the Wrox P2P, be sure to read the P2P FAQs for answers to questions about how the forum software works as well as many common questions specific to P2P and Wrox books. To read the FAQs, click the FAQ link on any P2P page.

Welcome to SSIS

SQL Server Integration Services (SSIS) is one of the most powerful applications in your arsenal for moving data in and out of various databases and files. Like the rest of the business intelligence (BI) suite that comes with SQL Server, SSIS is already included in your SQL Server license when you pay for the Standard, BI, or Enterprise editions of SQL Server. Even though SSIS is included in SQL Server, you don't even need to have SQL Server installed to make it function. Because of that, even if your environment is not using a lot of SQL Server, you can still use SSIS as a platform for data movement.

Though ultimately this book is more interactive in nature, this introduction first walks you through a high-level tour of SSIS so you have a life preserver on prior to jumping in the pool. Each topic touched on in this introduction is covered in much more depth throughout the book in lesson form and in the supporting videos on the DVD.

IMPORT AND EXPORT WIZARD

If you need to move data quickly from almost any data source to a destination, you can use the SSIS Import and Export Wizard (shown in Figure 1). The wizard is a quick way to move the data and perform very light transformations of data, such as casting of the data into new data types. You can quickly check any table you want to transfer, as well as write a query against the data to retrieve only a selective amount of data.

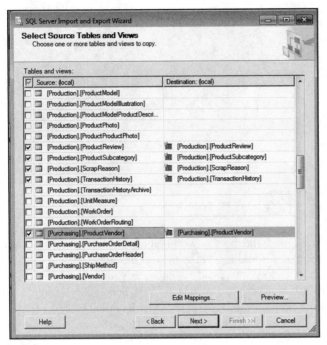

FIGURE 1

SQL SERVER DATA TOOLS

SQL Server Data Tools (SSDT) is the central tool that you'll spend most of your time in as an SSIS developer (really as a SQL Server developer). Like the rest of SQL Server, the tool's foundation is the Visual Studio 2010 interface (shown in Figure 2), and SSDT is installed when you install SQL Server 2012. The nicest thing about the tool is that it's not bound to any particular SQL Server. In other words, you won't have to connect to a SQL Server to design an SSIS package. You can design the package disconnected from your SQL Server environment and then deploy it to your target SQL Server or the filesystem on which you'd like it to run.

ARCHITECTURE

Although SSIS has been a major extraction, transformation, and loading (ETL) platform for several releases of SQL Server, SQL Server 2012 has simplified the platform for developers and administrators. Because of its scalability and lower cost, SSIS is also a major player in the ETL market. What's especially nice about SSIS is its price tag, which is free with the purchase of SQL Server. Other ETL tools can cost hundreds of thousands of dollars based on how you scale the software.

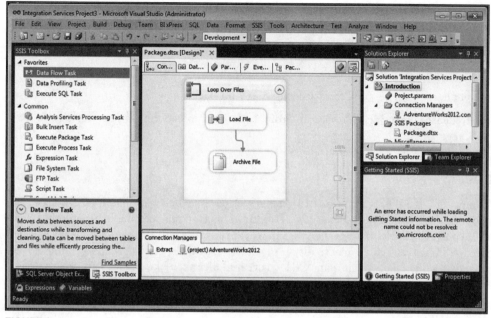

FIGURE 2

The SSIS architecture consists of five main components:

➤ The SSIS service (there for legacy SSIS packages)

➤ The SSIS runtime engine and the runtime executables

➤ The SSIS catalog

➤ The SSIS Data Flow engine and the Data Flow components

➤ The SSIS clients

Let's boil this down to the essentials that you need to know to do your job. The SSIS service (for packages running in legacy mode) and now the SSIS catalog handle the operational aspects of SSIS. The service is a Windows service that is installed when you install the SSIS component of SQL Server 2012, and it tracks the execution of packages (a collection of work items) and helps with the storage of the packages. You don't need the SSIS service to run SSIS packages, but if the service is stopped, all the SSIS packages that are currently running will, in turn, stop by default.

This service is mainly used for packages stored in the older style of storing packages, the package deployment model. The new model, the project deployment model, uses something called the *package catalog*. The catalog is the newer way of storing packages that gives you many new options, like running packages with T-SQL. The catalog also stores basic operational information about your package.

The SSIS runtime engine and its complimentary programs actually run your SSIS packages. The engine saves the layout of your packages and manages the logging, debugging, configuration, connections, and transactions. Additionally, it manages handling your events to send you e-mails or log in to a database when an event is raised in your package. The runtime executables provide the following functionality to a package; these are discussed in more detail throughout this book:

➤ **Containers**—Provide structure and scope to your package

➤ **Tasks**—Provide the functionality to your package

➤ **Event handlers**—Respond to raised events in your package

➤ **Precedence constraints**—Provide an ordinal relationship between various items in your package

Packages

A core component of SSIS is the notion of a *package*. A package best parallels an executable program in Windows. Essentially, a package is a collection of tasks that execute in an orderly fashion. Precedence constraints help manage the order in which the tasks will execute. A package can be saved onto a SQL Server, which in actuality is saved in the msdb or package catalog database. It can also be saved as a .dtsx file, which is an XML structured file much like .rdl files are to Reporting Services. The end result of the package looks like what's displayed in Figure 2, which was shown earlier.

Tasks

A *task* can best be described as an individual unit of work. Tasks provide functionality to your package, much like a method does in a programming language. A task can move a file, load a file into a database, send an e-mail, or write a set of .NET code for you, to name just a few of the things it can do. A small subset of the common tasks available to you comprises the following:

➤ **Bulk Insert Task**—Loads data into a table by using the BULK INSERT SQL command.

➤ **Data Flow Task**—This is the most important task that loads and transforms data into an OLE DB Destination.

➤ **Execute Package Task**—Enables you to execute a package from within a package, making your SSIS packages modular.

➤ **Execute Process Task**—Executes a program external to your package, like one to split your extract file into many files before processing the individual files.

➤ **Execute SQL Task**—Executes a SQL statement or stored procedure.

➤ **File System Task**—This task can handle directory operations like creating, renaming, or deleting a directory. It can also manage file operations like moving, copying, or deleting files.

➤ **FTP Task**—Sends or receives files from an FTP site.

➤ **Script Task**—Runs a set of VB.NET or C# coding inside a Visual Studio environment.

➤ **Send Mail Task**—Sends a mail message through SMTP.

➤ **Analysis Services Processing Task**—This task processes a SQL Server Analysis Services cube, dimension, or mining model.

➤ **Web Service Task**—Executes a method on a web service.

➤ **WMI Data Reader Task**—This task can run WQL queries against the Windows Management Instrumentation (WMI). This enables you to read the event log, get a list of applications that are installed, or determine hardware that is installed, to name a few examples.

➤ **WMI Event Watcher Task**—This task empowers SSIS to wait for and respond to certain WMI events that occur in the operating system.

➤ **XML Task**—Parses or processes an XML file. It can merge, split, or reformat an XML file.

These are only a few of the many tasks you have available to you. You can also write your own task or download a task from the web that does something else. Writing such a task only requires that you learn the SSIS object model and know VB.NET or C#. You can also use the Script Task to do things that the native tasks can't do.

Data Flow Elements

Once you create a Data Flow Task, the Data Flow tab in SSDT is available to you for design. Just as the Control Flow tab handles the main workflow of the package, the Data Flow tab handles the transformation of data. Every package has a single Control Flow, but can have many Data Flows. Almost anything that manipulates data falls into the Data Flow category. You can see an example of a Data Flow in Figure 3, where data is pulled from an OLE DB Source and transformed before being written to a Flat File Destination. As data moves through each step of the Data Flow, the data changes based on what the transform does. For example, in Figure 3, a new column is derived using the Derived Column Transform and that new column is then available to subsequent transformations or to the destination.

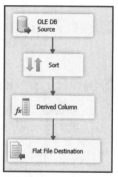

FIGURE 3

You can add multiple Data Flow Tasks onto the Control Flow tab. You'll notice that after you click on each one, it jumps to the Data Flow tab with the Data Flow Task name you selected in the drop-down box right under the tab. You can toggle between Data Flow Tasks easily by selecting the next Data Flow Task from that drop-down box.

Sources

A *source* is where you specify the location of your source data to pull from in the data flow. Sources will generally point to a connection manager in SSIS. By pointing them to the connection manager, you can reuse connections throughout your package because you need only change the connection in one place. Here are some of the common sources you'll be using in SSIS:

➤ **OLE DB Source**—Connects to nearly any OLE DB Data Source like SQL Server, Access, Oracle, or DB2, to name just a few.

➤ **Excel Source**—Source that specializes in receiving data from Excel spreadsheets. This source also makes it easy to run SQL queries against your Excel spreadsheet to narrow the scope of the data that you want to pass through the flow.

➤ **Flat File Source**—Connects to a delimited or fixed-width file.

➤ **XML Source**—Can retrieve data from an XML document.

➤ **ODBC Source**—The ODBC Source enables you to connect to common data sources that don't use OLE DB.

Destinations

Inside the Data Flow, *destinations* accept the data from the data sources and from the transformations. The flexible architecture can send the data to nearly any OLE DB–compliant data source or to a flat file. Like sources, destinations are managed through the connection manager. Some of the more common destinations in SSIS and available to you are as follows:

➤ **Excel Destination**—Outputs data from the Data Flow to an Excel spreadsheet that must already exist.

➤ **Flat File Destination**—Enables you to write data to a comma-delimited or fixed-width file.

➤ **OLE DB Destination**—Outputs data to an OLE DB data connection like SQL Server, Oracle, or Access.

➤ **SQL Server Destination**—The destination that you use to write data to SQL Server most efficiently. To use this, you must run the package from the destination.

Transformations

Transformations (or transforms) are a key component to the Data Flow that change the data to a format that you'd like. For example, you may want your data to be sorted and aggregated. Two transformations can accomplish this task for you. The nicest thing about transformations in SSIS is they are all done in-memory, and because of this they are extremely efficient. Memory handles data manipulation much faster than disk IO does, and you'll find if disk paging occurs, your package that ran in 20 minutes will suddenly take hours. Here are some of the more common transforms you'll use on a regular basis:

➤ **Aggregate**—Aggregates data from a transform or source similar to a GROUP BY statement in T-SQL.

➤ **Conditional Split**—Splits the data based on certain conditions being met. For example, if the State column is equal to Florida, send the data down a different path. This transform is similar to a CASE statement in T-SQL.

➤ **Data Conversion**—Converts a column's data type to another data type. This transform is similar to a CAST statement in T-SQL.

➤ **Derived Column**—Performs an in-line update to the data or creates a new column from a formula. For example, you can use this to calculate a Profit column based on a Cost and SellPrice set of columns.

➤ **Fuzzy Grouping**—Performs data cleansing by finding rows that are likely duplicates.

➤ **Fuzzy Lookup**—Matches and standardizes data based on fuzzy logic. For example, this can transform the name Jon to John.

➤ **Lookup**—Performs a lookup on data to be used later in a transformation. For example, you can use this transformation to look up a city based on the ZIP code.

➤ **Multicast**—Sends a copy of the data to an additional path in the workflow and can be used to parallelize data. For example, you may want to send the same set of records to two tables.

➤ **OLE DB Command**—Executes an OLE DB command for each row in the Data Flow. Can be used to run an UPDATE or DELETE statement inside the Data Flow.

➤ **Row Count**—Stores the row count from the Data Flow into a variable for later use by, perhaps, an auditing solution.

➤ **Script Component**—Uses a script to transform the data. For example, you can use this to apply specialized business logic to your Data Flow.

➤ **Slowly Changing Dimension**—Coordinates the conditional insert or update of data in a slowly changing dimension during a data warehouse load.

➤ **Sort**—Sorts the data in the Data Flow by a given column and removes exact duplicates.

➤ **Union All**—Merges multiple data sets into a single data set.

➤ **Unpivot**—Unpivots the data from a non-normalized format to a relational format.

SSIS CAPABILITIES AVAILABLE IN EDITIONS OF SQL SERVER 2012

The features in SSIS and SQL Server that are available to you vary widely based on what edition of SQL Server you're using. As you can imagine, the higher-end edition of SQL Server you purchase, the more features are available. As for SSIS, you'll have to use at least the Standard Edition to receive the bulk of the SSIS features. In the Express and Workgroup Editions, only the Import and Export Wizard is available to you. You'll have to upgrade to the Enterprise or Developer Editions to see some features in SSIS. The advanced transformations available only with the Enterprise Edition are as follows:

➤ Data Mining Query Transformation

➤ Fuzzy Lookup and Fuzzy Grouping Transformations

➤ Term Extraction and Term Lookup Transformations

➤ Data Mining Model Training Destination

➤ Dimension Processing Destination

➤ Partition Processing Destination

➤ Change Data Capture components

➤ Higher speed data connectivity components such as connectivity to SAP or Oracle

SUMMARY

This introduction exposed you to the SQL Server Integration Services (SSIS) architecture and some of the different elements you'll be dealing with in SSIS. Tasks are individual units of work that are chained together with precedence constraints. Packages are executable programs in SSIS that are a collection of tasks. Finally, transformations are the Data Flow items that change the data to the form you request, such as sorting the data the way you want. Now that the overview is out of the way, it's time to start the first section and your first set of lessons, and time for you to get your hands on SSIS.

As mentioned earlier, the print book comes with an accompanying DVD containing hours of instructional supporting video. At the end of each lesson in the book, you will find a box like this one pointing you to a video on the DVD that accompanies that lesson. In that video, one of us will walk you through the content and examples contained in that lesson. So, if seeing something done and hearing it explained helps you understand a subject better than just reading about it does, this text and video combination provides exactly what you need. There's even an Introduction to SSIS video that you can watch to get started. Simply select the Intro to SSIS lesson on the DVD. You can also view the instructional videos online at `www.wrox.com/go/ssis2012video`*.*

SECTION 1
Installation and Getting Started

▶ **LESSON 1:** Moving Data with the Import and Export Wizard

▶ **LESSON 2:** Installing SQL Server Integration Services

▶ **LESSON 3:** Installing the Sample Databases

▶ **LESSON 4:** Creating a Solution and Project

▶ **LESSON 5:** Exploring SQL Server Data Tools

▶ **LESSON 6:** Creating Your First Package

▶ **LESSON 7:** Upgrading Packages to SQL Server 2012

▶ **LESSON 8:** Upgrading to the Project Deployment Model

Moving Data with the Import and Export Wizard

The Import and Export Wizard is the easiest method to move data from sources like Excel, Oracle, DB2, SQL Server, and text files to nearly any destination. This wizard uses SSIS as a framework and can optionally save a package as its output prior to executing. The package it produces will not be the most elegant, but it can take a lot of the grunt work out of package development and provide the building blocks that are necessary for you to build the remainder of the package. Oftentimes as an SSIS developer, you'll want to relegate the grunt work and heavy lifting to the wizard and do the more complex coding yourself. The wizard does no transformations or cleansing, but instead only moves data from point A to point B.

As with most SQL Server wizards, you have numerous ways to open the tool:

➤ To open the Import and Export Wizard, right-click the database you want to import data from or export data to SQL Server Management Studio and select Tasks ➪ Import Data (or Export Data based on what task you're performing).

➤ You can also open the wizard by right-clicking SSIS Packages in SQL Server Data Tools (SSDT) and selecting SSIS Import and Export Wizard.

➤ Another common way to open it is from the Start menu under SQL Server 2012 by choosing Import and Export Data.

➤ The last way to open the wizard is by typing **dtswizard.exe** at the command line or Run prompt.

Regardless of whether you need to import or export the data, the first few screens in the wizard look very similar.

Once the wizard comes up, you see the typical Microsoft wizard welcome screen. Click Next to begin specifying the source connection. If you opened the wizard from Management Studio by selecting Export Data, this screen is prepopulated. In this screen, you specify where your data is coming from in the Source drop-down box. Once you select the source, the rest of the options on the dialog box may vary based on the type of connection. The default source is SQL Native Client, and it looks like Figure 1-1. You have OLE DB Sources like SQL Server, Oracle, and Access available out of the box. You can also use text files and Excel files. After selecting the source, you have to fill in the provider-specific information.

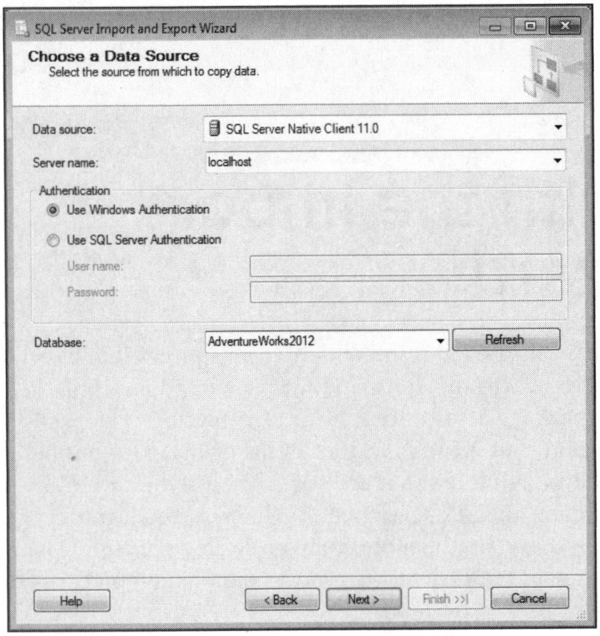

FIGURE 1-1

For SQL Server, you must enter the server name (localhost means go to your local machine's SQL Server instance, if applicable) and the username and password you want to use. If you're going to connect with your Windows account, simply select Use Windows Authentication. Windows Authentication will pass your Windows local or domain credentials into the data source. Lastly, choose a database that you'd like to connect to. For most of the examples in this book, you use the AdventureWorks2012 database. You can see Lesson 3 of this book for more information on installing this sample database.

> **NOTE** *You can find the sample databases used for this book at the Wrox website at* www.wrox.com/go/SQLSever2012DataSets.

> **NOTE** *Additional sources such as Sybase and DB2 can also become available if you install the vendors' OLE DB or ODBC providers. You can download additional providers for free if you're using Enterprise Edition by going to the SQL Server 2012 Feature Pack on the Microsoft website. You also have ODBC and ADO.NET providers available to you in SQL Server 2012.*

After you click Next, you are taken to the next screen in the wizard, where you specify the destination for your data. The properties for this screen are exactly identical to those for the previous screen with the exception of the database. On the next screen, if you select the Copy data from one or more tables or views option, you can simply check the tables you want. If you select the Write a query to specify the data to transfer option, you can write an ad hoc query (after clicking Next) addressing where to select the data from or what stored procedure to use to retrieve your data.

The next screen enables you to select the table or tables you want to copy over and which table names you want them to be transferred to. If you want, you can click the Edit button to go to the Column Mappings dialog box (shown in Figure 1-2) for each table. Here you can change the mapping between each source and destination column. For example, if you want the DepartmentID column to go to the DepartmentID2 column on the destination, simply select the Destination drop-down box for the DepartmentID column and point it to the new column, or choose <ignore > to ignore the column altogether. By checking the Enabled identity insert box, you allow the wizard to insert into a column that has an identity (or autonumber) value assigned. If the data types don't match between the source and destination columns, the wizard will add the necessary components to convert the data to a proper data type if possible.

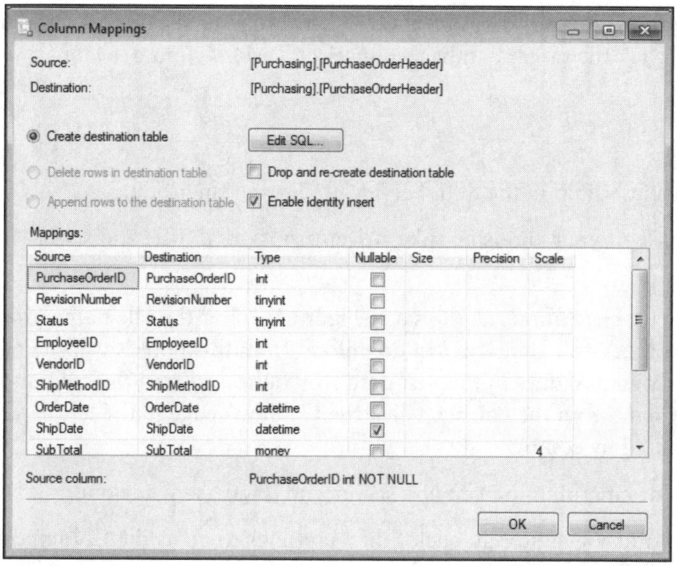

FIGURE 1-2

The next screen enables you to save the package or just choose to run it immediately. You can uncheck Execute Immediately to just save the package for later modification and execution. You can open the package that executed in SQL Server Data Tools (SSDT) if you'd like. You do this by creating a project in SSDT and adding the package to the project. You cannot edit the package without an SSDT project to contain the package. We discuss how to create a project in Lesson 4 later in this book. The final screen executes the process and shows you the output log.

TRY IT

In this Try It, you learn how to quickly load a flat file into a database using the Import and Export Wizard. After this lesson, you'll have a clear understanding of how the Import and Export Wizard is the easiest way to load data into almost any destination and how it is accessed from Management Studio or SSDT.

You can find the file associated with Lesson 1 on the companion website for this book at www.wrox.com.

Lesson Requirements

Load the ZipCodeExtract.csv file (which you can download at this book's website at www.wrox.com) into any database of your choosing. We are using the AdventureWorks2012 database as our target, but that's not a dependency. Note: The file's first row holds the column names.

Hints

➤ One of the fastest ways to access the Import and Export Wizard to load the data is through Management Studio. Right-click the target database and select Tasks ➪ Import Data.

Step-by-Step

1. Open SQL Server Management Studio in the SQL Server 2012 program group.

2. Right-click the target database of your choosing (like AdventureWorks2012) and select Tasks ➪ Import Data.

3. For the Data source, select Flat File Source, as shown in Figure 1-3. For the File name property, select the ZipCodeExtract.csv file that you can download from this book's website at www.wrox.com. Check the Column names in the first data row option to read the column names from the first row of data from the flat file. Click the Columns page in the left pane to confirm that the file is delimited by commas.

4. Click Next to configure the destination. Point to any server and database you want.

5. On the Select Source Tables and Views screen, click Edit Mappings to go to the Column Mappings page. Change the StateAbbr to a size of 2 and the Population column to an int data type, as shown in Figure 1-4. Normally, you would evaluate each column to use the proper data length in an effort to save space.

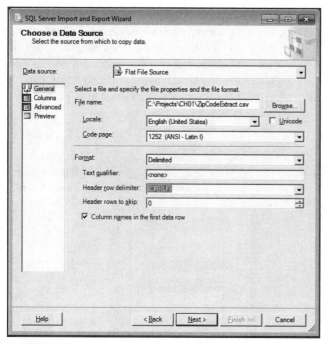

FIGURE 1-3

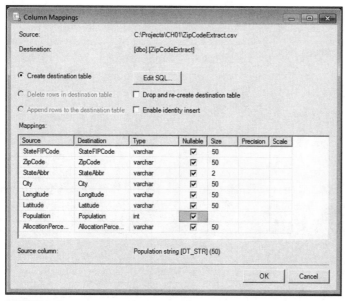

FIGURE 1-4

6. Click OK to leave the Column Mappings page and then click Next to review any data type mapping warnings. The Data Mapping Warnings screen shows you where you have any columns for which the data types don't match. You can ignore those warnings for the time being and click Next a few times to execute the package. If you are successful, you should see a total of 29,470 rows. You will see a truncation warning, which is a warning that you receive when you try to insert a 50-character string into a smaller sized column like a varchar(2), that you can also ignore.

> *Please select Lesson 1 on the DVD, or online at* www.wrox.com/go/ssis2012video, *to view the video that accompanies this lesson.*

Installing SQL Server Integration Services

This book requires that you have SQL Server Data Tools (SSDT) and the SQL Server Integration Services (SSIS) service installed. To develop SSIS, you cannot use SQL Express. The SSIS run time to run packages does ship with all editions, but on some of the lower editions that run time may not work with all SSIS components.

On the subject of editions of SQL Server, you have a decision to make as to which edition you want to install: Standard Edition, Business Intelligence (BI), or Enterprise Edition. Developer Edition is also available. It contains all the components of Enterprise Edition at a tiny fraction of the cost but is licensed for development only. Enterprise Edition gives you a few additional SSIS components that you may be interested in for SQL Server 2012:

- ➤ Data Mining components

- ➤ Fuzzy Lookup and Group transforms

- ➤ Dimension and Partition Processing destinations

- ➤ Term Extraction and Lookup transforms

- ➤ Higher performance components for ODBC, Oracle, and SAP

- ➤ Change Data Capture components

Additionally, the Enterprise Edition of SQL Server gives you database engine features that complement or may affect SSIS. One such feature is the *Change Data Capture* (CDC) feature, which enables you to easily synchronize two systems by querying SQL Server 2012 for only the changes that have occurred after a given date or time. Data compression is another key feature that may speed up your database reads and reduce your disk cost by 60–75 percent.

Oftentimes, if you care about the Enterprise Edition features enough, but don't need Enterprise Edition for the database engine, you might decide to license an SSIS server with just the minimum number of client access licenses (CALs) instead of doing a per-core license. This approach reduces your SQL Server licensing cost sizably, but you now have new hardware cost to add.

When you're installing SQL Server, you need to ensure that the SQL Server Data Tools, Integration Services, and Management Tools - Complete check boxes are selected in the Feature Selection screen (shown in Figure 2-1). The Integration Services option installs the run time and service necessary to run the packages, and is likely all you would need on a production server. The SQL Server Data Tools option installs the designer components, and the Management Tools option installs the DBA tools necessary to manage the packages later.

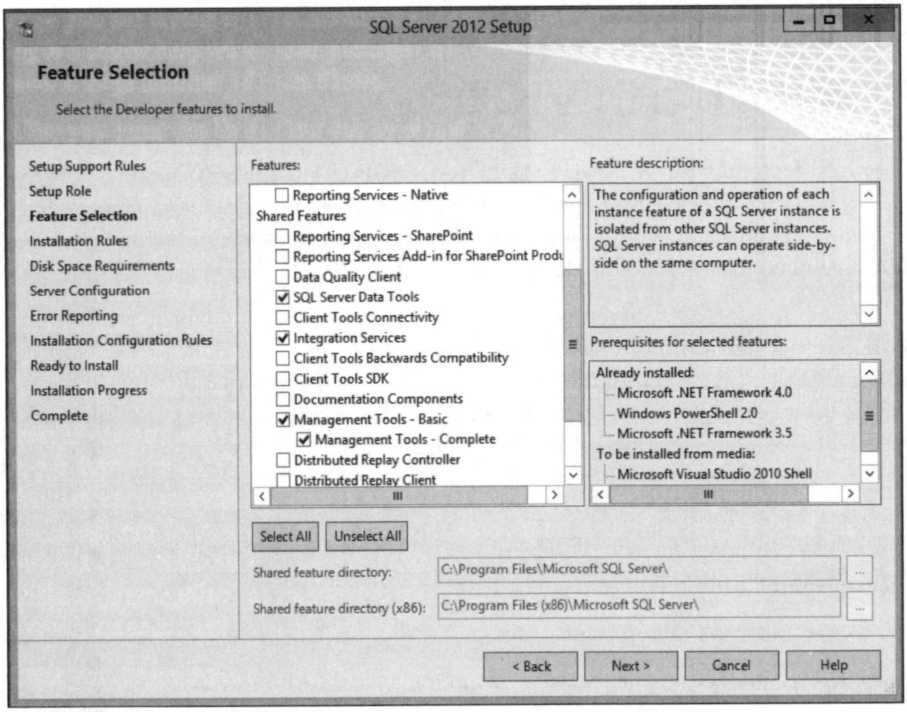

FIGURE 2-1

After you complete the Feature Selection screen, SQL Server installs all the necessary components without any wizard configuration required for SSIS. Once the installation is complete, open the configuration file located at C:\Program Files\Microsoft SQL Server\110\DTS\Binn\MsDtsSrvr.ini.xml. This file configures the SSIS service. Change the <ServerName> node where it currently says "." to your SQL Server's instance name where you want to store your packages. You can also change the directory from ..\Packages to the directory of your choice.

```
<?xml version="1.0" encoding="utf-8"?>
<DtsServiceConfiguration xmlns:xsd="http://www.w3.org/2001/XMLSchema"
xmlns:xsi="http://www.w3.org/2001/XMLSchema-instance">
  <StopExecutingPackagesOnShutdown>true</StopExecutingPackagesOnShutdown>

  <TopLevelFolders>
    <Folder xsi:type="SqlServerFolder">
      <Name>MSDB</Name>
      <ServerName>.</ServerName>
    </Folder>

    <Folder xsi:type="FileSystemFolder">
      <Name>File System</Name>
      <StorePath>..\Packages</StorePath>
    </Folder>

  </TopLevelFolders>
</DtsServiceConfiguration>
```

Once you modify this file, you need to restart the SSIS service from the SQL Server Configuration Manager under the SQL Server 2012 node in the Start menu or the Services applet.

> *Please select Lesson 2 on the DVD, or online at* www.wrox.com/go/ssis2012video, *to view the video that accompanies this lesson.*

Installing the Sample Databases

You will need two sample databases for the future tutorials in this book and for many tutorials on the web; both are provided by Microsoft. The AdventureWorks2012 database is an example database that simulates a bike retailer. It contains HR, accounting, and sales data for online transactions and store sales. The AdventureWorksDW2012 database is an example data warehouse for the same bike reseller.

The two sample databases are not installed by default with SQL Server 2012. You can download the sample databases used for this book at the Wrox website at www.wrox.com/go/ SQLSever2012DataSets.

To use the AdventureWorks2012 database, you must enable the Full Text Search feature and enable the FileStream feature in SQL Server 2012. In addition, the SQL Server Full Text service must be running. You can still install the AdventureWorksDW2012 database without these, but not the AdventureWorks2012 database.

To install the Full Text Search feature, you must go back to the SQL Server Installation Center under SQL Server 2012 ➪ Configuration Tools ➪ SQL Server Installation Center. Walk through the installation wizard again as if you were doing a new installation, but when you get to the Feature Selection screen, ensure Full Text Search and Semantic Extractions for Search are selected.

The FileStream feature enables you to store files quickly and easily on the filesystem of the server, but they are treated like columns in a table. When you back up the database, it also backs up all files to which the table may refer. The feature is initially enabled in the installation wizard, but you can also enable it after the installation in the SQL Server Configuration Manager under SQL Server 2012 ➪ Configuration Tools. Once the Configuration Manager is open, double-click the SQL Server database instance on which you want to enable the feature. This opens up the properties of the service, where you can go to the FILESTREAM tab to enable the feature, as shown in Figure 3-1.

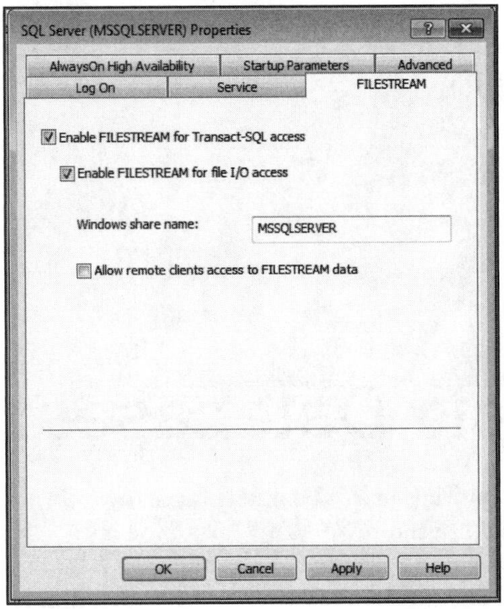

FIGURE 3-1

Enabling FileStream requires that you restart the SQL Server instance.

To install the sample databases, download the AdventureWorks2012 and AdventureWorksDW2012 (data warehouse) MDF data files from the Wrox website and attach them to your server using the CREATE DATABASE command, as shown in the following code:

```
CREATE DATABASE AdventureWorksDW2012 ON (FILENAME =
'C:\Data\AdventureWorksDW2012_Data.mdf') FOR ATTACH_REBUILD_LOG
```

TRY IT

In this Try It, you download and install the necessary example databases to work through the rest of the lessons in this book.

Lesson Requirements

To do the examples in the book, you'll need at least 300 MB of hard drive space and the SQL Server 2012 database engine installed.

Hints

➤ Navigate to `www.wrox.com/go/SQLSever2012DataSets` to download the sample databases and make sure the Full Text service is installed and running prior to the installation.

Step-by-Step

1. Browse to www.wrox.com/go/SQLSever2012DataSets in the browser of your choice.

2. Download the two MDF files for AdventureWorks2012 and AdventureWorksDW2012.

3. Run the following script in Management Studio to install the two databases, substituting your own path:

```
CREATE DATABASE AdventureWorks2012 ON (FILENAME = '{drive}:\{file
path}\AdventureWorks2012_Data.mdf') FOR ATTACH_REBUILD_LOG;

CREATE DATABASE AdventureWorksDW2012 ON (FILENAME = '<drive>:\<file
path>\AdventureWorksDW2012_Data.mdf') FOR ATTACH_REBUILD_LOG
```

> **WARNING** *Prior to installation, open the SQL Server Configuration Manager to start the SQL Full-text Filter Daemon Launcher for your instance. Failure to do this will cause the installation to fail.*

4. The sample databases are now installed and ready to use in Management Studio and for the rest of the examples.

> *Please select Lesson 3 on the DVD, or online at* www.wrox.com/go/ssis2012video, *to view the video that accompanies this lesson.*

Creating a Solution and Project

You cannot create an SSIS package in SQL Server Data Tools (SSDT) without first having a solution and project. Additionally, for execution of the package in debug mode, which you use when troubleshooting, your package must be in a project and solution. Projects and solutions are containers for your packages that help you keep every component together and make you a more efficient SSIS developer.

SSDT is the program in which you're going to develop your SSIS packages. In SQL Server 2012, SSDT is a Visual Studio 2010 shell. You can either open SSDT by itself under the SQL Server 2012 program group or open it by opening the full Visual Studio 2012 program.

An SSIS *project* is a container of one or more packages and other SSIS components. All the Visual Studio suite of products use the project construct to hold their files. For example, Reporting Services uses projects to hold its reports, and VB.NET uses projects to hold its VB.NET class files. In general, you want to align an SSIS project with a business project you're working on. For example, you may have an SSIS project called "Data warehouse ETL."

Projects mean much more in SQL Server 2012 than they did in SQL Server 2005 and 2008. This is because you now deploy projects, not packages, to production if your project is using the project deployment model. If you want to use the legacy deployment model where you deploy a package at a time, you will use the package deployment model. The new project deployment model is where many of the new SQL Server 2012 features that are discussed later in this book are used.

A *solution* is a container of one or more projects. Solutions enable many disparate types of projects to live under one container. For example, you may have a solution called "Enterprise Data Warehouse" with a SQL Server Reporting Services (SSRS) project called "Data warehouse reports," another project for SSIS called "Data warehouse ETL," and a final one for C# called "SharePoint code." All of those projects could live under one roof, so if a report developer makes a change in his SSRS project, the SSIS developer is aware of that change.

When you create a project in SSDT, a solution is automatically created at the same time. To create a project, you can open SSDT and select File ➪ New ➪ Project. As you can see in Figure 4-1, the solution name is "Enterprise Data Warehouse" and its project is called "Datawarehouse Load."

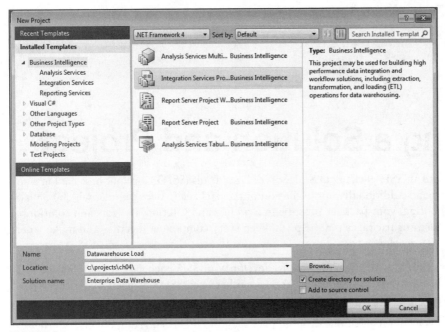

FIGURE 4-1

At first, the solution will not appear in your Solution Explorer because you have only a single project. Once you add a second project, it will appear. You can add subsequent projects into the same solution by going back to File ➪ New ➪ Project and selecting Add to Solution from the Solution drop-down box (which is shown in Figure 4-3 in the "Step-by-Step" later in this chapter). When you create your first project, you'll notice in the Solution Explorer, which shows you all the projects and files, that there appears to be no solution. This is because solutions are hidden from you when you have only a single project in the solution. You can choose to always see the solution file in the Solution Explorer by going to Tools ➪ Options and checking the Always show solution option in the Projects and Solutions page (shown in Figure 4-2).

TRY IT

In this Try It, you learn how to create your first solution and project, which you'll be using throughout the rest of the book.

You can download examples of completed package, project, and solution files for this lesson from the book's website at www.wrox.com.

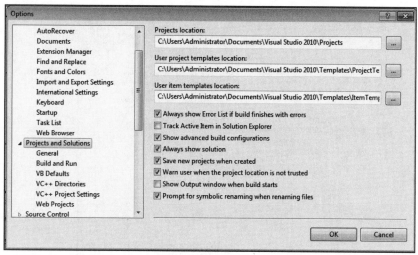

FIGURE 4-2

Lesson Requirements

To successfully complete this lesson, you need to create a solution called **Personal Trainer Solution** and a project called **Personal Trainer SSIS Project** that will be used throughout this book.

Hints

➤ To create the project, open SQL Server Data Tools and select File ➪ New ➪ Project.

Step-by-Step

1. Open SSDT from the SQL Server 2012 program group.
2. Click File ➪ New ➪ Project.
3. Select Business Intelligence Projects for the project type.
4. Select Integration Services Project for the template.
5. Type **Personal Trainer SSIS Project** for the Name property, as shown in Figure 4-3.
6. Type **C:\projects** for the Location property.
7. Type **Personal Trainer Solution** for the Solution Name property.

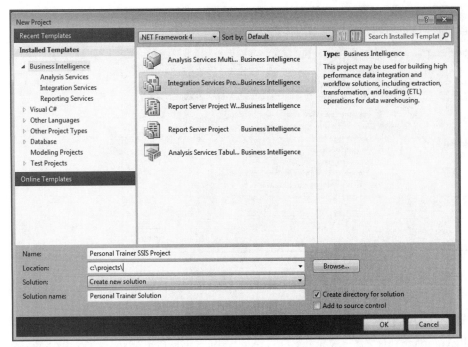

FIGURE 4-3

Please select Lesson 4 on the DVD, or online at www.wrox.com/go/ssis2012video, to view the video that accompanies this lesson.

5

Exploring SQL Server Data Tools

SQL Server Data Tools (SSDT) is a Visual Studio 2010 tool that helps you create, debug, and execute SSIS packages. When you're a business intelligence developer, it can also help you create reports in SQL Server Reporting Services (SSRS) or design cubes in SQL Server Analysis Services (SSAS). You'll be using SSDT extensively throughout this book, so it's important that in this lesson, you learn everything you need to know to make your life easier in this critical environment.

> **NOTE** *Because this is a more exploratory, introductory lesson, it doesn't have a task-based tutorial as the other lessons have.*

You can open SSDT through the SQL Server 2012 program group. Depending on your PC, SSDT may take some time to open.

> **NOTE** *One hint that you can use to reduce your load time is to eliminate the splash screen. To eliminate the SSDT splash screen and reduce your load time by a few seconds each time, right-click the SSDT shortcut and select Properties. Next, add the* -NOSPLASH *switch at the end of the shortcut as shown here:*
>
> ```
> "C:\Program Files (x86)\Microsoft Visual Studio 10.0\Common7\IDE\
> devenv.exe" -NOSPLASH
> ```

THE SOLUTION EXPLORER

Once you create your project from Lesson 4, you're ready to begin exploration of the environment. The most important pane, the Solution Explorer, is on the right. The Solution Explorer is where you can find all of your created SQL Server Integration Services (SSIS) packages, shared connection managers, and parameters. As discussed in Lesson 4, a solution is a container that holds a series of projects. Each project holds a myriad of objects for whatever type of project you're working in. For SSIS, it holds your packages, shared parameters, and shared connections (the latter two are available only in the project deployment model, which is discussed in this lesson shortly in the "Deployment Models" section). Once you create a solution, you can store many projects inside of it. For example, you might have a solution that has your VB.NET application and all the SSIS packages that support that application. In this case, you would probably have two projects: one for VB and another for SSIS.

After creating a new project, your Solution Explorer window contains a series of empty folders and a single package in the Packages folder. Figure 5-1 shows you a partially filled Solution Explorer. In this screenshot, you see a solution named Enterprise Data Warehouse with one project, an Integration Services project called Datawarehouse Load. Inside the project, you'll find the single default package, Package.dtsx.

FIGURE 5-1

If you don't see the solution name in your Solution Explorer, it's because solutions are hidden when you have only a single project. In this scenario, the solution won't appear by default. To always show the solution, you can select Tools ⇨ Options to open the Visual Studio options pane. Under Projects and Solutions, check Always show solution, as shown in Figure 5-2.

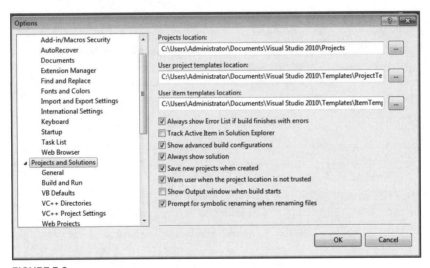

FIGURE 5-2

If you look into the directory that contains your solution and project files, you can see all the files that are represented in the Solution Explorer window. Some of the base files you might see will have the following extensions:

➤ .dtsx—An SSIS package

➤ .ds—A shared data source file

➤ `.sln`—A solution file that contains one or more projects

➤ `.dtproj`—An SSIS project file

➤ `.params`—A shared parameter file

➤ `.conmgr`—A shared connection manager

If you copy any file that does not match the `.params`, `.conmgr`, or `.dtsx` extension, it is placed in the Miscellaneous folder. This folder is used to hold any files such as Word documents that describe the installation of the package or requirements documents. Anything you'd like can go into that folder, and it can all potentially be checked into a source control system like SourceSafe with the code.

DEPLOYMENT MODELS

In SQL Server 2012, you have two models for developing and deploying packages: package and project deployment models.

➤ The *package deployment model* used to be the only deployment model that existed in SQL Server 2005 and 2008 and was where you could deploy only a package at a time to the server. It also had ways of configuring the packages to change properties like connections with XML files or tables.

➤ With the new *project deployment model*, you can only deploy the entire project of packages, and packages can be configured by the database administrator (DBA) through parameters.

You can switch back and forth between these models, but the new project deployment model is much more robust with features. You can switch back and forth between the models by right-clicking the project in the Solution Explorer and selecting Convert to Project (or Package) Deployment Model. You learn much more about this functionality in Lessons 52 and 53.

THE PROPERTIES WINDOW

The Properties window (shown in Figure 5-3) is where you can customize almost any item that you have selected. For example, if you select a task in the design pane, you receive a list of properties to configure, such as the task's name and what query it's going to use. The view varies widely based on what item you have selected. Figure 5-3 shows the properties of the Execute SQL Task. You can also click the white background of the Control Flow tab to see the package properties in the Properties window. Sometimes, you can see some more advanced properties in the Properties pane than what the task's editor user interface provides you.

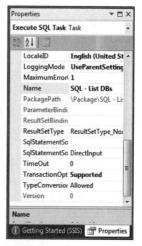

FIGURE 5-3

THE TOOLBOX

The Toolbox contains all the items that you can use in the particular tab's design pane at any given point in time. For example, the Control Flow tab has a list of tasks and containers (a partial list is shown in Figure 5-4). This list may grow based on what custom tasks are installed. The list is completely different when you're in a different tab, such as the Data Flow tab. Many of the core tasks you see in Figure 5-4 are covered in Section 2 of this book in much more detail.

The Toolbox is organized into sections such as Common, Containers, and Other Tasks. These tabs can be collapsed and expanded for usability. As you use the Toolbox, you may want to customize your view by moving items to your favorites by right-clicking a given task or container and selecting Add to Favorites. Also, after you install a custom component, it automatically shows up in your Toolbox. When you select a component like a task from the Toolbox, notice that below the Toolbox pane, an interactive help section appears that enables you to see samples and a short description of the component.

FIGURE 5-4

> **NOTE** *At some point, you may accidentally close a window like the Properties window. If this happens to you, you can bring that window back through the View menu. You can also click the pushpin on any particular window to hide the window because real estate is at a premium when you begin development of SSIS.*

THE SSDT DESIGN ENVIRONMENT

The SSDT environment contains two key tabs for designing packages: the Control Flow and Data Flow tabs. Each of these handles different parts of your packages. The *Control Flow* tab controls the execution of the package and the *Data Flow* tab handles the movement of data.

The Control Flow tab orchestrates the execution of your package, dictating that one task, such as an FTP Task, should execute ahead of another; for example, an Execute SQL Task. Inside the tab are tasks and containers you can drag over from the Toolbox onto the design pane. Each of those tasks has its own user interface that you can use to configure the task, and you can access it by double-clicking the component.

Each package has only a single Control Flow, but can have many Data Flows. The user interface for the Data Flow task is quite different. Its user interface is the Data Flow tab. In the Data Flow tab, you can configure one or more Data Flow tasks by dragging over sources, transforms, and destinations onto the design pane. Each Control Flow can have any number of Data Flow tasks, each of which results in a new item in the Data Flow tab's drop-down list of tasks. The Data Flow is essentially where you're going to configure the movement of your data from nearly any source to nearly any destination.

When you execute a package by right-clicking it in the Solution Explorer and selecting Execute Package, you enter debug mode. Notice a new tab called Progress immediately opens. The Progress tab is where you go to debug when a package has a problem. You can also go to the Output window below to see a textual view of the same Progress tab. Once you stop debug mode by clicking the Stop button or by going to Debug ➪ Stop Debugging, the Progress tab changes to an Execution Results tab, which shows you the last run of a package. Each of those tabs shows you more than the Output window at the bottom, which shows you only critical issues.

One other handy thing you can do from within SSDT is open Server Explorer. Server Explorer enables you to create a connection to a SQL Server database that you can manage just as you would in Management Studio. You can do this by selecting Tools ➪ Connect to Database. Type in the credentials for the database, and then you're ready to run queries against the database, create stored procedures, or redesign tables, to name just a few things you can do.

Now that you've taken a look at the SSDT environment, Lesson 6 covers using the environment to create your first package.

> *Please select Lesson 5 on the DVD, or online at* www.wrox.com/go/ssis2012video, *to view the video that accompanies this lesson.*

Creating Your First Package

Creating packages in SQL Server Integration Services (SSIS) is a bit like LEGO-block programming. You drag various tasks over, configure the tasks, chain them together, and then *voila*, execute. Well, it's not quite that easy, but you'll find it much easier than writing any program. In this lesson, you learn how to create your first SSIS package. Granted, the package does very little here, but it shows you many of the concepts that will be critical throughout the rest of the book. Many of the concepts may not make complete sense yet when it comes to configuring various components, but no worries—the concepts are deeply covered throughout the rest of the book.

To create your first package, you need an SSIS project. Creating a project is covered extensively in Lesson 4. After you create your first project, a package called Package.dtsx is automatically created. If you want to rename this package, simply right-click the package in Solution Explorer and select Rename, leaving the .dtsx extension.

To create a new package, you can also right-click SSIS Packages in the Solution Explorer and select New Package. This action creates a new package that you will want to rename as soon as it's created because it, too, will be called Package.dtsx or some variation of it. The final result will resemble Figure 6-1, which shows a partially complete SSIS project.

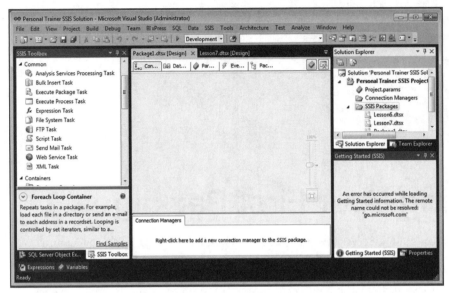

FIGURE 6-1

CREATING AND USING CONNECTION MANAGERS

To design a package, you want to first create connections, which are called connection managers in SSIS. A *connection manager* is a connection that can be leveraged and consumed once or many times in a package. To create a connection manager, right-click in the Connection Manager pane at the bottom of the screen in SSDT and select New <type of connection>. Any connection that you would use in SSIS, whether to a file or a database, will be stored as a connection manager here. Some of those common items would include the connections in the following table.

TYPE OF CONNECTION	CONNECTION MANAGER
Database	OLE DB Connection Manager for Oracle, SQL Server, DB2.ADO.NET and ODBC Connection Manager for ODBC types of connections and in some cases OLE DB Data Sources.
File	Flat File Connection Manager when you want to load the file using a Data Flow Task. There is also an additional connection manager called the File Connection Manager that you can use if all you want to do is rename, delete, or perform some other type of file operation.
Excel	Excel Connection Manager.
Internet Connection	SMTP Connection Manager for mail servers. FTP Connection Manager for FTP servers. HTTP Connection Manager for websites or web services.

You can access some of the connections by right-clicking in the Connection Manager pane and selecting New Connection. This brings up a list of all the available connection managers (shown in Figure 6-2), including third-party ones that you have installed. The handy thing about connection managers is that they're externally available to a DBA at run time. In other words, when a DBA goes to schedule this package, he or she can point the connection to a new database or file on-the-fly for that one job.

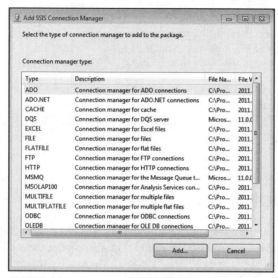

FIGURE 6-2

Once you create an OLE DB connection, it is available to you anywhere in the package from any component that can use the connection. If you'd like, you can create a connection that can be leveraged from multiple packages by creating a project connection manager. To do this, right-click Connection Managers in the Solution Explorer and select New Connection Manager. These data sources can be leveraged from multiple packages in the project and can be changed by the DBA later. By creating a connection here, you type the password one time for your connection, and if you ever change any type of connection information, it changes across any package using that connection. No negative consequences result from doing this, so generally speaking, it's a great design-time practice to use project connection managers if you see yourself using the connection a few times.

> **NOTE** *At any time, you can convert a regular connection manager to a project connection manager by right-clicking the connection in the Connection Manager pane.*

USING AND CONFIGURING TASKS

Your package would be nothing without tasks. *Tasks* in the Control Flow tab orchestrate the work that you want to do in the package. For example, one task may copy a file over from a different server while another task may load the file into a database. To use a task, simply drag it onto the design pane in the Control Flow tab from the Toolbox. A common task that you'll use in this book is the Script Task because it requires no configuration, which makes it a great training tool.

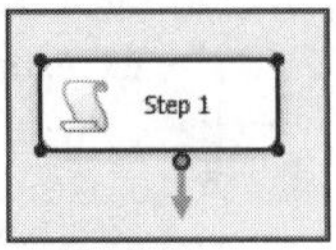

Until most tasks are configured by double-clicking the task, you may see a yellow warning or red error indicator on the task. After you configure the task, you can link it to other tasks by using precedence constraints. Once you click the task, you'll notice a green arrow (the precedence constraint) pointing down from the task, as shown in Figure 6-3. This precedence constraint controls the execution order of the various tasks in your package, and you can use it by dragging the green arrow to the next task that you want to chain together. You read more about most of the core tasks and the topic of precedence constraints in Section 2 of this book.

FIGURE 6-3

You should never keep the default name of your tasks. Instead, you should rename them to something that you can recognize in the log later. We prefer to name all of our tasks with some two- or three-digit qualifier, such as SCR for a Script Task, and then the purpose of the task such as SCR - Encrypt File. This name then shows up in your logs when a problem occurs and can also help you self-document your package.

EXPLORING PACKAGE ENCRYPTION

A package is essentially an XML file behind the scenes. To prove this, you can right-click any package and select View Code to see the package's XML. As you can imagine, though, storing secure information inside an XML file could create some security problems. Luckily, Microsoft already thought of that problem and has a solution—encrypting your packages.

Microsoft encrypts your package by default with your Windows user key, which is a key that protects your Windows user credentials on your PC. You can look at the property that encrypts your package by going to the Properties pane and looking at the ProtectionLevel package-level property. This property is set to EncryptSensitiveWithUserKey by default, which means that all the usernames, passwords, or any other sensitive data are locked down with your credentials. If you were to pass the package to another user, the package's encrypted data would not be visible, and the user would have to retype the secure information, such as the login information.

Another option is to change the property to EncryptSensitiveWithPassword, which locks down the package with a password instead. You can also use EncryptAllWithPassword (or UserKey). This property value locks down the entire package to where no one can open it without a proper password.

> **WARNING** *This property is usually one of the top reasons why packages fail in production. For example, if your package has sensitive information inside of it to connect to a database, the package would potentially fail when you ran the job because it was running under the SQL Server Agent's (SQL Server's scheduler) service account. You can also avoid this problem by setting the property to EncryptAllWithPassword and simply pass in the password when running the package or scheduling it.*

EXECUTING PACKAGES

Once your package is ready to execute, you can run it in debug mode by right-clicking it in Solution Explorer and selecting Execute Package. By running the package in debug mode, you have enhanced logging views and breakpoints available to you to determine why your package is not working. While in debug mode, however, you will not be able to sizably change the package. To stop debug mode, click the Stop button or click Debug ➪ Stop Debugging.

TRY IT

In this Try It, you learn how to create your first basic package that will do very little other than demonstrate some of the SSIS functionality.

You can find the complete package (Lesson6.dtsx) as part of the download for this lesson on the companion website for this book at www.wrox.com.

Lesson Requirements

To create your first package, you can reuse the project from Lesson 4 or create a brand new project. Once created, you'll notice that one such package in your project is Package.dtsx. Rename or create a new package called Lesson6.dtsx that has two Script Tasks in it that are connected. One Script Task should be named Step 1 and the other Step 2. These two tasks will do nothing at all. Create a connection manager that points to AdventureWorks2012 and create a password on the package of your choosing that will always pop up when you open the package and execute it.

Hints

➤ Create a new package by right-clicking the word Packages in Solution Explorer in SSDT.

➤ Drag over the two Script Tasks and connect them together using the green precedence constraint coming out of the task.

Step-by-Step

1. Create a new package in a new solution or the existing solution you created in Lesson 4 by right-clicking Packages in Solution Explorer and selecting New Package. Rename the package to **Lesson6.dtsx**.

2. Drag over two Script Tasks from the Toolbox into the Control Flow design pane.

3. Right-click in each Script Task and select Rename. Rename one task **Step 1** and the other **Step 2**.

4. Select Step 1 and drag the green line (called a precedence constraint) onto Step 2.

5. Right-click in the Connection Manager pane at the bottom of the screen in SSDT and select New OLE DB Connection. In the Configure OLE DB Connection Manager dialog box, you may have to click New to create a new connection, or it may already be cached from a

previous package. If you had to click New, type the credentials to the AdventureWorks2012 database and click OK twice.

6. Rename the newly created connection manager **AdventureWorks2012** (removing the instance name from the connection manager name).

7. Select the blank white area of the design pane in the Control Flow tab and then go to the Properties pane. Change the ProtectionLevel property to EncryptAllWithPassword and type the password of whatever you want above it by selecting the ellipsis button in the Password property right above ProtectionLevel.

8. Execute the package by right-clicking it in Solution Explorer and selecting Execute Package. The final package should look like Figure 6-4.

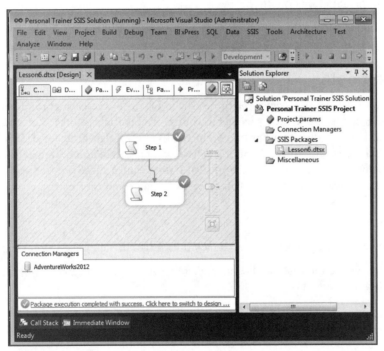

FIGURE 6-4

Please select Lesson 6 on the DVD, or online at www.wrox.com/go/ssis2012video, *to view the video that accompanies this lesson.*

Upgrading Packages to SQL Server 2012

With every new version of Integration Services, there is a path you must follow to upgrade your existing solution to the latest version of the tool. In SQL Server 2012, you can upgrade your 2005 or 2008 SSIS package using the SSIS Package Upgrade Wizard.

The SSIS Package Upgrade Wizard fully upgrades your packages, but you should note a few things upon the completion of the upgrade. The wizard automatically updates connection strings that use an outdated data provider to the latest drivers that come natively with SQL Server. This is a nice feature, but if the packages you are upgrading use configurations to overwrite data source information, as described in Section 7 of this book, you must manually upgrade the providers in the configurations; this wizard, by default, does not upgrade configuration values.

The wizard also does not upgrade packages to utilize many of the new features available in SSIS 2012. For example, it does not upgrade Execute Package Tasks to use the new internal project reference. Also, after converting, the wizard leaves your packages set to the old package deployment model. New packages that are developed in SSIS use the project deployment model, which is detailed in Lesson 8.

You can invoke the SSIS Package Upgrade Wizard by simply opening your packages in SQL Server Data Tools (SSDT) or you can upgrade your packages manually by running SSISUpgrade.exe, the SSIS Package Upgrade Wizard executable (Figure 7-1). If you've installed SQL Server in the default paths, you will find the upgrade wizard in the folder location C:\Program Files\Microsoft SQL Server\110\DTS\Binn\SSISUpgrade.exe.

FIGURE 7-1

The SSIS Package Upgrade Wizard walks you through selecting the packages targeted for upgrade and then enables you to apply a set of rules that the wizard should adhere to during the conversion. Figure 7-2 shows the Select Package Management Options screen where you can configure the conversion rules.

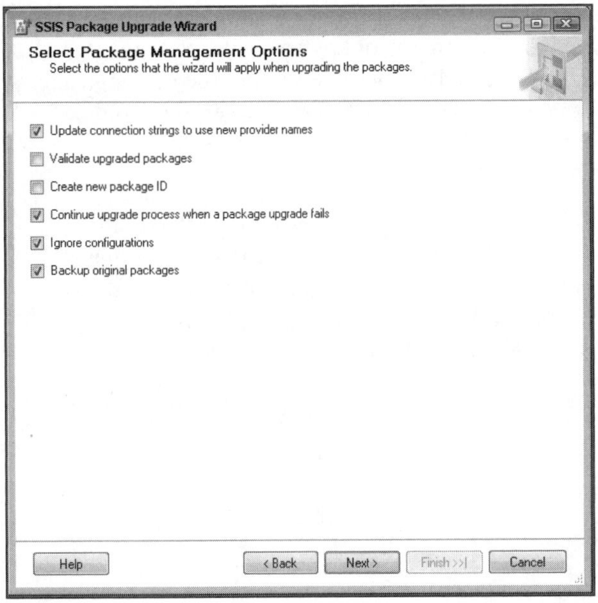

FIGURE 7-2

TRY IT

In this Try It, you convert an existing ETL solution that loads a datamart from SSIS 2008R2 to an SSIS 2012 solution. The solution includes several packages for loading dimension tables, a fact table, and a master package that runs all of these in the correct order. After this lesson, you will know how to use the SSIS Package Upgrade Wizard to upgrade packages to SSIS 2012.

You can download the complete project both prior to conversion (Lesson 7.zip) and following the conversion (Lesson 7_Completed.zip) from www.wrox.com.

Lesson Requirements

Make the following changes to convert the SSIS project to SSIS 2012. You can also find the fully converted Lesson 7 project at www.wrox.com:

➤ Download the completed SSIS 2008R2 project that will be converted from www.wrox.com, and then unzip and save it to C:\Projects\SSISPersonalTrainer\.

➤ Use SSDT to convert the packages.

➤ Do not execute the packages after completing the conversion.

Hints

➤ Open the solution in SSDT and use the SSIS Package Upgrade Wizard to convert the packages.

Step-by-Step

1. Open the Datamart Load.sln file in SQL Server Data Tools. This file is in the folder C:\Projects\SSISPersonalTrainer\Lesson 7, which you downloaded from www.wrox.com.

2. Open the solution file to bring up the Visual Studio Conversion Wizard. Click Next when the welcome screen appears.

3. The Visual Studio wizard creates a backup of your original files by default. On the Choose Whether To Create a Backup screen, accept the default location for storing a backup of the original files and then click Next.

4. Click Finish to complete the Visual Studio upgrade and begin the SSIS Package Upgrade Wizard.

5. When the SSIS Package Upgrade Wizard welcome screen appears, click Next.

6. Select the packages targeted for the upgrade. Figure 7-3 shows all packages selected, but you can uncheck packages you do not want to upgrade. Also, if any package had been encrypted with a password, you would enter that password here. These packages do not have a password, so click Next.

FIGURE 7-3

7. On the Select Package Management Options screen, use the default conversion rules as shown in Figure 7-4 and click Next.

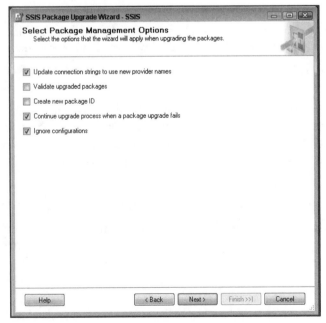

FIGURE 7-4

8. Before the conversion starts, a confirmation screen appears that shows the work the wizard is about to begin. Click Finish to begin the upgrade.

9. A successful conversion should match Figure 7-5. Click Close to end the SSIS Package Upgrade Wizard. You may have to click Close a second time to end the Visual Studio Conversion Wizard as well. You can now explore the converted packages in the Solution Explorer, but do not execute them because they reference nonexistent tables.

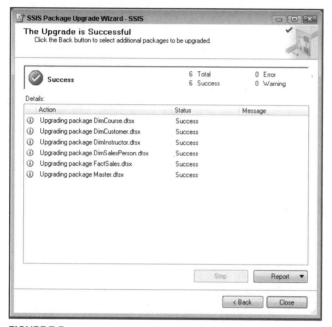

FIGURE 7-5

Please select Lesson 7 on the DVD, or online at www.wrox.com/go/ssis2012video, *to view the video that accompanies this lesson.*

Upgrading to the Project Deployment Model

In SSIS 2012, the project deployment model has become the new standard for how packages are created, configured, and deployed. Any new packages that are developed are automatically set up to use the project deployment model.

Having this new deployment model means several things for you, especially if you developed SSIS packages in previous versions of SQL Server. For example, these features, which you may have used previously, are no longer available in the project deployment model:

> Data sources

> Configurations

> Package deployment

Although the features have been removed in the project deployment model, they are easily replaced with new tools. Following are some of the major features that are either new or have been changed in the project deployment model:

> Project connection managers (discussed in Lesson 6)

> Project deployment (discussed in Lesson 53)

> Project parameters (discussed in Lesson 33)

> Environments and environment variables (discussed in Lesson 54)

As you can see, much of what you can do when developing is focused more on the project than the package, as it was in the past. This may change how you organize your packages because, as "project deployment" implies, you will now be deploying entire projects and not just individual packages. So if you put all your packages into a single project, regardless of what part of the business they affect, they will all have to go into the same deployment path with the new model.

So, if all new packages developed use the project deployment model by default, what about packages that have been upgraded from SSIS 2005 or 2008? Remember in Lesson 7 you learned that when you upgrade packages to SSIS 2012, they are converted to use the package deployment model by default, which is the legacy way of developing packages. If you want to fully upgrade your packages to use the new deployment model, you must run the Integration Services Project Conversion Wizard.

To launch the Integration Services Project Conversion Wizard, right-click a project in the Solution Explorer and select Convert to Project Deployment Model, as shown in Figure 8-1. This wizard walks you through the steps of applying project encryption, updating Execute Package Tasks to use internal project references, and converting configurations to parameters. The Try It section of this lesson walks you through the detailed steps of using this wizard.

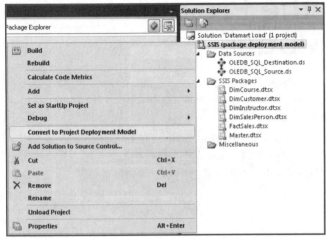

FIGURE 8-1

You can also choose to leave your packages in the package deployment model if you prefer the old method of administrating packages. However, if you decide to stay in the package deployment model, you will miss the features like executing packages with T-SQL and monitoring package execution reports. These features are detailed later in this book.

TRY IT

In this Try It, you use the solution you upgraded in the previous lesson and convert it to use the project deployment model.

If you did not complete the previous lesson, you can download the files you need from www.wrox .com. The Lesson 8.zip file contains the completed Try It files from Lesson 7 and the Lesson 8_ Completed.zip file contains the completed files from this lesson.

Lesson Requirements

Make the following changes to convert the solution to a project deployment model. You can also find the fully converted Lesson 8 project at www.wrox.com:

➤ Use the Integration Services Project Conversion Wizard to convert to the project deployment model.

➤ Apply project-level encryption.

➤ Update Execute Package Tasks to use internal project references.

➤ Replace configurations with project parameters.

Hints

➤ Right-click the SSIS project in the Solution Explorer to launch the Integration Services Project Conversion Wizard.

Step-by-Step

1. Open the Datamart Load.sln file in SQL Server Data Tools. This file is in the folder C:\ Projects\SSISPersonalTrainer\Lesson 8, which you downloaded from www.wrox.com. If you completed the Try It section of Lesson 7, then you can also use that.

2. After opening the solution file, open the Solution Explorer and right-click the project named SSIS. Click Convert to Project Deployment Model to launch the Integration Services Project Conversion Wizard.

3. As soon as you select to convert the packages, a prompt appears (Figure 8-2) warning you that data sources you have in the Solution Explorer will be removed with the project deployment model. Click OK to continue past the warning.

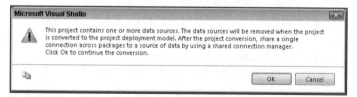

FIGURE 8-2

4. The Introduction screen briefs you on the steps the wizard will take to convert your package. Click Next.

5. Select the packages you want to convert and apply any password you may have on the packages, as shown in Figure 8-3. Click Next after reviewing the selection.

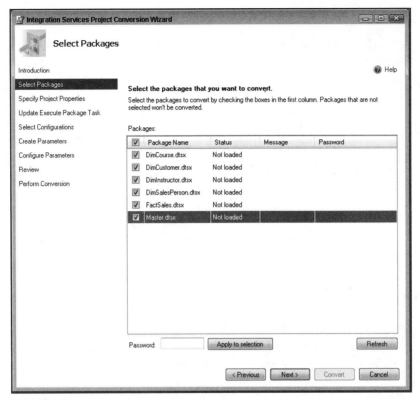

FIGURE 8-3

6.   You are prompted to add a package protection level. If you've developed in SSIS in prior versions, this may be familiar to you because you could do this on individual packages. Now this capability has been extended to projects. Change the protection level to DontSaveSensitive, then click Next. DontSaveSensitive means that any "sensitive" information, usually referring to connection string passwords, will not be saved for others to open and use.

7.   On the Update Execute Package Task screen, use the default assign reference as shown in Figure 8-4 and click Next. This updates the Execute Package Task in Master.dtsx to no longer use a file connection, but instead use an internal project reference.

8.   The next step identifies all configurations that are being used to convert them to parameters. With the project deployment model, configurations are no longer used and are replaced with either package or project parameters. Figure 8-5 shows each of my packages has two configuration files being used. These will be replaced with parameters on the next screen. Use the default selection here and click Next.

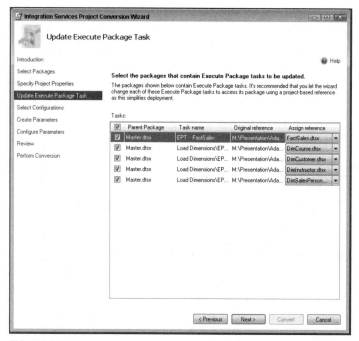

FIGURE 8-4

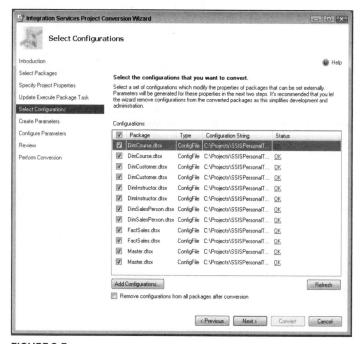

FIGURE 8-5

9. The wizard suggests that two project parameters be created to replace the configuration files. A project parameter is used because it can be shared across the entire project. A package parameter would only be available in a single package. In Figure 8-6, it appears as though several parameters will be created, but keep in mind that these are project parameters and they can be shared in multiple packages, so only two will be created on the next screen. Click Next.

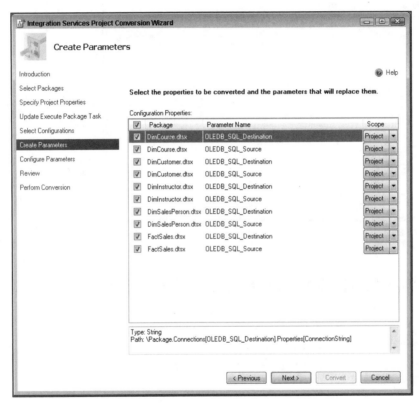

FIGURE 8-6

10. Next, the wizard creates the two parameters identified in the previous screen, but you can make changes to them prior to completing the wizard. Go with the default configuration (Figure 8-7) and click Next.

11. The final review screen enables you to evaluate your settings. Click Convert to begin the conversion process.

12. Once the conversion completes, your screen should look like Figure 8-8. You will see an information pop-up telling you that the changes will not be saved until you save your Visual Studio session. Click OK on the information pop-up and click Close on the Integration Services Project Conversion Wizard.

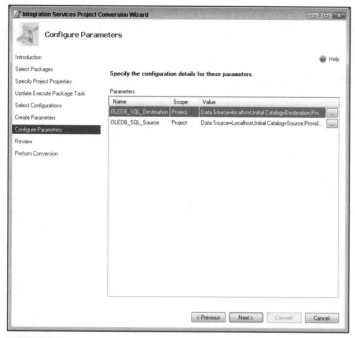

FIGURE 8-7

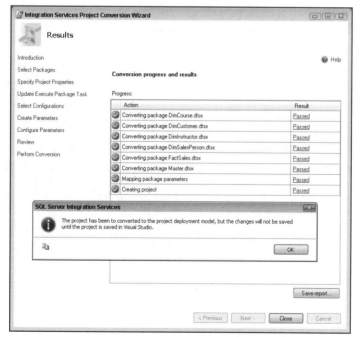

FIGURE 8-8

13. If you would like to review the changes the wizard made, open the Master.dtsx package and take a look at the configuration for one of the Execute Package Tasks. Figure 8-9 shows the ReferenceType property changed to Project Reference.

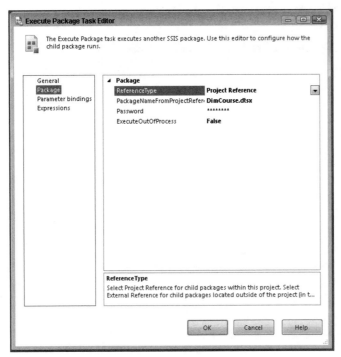

FIGURE 8-9

14. The wizard also created two project parameters called OLEDB_SQL_Destination and OLEDB_SQL_Source, which replace the previously-used configurations. These parameters fully replace the configurations by applying expressions on the connection managers that reference the project parameter values. Figure 8-10 shows the expression the wizard applied to the one of the connection managers. Read Lesson 54 to see how these parameters can easily be changed from outside the package using environments in the Integration Services Catalog.

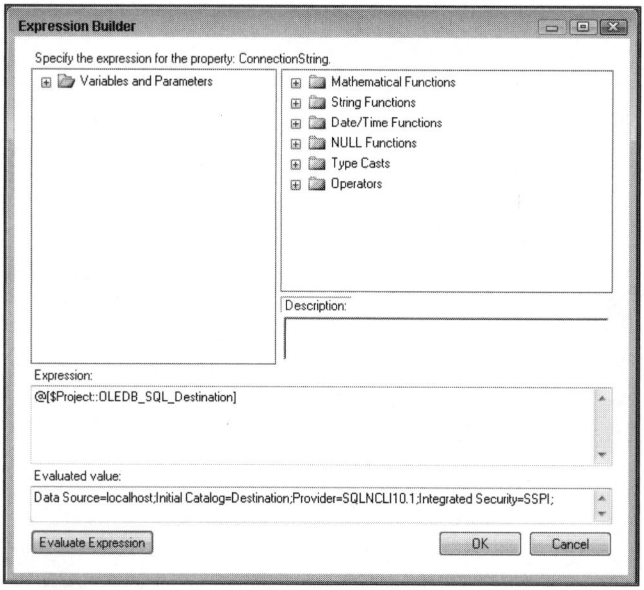

FIGURE 8-10

> *Please select Lesson 8 on the DVD, or online at* www.wrox.com/go/ssis2012video, *to view the video that accompanies this lesson.*

SECTION 2
Control Flow

9

Using Precedence Constraints

When using tasks in SQL Server Integration Services (SSIS), you need a way to connect these tasks in most cases. *Precedence constraints* are the connections between the tasks that control the execution order of each task. After you drag in more than one task in the Control Flow in SSIS, you can link them together by using these precedence constraints. Click once on a task, and you see a green arrow pointing down from the task; this is the precedence constraint line for this task. For example, in Figure 9-1, you can see a Script Task with a green arrow below the task. This is the precedence constraint arrow to connect to the next task you need to run after this task completes successfully. These arrows control the order of tasks in a package, and they also control whether tasks will run at all.

FIGURE 9-1

To create an On Success Precedence Constraint, click the green arrow coming out of the task and drag it to the task you want to link to the first task. In Figure 9-2, you can see the On Success Precedence Constraint between the two Script Tasks. Only if the first Script Task completes successfully will the second Script Task run. To delete the constraint, click once on the constraint line and press Delete on the keyboard, or right-click the constraint line and left-click Delete.

FIGURE 9-2

The precedence constraint arrows can be different colors to represent different commands. They can also have an FX logo to represent an expression, as shown in Figure 9-3. Placing expressions on precedence constraints gives you more advanced ways to control the execution of each package. For example, you could state that you want Script Task 1 to execute only if you're processing a month-end cycle. Each color represents a status of when a task will execute:

FIGURE 9-3

➤ **Green** = On Success

➤ **Red** = On Failure

➤ **Blue** = On Completion

➤ **Any color with FX Logo** = Expression, or Expression with a Constraint

The arrows that connect tasks in a Data Flow tab look similar to the precedence constraints in the Control Flow. These Data Flow connections do not have the same properties as the Control Flow. Click a source or a transformation in the Data Flow tab, and you see a blue and red arrow pointing down, as in Figure 9-4 (though in this figure you won't be able to see the colors). The blue arrow is the flow of good data, and the red arrow is the flow of data with errors. This allows data with errors to be sent to another destination separate from the good data.

FIGURE 9-4

In the Control Flow, you need to use a different approach. If you'd like the next task to execute only if the first task has failed, create a precedence constraint as explained previously for the On Success Constraint. After the constraint is created, double-click the constraint arrow and the Precedence Constraint Editor opens, as shown in Figure 9-5. This is where you set the conditions that decide if the next task will execute at run time. The first option you want to change is Value to Failure, which changes the precedence constraint to an On Failure event.

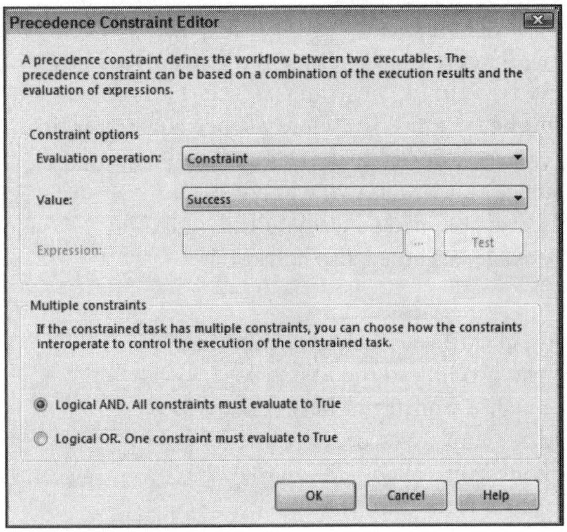

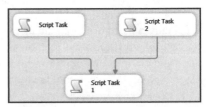

FIGURE 9-5

In the Precedence Constraint Editor, you can also set the logical AND/OR for the preceding task. SSIS gives you the option of adding a logical AND or a logical OR when a task has multiple constraints. In the Precedence Constraint Editor, you can configure the task to execute only if the group of predecessor tasks has completed (AND), or if any one of the predecessor tasks has completed (OR). A predecessor task is any task with a precedence constraint that is connected to another task. If a precedence constraint is a logical AND, the connecting lines are solid (Figure 9-6). If a precedence constraint is a logical OR, the lines are dotted (Figure 9-7), which allows the task to perform even if one or more predecessor tasks have failed.

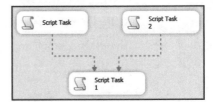

FIGURE 9-6

FIGURE 9-7

In the Evaluation Operation drop-down box of the Precedence Constraint Editor, you can edit how the task will be evaluated. The drop-down menu has four options:

➤ **Constraint**—Evaluates the success, failure, or completion of the predecessor task or tasks

➤ **Expression**—Evaluates the success of a customized condition that is programmed using an expression

➤ **Expression and Constraint**—Evaluates both the expression and the constraint before moving to the next task

➤ **Expression or Constraint**—Determines if either the expression or the constraint has been successfully met before moving to the next task

If you select any constraint with an expression, the expression box requires a valid expression. An SSIS expression is most often used to evaluate a variable before proceeding to the next task. New in SQL Server 2012 is the ellipse button next to the expression. This button opens the Expression Builder, making it easier to write your expressions. Expressions are covered in detail in Lesson 14. One example of an SSIS expression is comparing two variables. This is done using the following syntax:

```
@Variable1 == @Variable2
```

TRY IT

In this Try It, you create four Script Tasks in a package and control when they execute with precedence constraints. After this lesson, you will understand how to use precedence constraints to decide which tasks will execute in a package.

You can download the completed Lesson9.dtsx from www.wrox.com.

Lesson Requirements

Drag four Script Tasks into a blank package. The names of the Script Tasks will automatically be Script Task, Script Task 1, Script Task 2, and Script Task 3. Connect the Script Task so that Script Task 1 runs if Script Task is successful. Connect Script Task 1 to Script Task 2 with a success constraint. Connect Script Task 3 before Script Task 2 with a success constraint and run the package once with the logical constraints on Script Task 2 set to AND. Then change the logical constraint on Script Task 2 to OR and change the properties of Script Task 3 to Force Failure and run the package again. You should see a green check above Script Task 2 each time, indicating success.

Hints

➤ Script Task 2 should have two incoming precedence constraint lines.

➤ Look in the Properties window in the bottom right of Visual Studio to find the ForceExecutionResult property for the Script Task.

Step-by-Step

1. Drag four Script Tasks into the Control Flow.

2. Drag the precedence constraint from Script Task to Script Task 1.

3. Drag the precedence constraint from Script Task 1 to Script Task 2.

4. Drag the precedence constraint from Script Task 3 to Script Task 2. The result should match Figure 9-8.

5. Run the package; a green check mark indicating success should appear in the top right of each task, as shown in Figure 9-9.

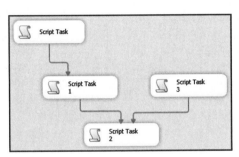

FIGURE 9-8

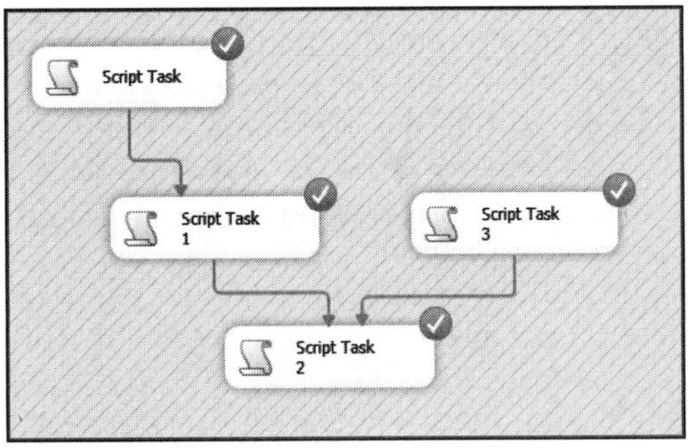

FIGURE 9-9

6. Stop the debugging using the square Stop button on the toolbar.

7. Double-click one of the constraint arrows going into Script Task 2.

8. Change the logical constraint to OR; the two lines in Script Task 2 change to dotted lines.

9. Click Script Task 3.

10. In the Properties window, change the ForceExecutionResult to Failure (Figure 9-10).

11. Run the package. Script Task 3 should have a red "X" in the top right indicating failure, and all other tasks should have a green check mark in the top right. Notice that Script Task 2 ran even though Script Task 3 failed.

FIGURE 9-10

> *Please select Lesson 9 on the DVD, or online at* www.wrox.com/go/ssis2012video, *to view the video that accompanies this lesson.*

10

Manipulating Files with the File System Task

When you need to move, delete, or rename a file, or make just about any other changes to it, the File System Task is the task to use. The File System Task enables you to make changes to files or directories and move them around without having to write custom scripts. The File System Task is a commonly used and powerful task in SSIS. A File System Task can:

➤ Copy a directory

➤ Copy a file

➤ Create a directory

➤ Delete a directory

➤ Delete the contents of a directory

➤ Delete a file

➤ Move a directory

➤ Move a file

➤ Rename a file

➤ Change the attributes of a file

You can bring up the File System Task Editor by double-clicking the File System Task or by right-clicking and selecting Edit. In the editor, you see several fields that you can set to perform the needed operation. The Operation property is the action the task performs when executing. In Figure 10-1 you can see the drop-down menu for the Operation property. What you select in this menu determines which properties will be available to you. For

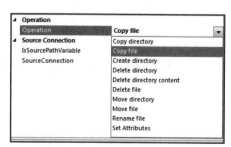

FIGURE 10-1

example, when you select Delete file, you do not need a destination, just a source file to delete, so a destination will not be available.

The property IsSourcePathVariable enables you to use a variable for the source. This variable will be a string variable that holds the location of the file, for example, C:\SSIS\FlatFile.csv. Instead of placing this path directly in the task, you have the location entered into a variable. The same holds true for the IsDestinationPathVariable property. The destination will not be a filename, but a folder location. Figure 10-2 shows the File System Task with both the source and destination set to a variable.

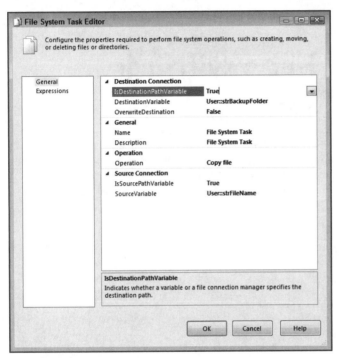

FIGURE 10-2

If you prefer to enter a connection instead of a variable, the connection must exist in the connection manager. You can also click <New Connection> in the Source Connection or the Destination Connection drop-down menu to create the connection in the connection manager. When you click <New Connection>, you see the screen in Figure 10-3. Here, you can browse to the file or folder location and save it as the source or destination; after it is saved, it appears in the connection manager of the package. (If you are unfamiliar with the concept of connections and connection managers in SSIS, please refer to Lesson 6 for more explanation.)

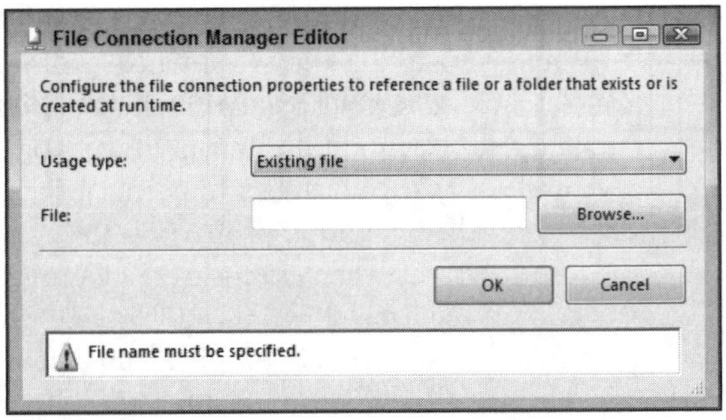

FIGURE 10-3

To copy a directory's contents with the File System Task, you need to set up a source and destination either in the connection manager or in variables. The DestinationConnection is the location the directory is copied into for this operation. If you set IsDestinationPathVariable to True, the option is DestinationVariable. Clicking the field shows a drop-down box with a list of variables. If the variable is not listed, you can click New Variable to create a variable to hold the destination name in the variable creation screen shown in Figure 10-4.

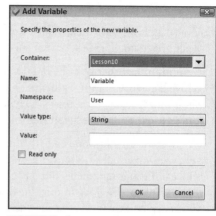

FIGURE 10-4

OverwriteDestination is the next option in the File System Task Editor. When you are setting this field, consider the package failures that can occur due to this setting. With this field set to True, the File System Task overwrites a directory if it already exists. This prevents errors, but may overwrite a needed file. With OverwriteDestination set to False, you do not risk overwriting a file inadvertently, but if a destination file already exists, the task will fail with an error stating that the file already exists.

SourceConnection is the directory that is going to be copied. In the drop-down menu, you see the sources that are in the connection manager. If you do not see the directory, click <New Connection>. This enables you to create the source connection in the connection manager just as in the DestinationConnection.

With a source folder and a destination folder set, the File System Task transfers all of the contents of the source folder and the contents of all subfolders to the destination folder. Figure 10-5 shows a completed File System Task set to back up a drive. Notice the name and description make it easy to see what the task is supposed to perform.

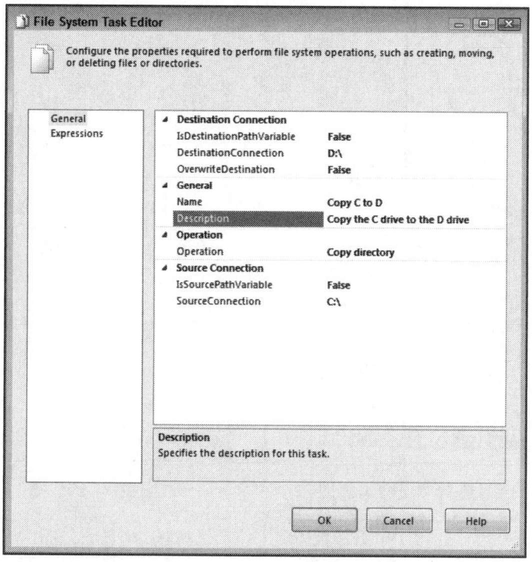

FIGURE 10-5

The next two properties are Name and Description. The name shows in the Control Flow on the task, as in Figure 10-6, and should describe what the task is designed to do. The description should be a longer explanation.

FIGURE 10-6

Several of the other options in File System Task, such as Copy file, Move file, Move directory, and Rename file, have the same options as Copy directory. You set up these tasks using the same fields. Copy file copies a file from the source to the destination. Move file moves a file from the source to the destination.

The Rename file option is a little different. It actually performs two actions at once. It not only renames a file, but also moves a file if the destination is different from the source. If you need to move a file and rename it, there is no need to create a Rename Task and a separate Move File Task. Both steps can be done in one File System Task. Set the source to the location of the file and set the destination to the new location the file should be moved to with this task. If you do not want to move the file and just need to rename it, set the source and destination to the same directory.

When you select Create directory, the first property in the File System Task is UseDirectoryIfExists, shown in Figure 10-7. If this is set to True, the task checks for the existence of the directory. If the directory exists, the File System Task takes no action. If the directory does not exist, it creates it. If UseDirectoryIfExists is set to False and the directory already exists, the task fails with an error stating that the directory already exists.

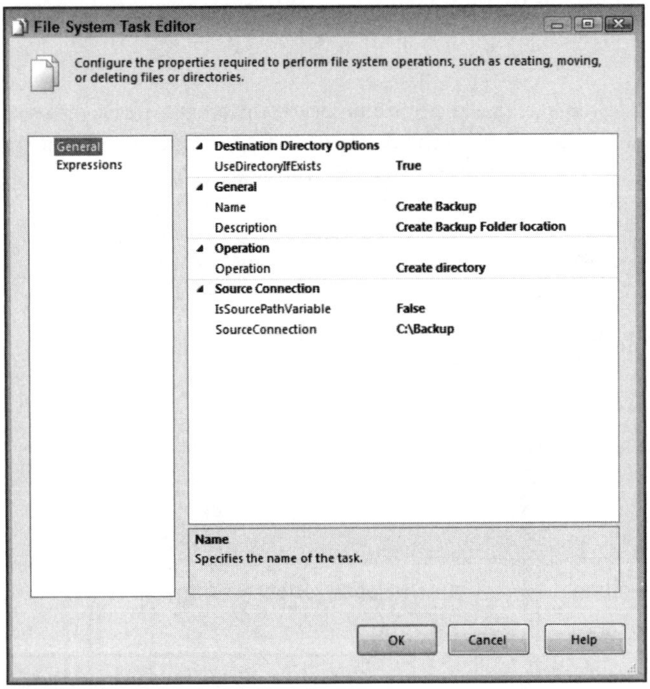

FIGURE 10-7

When you are setting up a File System Task to delete a directory or a file, only a source is needed. You can set the source to an existing connection manager source or to a variable. This task will delete a directory and all of its contents, including all subfolders and files in the subfolders. The Delete directory content operation needs only a source as well. This task leaves the directory and just deletes the contents of the directory.

When you are using a File System Task to set attributes of a file or folder, you can set four attributes for a source file. These attributes are:

➤ Hidden

➤ ReadOnly

➤ Archive

➤ System

You can set each file attribute to either True or False. The source is changed to match the settings in the File System Task. If the source file properties match the settings in the File System Task, no changes are made to the source file.

TRY IT

In this Try It, you create a package with a File System Task that moves a file and renames it at the same time. After this lesson, you will understand how to use the File System Task to manipulate files.

You can download Lesson10.dtsx from www.wrox.com.

Lesson Requirements

Create a file on the C: drive named CreatedFile.txt. The file will have nothing in it and you can create it by using Notepad or any other tool. Create a directory named Backup on the C: drive. Then use SSIS to move and rename the CreatedFile.txt to MovedFile.txt and move it into the Backup folder on the C: drive.

Hints

➤ You need only one File System Task.

➤ The rename operation can also move the file.

Step-by-Step

1. Create a new SSIS package called **Lesson10.dtsx** (or download Lesson10.dtsx from www.wrox.com).

2. Navigate to the C: drive on the local machine and create a file named **CreatedFile.txt** (right-click in Windows Explorer and select New ➪ Text Document).

3. Create a folder in the C: drive named **Backup** (right-click in Windows Explorer and select New Folder).

4. Create a new file connection in the SSIS package for C:\CreatedFile.txt (Figure 10-8) by right-clicking in the connection manager and selecting New File Connection.

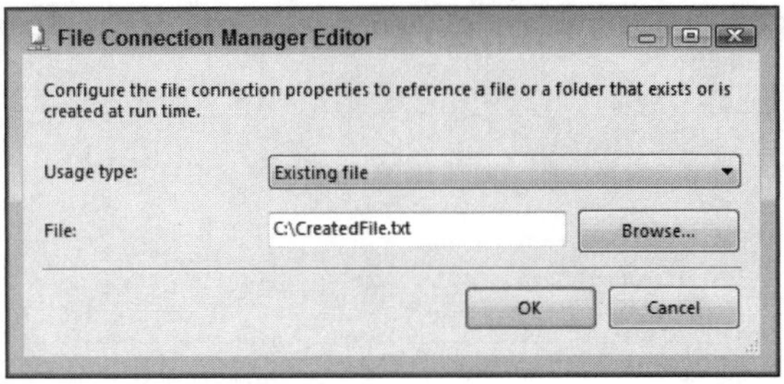

FIGURE 10-8

5. Create a new file connection in the SSIS package to C:\Backup\MovedFile.txt (Figure 10-9) by right-clicking in the connection manager and selecting New File Connection.

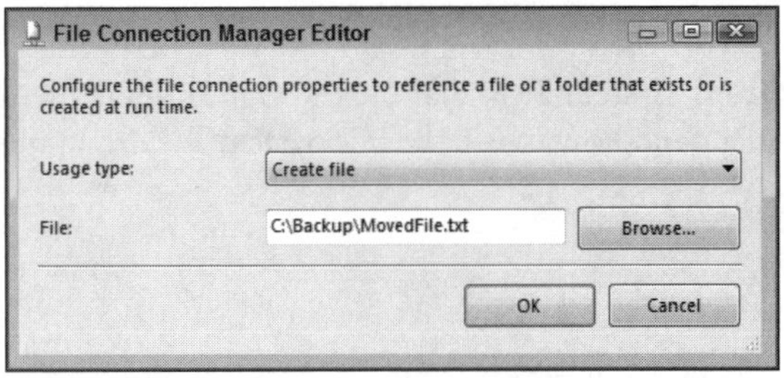

FIGURE 10-9

6. Drag over a File System Task into the Control Flow.

7. Change the Name to **Backup Created File**.

8. Enter a description that describes this operation.

9. Select Rename in the operation menu.

10. Select CreatedFile.txt as the source.

11. Select MovedFile.txt as the destination.

12. Set OverwriteDestination to True. The screen should now look like Figure 10-10.

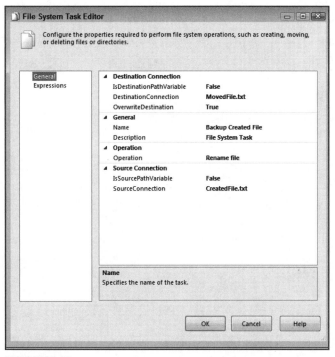

FIGURE 10-10

13. Click OK and run the package; a green check should appear next to the task, indicating success, as shown in Figure 10-11.

FIGURE 10-11

Please select Lesson 10 on the DVD, or online at `www.wrox.com/go/ssis2012video`, *to view the video that accompanies this lesson.*

11

Coding Custom Script Tasks

When you create a new SQL Server Integration Services (SSIS) package, you may find yourself wanting some functionality that the built-in tasks cannot accomplish. This situation is where the Script Task comes into play. This task can accomplish anything that can be done with any .NET programming. Interestingly, the Script Task is not a scripting language at all. In SSIS, you can use VB.NET or C# to write complete coding solutions to perform just about any task your imagination can come up with.

When you drag over a Script Task and double-click it to open the Script Task Editor, you first see three nodes listed on the left: Script, General, and Expressions, as shown in Figure 11-1. Expressions are discussed later in this book (see Lesson 14). This lesson focuses on the General and Script nodes.

FIGURE 11-1

Under the General node, you see the name and description of the Script Task. This does not affect the code in the script; it is used for ease of reference when viewing the tasks in the Control Flow. The name shows on the tasks in the Control Flow. The description is usually a longer line of text describing the purpose of the Script Task. It is a best practice to always change the values of these fields to values that will make it easy for anyone to see and understand the function of the task.

In the Script node you have four properties to set:

➤ The first is the ScriptLanguage. VB.NET is used for all of the examples in this lesson.

➤ EntryPoint is the next property. This is the location in the code where the task looks to execute the code first. Generally, this is left at Main because Main is automatically set up in the built-in starting script.

The next two properties enable you to list the variables from the package that you can use in the Script Task code:

➤ ReadOnlyVariables are variables that you want to use in the Script Task code, but you do not want the values of the variables edited.

➤ The ReadWriteVariables are variables used in the Script Task that can have their values changed, meaning you can change the values of the variables to be used in the package after the Script Task completes.

At the bottom of this node, you can see a button labeled Edit Script. The default script language is C#.

> **NOTE** *To change the default script language in SSDT, click Tools ⇨ Options at the top of SSDT in the text toolbar. Click the arrow next to Business Intelligence Designers and then click Integrated Services Designers. Change the default language on the right to VB in the Language drop-down menu.*

When you click the Edit Script button, it opens the Visual Studio Script Editor. If this is your first time opening the script editor, you see the first-time configuration window. After the environment is configured, you see a screen similar to the one shown in Figure 11-2, which is very similar to the Visual Studio coding environment. Developers should feel right at home with this interface.

On the right hand side you will see the ScriptMain.Vb window. This window contains the beginning code needed to start writing your script. This Main section is where you will write most of your code.

Most Script Tasks use ReadOnlyVariables, ReadWriteVariables, or a combination of both. As mentioned earlier in the lesson, to get a variable to be available in the Script Task, you need to add it to the ReadWriteVariables or ReadOnlyVariables in the Script node on the Properties screen of the task. One of the most common tasks is changing a filename based on the conditions in a Script Task. You can accomplish this by passing in a ReadWriteVariable with the filename and using the VB.NET code to change the variable.

First, you have to add the variable name to the ReadWriteVariables variable property. When you click the ReadWriteVariables line, an ellipsis appears on the right. Click this ellipsis button to see the list of all variables in the package, as shown in Figure 11-3. Place a check next to the variable name and click OK. Now the variable shows in the variable property as User::*Variable name*. You can now use this variable in the Script Task code.

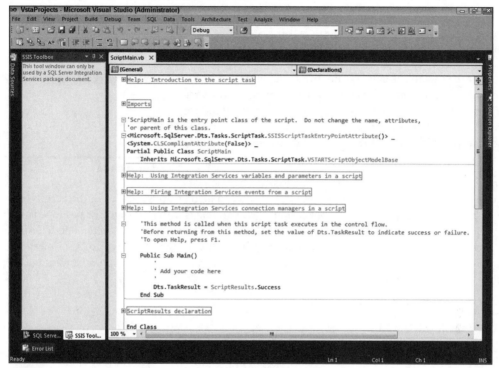

FIGURE 11-2

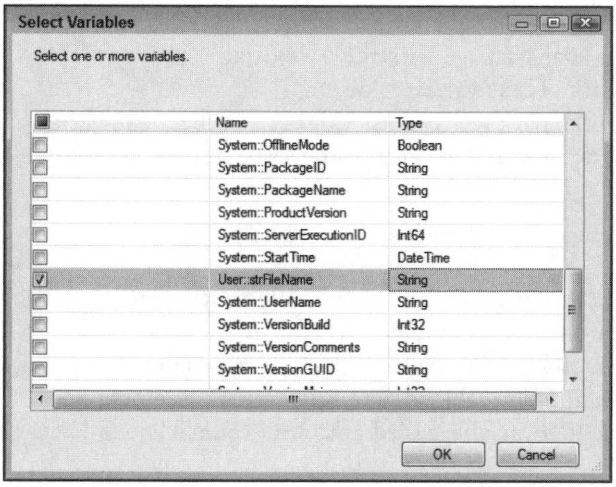

FIGURE 11-3

Now you can click the Edit Script button and write some code to change the value of the variable. Change the variable to `"newvalue"` and then make a popup box appear showing the value of the variable. Write this code below the `public sub main` starting code. Remember the entry point was left at Main in the properties of the Script Task. The following code shows how to accomplish this function:

```
Dts.Variables("strFileName").Value = "newvalue"
MsgBox(Dts.Variables("strFileName").Value)
```

Notice that the variable is called using the string literal name of the file and it is case-sensitive. Use the value property of the variable to set it to a `"newvalue"`. The next line is the typical message box in VB.NET. This causes a popup box to appear showing the value of the variable. If the value is set correctly, you see a popup box as shown in Figure 11-4.

FIGURE 11-4

You can use two types of variables in Script Tasks. The one just shown is the variable from the package. However, you can also create variables in the Script Task just as you would in a regular .NET application. This variable is different than the package variable and is not used outside of the Script Task. You create this variable with a `Dim` statement. The value of the variable is changed directly and does not require the use of the `DTS.Variables()` method. The following code shows how to create a variable, give it a value, and then pop up a message box with the value of the variable:

```
Dim strInternal As String
strInternal = "test"
MsgBox(strInternal)
```

This code causes a popup box to appear, as shown in Figure 11-5. Notice the value of `test` was saved in the variable value and then shown in the popup box. Again, you did this directly without using the `Dts.Variables()` method. The variable cannot be called by the package directly.

FIGURE 11-5

Keep in mind that you can have variables in your package with the same name as the variables in your Script Task. These variables do not pass values between the Script Task and the package. To pass values from the script variables to the package variables you need to set the package variable value to the value of the script variable. The following code shows how to do this:

```
Dts.Variables("strFileName").Value = strInternal
```

Another common function of Script Tasks is the creation of "if then" statements. You can use these statements to make decisions based on certain values. A common use for this functionality is to have an Execute SQL Task to count values from a table and pass that value into a variable. For example, say you want to see if a filename exists in an auditing table to determine if the file should be used. The Execute SQL Task saves the count value to a variable called `intAuditCount`. This value is compared with the "if then" statement and then used in further code. The following code shows an example of the "if then" statement:

```
If Dts.Variables("intAuditCount").Value > 0 Then
    'code for the file found in the audit table
Else
    'code for the file not found in the audit table
End If
```

Altering connections is another common task that Script Tasks can perform. First, the connection must exist in the connection manager of the package. Connection managers are explained in Lesson 6. Assume the connection is named AdventureWorks2012. To alter this connection, use the Dts.Connections() method. The following code shows an example of changing a connection string. Notice the literal name is in parentheses and double quotes, and is case-sensitive. The ConnectionString property of the connection follows. You can then set the connection string to be equal to the needed string. This enables you to change the connection during the package run time.

```
Dts.Connections("AdventureWorks2012").ConnectionString = _
"Data Source=localhost;Initial Catalog=AdventureWorks2012;" + _

"Provider=SQLNCLI10.1;Integrated Security=SSPI;"
```

Checking for the existence of a file is a common need in SSIS packages. To perform this function, you must import the System.IO into the Script Task. Simply add the line Imports System.IO after the last Import line at the top of the Script Task code. You must create two variables on the package: a string variable to hold the filename and a boolean variable to set to true if the file exists and false if it does not exist. Name them strFileName and bolFileExist. The code would then be:

```
If File.Exists(Dts.Variables("strFileName").Value) Then
    Dts.Variables("bolFileExist").Value = True
Else
    Dts.Variables("bolFileExist").Value = False
End If
```

Checking to see if a file is in use is another common task that can be performed with a Script Task in SSIS. Use the variables strFileName as the filename and bolFileInUse as the boolean variable and set this to true if the file is in use. The code would be:

```
Try
    File.SetLastAccessTime(Dts.Variables("strFileName").Value, Today)
Catch e As Exception
    Dts.Variables("bolFileInUse").Value = True
End Try
```

Notice that the code is catching an exception. The Script Task attempts to set the last access date of the file to today's date. If this process fails, the exception will set the boolean variable to true to indicate that the file is in use. Before running this code, you may want to use the previous code that checks if a file exists to determine whether the file does exist. That ensures that you don't catch an exception because the file does not exist when you really want to catch it because the file is being used.

After these boolean variables are set with the Script Task, you can use the expression on the precedence constraints coming from the Script Task to determine which direction the Control Flow should go. You may have two precedence constraints leaving the Script Task, both with expressions on them. One precedence constraint expression checks for a value of true and the other checks for false. The value of the boolean variable will be evaluated, and the Control Flow will continue down the proper precedence constraint line.

Now you can use the Script Task to perform complicated decision making based on the values of the variables in the package and the values of the variables in the script. You can write these values into the ReadWriteVariables and use them later in the package. The Script Task is a very powerful component that enables developers to write complex code components to perform functions that might not exist in the built-in tasks in SSIS.

TRY IT

In this Try It, you create a Script Task that changes the value of a variable based on the value of another variable. After completing this lesson you will understand how to use the Script Task to make changes to a package.

You can download Lesson11.dtsx and the sample code from www.wrox.com.

Lesson Requirements

You need to create two variables called intVar and strVar. You want to check the value of the intVar, and if it is above 10, you want to display the word "Big". If the value is 10 or less, you want to display "Small". The message box should display the value of the variable strVar and not the literal string of the words.

Hints

➤ You need only one message box code line in the Script Task.

➤ Set the value of the strVar to "Big" or "Small".

Step-by-Step

1. Right-click the Control Flow area in a blank package and left-click Variables.

2. Create a variable named **strVar** and set the type to string.

3. Create a variable named **intVar** and set the type to int.

4. Set the value of intVar to 5.

5. Drag over a Script Task and double-click it to open the Script Task Editor.

6. Ensure that the script language is set to Microsoft Visual Basic 2010.

7. Click the ReadWriteVariables property and click the ellipsis button.

8. Place a check next to User::intVar and User::strVar and click OK; the variables should show in the property window, as shown in Figure 11-6.

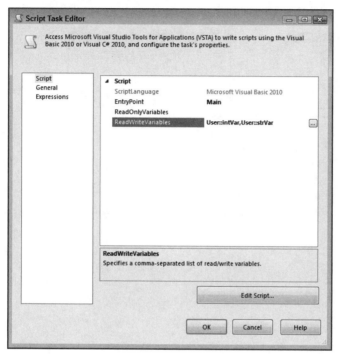

FIGURE 11-6

9. Click the Edit Script button in the task window.

10. Below the `public sub main()` section, type in the following code:

```
If Dts.Variables("intVar").Value > 10 Then
    Dts.Variables("strVar").Value = "Big"
Else
    Dts.Variables("strVar").Value = "Small"
End If

MsgBox(Dts.Variables("strVar").Value)
```

11. Close the script editor.

12. Click OK in the Script Task Editor window.

13. Right-click the Script Task and left-click Execute Task.

14. You should see a popup message showing the word "Small", as shown in Figure 11-7.

15. Click OK in the message box and click the Stop Debug button on the toolbar.

16. Change the value of the intVar variable to **11**.

17. Execute the Script Task again; you should see a message box appear showing the word "Big", as shown in Figure 11-8.

18. Click the OK button and stop debugging.

FIGURE 11-7   **FIGURE 11-8**

Please select Lesson 11 on the DVD, or online at www.wrox.com/go/ssis2012video, *to view the video that accompanies this lesson.*

12

Using the Execute SQL Task

When you are creating a SQL Server Integration Services (SSIS) package, you will find that one of the most commonly used tasks is the Execute SQL Task. This task is used to insert, update, select, and truncate data from SQL tables. Any normal SQL commands you would use can be used in this task. You can use parameters just like a stored procedure and can even call stored procedures from the task. A connection to the database must exist in the connection manager for the Execute SQL Task to reference.

Double-click an Execute SQL Task in the Control Flow to open the Execute SQL Task Editor. The first screen on the editor lists four nodes in the left pane:

➤ General

➤ Parameter Mapping

➤ Result Set

➤ Expressions

In the General node, shown in Figure 12-1, you see the main properties that you need to set for the Execute SQL Task. The first two properties are Name and Description. These properties do not affect the task. They are used for ease of reference when viewing the task in the Control Flow. The name shows on the task in the Control Flow. The description is usually a longer line of text describing the purpose of the Execute SQL Task. It is a best practice to always change the values of these fields to values that make it easy for anyone to see and understand the function of the task.

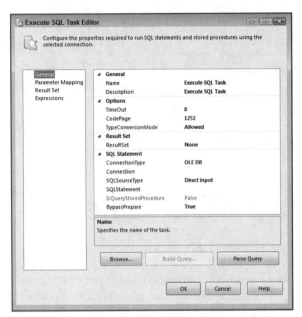

FIGURE 12-1

The next two options are the TimeOut and CodePage. The timeout is the number of seconds you want the Execute SQL Task to run before the task stops and reports a timeout failure. A setting of zero is infinite.

Code pages are set based on the code page that is used on the SQL server. In the United States, the common code page is Western European (1252). If you are using a different code page, such as Korean (949), you would need to change the code page to match the code page of the server. The code page option is available only for the following connection types:

➤ Excel

➤ OLE DB

➤ ADO.NET

➤ SQL Mobile

The TypeConversionMode option is new in SQL Server 2012. This option allows the Execute SQL Task to convert data types when saving to a variable. The data types for SSIS variables do not match exactly to the data types in SQL Server. This mismatch can cause headaches due to needed data conversions. In SQL Server 2012, that headache is relieved with the new TypeConversionMode option. Set this mode to Allowed and the Execute SQL Task will convert some items to match the variable types when necessary.

To see this in action, run the following query in an Execute SQL Task and map the results to an int32 variable in SSIS (mapping is covered later in this chapter):

```
Select Cast(1 as decimal) as Col1
```

If you have the TypeConversionMode set to Allowed, the task succeeds. If you have the TypeConversionMode set to None, the Execute SQL Task fails with the following error:

```
[Execute SQL Task] Error: An error occurred while assigning a value to variable
"intVar": "The type of the value (String) being assigned to variable
"User::intVar" differs from the current variable type (Int32). Variables may not
change type during execution. Variable types are strict, except for variables
of type Object.
```

The ResultSet property is the type of returned data from the SQL command. This can be None when the SQL command is not returning data, as with an insert command. The result set can be a single row. This single row can be stored in a string or integer variable. It can also be a full result set or XML, which can be stored in an object variable. These variables are set in the Result Set node.

When you click the Result Set node in the left pane of the Execute SQL Task Editor, you see the Result Set pane, as shown in Figure 12-2, where you can create new result set variables by clicking the Add button. The Add button is not available here if the ResultSet property on the General node is set to None. The result set name is the name of the returning data. This can be an alias you gave to a selected set of data. If you did not give the data an alias, you would enter the number 0 to indicate the first result set returned.

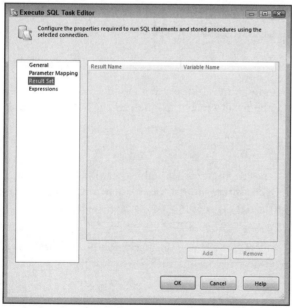

FIGURE 12-2

The Parameter Mapping node (also in the left pane of the Execute SQL Task Editor) is where you set up the parameters that you want to pass into the SQL query. The SQL query can handle multiple parameters. In this screen, as shown in Figure 12-3, you can create the parameter mappings to connect the parameter in the SQL command to a package variable. You see an example of parameters later in this lesson.

FIGURE 12-3

You can use the Execute SQL Task to count data in a table and return a number for the result set. If the count is returned as an alias, you can name the result set. For example, if the SQL query looks like this:

```
Select Count(*) as Counter From Production.Product
```

the result set will be `Counter`, and you can assign it to an integer variable that you create in the package using the Result Set node. If the SQL query is returning more than one row, you need to store that in an object variable. Once you have the data stored in a package variable, you can use this data throughout the rest of the package and in other tasks or expressions.

Returning to properties in the General node, you can see the next property you need to address is the ConnectionType. The Connection Type drop-down box contains six options:

➤   Excel

➤   OLE DB

➤   ODBC

➤   ADO

➤   ADO.NET

➤   SQL Mobile

These connections can be used to retrieve data from the connection types using the SQL language. This lesson covers the OLE DB connection and selecting data from a SQL Server table because this is very common.

Once you have selected the connection type, you can click the Connection drop-down menu. If the connection you want to use already exists in the connection manager, you can select the connection from the drop-down menu. However, at the top you see the <New Connection> option. Clicking <New Connection> opens a corresponding connection creation window depending on the connection type you select. If you select the OLE DB connection type, you see the window shown in Figure 12-4, where you can create a new OLE DB connection.

FIGURE 12-4

The next property to set is the SQLSourceType. It has three options:

➤ **Direct Input**—SQL command typed into the Execute SQL Task

➤ **File Connection**—SQL command saved in an external file

➤ **Variable**—SQL command stored in a package variable

Direct Input is the easiest to use. This method enables you to type the SQL command directly into the Execute SQL Task. The advantage of this method is that the SQL command is easy to enter. The disadvantage is that the SQL command cannot be altered outside of the package. So, maintenance is more difficult and requires the package to be altered and redeployed. This can be cumbersome and time consuming.

The File Connection option makes it easy to alter the SQL command from outside of the package. So, as business needs change and you need to select different data for your package, you can accomplish those changes very easily. The disadvantage here concerns maintaining and securing your files. Imagine if someone inadvertently deletes all of the SQL command files that your company's packages use daily. Any packages using these files would then fail at run time.

The Variable option as the SQL source is similar to Direct Input because the variable is stored in the package. However, because configuration files make it easy to alter variables outside of the package, you can alter the package without altering and redeploying it, giving you the best of both worlds in this situation.

Once you have selected the SQL source type, you are given an option to enter a SQL statement, select a file connection, or select a variable. The option shown changes depending on the SQL source type selected.

If you have selected Direct Input, you see a SQL statement option, and clicking the property makes an ellipsis appear. Clicking this ellipsis opens a small editor window in which to enter the SQL command, as shown in Figure 12-5. The editor is not much more than a small notepad with fewer options. It's not an optimal place to enter SQL, and there is no color coding to help developers entering SQL code. You might find it a better option to go to SQL Server Management Studio and type the SQL command there so you receive the benefits of color coding and IntelliSense. This will make the SQL coding much easier. Then, copy and paste the SQL command into the Direct Input window.

FIGURE 12-5

Parameters enable you to select different data with the same SQL command. The parameters are entered into the direct SQL command using question marks, as shown in the following code:

```
Select Count(*) as Counter from Production.Product where ProductID = ?
```

This SQL command selects the number of products in a table that have the product ID in the parameter you pass into the tasks. You set this up with variables in the Parameter Mapping node. You can click the Parameter Mapping node and click the Add button to create a parameter mapping for the task. The names of the parameters start at 0 and count up. So, if you have three question marks in your SQL query, representing three parameters, your parameter mappings will be 0, 1, and 2.

Once again returning to properties in the General node, you can see the next property is IsQueryStoredProcedure. This property is available on the ADO and ADO.NET options only. This is set to True when the SQL command is calling a stored procedure from the ADO connection. This stored procedure name can be stored in direct input, a file connection, or a variable.

The BypassPrepare property indicates whether the task should prepare the query before the execution of the query. Preparing a query is similar to compiling. A prepared SQL statement does not need to be analyzed every time it is used. This property must be set to False before the Parse Query button will actually parse the SQL query.

The three buttons at the bottom of the Execute SQL Task on the General node are:

➤   **Browse**—Searches for .SQL files in the filesystem

➤   **Build Query**—Query builder, similar to the query builder in SQL Management Studio

➤   **Parse Query**—Parses the SQL query checking for syntax errors

These can be used to help build the SQL query for the task. The browse features allow users to find SQL queries stored in files in the structured filesystem. The query builder helps build an error-free SQL query with a visual representation of the tables and their joins. And as already mentioned, the Parse Query button will not parse the query unless the BypassPrepare property is set to False.

TRY IT

In this Try It, you build an Execute SQL Task to return data from a table in the AdventureWorks2012 database. After this lesson, you will have a grasp of how to use the Execute SQL Task to query data from a data source and store the results in a variable.

You can download the completed Lesson12.dtsx and sample code from `www.wrox.com`.

Lesson Requirements

First, you want to count the number of products with a certain product ID. Then, you are going to have a Script Task pop up the value of the variable.

Hints

➤   You need a Script Task and an Execute SQL Task.

➤   Create a variable to hold the return value.

➤   Create a variable to hold the product ID.

➤   Create a Script Task with a popup message showing the variable value.

Step-by-Step

1.   Drag in an Execute SQL Task and double-click the task to open the editor.

2.   Click the connection and select New Connection.

3.   Create a connection to the AdventureWorks2012 database.

4.   Select Single Row as the result set.

5.   Select Direct Input as the SQL type.

6.   Click the SQL command and enter the following query:

```
Select Count(*) as Counter from Production.Product Where ProductID = ?
```

7.   In the Parameter Mapping node, click Add and create a parameter with the name of 0.

8. While in the Parameter Mapping node, click the Variable Name drop-down menu and select New Variable.

9. Create an integer (int32) variable named **intProductID** and set the value to 316.

10. Click the Result Set node and click Add to create a result set with the name of 0.

11. In the Result Set node, click the Variable Name drop-down and select New Variable.

12. Create another Int32 variable named **intProductCount**.

13. Drag a Script Task into the Control Flow of the package.

14. Connect the Execute SQL Task to the Script Task with an On Success Precedence Constraint.

15. Double-click the Script Task and select intProductCount in the ReadOnlyVariables of the Script Task.

16. Click the Edit Script button.

17. Type the following VB code in the script editor (refer to Lesson 11 for a Script Task explanation):

```
Msgbox(DTS.Variables("intProductCount").Value)
```

18. Close the script editor.

19. Click OK in the Script Task.

20. The package should look like Figure 12-6. Click Debug on the toolbar to run the package.

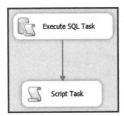

FIGURE 12-6

21. A popup message should appear showing the intProductCount variable, which should have a value of 1, as shown in Figure 12-7.

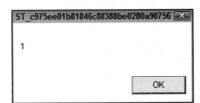

FIGURE 12-7

> *Please select Lesson 12 on the DVD, or online at* www.wrox.com/go/ssis2012video, *to view the video that accompanies this lesson.*

13

Using the Execute Process Task

When creating SSIS packages, you will sometimes find that you need to run a process or executable outside of your SSIS package. A good example of this is the need to compress or decompress files for a package before loading the data from those files into a database. There is no built-in compression task in the SSIS Toolbox. The Execute Process Task enables you to call these windows or console applications.

Errors that occur in the outside programs can be captured in the SSIS package in a variable. This variable value can be written to a log file or a table for auditing.

The Execute Process Task is shown in Figure 13-1, where the Process node is selected on the left. In this screen, you select the executable the task will call and enter any arguments you need to pass to the executable. Arguments can be thought of as parameters and are not always required by the executable. The figure has an executable set and an argument for example purposes.

You can see several other properties in the Process node of the Execute Process Task. The following list explains each of these properties.

- ➤ **RequireFullFileName**—Tells the task whether it needs the full path to execute the command. If the file is not found at the full path or in the PATH environment variables of the machine, the task will fail. Typically, a full path is used only if you want to explicitly identify the executable you want to run. However, if the file exists in the System32 directory, you wouldn't normally have to type the full path to the file because this path is automatically known to a typical Windows system.

- ➤ **Executable**—Identifies the path and filename for the executable you want to run. Be careful not to provide any parameters or optional switches in this property that would be passed to the executable. Use the Arguments property to set these types of options separately. For example, Figure 13-1 shows that the task will execute PingParameter. bat and pass in the site to ping, which in this case is www.bing.com.

- ➤ **WorkingDirectory**—Contains the path from which the executable or command file will work.

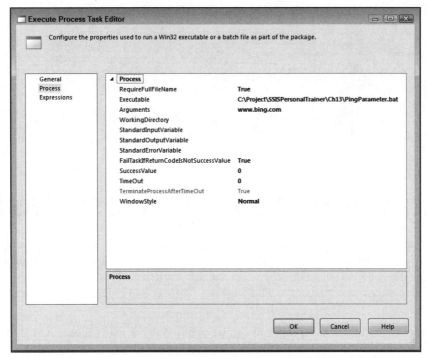

FIGURE 13-1

➤ **StandardInputVariable**—Variable used to pass into the process as an argument. Use this property if you want to dynamically provide a parameter to the executable based on a variable.

➤ **StandardOutputVariable**—Captures the result of the execution by setting the StandardOutputVariable property to a variable.

➤ **StandardErrorVariable**—Any errors that occurred from the execution are captured in the variable you provide in this property.

The variables mentioned in the preceding list can be sent to an Execute SQL Task to log or can be used in a precedence constraint later in the package that checks the length of the variables to determine whether you should go to the next task. This enables you to loop back to the process task again if need be.

Other options in the Process tab include:

➤ **FailTaskIfReturnCodeIsNotSuccessValue property**—Another option for validating if the executable completed successfully.

➤ **SuccessValue option**—The Execute Process Task will fail if the exit code passed from the program is different from the value provided in the SuccessValue option. The default value of 0 indicates that the task was successful in executing the process.

➤ **Timeout/TerminateProcessAfterTimeOut properties**—The Timeout property determines the number of seconds that must elapse before the program is considered a runaway process. A value of 0, which is the default, means the process can run for an infinite amount of time. This property is used in conjunction with the TerminateProcessAfterTimeOut property, which if set to true terminates the process after the timeout has been exceeded.

➤ **WindowStyle option**—You can set the executable to be run minimized, maximized, hidden, or normal. If this is set to any option other than hidden, users will be able to see any windows that potentially pop up and may interact with them during run time. Typically, these are set to hidden once a package is fully tested and deployed to a server to be run on a schedule unattended.

With the Execute Process Task, you can use command-line or out-of-process executables to perform work for ETL tasks. This extends SSIS beyond just what can be accomplished in the Toolbox.

The code supplied with this lesson on the book's website at www.wrox.com contains two batch files that are set up to ping a URL. The one named PingBing.bat is hard-coded to ping the URL www.bing.com. The following is the code used in this batch file:

```
ECHO Start Ping of Bing
PING www.Bing.com
ECHO Finished Ping of Bing
```

In the second batch file named PingParameter.bat the code is set to ping the argument passed to the executable. It is almost identical except that it uses a parameter instead of the hard-coded site name. The following is the code found in this batch file:

```
ECHO Start Ping of %1
PING %1
ECHO Finished Ping %1
```

There is also an SSIS package in the code with this book that contains two Execute Process Tasks, each one calling one of the batch files just described. In the following section, you build a package to call the PingParameter.bat file. You will need Internet connectivity for the batch file to ping the URLs.

TRY IT

In this Try It, you create an Execute Process Task to ping a website. This will show success when the task is able to ping the website. After this lesson you should have an understanding of how you can use the Execute Process Task to extend the capability of SSIS.

You can download the completed Lesson13.dtsx and the two batch files mentioned earlier in this lesson from www.wrox.com.

Lesson Requirements

You need to create an Execute Process Task. The executable information needs to be the name of the bat file. The argument can be changed to any website.

Hints

➤ You need one Execute Process Task.

➤ You need the bat file that is included in the code with this book.

Step-by-Step

1. Drag an Execute Process Task to a blank package.

2. Open the Execute Process Task and set the Executable to **C:\Project\SSISPersonalTrainer\Lesson13\PingParameter.bat**.

3. Set the Argument to **www.bing.com**.

4. Click OK to save the Execute Process Task.

5. Execute the package. You should see a window appear that shows the pinging of the URL, as shown in Figure 13-2.

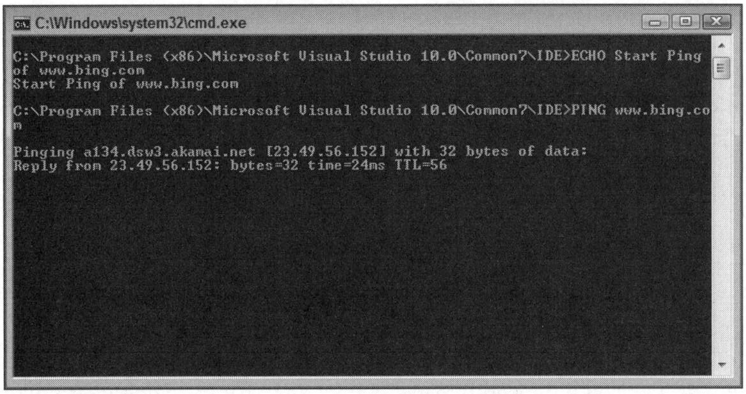

FIGURE 13-2

6. Now you will set the argument to an SSIS variable on the package. Right-click the Control Flow background in the package and select Variables.

7. Create a String Variable named **strURL** and set the value to **www.MikeDavisSQL.com**.

8. Close the variables window.

9. Double-click the Execute Process Task you created in step 1.

10. Click the Expressions node on the left.

11. Click the ellipses on the right, as shown in Figure 13-3.

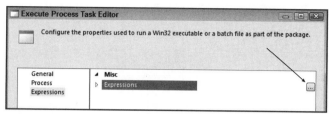

FIGURE 13-3

12. Set the Property on the right column to Arguments.

13. Click the ellipses under Expression.

14. Drag the strURL variable in the expression box below.

15. Click the Evaluate Expression button and you should see the URL appear as in Figure 13-4.

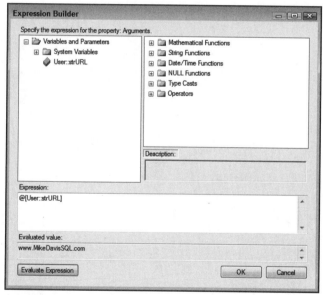

FIGURE 13-4

16. Click OK in all of the open windows.

17. Execute the package, and you will see it ping the new URL.

Feel free to change the value of the variable and execute the package again and you should see it ping the sites you enter.

> *Please select Lesson 13 on the DVD, or online at* www.wrox.com/go/ssis2012video, *to view the video that accompanies this lesson.*

14

Using the Expression Task

A new task introduced in this release of SQL Server is the Expression Task. Expression building is covered more in depth in Lesson 35 of this book, so this lesson focuses on using the Expression Task in the Control Flow.

In previous versions of SSIS, if you wanted to manipulate SSIS variables in a Control Flow, you would need to use a Script Task. This required some .NET programming knowledge and the package had to compile a script. Now you can skip the Script Task and use the new Expression Task.

The editor for the Expression Task is identical to the Expression Builder found in the Expression property of the Control Flow tasks and variable expressions. The common SSIS expression syntax is used in this task also. Figure 14-1 shows the Expression Task Editor. Notice that the title at the top is Expression Builder. One more difference in this version of SSIS is that the folder in the top left is titled Variables and Parameters. Parameters are a new addition in SQL Server 2012 and are covered in Lesson 33 of this book.

One of the common scenarios in which the Expression Task would come in handy is incrementing variables in a loop. Loops are covered in Lessons 42 and 43 of this book. Looping through a set of files to load into a database is a common use of

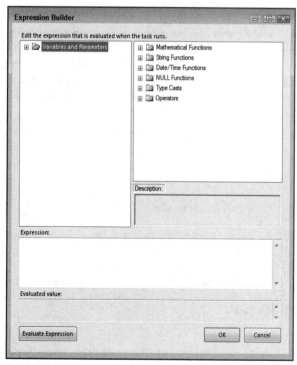

FIGURE 14-1

SSIS. Auditing the number of files that run through the loop is also commonly done. The Expression Task makes this easy now.

In Figure 14-2, you can see a package set up with a Foreach Loop, and in the container you have a Data Flow Task to load the file into a database and an Expression Task to increment a variable.

If you open the Expression Task Editor, you will see the screen in Figure 14-3. Notice that the expression is simply incrementing the variable by adding 1.

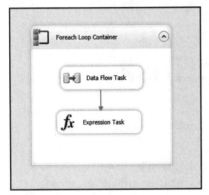

FIGURE 14-2

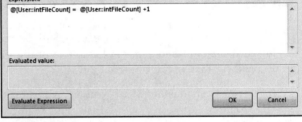

FIGURE 14-3

You can also use the Expression Task in conjunction with the precedence constraints in the Control Flow. With this combination, you can control which task will execute. Figure 14-4 shows an example Control Flow where two Execute SQL Tasks retrieve row counts from two different tables on two different servers. The variables are then added together in the Expression Task. You can see the expression after the Expression Task on the precedence constraint line. This is checking the value of the combined variables against a certain amount. If the precedence constraint expression is True, the Data Flow executes.

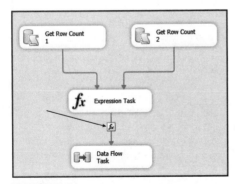

FIGURE 14-4

In the top right of the Expression Builder are the function folders. These contain all of the SSIS functions that are available to you. If you are unsure how to create an expression, you can open these folders and find examples of code; they will aid you in building the expression you need.

If you need to perform a date operation, like finding the difference between two dates, open the Date/Time Function folder as shown in Figure 14-5. Here, you see the DATEDIFF function. If you are unsure what a function does, you can read the description below the function window. This categorized layout makes it easy to find the functions you need.

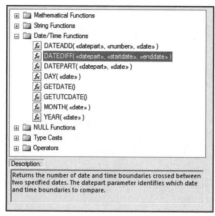

FIGURE 14-5

The Expression Task is a great addition to the Control Flow and will help developers avoid unnecessary Script Tasks in the future. In the next section, you build a package using an Expression Task.

TRY IT

In this Try It, you create an Expression Task to increment a variable in a loop. This task will add an integer variable to itself in each completed loop. When the package is successful, you will see the variable value increase as the loop runs. This exercise should give you an understanding of how the Expression Task can be used in a package.

You can download the completed Lesson14.dtsx from www.wrox.com.

Lesson Requirements

You will start with a blank package. You need to create an Expression Task and a For Loop.

Hints

➤ You need one Expression Task.

➤ You will need a For Loop Task.

➤ You need to create two integer variables.

Step-by-Step

1. Create a blank SSIS package and name it **Lesson14.dtsx**.

2. Right-click in the background of the package and select Variables.

3. Click the Create Variable button and create an integer variable named **intLoop**.

4. Click the Create Variable button again and create an integer variable named **intValue**. Set its value to **10**.

5. Close the Variable window.

6. Drag a For Loop into the package.

7. Set the For Loop Properties to match Figure 14-6.

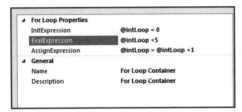

FIGURE 14-6

8. Click OK in the For Loop.

9. Drag an Expression Task into the For Loop.

10. Set the expression in the Expression Task to match Figure 14-7.

FIGURE 14-7

If you run the package at this point, it will execute successfully. But to see the value of the variable change, you will need to place a breakpoint on the For Loop and open the Locals window.

11. Right-click the For Loop and select Edit Breakpoints.

12. Select the last breakpoint option that will break on the iterations of the loop.

13. Click OK in the Breakpoints window.

14. Execute the package.

15. While in debug mode, press Ctrl+D, L. This opens the Locals window. You can also open in Debug menu at the top under the Windows section, as shown in Figure 14-8.

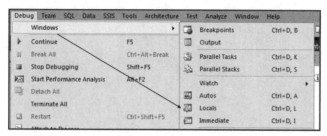

FIGURE 14-8

16. Click the plus sign (+) next to Variables in the Locals window.

17. Scroll down and find the two variables you created.

18. Press F5 to continue the package to the next breakpoint. You should see variables change value each time you continue, as shown in Figure 14-9.

Name	Value	Type
⊞ System::InteractiveMode	{True}	Boolean
⊞ User::intLoop	{2}	Int32
⊞ User::intValue	{11}	Int32
⊞ System::LastModifiedProductV	{11.0.2100.60}	String
⊞ System::LocaleID	{1033}	Int32
⊞ System::MachineName	{KIWI}	String
⊞ System::OfflineMode	{False}	Boolean
⊞ System::PackageID	{{25295CFB-1BF5-47F6-8E9C-2B747B44BD0E}}	String
⊞ System::PackageName	{Ch14Lesson}	String

FIGURE 14-9

Please select Lesson 14 on the DVD, or online at www.wrox.com/go/ssis2012video, *to view the video that accompanies this lesson.*

15

Using the Send Mail Task

The Send Mail Task sends e-mail via Simple Mail Transfer Protocol (SMTP) from a SQL Server Integration Services (SSIS) package. This task enables you to receive information about the package that can be passed into the mail task through variables—system variables or user-defined variables. The Send Mail Task is most commonly used as a notification tool. The system variables in an SSIS package hold information such as package start time, errors, and warnings.

You can place the Send Mail Task at the end of a Control Flow to send e-mail on the successful completion of a package. The event handler of a package is also a great place to place the Send Mail Task (event handlers are covered in Lesson 48). You can place the task in the OnPreExecute Event Handler to notify you via e-mail that a package has begun. The OnPostExecute Event Handler can send mail at the end of a package showing the start and end for a package, therefore enabling you to track the run time of a package. When you place a Send Mail Task in the OnError or the OnWarning Event, you can be notified when an error or warning occurs anytime during the running of a package.

You can also use the Send Mail Task to send files, because it can send attachments. A Data Flow can exist in a package that creates a file, and a Send Mail Task can then send that file via e-mail. The file can be created in a Data Flow or by a File System Task. It can also be any file not created or altered by the package.

When you first open the Send Mail Task Editor by double-clicking a Send Mail Task, you see the General node, as shown in Figure 15-1. This contains the name and description of the task. These properties are used for ease of reference when viewing the task in the Control Flow; the name shows on the tasks in the Control Flow and the description is usually a longer line of text describing the purpose of the Send Mail Task. It is a best practice to always change the values of these fields to values that make it easy for anyone to see and understand the function of the task.

FIGURE 15-1

Clicking the Mail node in the left-hand pane opens the Mail properties. Here, you see the main properties of the Send Mail Task, as shown in Figure 15-2. The first property is the SMTP connection. This connection must exist in the connection manager.

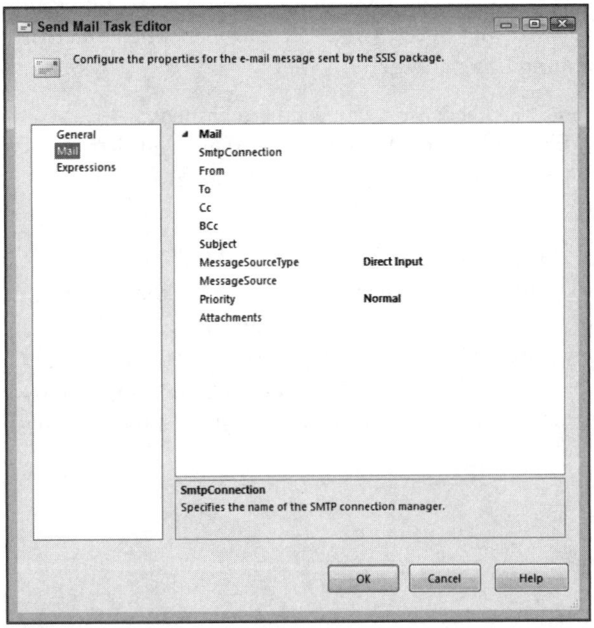

FIGURE 15-2

If the SMTP connection does not exist, you can create it by clicking <New Connection...> in the SmtpConnection drop-down menu, which opens the SMTP Connection Manager Editor, as shown in Figure 15-3. This enables you to create an SMTP connection in the connection manager. Once an SMTP connection exists in the connection manager, you can use this connection in all Send Mail Tasks.

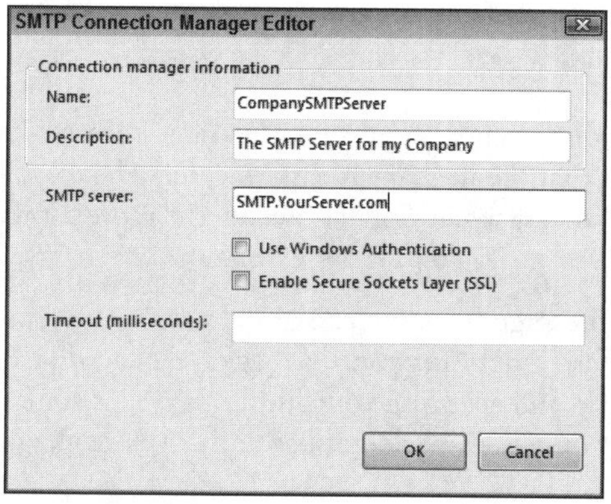

FIGURE 15-3

Just as in the Send Mail Task, the SMTP connection (which is created in the connection manager) has a name and description. The name shows in the connection manager area below the Control Flow. The description is usually a longer line of text describing the purpose of SMTP connection. The SMTP server is the name of your server that will handle e-mail sent via SMTP. Below the server name, you see two check boxes: Use Windows Authentication and Enable Secure Sockets Layer (SSL). When you check Use Windows Authentication, the package passes the user credentials of the person running the package through to the SMTP server for verification to send the e-mail. Checking Enable Secure Sockets Layer (SSL) sends the e-mail via Secure Sockets Layer. The security type you select will vary based on your environment. One new feature of the SMTP Connection is the Timeout option. Set this to the number of seconds you want the SMTP Connection to attempt to connect before timing out if it has trouble connecting.

Returning to the Send Mail Task Editor, you see that the next properties of the Send Mail Task are the basic fields of an e-mail:

➤ **From**—The e-mail address that will show as the sender

➤ **To**—The receiver of the e-mail

➤ **Cc**—Sends a carbon copy e-mail

➤ **Bcc**—Sends a blind carbon copy e-mail

➤ **Subject**—Shows in the subject line of the e-mail

The From, To, and Subject properties should be very familiar to anyone who has sent an e-mail. The carbon copy sends a copy of the e-mail to another e-mail address along with the To e-mail address. The recipients can see both of the e-mail addresses receiving the e-mail. Blind carbon copy sends the e-mail to another recipient along with the user in the To field, but the To recipient cannot see the Bcc e-mail address.

The next property to set is the MessageSourceType. It has three options:

➤ **Direct Input**—Message is typed into the Send Mail Task

➤ **File Connection**—Message is saved in an external file

➤ **Variable**—Message is stored in a package variable

Direct Input is the easiest to use. This method enables you to type the message command directly into the Execute SQL Task. The advantage of this method is that the message is easy to enter. The disadvantage is that the message cannot be altered outside of the package. So, maintenance is more difficult and requires you to alter and redeploy the package, which can be cumbersome and time consuming.

The File Connection option makes it easy to alter the message from outside of the package. So, as your business needs change and you need to select different data for your package, you can do this very easily. The disadvantage here concerns maintaining and securing your files. Imagine if someone inadvertently deletes all of the message files that your company's packages use daily. Any packages using these files would then fail at run time.

The Variable option as the message source is similar to Direct Input because the variable is stored in the package. However, configuration files make it easy to alter variables outside of the package. Thus, you can alter the package without altering and redeploying it, giving you the best of both worlds in this situation.

Once you have selected the MessageSourceType, you have an option to enter a message statement, select a file connection, or select a variable. The option shown changes based on the MessageSourceType you selected.

If you selected Direct Input, you see a message source option, and clicking the property makes an ellipsis appear. Clicking this ellipsis opens a small editor window in which to enter the message, as shown in Figure 15-4. The editor is not much more than a small notepad with fewer options. This is not an optimal place to enter a message. When you select Variable or File Connection for the MessageSourceType, the message source changes to a drop-down menu that enables you to select the file or variable. Files and variables are easier to edit than direct input and are, therefore, a better practice.

FIGURE 15-4

The Priority property enables you to set the priority mail flag on an e-mail. These are the small symbols you see in Outlook. High priority shows a red exclamation point, normal priority shows no icon, and low priority shows a blue arrow pointing down. However, remember that although this is true in Outlook, other e-mail programs may not show icons.

The last option is Attachments. Here, you can select a file that you would like to send to the recipients. This attaches the file to the e-mail just the same as if you attached it to a standard e-mail. This can be a file that was created in the package by a File System Task, or a completely separate file not used anywhere else in the package.

TRY IT

In this Try It, you create a Send Mail Task to send an e-mail. This e-mail will be in a Control Flow. When the package is successful, the e-mail will be sent and tell you the package has finished running, giving you an understanding of how the task can be used as a notification tool.

You can download the completed Lesson15.dtsx from www.wrox.com.

Lesson Requirements

You need to create a Send Mail Task. The SMTP information needs to be your own SMTP connection information so that the e-mail can be sent via your SMTP connection.

Hints

- ➤ You need one Send Mail Task.
- ➤ You need to set up an SMTP connection.

Step-by-Step

1. Drag a Send Mail Task into a blank package.
2. Right-click in the connection manager and select New Connection.
3. Select the SMTP connection from the list and click Add, as shown in Figure 15-5.

FIGURE 15-5

4. Change the SMTP connection name to your company name and SMTP, for example, **Your Server Name**.

5. Set the SMTP connection description to **My companys SMTP Server**.

6. Set the SMTP connection server to the actual SMTP Server connection.

7. Place a check in Windows Authentication if your company uses Windows Authentication to send SMTP e-mail.

8. Place a check in Enable Secure Sockets Layer (SSL) if your SMTP server requires a secure connection.

9. Once you have completed the previous steps, the SMTP connection should look like Figure 15-6.

FIGURE 15-6

10. Click OK in both open windows to return to the Control Flow.

11. Double-click the Send Mail Task to open the editor.

12. Name the Send Mail Task **Send Package Info**.

13. Set the Send Mail Task description to **Send email to users containing the package information**.

14. Click the Mail node on the left-hand side of the Send Mail Task Editor window.

15. Set the SMTPConnection to the SMTP connection you created in Steps 2–9.

16. Set the From address to your e-mail address.

17. Set the To address to your e-mail address. (If you have two e-mail addresses, you can set From and To to the two different e-mail addresses. This is true as long as the SMTP server allows you to send and receive e-mail from these e-mail addresses.)

18.   Set the Subject line to **Email From Package**.

19.   Set the MessageSourceType to Direct Input.

20.   Set the MessageSource to **The Send Mail Package Finished**. The Send Mail Task should look similar to Figure 15-7.

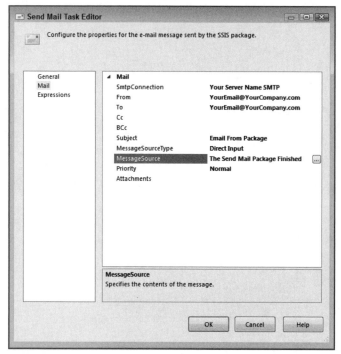

FIGURE 15-7

21.   Click OK.

22.   Run the package by clicking the green debug arrow on the toolbar; you should receive an e-mail from yourself.

> **NOTE** *If you do not receive an e-mail, but the package completes, check your SMTP server logs to see why the e-mail was stopped.*

> *Please select Lesson 15 on the DVD, or online at* www.wrox.com/go/ssis2012video, *to view the video that accompanies this lesson.*

16

Using the FTP Task

The FTP Task works very similarly to any FTP utility. It enables you to send and receive files from an FTP location along with other FTP commands. The FTP Task comes in handy when you need to move files from an FTP server to your environment for processing or when you need to send a file to an FTP server. A common example is sending an extract file created in a Data Flow or receiving a flat file to be processed by a Data Flow and inserted into a table in your server.

Double-click the FTP Task to open the task editor. The first screen of the FTP Task Editor shows the General node with some basic properties of the task. Under the General node, you see the name and description of the FTP Task. These do not affect the FTP Task; they are used for ease of reference when viewing the tasks in the Control Flow. The name shows on the tasks in the Control Flow, and the description is usually a longer line of text describing the purpose of the FTP Task. It is a best practice to always change the values of these fields to values that make it easy for anyone to see and understand the function of the task.

The General node also has two other properties: FTP Connection and Stop on Failure. The FTP Connection is the connection to the FTP server that must exist in the connection manager. You can create this FTP connection either by clicking the drop-down menu next to the FTP Connection field and selecting <New Connection...> or by right-clicking in the connection manager and selecting New Connection. Then select FTP in the menu of connection types. Either way opens the FTP Connection Manager Editor, as shown in Figure 16-1.

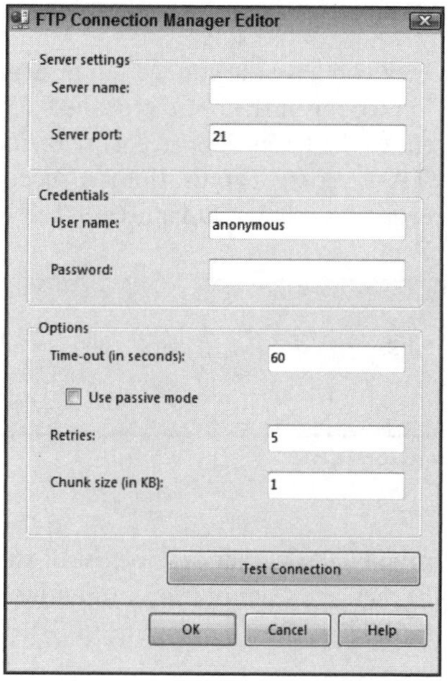

FIGURE 16-1

The first property of the FTP Connection Manager is the FTP Server location. The examples in this chapter use FTP.Microsoft.com. It is an FTP server that allows anonymous connections, so you should be able to connect to it with no issues. So in the Server name box, you would type in FTP. Microsoft.Com. The port is usually 21, but if your company uses a different port for FTP, which can be due to security concerns, type the appropriate port in the Server port property.

Under the Credentials section are two properties, the User name and Password. These are the credentials used to log in to the FTP server. The Microsoft FTP Server allows Anonymous connections, so a password is not required. If you are connecting to another server, you would type in the proper username and passwords in this section.

In the Options section are four other options. The first is Time-out. The Time-out is the number of seconds the FTP connection tries to connect before failing. The default is 60 seconds. Keep in mind that when an FTP Task is trying to connect, the package is stopped at that point in the Control Flow. So if the Time-out is set to a large number and has trouble connecting, the package may run for an extended period of time without actually performing any task. This is especially true if the package is contingent on the success of the FTP Task. So keeping this at a shorter time allows the package to fail faster due to the FTP connection issues. However, if you have an FTP server that takes a long time to validate the connection, the time may need to be higher.

The next option is Use passive mode. If checked, this option connects the FTP server using the passive mode instead of active mode. The Retries option is the number of times the FTP Task tries to connect to the FTP server before failing out. The last property of the FTP Connection Manager Editor is the Chunk size. This is the size of the data that is sent out in succession until the entire file is sent or received. Some networks have restrictions that may require this to be adjusted, so check with your network admin for your restrictions. Generally, the 1 KB default is acceptable.

Once you have the connection information set up to connect to the FTP location, you can click Test Connection at the bottom of the FTP Connection Manager Editor window, and a test message is sent to the FTP server to ensure the connection exists and that the username and password meet the FTP server credentials. If it is a successful connection, you receive the message "Test connection succeeded," as shown in Figure 16-2.

FIGURE 16-2

If the FTP server does not exist or the user credentials fail to pass the login process, you receive the message "Connection cannot be established. Server name, port number, or credentials may be invalid," as shown in Figure 16-3.

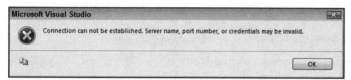

FIGURE 16-3

After you have created the FTP server connection in the connection manager, you can then rename the connection by clicking it in the connection manager one time, and the name will highlight blue. Then you can type a more meaningful name for the FTP connection. This capability is particularly helpful when you have multiple FTP connections in the connection manager.

Once you have the FTP connection set up in the connection manager, you can select it in the FTP Connection drop-down menu in the FTP Task. The next property is Stop on Failure. This property stops the FTP from performing a transfer if there is a failure during the transfer process. Keep in mind that the task will still send a failure message to the package or parent container if it has a failure regardless of this property's setting. The Stop on Failure property is available simply to allow the transfer to continue if part of the transfer fails.

When you click the File Transfer node in the FTP Task Editor, you see the operations that are available for the FTP Task to perform and the parameters for these operations. Of course, the parameters change based on the operation you select. The Operation drop-down menu has several options, as shown in Figure 16-4:

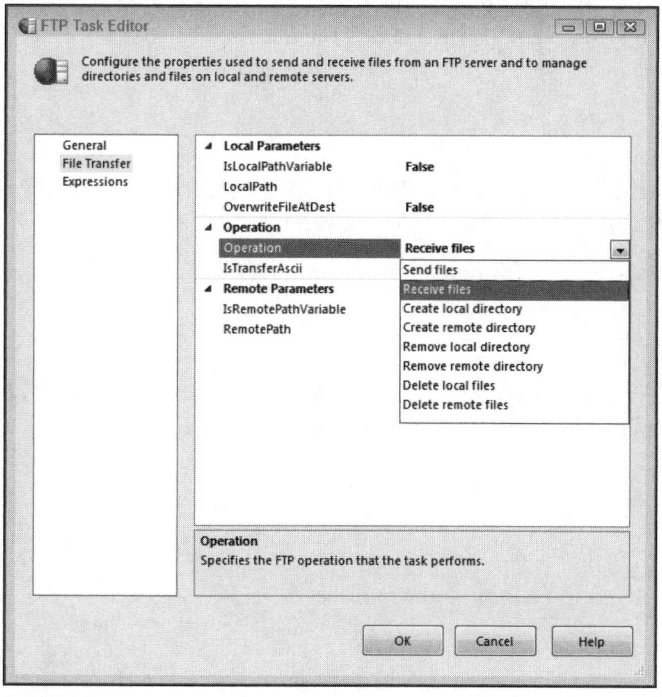

FIGURE 16-4

➤ **Send files**—Send files to the FTP server from a local source

➤ **Receive files**—Retrieve files from the FTP server to a local destination

➤ **Create local directory**—Create a folder on a local drive

➤ **Create remote directory**—Create a folder on the remote directory

➤ **Remove local directory**—Delete a local folder and all of the contents

➤ **Remove remote directory**—Delete a remote folder and all of its contents

➤ **Delete local files**—Delete files on the local directory

➤ **Delete remote files**—Delete files on the remote FTP server

If you select Receive files, you see the most common options used in an FTP Task. IsLocalPathVariable is a boolean property that tells the FTP Task whether the location on the local destination is saved in a variable. When this is set to true, the drop-down menu of the LocalPath changes to a drop-down menu of variables. When the IsLocalPathVariable option is set to false, the LocalPath drop-down shows the available folder location in the connection manager.

If the IsRemotePathVariable is true, the RemotePath shows a drop-down of variables to choose from. If the IsRemotePathVariable is false, the RemotePath shows an ellipsis that will connect to the FTP server and show a browse window enabling you to select the file to be retrieved with the FTP Task.

The last property to set is OverwriteFileAtDest. If set to true, this property allows the FTP Task to overwrite an existing file if the FTP Task attempts to move the file into a directory that already contains the file being moved. If it is set to false, the FTP Task fails if the file already exists.

TRY IT

In this Try It, you retrieve a file from the FTP server from Microsoft. After this lesson, you will understand how you can use the FTP Task to download a file to a local destination.

You can download the completed Lesson16.dtsx from `www.wrox.com`.

Lesson Requirements

You need to create an FTP Task with the proper credentials and server settings to connect to FTP. Microsoft.Com. You then look in a folder on the FTP server and retrieve a single file.

Hints

➤ You need a single FTP Task.

➤ Microsoft's FTP server enables you to connect anonymously.

Step-by-Step

1. Drag an FTP Task into a blank package and double-click the task to open the FTP Task Editor.

2. Click the FTP Connection drop-down menu and select the only option, <New Connection...>. This opens the FTP Connection Manager Editor.

3. In the FTP Connection Manager Editor, set the Server name to **FTP.Microsoft.Com** and leave the other options at the defaults. The window should match Figure 16-5.

FIGURE 16-5

4. Click Test Connection to ensure you have a connection to the FTP server. If your connection fails, check with your network admin to determine your FTP abilities in your environment.

5. Click OK in the FTP Connection Manager Editor; the FTP Task Editor should still be open.

6. Change the name of the FTP Task to **Get MS File**.

7. Change the description to **Retrieve File from Microsoft**.

8. Click the File Transfer node in the left pane of the FTP Task Editor.

9. Select Receive Files in the Operation drop-down menu.

10. From the drop-down menu for LocalPath, select <New Connection...>. This selection opens the File Connection Manager Editor.

11. Set the usage type to Existing Folder.

12. Click Browse and select the C:\Projects\SSISPersonalTrainer.

13. Click the ellipsis next to RemotePath and browse to the SoftLib directory in the Microsoft FTP Server.

14. Select the index.txt file. Click OK.

15. Click OK in the FTP Task.

16. Click the green debug arrow on the toolbar. The FTP Task should turn green to indicate success.

17. Ensure you have the index.txt file in the SSISPersonalTrainer folder on your local drive.

> *Please select Lesson 16 on the DVD, or online at* www.wrox.com/go/ssis2012video, *to view the video that accompanies this lesson.*

17

Creating a Data Flow

This lesson covers the basics of the Data Flow Task. Section 3 comprises lessons covering the sources, destinations, and transformations in detail. However, this lesson gives you the tools to get started creating a Data Flow and understanding its purpose.

The Data Flow Task is used to transfer data from a source to a destination and can transform the data as needed. The Data Flow Task is capable of handling large amounts of data. The source and destination can be any of several different types, such as a flat file or database, and can contain millions of rows of data. The destination can also be of several types.

You can use the Data Flow Task to extract data from a database and write to a flat file location or to move the data from a flat file to a database. This capability enables you to receive files from outside sources and write this data to your database. You can also use the Data Flow Task to move data from one database to another.

The transforms that exist in the Data Flow enable you to make changes to the data as you move it from a source to a destination. For example, if you are receiving flat files from a vendor and the data is not formatted correctly (say, the Social Security numbers need to have dashes) you can fix that before writing it to a database. Fixing things like that prior to writing to your database prevents you from having to run updates on your database later.

Additionally, these transforms are faster in SSIS. SSIS performs the transforms in memory, which is why it is much faster than reading and writing the data to a drive. This speed is especially evident in the case of running updates to a table. SQL update commands read data from a database and write data back to the same database. This reading and writing to the same location makes the process very slow compared to SSIS.

The Data Flow enables you to save data to multiple locations simultaneously, which also improves performance when you are saving data. You can receive a flat file from a vendor, open it with an SSIS package, parse through the data, make decisions on where data needs to be written, and write the data to multiple locations, all in one Data Flow.

You have two ways to create a Data Flow in a package. You can drag out the Data Flow Task from the Toolbox, or you can click the Data Flow tab at the top and click the blue link in the middle of the screen. This link states, as shown in Figure 17-1, "No Data Flow tasks have been added to this package. Click here to add a new Data Flow task."

If there is already a Data Flow in the package, clicking the Data Flow tab shows that Data Flow. If multiple Data Flows are in a package, you see a drop-down menu at the top of the Data Flow screen showing the list of all the Data Flows in the package. It is a best practice to give the Data Flows a name that is descriptive. With descriptive names, you can then easily select the correct Data Flow you are trying to alter. Descriptive naming is a major help when your package contains a large number of Data Flows.

FIGURE 17-1

After you enter the Data Flow tab by either method previously mentioned, the Toolbox will contain a new set of tools. The top section contains the Favorites, the middle contains the common transforms, and the bottom contains the source and destinations. These tasks can be used only in the Data Flow Task and cannot be used in the Control Flow screen. You can move any item in the Toolbox to the Favorites section by right-clicking on it and clicking Move to Favorites.

Several sources have the same type as a destination. For example, there is an Excel Source and an Excel Destination. These tasks are not interchangeable. A source can only read data and a destination can only write data. Keep in mind that any connections you add to the Connection Managers in a package can be reused in other Data Flows or even in the Control Flow of the package (connection managers are explained in Lesson 6). So, a source in a Data Flow can connect to an Excel file, and an Excel Destination can connect to the same Excel file. The connection exists just once in the connection manager but can be used multiple times in a package.

Once you drag a source into a Data Flow, two lines appear from the bottom of the task. The blue line is the good data. The red line is the bad data. Sources and destinations, including how to use these blue and red lines, are explained in detail in the lessons following this one. Double-clicking the source opens the source editor for that source type. In the editor, you can select the location of the source.

After your source is established, you can connect it to a transform from the transformation section of the Toolbox. This transform can manipulate the data to be in the form you want for your destination. The transform can also make complex decisions to send data to different destinations.

Once the sources and transforms are created, you can drag out a destination and connect the last step of the transforms to the destination. If the Data Flow does not contain any transforms, the source can be connected directly to the destination, which simply moves data from one location to another without changing the data. This arrangement is the simplest form of a Data Flow.

TRY IT

In this Try It, you create a package with a Data Flow Task. The Data Flow is going to move data from a SQL database table to a flat file. After this lesson, you will have an understanding of how to create a Data Flow Task in the Control Flow of a package.

Lesson Requirements

You need to create a Data Flow in a package and create a source and a destination. The source is going to be an OLE DB connection to the AdventureWorks2012 database to the Products table. The destination is going to be a flat file you create.

You can download the completed Lesson17.dtsx from www.wrox.com.

Hints

➤ You need only one Data Flow Task for this example.

➤ The Data Flow needs a source and a destination.

➤ The package needs two connections in the connection manager.

Step-by-Step

1. Drag a Data Flow Task into a blank package.

2. Double-click the Data Flow Task to enter the Data Flow tab.

3. Drag in an OLE DB Source.

4. Double-click the OLE DB Source to open the Source Editor.

5. Click the New button. The Configure OLE DB Connection Manager dialog box opens (see Figure 17-2). Select the source connection to AdventureWorks2012 and click OK. Note: If the connection exists in this window, you can skip steps 6–8.

6. If the AdventureWorks2012 connection is not shown in the Configure OLE DB Connection Manager dialog box, click the New button, which takes you to the Connection Manager dialog box (see Figure 17-3).

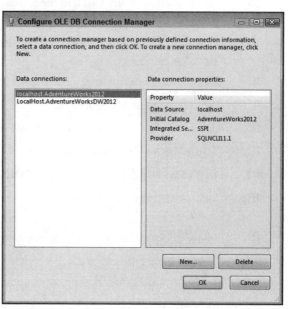

FIGURE 17-2

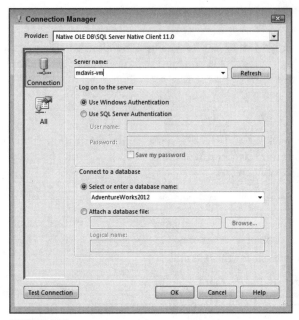

FIGURE 17-3

7. Set the Server Name to the location of the server with the AdventureWorks2012 database. Usually this name is LocalHost if the server is on your machine.

8. Select AdventureWorks2012 in the Select or enter a database name drop-down and click OK twice.

9. In the OLE DB Source Editor, click the drop-down menu of tables and select the Production.Product table.

10. Click the Columns node in the left-hand pane. You should see columns in the Products table.

11. Click OK to close the Source Editor.

12. Right-click the OLE DB Source and select Rename.

13. Change the Name to **AW Products**.

14. Drag a Flat File Destination into the Data Flow.

15. Connect the blue line from the bottom of the AW Products Source to the Flat File Destination.

16. Double-click the Flat File Destination to open the Flat File Destination Editor.

17. Click the New button.

18. Select Delimited in the Flat File format window and click OK.

19. In the Flat File Connection Manager Editor, change the name to **AW Products Extract**.

20. Change the Description to **All AW product data**.

21. Type **C:\AWProducts.txt** in the File Name text box.

22. Click OK to close the Connection Manager.

23. Click the Mappings node in the left-hand pane; the mappings should look like Figure 17-4.

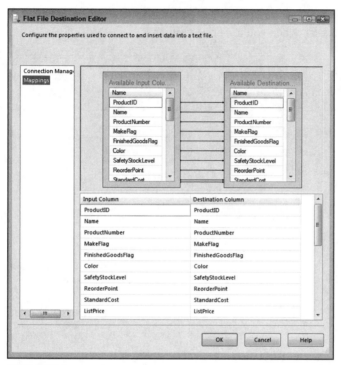

FIGURE 17-4

24. Click OK to close the Flat File Destination Editor.

25. Right-click the Flat File Destination and click Rename. Change the name to **AW Products Extract File.** The Data Flow should match Figure 17-5.

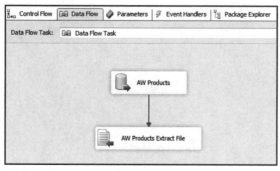

FIGURE 17-5

26. Click the blue debug arrow on the toolbar. A new file will be created in your C: drive containing all the data from the product table. (If you do not see a file, you may not have rights to create a file and may need to start SQL Server Data Tools MD in administrative mode.)

27. Click the Stop Debug button on the toolbar and look at the contents of the file on your C: drive.

28. You can delete the text file when you are done viewing it.

Please select Lesson 17 on the DVD, or online at www.wrox.com/go/ssis2012video, *to view the video that accompanies this lesson.*

SECTION 3
Data Flow

18

Extracting Data from Sources

Generally, when you create SQL Server Integration Services (SSIS) packages, it is for the purpose of moving data from one point to another. A *source* is where you specify the location of the data you want to move or transform.

Most sources point to a connection manager in SSIS. By pointing to a connection manager, you can reuse connections throughout your package because you need only change the connection in one place. In this lesson, the most frequently used sources (OLE DB, Excel, and flat file) are described thoroughly.

> **NOTE** *In August 2011, Microsoft announced that SQL Server 2012 would be the last release to support the Microsoft SQL Server OLE DB provider, and recommended that new development using SQL Server 2012 be done using ODBC connections. Although this announcement stunned many because of Microsoft's investment in OLE DB over the past years, it shouldn't be surprising with the emphasis on cloud computing, which frequently uses ODBC. This is a significant change, but it should not change your design style at this point in time. When it comes to SSIS development, using ODBC connections is still missing some functionality. This could cause your development to stall at points, so you should stick with the OLE DB provider.*

SOURCE ASSISTANT

The *Source Assistant* is a new feature of SSIS that helps guide you through the process of defining a connection manager and source. From inside the Data Flow tab, select the Source Assistant from the SSIS Toolbox. Figure 18-1 shows the Source Assistant displaying the available source types you can choose from, and it even creates a connection manager to the selected source type if one does not already exist. If you believe you have a source type installed on your machine, but it does not appear, uncheck the Show only installed source types option and all source types will appear.

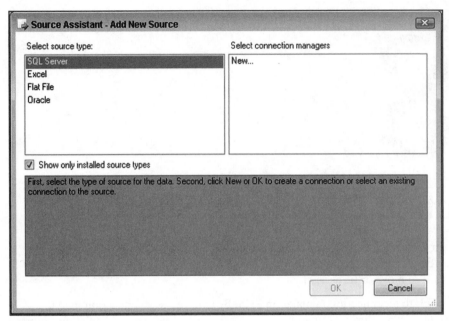

FIGURE 18-1

After selecting the appropriate source and connection manager for your design, click OK and a source appears in your Data Flow Task with the features you selected. The next sections dive deeper into the most frequently used connection types.

OLE DB SOURCE

The most common type of source used is the OLE DB Source, which can point to any Object Linking and Embedding Database (OLE DB)–compatible data source, such as SQL Server, Oracle, or DB2. To configure the OLE DB Source, add the source to the design pane in the Data Flow tab and double-click on it. In the Connection Manager page of the OLE DB Source Editor, shown in Figure 18-2, select the connection manager of your OLE DB Source from the OLE DB connection manager drop-down box. You can also add a new connection manager in the editor by clicking the New button.

The Data access mode option sets how you can retrieve the source data. The OLE DB Source has four different data access modes available:

➤   A table or view

➤   A table or view indicated in a variable

➤   The results of a SQL statement

➤   The results of a SQL statement initiated in a variable

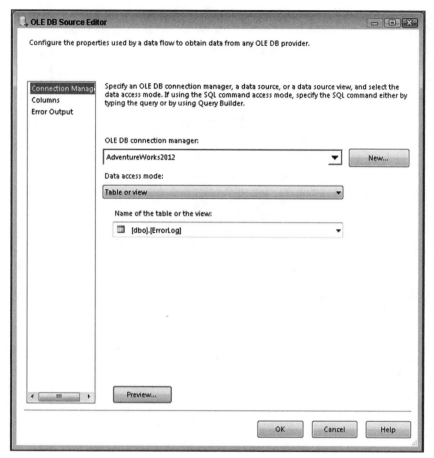

FIGURE 18-2

SSIS does not easily allow a stored procedure to be accessed when using the SQL command mode. Additionally, you can pass a variable into the query by substituting a question mark (?) for where the parameter should be and then clicking the Parameters button.

After these configurations have been completed, you can go to the Columns page to check each column you need from the table. Figure 18-3 shows that once the needed columns are checked, you can assign a new name by typing the new name in the Output Column.

> **NOTE** *Here's a best practice: when you are selecting columns, check only what you will need to use. With a smaller data set, you gain better performance. For the same reason, it is always better to type a query with only the needed columns instead of selecting a table. Using the select table option essentially does a* Select * *on the table, bringing all that data across the network when you might need only 5 out of 25 columns.*

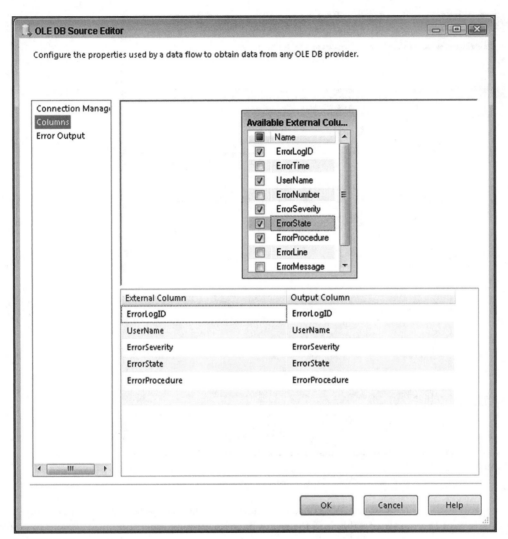

FIGURE 18-3

Sometimes incompatible data types can cause conversion issues, and you may want to send these errors to a different path in the Data Flow. You can do this within the Error Output page shown in Figure 18-4, where you specify how to handle these issues when they occur. On each column, you can specify that if an error occurs, you want the row to be ignored, be redirected, or fail. If you choose to ignore failures, the column for that row is set to NULL. If you redirect the row, the row is sent down the red path in the Data Flow coming out of the OLE DB Source.

FIGURE 18-4

Try It

In this Try It, you set up an OLE DB Source to bring in transaction history data from the AdventureWorks2012 database. You can download the AdventureWorks2012 database used for this book at the Wrox website at www.wrox.com/go/SQLSever2012DataSets. (Please see Lesson 3 if you haven't yet installed the AdventureWorks2012 database.) After this lesson, you will know how to use an OLE DB Source to extract data from a SQL Server table.

You can download the completed Lesson18.dtsx from www.wrox.com.

Lesson Requirements

Create a new package named **Lesson18** and make the following change:

➤   Use the following query to return needed rows from AdventureWorks2012:

```
SELECT TransactionID
      ,ProductID
      ,TransactionDate
      ,Quantity
```

```
        ,ActualCost
        ,ModifiedDate
  FROM Production.TransactionHistory
WHERE Quantity > 2
```

Hints

➤ You need only one OLE DB Source and one OLE DB Connection Manager.

Step-by-Step

1. Create an SSIS package and name it **Lesson18** or download Lesson18.dtsx from
   www.wrox.com. Add a Data Flow Task to the Control Flow design surface and name it
   OLE DB Extract.

2. Drag an OLE DB Source in the Data Flow design surface and double-click to open the OLE
   DB Source Editor.

3. Click the New button for the OLE DB Connection Manager to create a new connection to a
   SQL Server Source, which is shown in Figure 18-5. Click OK to create the connection.

FIGURE 18-5

4. Back in the OLE DB Source Editor, once the connection manager is created select SQL Command as the data access mode and type the following query:

```
SELECT TransactionID
      ,ProductID
      ,TransactionDate
      ,Quantity
      ,ActualCost
      ,ModifiedDate
  FROM Production.TransactionHistory
WHERE Quantity > 2
```

Once your screen looks like Figure 18-6, click OK to continue.

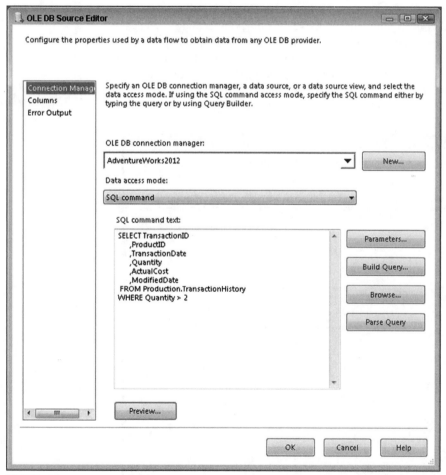

FIGURE 18-6

5. Drag a Union All onto the Data Flow design surface. The Union All serves as a placeholder until you learn about destinations in the next lesson. Connect the OLE DB Source to the Union All and execute just this Data Flow by right-clicking in the design surface and selecting Execute Task. Figure 18-7 shows the results.

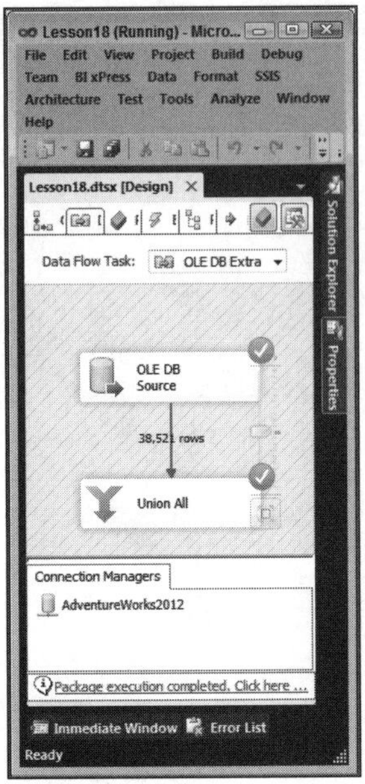

EXCEL SOURCE

The Excel Source is used to extract data from an Excel spreadsheet. To use an Excel Source, you must first create an Excel Connection Manager that points to the location of the spreadsheet. Figure 18-8 shows that once you point to an Excel Connection Manager, you can select the sheet from the Name of the Excel sheet drop-down box. The Excel Source works much the same as the OLE DB Source, which means you can even run a query by changing the data access mode to SQL Command. This source treats Excel just like a database, where an Excel sheet is the table and the workbook is the database.

FIGURE 18-7

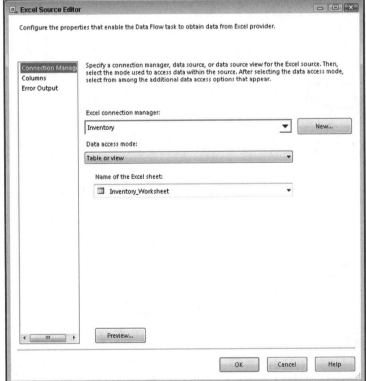

FIGURE 18-8

SSIS supports Excel data types, but unfortunately Excel does not translate well to how most databases are constructed. If you right-click a column in Excel and select Format Cells, you will find that most of the columns in your Excel spreadsheet have probably been set to General. SSIS interprets the General format as a Unicode data type. In SQL Server, the Unicode translates into nvarchar, which is not typically what you find in databases. If you have a Unicode data type in SSIS and you try to insert it into a varchar column, it can fail. Lesson 20 shows you this exact problem and how to correct it.

If you are connecting to a spreadsheet from Excel 2007 or later, ensure that you select the proper Excel version when creating the Excel Connection Manager. You will not be able to connect to an Excel 2007 spreadsheet otherwise.

Additionally, the native Excel driver is a 32-bit driver only, and your packages will have to run in 32-bit mode if the workstation you develop on is 64-bit. To enable 32-bit mode, right-click and select Properties on the project file in the Solution Explorer window. Select the Debugging tab and change Run64BitRuntime to False, shown in Figure 18-9.

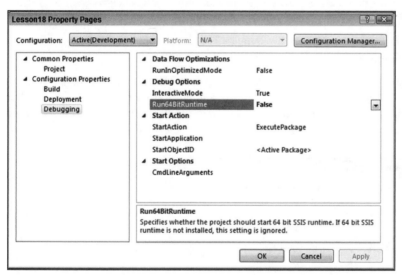

FIGURE 18-9

This is only necessary from within SQL Server Data Tools because it is a 32-bit application. When scheduling SSIS packages to run on a server, you can download the Microsoft Access Database Engine 2010 Redistributable, which includes a 64-bit driver for Excel, from `http://www.microsoft.com/en-us/download/details.aspx?id=13255`.

Try It

In this Try It, you set up an Excel Source to bring in inventory data. You use an Excel spreadsheet as your source, which you can download from `www.wrox.com`. After this lesson, you will know how to use an Excel Source to extract data from an Excel spreadsheet.

You can also download the completed Lesson18.dtsx from `www.wrox.com`.

Lesson Requirements

Make the following changes to your Lesson18 package:

➤ Download the file Inventory_Worksheet.xls as your source from www.wrox.com and save it to C:\Projects\SSISPersonalTrainer\

Hints

➤ You need only one Excel Source and one Excel Connection Manager.

Step-by-Step

1. Open the SSIS package named Lesson18 or download Lesson18.dtsx from www.wrox.com. Add a Data Flow Task to the Control Flow design surface and name it **Excel Extract**.

2. Drag an Excel Source in the Data Flow design surface and double-click to open the Excel Source Editor.

3. Click the New button for the connection manager. This opens the Excel Connection Manager dialog box.

4. For the Excel file path, click Browse to select the location C:\Projects\SSISPersonalTrainer\, where you downloaded the spreadsheet file. Once you have selected the correct spreadsheet, make sure the Microsoft Excel version is Excel 97-2003 and that the First row has column names option is checked. Figure 18-10 shows what your screen should look like.

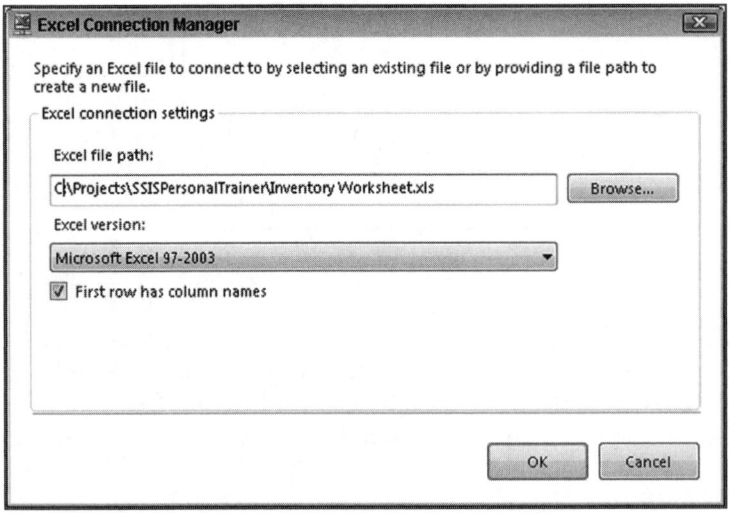

FIGURE 18-10

5. Back in the Excel Source Editor after the connection manager is created, select Inventory_
Worksheet in the Name of the Excel sheet drop-down menu and click OK, as shown in
Figure 18-11.

6. Drag a Union All onto the Data Flow design surface. The Union All serves as a placeholder
until you read about destinations in the next lesson. Connect the Excel Source to the Union
All and execute just this Data Flow by right-clicking in the design surface and selecting
Execute Task. Figure 18-12 shows the results.

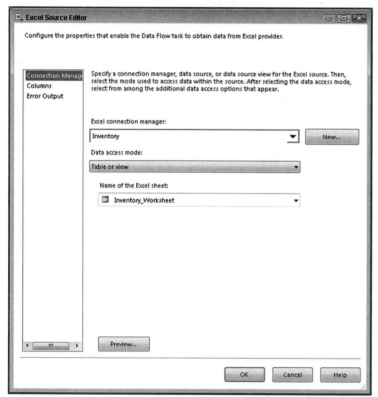

FIGURE 18-11

FIGURE 18-12

FLAT FILE SOURCE

The Flat File Source provides a data source for text files. Those files are typically comma– or tab-
delimited files, or they could be fixed-width or ragged-right. A fixed-width file is typically received
from the mainframe, and it has fixed start and stop points for each column. This method makes for
a fast load, but takes longer at design time for the developer to map each column.

You specify a Flat File Source the same way you specify an OLE DB Source. Once you add it to your Data Flow pane, point it to a connection manager connection that is a flat file. After that, go to the Columns tab of the Flat File Source Editor to specify what columns you want to be presented to the Data Flow. Figure 18-13 shows columns being selected from a Flat File Source. All the specifications for the flat file, such as delimiter type, were previously set in the Flat File Connection Manager.

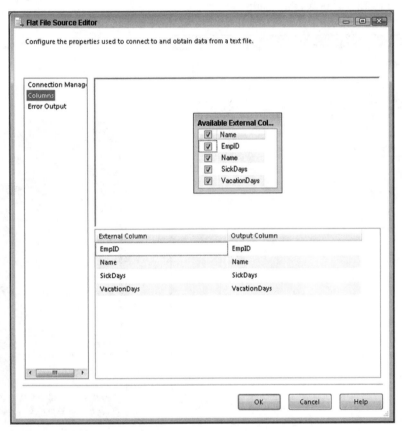

FIGURE 18-13

Similar to the Excel Source, the data types of a Flat File Source are set up by default, and SSIS may not assign them correctly. All columns are brought in as a string data type regardless of their true content. To correct this, go to the Advanced tab in the Flat File Connection Manager and select the column and then the correct data type.

Try It

In this Try It, you set up a Flat File Source to bring in employee benefits data from a flat file. The comma-delimited file to use for this example is called EmployeeList.txt, and you can find it at www.wrox.com. After this lesson, you will know how to use a Flat File Source to extract data from a text file.

You can also download the completed Lesson18.dtsx from www.wrox.com.

Lesson Requirements

Make the following changes to your Lesson18 package:

➤ Download the EmployeeList.txt file as your source from www.wrox.com and save it to C:\ Projects\SSISPersonalTrainer.

➤ Set the Flat File Connection Manager as comma-delimited.

➤ Note that the first row in the file comprises column names.

➤ Data types should be as follows:

  ➤ **EmpID**—int

  ➤ **Name**—string

  ➤ **SickDays**—int

  ➤ **VacationDays**—int

Hints

➤ You need only one Flat File Source and one Flat File Connection Manager.

Step-by-Step

1. Open the SSIS package named Lesson18 or download Lesson18.dtsx from www.wrox.com. Add a Data Flow Task to the Control Flow design surface and name it **Flat File Extract**.

2. Drag a Flat File Source in the Data Flow design surface and double-click to open the Flat File Source Editor.

3. Click the New button for the connection manager. This opens the Flat File Connection Manager Editor.

4. In the General tab, name the connection manager **Flat File Extract** and select the file named EmployeeList.txt for the source file. You can download this file from www.wrox.com. Last, check the Column names in the first data row check box. Once these changes have been made, your screen should look like Figure 18-14.

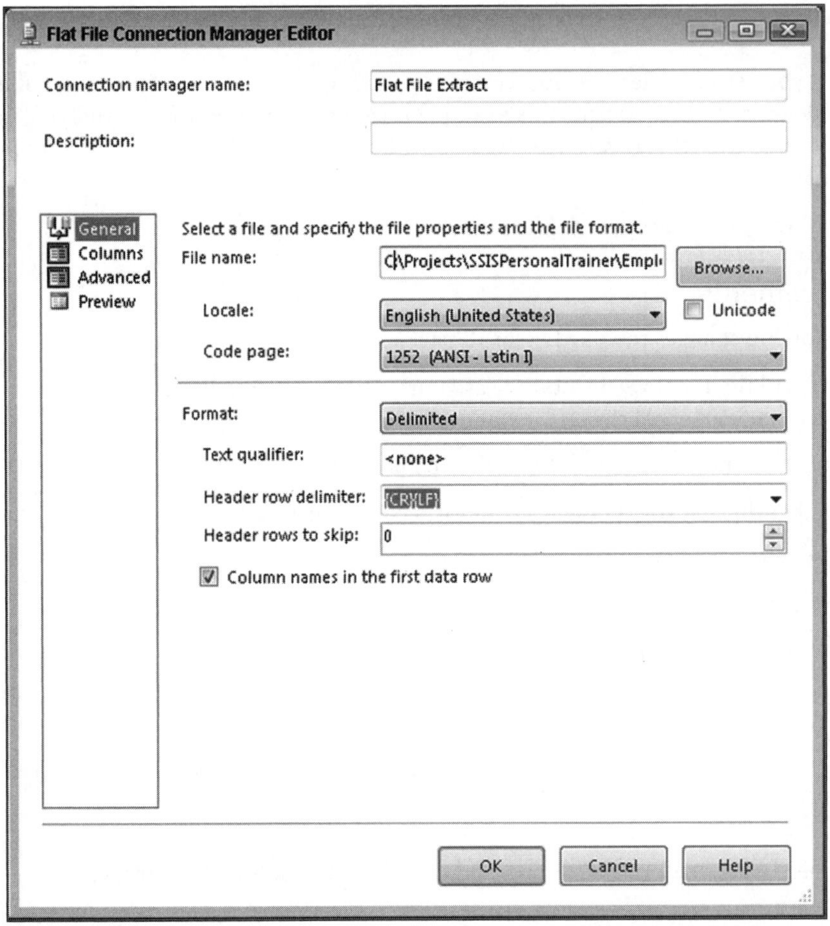

FIGURE 18-14

5. Select the Columns tab and ensure the Column delimiter drop-box has Comma {,} selected, as shown in Figure 18-15.

6. By default, all columns are assigned a string data type, but you can correct this in the Advanced tab of the Flat File Connection Manager Editor. In the Advanced tab, you can manually change the data type or have SSIS suggest the data type (click the Suggest Types button). SSIS suggestions are fairly accurate, but don't always give the desired results. For example, on the columns EmpID, SickDays, and VacationDays, change the DataType to four-byte signed integer (int). Had you done a Suggest Types for these columns, SSIS would have assigned these columns single-byte signed integer (tinyint), which is not what you want

this time. Once these changes have been made, your screen should look like Figure 18-16. Click OK to complete creating the Flat File Connection Manager.

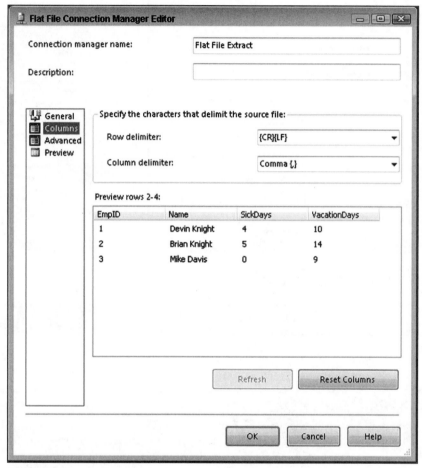

FIGURE 18-15

7. Click OK in the Flat File Source Editor and drag a Union All onto the Data Flow design surface. The Union All serves as a placeholder until you read about destinations in the next lesson. Connect the Flat File Source to the Union All and execute just this Data Flow by right-clicking in the design surface and selecting Execute Task. Figure 18-17 shows the results.

FIGURE 18-16

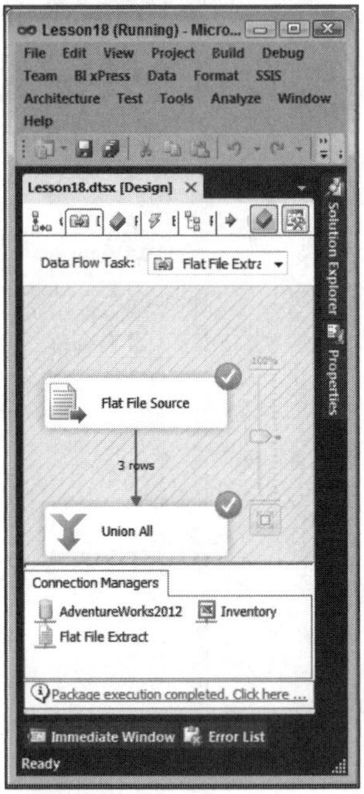

FIGURE 18-17

> **NOTE** Here's another best practice: using Fast Parse can drastically improve performance of your package when you are using a Flat File Source. By default, SSIS validates any numeric or date columns, but with Fast Parse set to True, this step will be bypassed. To enable Fast Parse, follow these steps:
>
> 1. Right-click the Flat File Source or Data Conversion Transformation, and click Show Advanced Editor.
>
> 2. In the Advanced Editor dialog box, click the Input and Output Properties tab.
>
> 3. In the Inputs and Outputs pane, click the column for which you want to enable Fast Parse (shown in Figure 18-18).
>
> 4. In the Properties window, expand the Custom Properties node, and set the FastParse property to True.
>
> 5. Click OK.

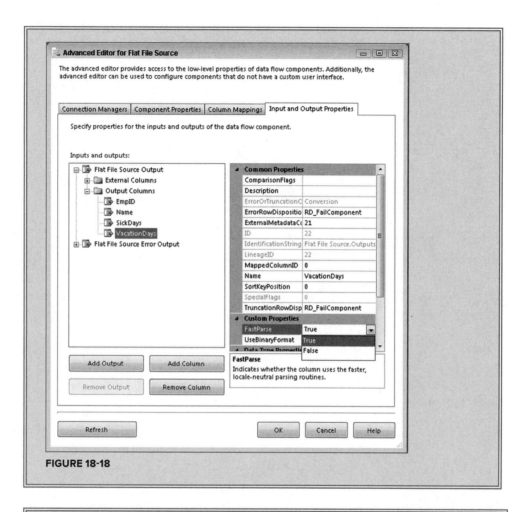

FIGURE 18-18

Please select Lesson 18 on the DVD, or online at www.wrox.com/go/ssis2012video, to view the video that accompanies this lesson.

19

Loading Data to a Destination

After you have set up a source to bring the needed data to the Data Flow, you need somewhere to put it. A *destination* accepts data from data sources or transformations and sends them to the location specified in the destination's connection manager.

The difference between configuration of sources and destinations is the Mappings page shown in Figure 19-1. The Mappings page points each column from your Data Flow's pipeline to each column that is available in your destination. By default, SSIS matches columns with the same name, but you can easily match columns by dragging one of Available Input Columns to the appropriate Available Destination Columns if your column names do not correspond. As you can see in the figure, it is not mandatory that these columns be in the same order from the source to the destination.

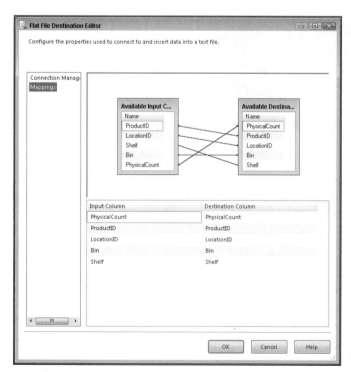

FIGURE 19-1

Until the destination is connected to the rest of pipeline, you cannot configure it. To make the connection, select the source or a transformation and drag the blue arrow to the destination. If you want to output a transformation's bad data to a destination, drag the red arrow to that destination. In this lesson, the most frequently used destinations (OLE DB, Flat File, and Excel) are demonstrated.

DESTINATION ASSISTANT

The *Destination Assistant* is a new feature of SSIS that helps guide you through defining a connection manager and destination. From inside the Data Flow tab, select the Destination Assistant from the SSIS Toolbox. Figure 19-2 shows the Destination Assistant and the default destination types that are available. In addition to selecting the type of Data Flow destination the Destination Assistant will also create a connection manager if one does not already exist. If you believe you should have a destination type installed on your machine but it does not appear, uncheck the "Show only installed destination types" option and all will appear.

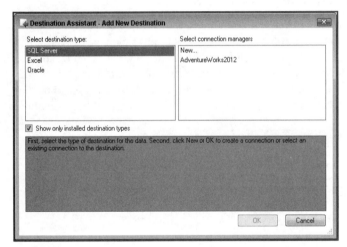

FIGURE 19-2

After selecting the appropriate destination and connection manager for your design, click OK and a destination appears in your Data Flow Task with the features you selected. The next sections dive deeper into the most commonly used destinations.

OLE DB DESTINATION

The most common type of destination is the OLE DB Destination. It can write data from the source or transformation to any Object Linking and Embedding Database (OLE DB)–compatible data source such as SQL Server, Oracle, or DB2. You configure it like any other source or destination, by using an OLE DB Connection Manager. The Connection Manager page of the OLE DB Destination Editor is shown in Figure 19-3.

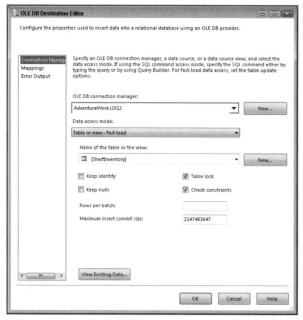

FIGURE 19-3

Selecting Table or view - fast load under Data access mode specifies that SSIS loads data in bulk into the OLE DB Destination's target table. The Fast Load option is available only for SQL Server database instances. When Fast Load is selected, you have options like Table Lock, Rows Per Batch, and Maximum Insert Commit Size available to configure.

➤ If you decide to employ **Table Lock**, it prevents others from accessing the table while your package is inserting to it, but speeds up the load.

➤ Setting **Rows Per Batch** allows you to specify how many rows are in each batch sent to the destination.

➤ The **Maximum Insert Commit Size** sets how large the batch size is going to be prior to sending a commit statement. Usually setting the Max Insert Commit Size to a number like 10,000 increases performance, but it really depends on how wide the columns are in the table.

Try It

In this Try It, you set up an OLE DB Destination to load a new EmployeeList table you create in the AdventureWorks2012 database. You can download the AdventureWorks2012 database used for this book at the Wrox website at `www.wrox.com/go/SQLSever2012DataSets`. (Please see Lesson 3 if you haven't yet installed the AdventureWorks2012 database.) After this lesson, you will know how to use an OLE DB Destination to load a SQL Server table.

You can download the Lesson19.dtsx from `www.wrox.com`.

Lesson Requirements

Open the package created from the previous lesson or download the completed package called Lesson19.dtsx from www.wrox.com and make the following changes:

➤ Using the following code, create a table in the AdventureWorks2012 database named EmployeeList to load the contents of the flat file to:

```
CREATE TABLE [EmployeeList] (
    [EmpID] int,
    [Name] varchar(50),
    [SickDays] int,
    [VacationDays] int
)
```

Hints

➤ You already created the source for this package in Lesson 18 so all you need is an OLE DB Destination this time.

Step-by-Step

1. Open the package created from the previous lesson or download the completed package called Lesson19.dtsx from www.wrox.com.

2. Open the Data Flow Task named Flat File Extract and drag an OLE DB Destination to the designer surface. If you have a Union All that was serving as a placeholder, delete it. Rename the destination **EmployeeList**.

3. Connect the blue arrow from the Flat File Source to the new destination and double-click to open the destination's editor.

4. By default, the destination assumes you are using the only OLE DB Connection Manager already created in the package. Click the New button next to the Name of the table or the view option to create a new SQL Server table to load.

5. The Create Table dialog box appears with a query to create the table already prepared, just like Figure 19-4. Ensure the query is the following and click OK:

```
CREATE TABLE [EmployeeList] (
    [EmpID] int,
    [Name] varchar(50),
    [SickDays] int,
    [VacationDays] int
)
```

FIGURE 19-4

6. Notice now that in the bottom of the OLE DB Destination Editor a warning flag has been raised. This warning flag is shown in Figure 19-5. This warning means you're not quite done yet. Select Mappings to go to the Mappings page.

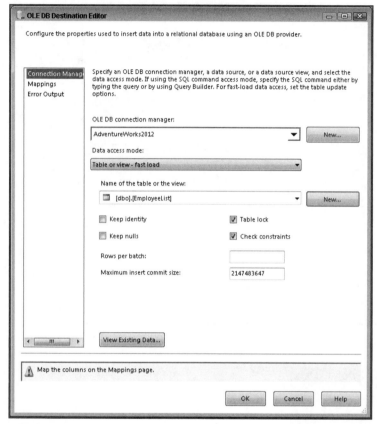

FIGURE 19-5

7. The Mappings page automatically matches columns with the same name; therefore, all your columns are now input columns and are now mapped to destination columns, as shown in Figure 19-6. Now, click OK to complete the configuration of this destination.

8. Execute just this Data Flow by right-clicking in the designer and selecting Execute Task. Figure 19-7 shows the results.

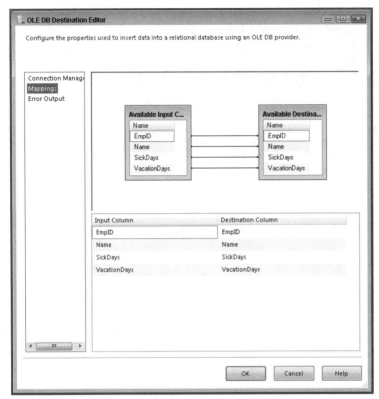

FIGURE 19-6

FIGURE 19-7

9. If you open the EmployeeList table now, you find the results shown in Figure 19-8.

	EmpID	Name	SickDays	VacationDays
1	1	Devin Knight	4	10
2	2	Brian Knight	5	14
3	3	Mike Davis	0	9

FIGURE 19-8

FLAT FILE DESTINATION

The Flat File Destination is used to load data into a flat file. The flat file can be either a fixed-width or delimited file. A file that is fixed-width uses width measurements to define columns and rows, whereas a delimited file uses special characters to define columns and rows. When you are configuring a Flat File Destination, you can choose to overwrite data in the file and add a custom header to the file by typing it into the Header window.

Try It

In this Try It, you set up a Flat File Destination to bring in inventory data from an Excel Source to a flat file. After this lesson, you will know how to use a Flat File Destination to load data into a text file.

You can download the Lesson19.dtsx and Excel file from www.wrox.com.

Lesson Requirements

Open the package you created from the previous lesson or download the completed package named Lesson19.dtsx from www.wrox.com and make the following changes:

➤ Create a new Flat File Connection Manager that is comma-delimited and save the file anywhere on your computer.

Hints

➤ This example requires one Flat File Destination and one Flat File Connection Manager, making a total of two Flat File Connection Managers for this package.

Step-by-Step

1. Open the package created from the previous lesson or download the completed package named Lesson19.dtsx from www.wrox.com.

2. Open the Data Flow Task named Excel Extract and drag a Flat File Destination to the designer surface. If you have a Union All that was serving as a placeholder, delete it.

3. Connect the blue arrow from the Excel Source to the new destination and double-click the destination to open the destination's editor.

4. By default, the destination assumes you are using the only Flat File Connection Manager already created in the package. However, in this case, you need to make a new connection manager, so click the New button next to the Flat File Connection Manager.

5. Make the file comma-delimited, find a location to save the file on your computer, and click OK.

6. Back in the Flat File Destination Editor, go to the Mappings page to ensure all columns are mapped appropriately, as shown in Figure 19-9. Then click OK.

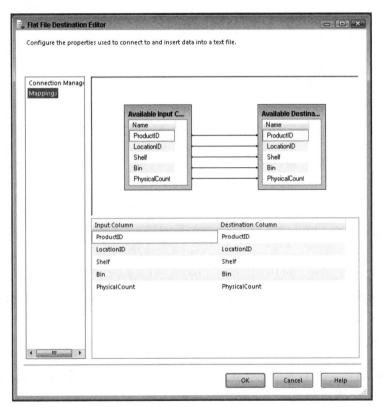

FIGURE 19-9

7. Execute just this Data Flow by right-clicking in the designer and selecting Execute Task. Figure 19-10 shows the results.

FIGURE 19-10

EXCEL DESTINATION

The Excel Destination basically works the same way the Excel Source does, except the destination takes in data instead of sending data out. As in all sources and destinations, a connection manager must be specified, in this case an Excel Connection Manager. The Excel Connection Manager must point to a worksheet you want to load data into. Unlike with the Flat File Destination, however, a spreadsheet must already exist to load; otherwise, you will receive an error.

Try It

In this Try It, you set up an Excel Destination to load a worksheet named TransactionHistory with data from an AdventureWorks2012 database source. After this lesson, you will know how to use an Excel Destination to load data into an Excel spreadsheet.

You can download the Lesson19.dtsx from www.wrox.com.

Lesson Requirements

Open the package created from the previous lesson or download the completed package named Lesson19.dtsx from www.wrox.com and make the following changes:

➤ Use the Inventory_Worksheet Excel file that you can download from www.wrox.com as the destination.

➤ Point the destination to the Excel sheet named TransactionHistory.

Hints

➤ You need only one Excel Destination for this example.

Step-by-Step

1. Open the package created from the previous lesson or download Lesson19.dtsx from www.wrox.com.

2. Open the Data Flow Task named OLE DB Extract and drag an Excel Destination to the designer surface. If you have a Union All that was serving as a placeholder, delete it. Rename the destination **Transaction History**.

3. Connect the blue arrow from the OLE DB Source to the new destination and double-click to open the destination's editor.

4. By default, the destination assumes you are using the only Excel Connection Manager already created in the package. Click the New button next to the Name of the Excel sheet option and click OK to create the sheet using the query SSIS has generated, as shown in Figure 19-11.

FIGURE 19-11

5. Back in the Excel Destination Editor, select the Mappings page and ensure all columns are mapped appropriately, as in Figure 19-12. Then click OK.

6. Execute just this Data Flow by right-clicking in the designer and selecting Execute Task. Figure 19-13 shows the results.

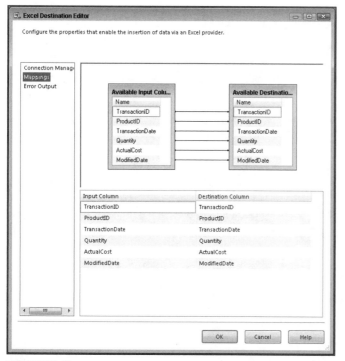

FIGURE 19-12

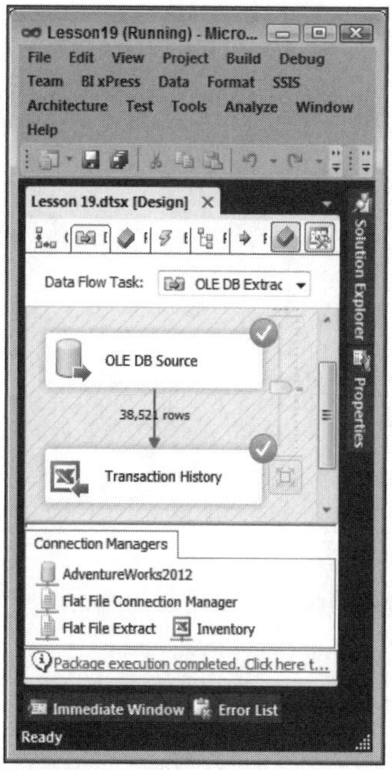

FIGURE 19-13

Please select Lesson 19 on the DVD, or online at www.wrox.com/go/ssis2012video, *to view the video that accompanies this lesson.*

20

Changing Data Types with the Data Conversion Transform

When working with data, you often have various reasons why you may need to make changes to a column's data type. For example, SQL Server Integration Services (SSIS) supports Excel data as a source, but it may not support the data the way you intend by default. By default, the general data type from Excel is set, which is brought in SSIS as a Unicode data type. In SQL Server, Unicode translates to an nvarchar, which is most likely not what you want because it requires twice the space and may be slower. If you have a Unicode data type in SSIS and you try to insert it into a varchar column, the execution may potentially fail.

The Data Conversion Transform performs the T-SQL equivalent of the CONVERT or CAST functions on a selected column. To configure this transform, first connect it to a source, then drag it onto the Data Flow designer and double-click it to open the Data Conversion Transformation Editor (shown in Figure 20-1). Here you check the columns you need to convert and use the Data Type drop-down menu to select the data type you want to convert to.

FIGURE 20-1

Something that can be frustrating with SSIS is how it deals with SQL Server data types. For example, a varchar maps in SSIS to a string datatyped column. It was made this way to translate well into the .NET development world. The following table shows how the data types translate from a SQL Server data type to an SSIS data type.

SQL SERVER DATA TYPE	SSIS DATA TYPE
Bigint	Eight-byte signed integer [DT_I8]
Binary	Byte stream [DT_BYTES]
Bit	Boolean [DT_BOOL]
Datetime	Database timestamp [DT_DBTIMESTAMP]
Decimal	Numeric [DT_NUMERIC]
Float	Float [DT_R4]
Int	Four-byte signed integer [DT_I4]
Image	Image [DT_IMAGE]
nvarchar or nchar	Unicode string [DT_WSTR]

SQL SERVER DATA TYPE	SSIS DATA TYPE
Ntext	Unicode text stream [DT_NTEXT]
Numeric	Numeric [DT_NUMERIC]
Smallint	Two-byte signed integer [DT_I2]
Text	Text stream [DT_TEXT]
Timestamp	Byte stream [DT_BYTES]
Tinytint	Single-byte unsigned integer [DT_UI1]
uniqueidentifier	Unique identifier [DT_GUID]
Varbinary	Byte stream [DT_BYTES]
varchar or char	String [DT_STR]
Xml	Unicode string [DT_WSTR]

The Output Alias is the column name you want to assign to the new column that is generated after it is converted. If you don't assign it a new name, it defaults to "Copy of *ColumnName*." It's always a good idea to give the Output Alias a new name so it can be identified as the converted column.

The Data Conversion Transform Editor dialog box also has length, precision, and scale columns.

➤ **Length** for a numeric data type is the total bytes required to store the number, and length for a string data type is the total characters the column can store.

➤ **Precision** is the total number of digits in a number (including the values to the right of the decimal). For example, the integer 9876543.21 has a precision of 9.

➤ **Scale** is the number of digits to the right of the decimal point. For instance, the integer 9876543.21 has a scale of 2.

The Data Conversion Transform is a synchronous transform, meaning rows flow into memory buffers in the transform and the same buffers come out. Essentially this means no rows are held or blocked, and typically these transforms perform very quickly with minimal impact to your Data Flow.

> **NOTE** *Here's a best practice: The Data Conversion Transform and the Flat File Source, discussed in Lesson 18, are the only two tools that can use the performance enhancement called Fast Parse. You can enable Fast Parse only in the tools' Advanced Editor. When you enable a column with Fast Parse, verification of that column is turned off. Use this feature only when you are certain your data is reliable.*

TRY IT

In this Try It, your company has an Excel file called Inventory Worksheet that needs to be imported into your AdventureWorks2012 database. Your requirements are to create a package that uses a Data Conversion Transform to convert all column data types. Your manager tells you that the results after the conversion should be populated into a new table. After this lesson, you'll know how to convert a column's data type using the Data Conversion Transform and load tables of different data types.

You can download the Inventory Worksheet.xls Excel file and the Lesson20.dtsx from www.wrox.com.

Lesson Requirements

Download the Inventory Worksheet.xls Excel file from www.wrox.com. This file will be your source for populating a new table you create called ShelfInventory in the AdventureWorks2012 database. Save the Excel file to a location on your computer called C:\Projects\SSISPersonalTrainer. You can also download the creation script for this lesson from www.wrox.com. Your goal in this lesson is to select all columns and convert them to the specified data types with a new destination table:

COLUMNS	CONVERT TO
Shelf	varchar(255)
Product	int
LocationID	int
Bin	int
PhysicalCount	int

Hints

➤ You need only one Excel Source and Excel Connection Manager.

➤ You need a Data Conversion Transform to convert the columns to the required data type.

➤ You need only one OLE DB Destination and OLE DB Connection Manager.

Step-by-Step

1. Create a new SSIS package called **Lesson20.dtsx** (or download Lesson20.dtsx from www.wrox.com).

2. Create a new Excel Connection Manager using the Inventory Worksheet.xls file you downloaded from www.wrox.com and make sure the First row has column names option is checked. (You can find more information on using an Excel Source in Lesson 18.)

3. Drag a Data Flow Task onto the design pane and name the new task **DFT – Data Conversion**.

4. In the Data Flow tab, drag a new Excel Source onto the Data Flow design pane and name it **Excel SRC - Inventory Worksheet**.

5. Double-click the Excel Source and change the OLE DB Connection Manager option to your only connection manager. Then change the Name of the Excel sheet option to **Inventory_ Worksheet** and click OK.

6. Drag a Data Conversion Transform onto the design pane and connect it to the Excel Source.

7. Open the Data Conversion Transformation Editor by double-clicking the new transform and check each column from the Available Input Columns table. Change the Output Alias of all columns to **Converted*ColumnName***, as shown in Figure 20-2.

FIGURE 20-2

8. For the Data Type, select string [DT_STR] for the Input Column Shelf and four-byte signed integer [DT_I4] for all other columns and click OK.

9. Back in the designer, drag an OLE DB Destination onto the design pane and connect it to the Data Conversion Transform.

10. Open the OLE DB Destination and click New next to the connection manager selection to create a new OLE DB Connection Manager, where you will select AdventureWorks2012.

11. Still in the OLE DB Destination Editor, click New next to the table selection to create a new table and ensure the following statement is used:

```
CREATE TABLE [ShelfInventory] (
    [Shelf] varchar(255),
    [ProductID] int,
    [LocationID] int,
    [Bin] int,
    [PhysicalCount] int
)
```

12. Go to the Mappings page and delete all connections between the Input Columns and Destination Columns. Now connect all Input Columns with the Converted prefix to the associated Destination Columns (Figure 20-3) and click OK.

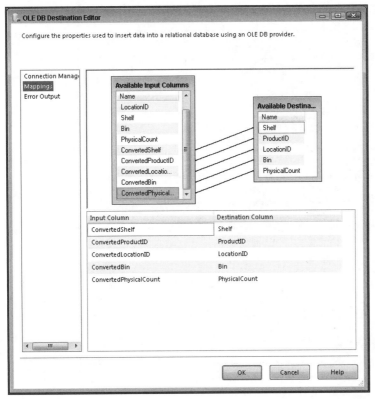

FIGURE 20-3

13. Execute the package. A successful run should look like Figure 20-4. Don't forget that you learned in Lesson 18 that when using an Excel source, you may need to set the designer to run in 32-bit mode if you're running on a 64-bit machine.

FIGURE 20-4

Please select Lesson 20 on the DVD, or online at www.wrox.com/go/ssis2012video, *to view the video that accompanies this lesson.*

21

Creating and Replacing Columns with the Derived Column Transform

The Derived Column Transform enables you to either create or replace a column in the data stream. You can use this component for many problems you may run into and, therefore, it is one of the most useful tools you have in the Data Flow. As you see in this lesson's Try It example, you can use the transform for things like auditing rows and editing incoming data using the available SQL Server Integration Services (SSIS) expressions.

You open the Derived Column Transformation Editor you open other transform editors, by dragging it into the Data Flow and then double-clicking. To configure this transform, drag the column or variable into the Expression column, as shown in Figure 21-1. Then you can add functions to it. You can find a list of functions to use as a reference in the top-right corner of the Derived Column Transformation Editor; you can drag the functions into the Expression property. You must then specify, in the Derived Column drop-down box, whether you want the output of the expression to replace an existing column or to create a new column. If you create a new column, give it a name in the Derived Column Name column.

In Figure 21-1, the expression states that if the column PhysicalCount is NULL, convert it to 0; otherwise, keep the existing data.

To get the most bang for your buck with this transform, explore the different functions available. The functions and the availability of variables makes the Derived Column Transform one of the top five transforms that you'll find yourself using to satisfy the need for T-SQL scripting in your package.

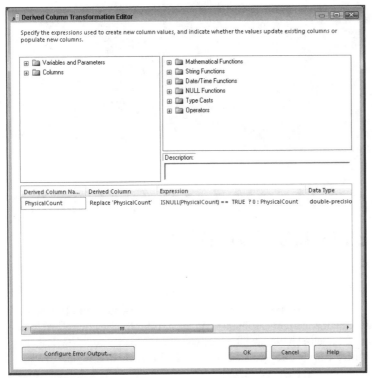

FIGURE 21-1

The expression language is marketed as being a heavily C#-based syntax. However, you can't just start writing C# because some quirks are mixed into the scripting language. Still, the following common operators are irrefutably from a C# ancestry:

EXPRESSION OPERATOR	DESCRIPTION
||	Logical OR operation
&&	Logical AND operation
==	Comparison of two expressions to determine if they are equivalent
!=	Comparison of two expressions to determine inequality
? :	Conditional operator

Now look at an example of how to write an expression using one of these operators. The following statement uses the conditional operator (? :) to check the column PhysicalCount to see if it contains any NULLs and, if it does, to change them to 0. Otherwise, it keeps the column the same. The shell of such a script uses code like this:

```
<<boolean_expression>> ? <<when_true>> : <<when_false>>
```

This shell translates the previously mentioned example into this code:

```
ISNULL( [PhysicalCount] ) ? 0 : [PhysicalCount]
```

Using the conditional operator has historically been a common way to handle NULL values, but in SSIS 2012, a new function has been added to make it even simpler to perform this same NULL-handling transform. The REPLACENULL works similarly to the ISNULL function in T-SQL. It accepts the value to check first, and the second value specifies what to replace it with when the first value is NULL. The shell of such a script uses code like this:

```
REPLACENULL( «expression», «expression» )
```

This shell translates the previously mentioned example into this code:

```
REPLACENULL( [PhysicalCount] ,0 )
```

Sometimes you run into functions that look like they would function like T-SQL. For example, the GETDATE() function is typically what you would use to return the current date in T-SQL. In this circumstance, GETDATE() performs exactly the same in the SSIS expression language. However, some functions look like T-SQL functions, but work in ways that are not the same:

EXPRESSION FUNCTION	DESCRIPTION	DIFFERENCE
DATEPART()	Parses the date part from a date	Requires quotes on the date part
ISNULL()	Tests an expression for NULL	Doesn't allow for default value

The statement that follows uses the DATEPART() function to return an integer representing the desired part of a date. In this example, the expression is returning the year from today's date. The shell of this script uses code that looks like this:

```
DATEPART( <<datepart>>, <<date>> )
```

This shell translates the previously mentioned code example into this code:

```
DATEPART( "yy",GetDate ( ) )
```

Many times, it is useful to build string data within an expression. You can use string data to populate the body of an e-mail message or to build file paths for processing. Here are some of the most commonly used string functions:

EXPRESSION OPERATOR	DESCRIPTION
REPLACE()	Replaces a character string
UPPER()	Converts lowercase characters to uppercase
SUBSTRING()	Returns a character value that starts at a specified position with a specified length

Using the REPLACE() function enables you to search through a string for a specific value and replace that value with another. In the example that follows, the expression searches the column named [Shelf] for the word "Development" and replaces it with "Production". The shell of this script uses code that looks like this:

```
REPLACE( <<character_expression>>, <<search_expression>>,
<<replace_expression>> )
```

This would translate the example into this code:

```
REPLACE( [Shelf] , "Development", "Production" )
```

Another common string function is UPPER(), which changes all lowercase characters to uppercase. The shell of this function is written like this.

```
UPPER( <<character_expression>> )
```

This example uses the system variable PackageName to return the name of the package in all upper-case. The result looks like this: LESSON 21.

```
UPPER(@[System::PackageName] )
```

The final example of a string function is SUBSTRING(). This function enables you to retrieve a pre-determined number of characters from a string field.

```
SUBSTRING( <<character_expression>>, <<start>>, <<length>> )
```

The following expression is bringing back just the first letter of the FirstName column with a period (.), followed by the entire contents of the LastName column. The results would look like this: D. Knight.

```
SUBSTRING( [FirstName] , 1, 1 )+". " +[LastName]
```

Many other string functions are available, so be sure to explore all the functions available in the reference guide in the top-right section of the Derived Column Transformation Editor.

It is very likely that you'll find it necessary to convert or cast certain values within an expression so they are compatible with the column's data type. Here are some of the most common cast functions available:

CAST OPERATOR	ADDITIONAL PARAMETERS
DT_STR(<<length>>, <<code_page>>)	length—Final string length code_page—Unicode character set
DT_WSTR(<<length>>)	length—Final string length

CAST OPERATOR	ADDITIONAL PARAMETERS
DT_NUMERIC(<<precision>>, <<scale>>)	precision—Max number of digits scale—Number of digits after decimal
DT_DECIMAL(<<scale>>)	scale—Number of digits after decimal

A common opportunity to use a cast operator involves converting dates to fit in inputs that accept only strings. The following example uses the DT_WSTR cast function to convert the date to a string. The code shell for this function looks like this:

```
(DT_WSTR, <<length>>)
```

This shell translates the previously mentioned code example into this code:

```
(DT_WSTR, 30) GETDATE()
```

For more on the SSIS expression language, read Lessons 34 and 35.

TRY IT

In this Try It, your company decides that it would be best to include the date on which each row is populated in your SSIS package from Lesson 20. Your manager tells you that this date is necessary for auditing purposes. Once you have made these changes to the package, delete the content of the table before you run the package again. After this lesson, you'll know how to add a derived column built by assigning an expression to the pipeline of an SSIS package.

You can download the completed Lesson21.dtsx from www.wrox.com.

Lesson Requirements

Make the following changes to the package you created in Lesson 20 or open the completed Lesson 21 package from www.wrox.com:

➤   Add a column to the pipeline that uses the system variable @[System::StartTime] to populate the RowStartDate column that is already in the ShelfInventory table.

➤   Delete the content of ShelfInventory table and repopulate it with the new column included.

Hints

➤   Use the Derived Column Transform to add the new date column to the file stream.

Step-by-Step

1. Open a query window in Management Studio and run this query to empty the table's data:

```
TRUNCATE TABLE ShelfInventory
```

2. Now run the following query to add a column to the ShelfInventory table:

```
ALTER TABLE ShelfInventory
ADD RowStartDate datetime
```

3. Open the SSIS package Lesson20.dtsx that you created in the previous lesson, or download the completed Lesson21.dtsx from www.wrox.com.

4. Click the Data Flow tab and delete the precedence constraint between the Data Conversion Transform and the OLE DB Destination.

5. Drag a Derived Column Transform into the Data Flow and connect it between the Data Conversion Transform and the OLE DB Destination.

6. Open the Derived Column Transformation Editor and add a new column by typing **RowStartDate** in the Derived Column Name property. Then, in the Expression property, add the system variable @[System::StartTime] by dragging it down from the variables list in the top-left section of the editor, as shown in Figure 21-2. Then click OK. This adds the current date and time to the column when the package is run.

FIGURE 21-2

7. Now that this column has been added, you need to make sure the destination knows to use it. Open the OLE DB Destination Editor and add the column RowStartDate to the mapping, as shown in Figure 21-3.

8. Now execute the package. A successful run should look like Figure 21-4. The ShelfInventory table has now been repopulated with the new column that holds the date and time the package was run. Don't forget that you learned in Lesson 18 that when using an Excel source, you may need to set the designer to run in 32-bit mode if you're running on a 64-bit machine.

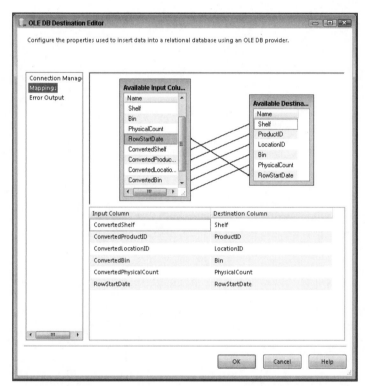

FIGURE 21-3

FIGURE 21-4

Please select Lesson 21 on the DVD, or online at `www.wrox.com/go/ssis2012video`, *to view the video that accompanies this lesson.*

22

Rolling Up Data with the Aggregate Transform

Do you have a large amount of data that you want to roll up to a different granularity? The Aggregate Transform enables you to essentially apply a GROUP BY statement on data that are entering it. Aggregate Transforms are one of the more expensive operations you can perform against data, much like a GROUP BY statement is in T-SQL, and they can be very memory intensive.

> **NOTE** *The Aggregate Transform is an asynchronous transform and is fully blocking. This means that every row must enter the transform prior to sending the first row out. Because of this, your transform will need as much RAM as the source retrieves. For example, if your Data Flow is reading a 1 GB file, your Aggregate Transform will require at least 1 GB of memory.*

Once you drag the transform over, simply check the columns in the Aggregations tab that you want to aggregate or sum. The Operation drop-down box enables you to select what type of aggregation function you want to apply to the data. The most important operation is a Group By operation, which enables you to roll the data up to that grain. For example, if you have a dozen sales of three products, and you grouped them by the ProductID, you'd have only three rows come out of the transform. You can see a list of all the operations allowed in the following table.

DATA TYPE	OPERATIONS ALLOWED
String	Group by, Count, Count distinct
Numeric	Group by, Count, Count distinct, Minimum, Maximum
Date	Group by, Count, Count distinct, Minimum, Maximum, Average, Sum

Like any GROUP BY statement, only the columns that are being grouped by or aggregated are returned. Other columns are dropped and will not be available to you in the next Data Flow transform or destination.

You can tune the Aggregate Transform by estimating how many distinct groups you will retrieve from the operation. In the Advanced tab of the Aggregate Transformation Editor (see Figure 22-1), you can type the estimated number of groups in the Number of keys text box. This optimizes the transform for that level of distinct values.

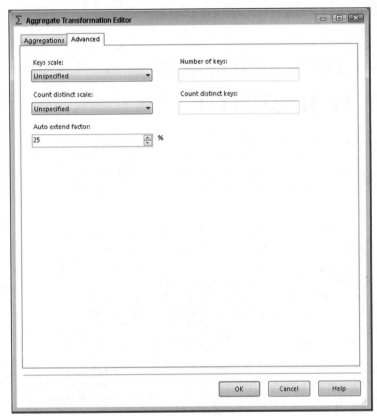

FIGURE 22-1

The Aggregate Transform is one of the most powerful and simple transforms to configure. However, you should use it sparingly due to its speed. If you pull data out of a flat file, it's a good application for the Aggregate Transform, but when you're pulling data out of a database, consider writing a SQL statement that pulls the data out already aggregated.

TRY IT

In this Try It, you create an extract file that contains a rolled-up version of the Production.
TransactionHistory table. The Production.TransactionHistory table has hundreds of thousands of
records in it containing very granular data of every transaction for your company's history. Your
partner only needs to know how many of each product you've sold, and other data such as the last
sale of that product. After this lesson, you'll know how to apply grouping to your data to see your
data at a higher grain.

You can download the completed Lesson22.dtsx package from the book's website at www.wrox.com.

Lesson Requirements

In this lesson, you need to read the Production.TransactionHistory table from the
AdventureWorks2012 database and create a new file with the following columns without using
T-SQL's GROUP BY statement:

➤ **ProductID**—One row for each product

➤ **LastTransactionDate**—The date of the last purchase

➤ **TotalQuantity**—The total quantity for all transactions for a given product

➤ **TotalCost**—The total cost for all transactions for a given product

Hints

➤ To perform a GROUP BY clause against data in a Data Flow, you use the Aggregate
Transform after pulling data out of the Production.TransactionHistory table with the
OLE DB Source.

➤ Write the data to a flat file with the Flat File Destination.

Step-by-Step

1. Create a new SSIS package called **Lesson22.dtsx**.

2. Create a new OLE DB Connection Manager that connects to your AdventureWorks2012
database.

3. Drag a Data Flow Task onto the design pane and call the new task **DFT - Aggregate Data**.

4. In the Data Flow tab, drag a new OLE DB Source onto the Data Flow design pane and name
it **OLE SRC – TransactionHistory**.

5. Double-click the OLE DB Source and change the OLE DB Connection Manager option to your only connection manager. Change the Data access mode to SQL Command and type the following query into the SQL Command text box:

```
SELECT
TransactionID, ProductID, TransactionDate,
TransactionType, Quantity, ActualCost, ModifiedDate
FROM Production.TransactionHistory
```

6. Drag an Aggregate Transform onto the design pane and connect it to the OLE DB Source. Rename the transform **AG – Roll up data.**

7. Open the Aggregate Transformation Editor by double-clicking the new transform and check the ProductID, TransactionDate, Quantity, and ActualCost columns.

8. Change the Output Alias column for each of the checked columns. Change the alias to LastTransactionDate for the TransactionDate column. Change the Quantity column to TotalQuantity, and ActualCost to TotalCost.

9. In the Operation column, change ProductID to Group by, LastTransactionDate to Maximum, TotalQuantity to Sum, and TotalCost to Sum, as shown in Figure 22-2.

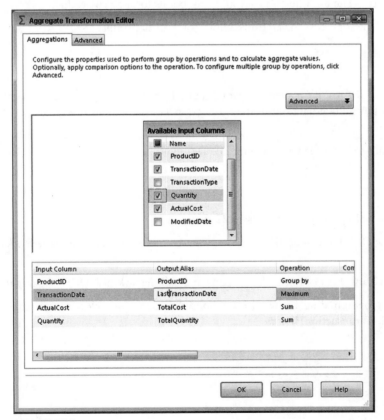

FIGURE 22-2

10. Back in the designer, drag a Flat File Destination onto the design pane and connect it to the Aggregate Transform. Rename the connection **FF DST – Create Extract**.

11. Open the Flat File Destination and click New to create a new Flat File Connection Manager. When prompted, select Delimited (separated by a given symbol).

12. Name the connection manager **Extract**. Place the file wherever you'd like and check the Column names in first data row option.

13. Go to the Mappings page and click OK.

14. Execute the package. A successful run should look like Figure 22-3.

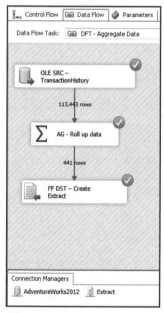

FIGURE 22-3

Please select Lesson 22 on the DVD, or online at www.wrox.com/go/ssis2012video, *to view the video that accompanies this lesson.*

23

Ordering Data with the Sort Transform

The Sort Transform enables you to sort data based on any column in the Data Flow path. To configure the Sort Transformation Editor after it's been connected, open the transform and check the columns you need to sort by (Figure 23-1). Uncheck any columns you don't want passed through the path from the Pass Through column. By default, every column passes through the Data Flow pipeline.

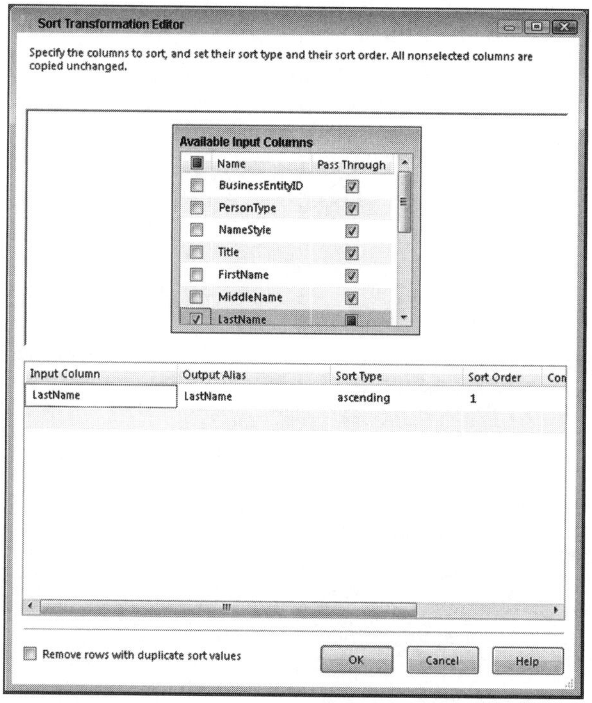

FIGURE 23-1

You can optionally check the Remove rows with duplicate sort values option. When this is checked, if a second value comes in that matches your same sort key, it is disregarded, and the row is dropped.

> **NOTE** *The Sort Transform is a fully blocking asynchronous transform and will slow down your Data Flow performance. Use these only when you have to, such as for sorting a Flat File Source, and sparingly.*

Sorting data in SSIS is one of the most frequently required operations. This is because many other transforms that can be used require that data be presorted with either a Sort Transform or an ORDER BY statement in the OLE DB Source. You should avoid using the Sort Transform when you can because of speed constraints.

If you place an ORDER BY statement in the OLE DB Source, SSIS is not aware of the ORDER BY statement because it can just as easily have been in a stored procedure, so you must notify SSIS that the data is presorted. To do this, right-click the source and select Advanced Editor; then go to the Input and Output Properties and select the OLE DB Source Output. In the Properties pane, change the IsSorted property to True (shown in Figure 23-2).

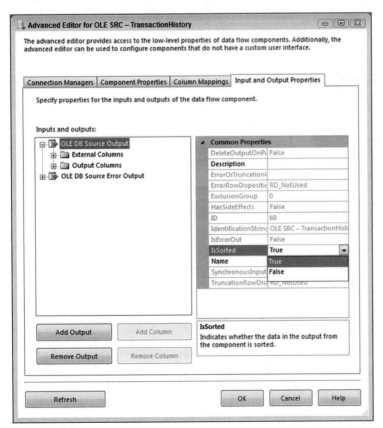

FIGURE 23-2

Then, under Output Columns, select the column you are ordering on in your SQL statement and change the SortKeyPosition to 1, if you're sorting only by a single column ascending, as shown in Figure 23-3. If you have multiple columns, you could change this SortKeyPosition value to the column position in the ORDER BY statement starting at 1. A value of –1 would sort the data in descending order.

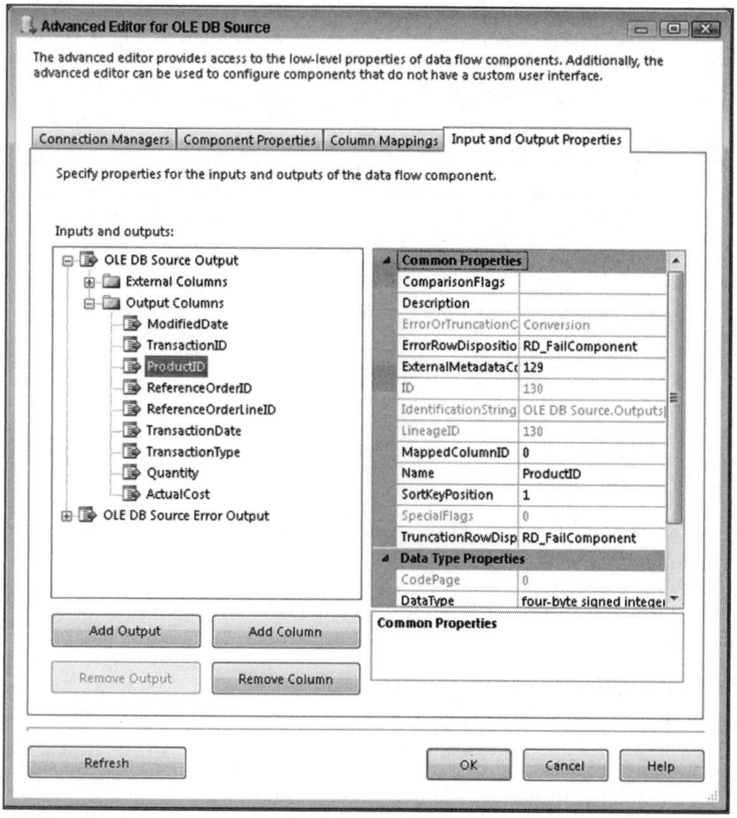

FIGURE 23-3

TRY IT

In this Try It, your company has decided it really needs the extract file you created in Lesson 22 to show the products in order by total sold. Your manager tells you to make sure that, once you've made these changes to your package, you delete the content of the extract file before you run the package again. After this lesson, you'll know how to sort data using SSIS.

You can download the completed Lesson23.dtsx package from the book's website at www.wrox.com.

Lesson Requirements

You can either make the following changes to the package you created in Lesson 22 or download the Lesson 22 package from www.wrox.com and make these changes:

➤ Set TotalQuantity to sort in descending order

➤ Delete the contents of the flat file and repopulate it with newly ordered records

> **NOTE** *Be sure you are using the Lesson 22 package as a starting place. The Lesson 23 package that you can download at* www.wrox.com *is the version of the package after this Step-by-Step example has already been completed.*

Hints

➤ You need to add only one Sort Transform to the package.

Step-by-Step

1. Open the SSIS package Lesson22.dtsx that you created in the previous lesson or download it from www.wrox.com.

2. Click the Data Flow tab and delete the precedence constraint between the Aggregate Transform and the Flat File Destination.

3. Drag a Sort Transform into the Data Flow and connect it between the Aggregate Transform and the Flat File Destination.

4. Open the Sort Transformation Editor, select TotalQuantity to sort by, and change the Sort Type to descending, as shown in Figure 23-4. Then click OK.

5. Now execute the package. A successful run should look like Figure 23-5. The flat file has now been repopulated sorted by TotalQuantity in descending order.

6. Upon completion, your package will look like the completed Lesson23.dtsx available from www.wrox.com.

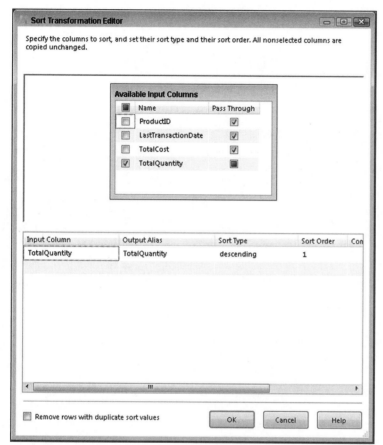

FIGURE 23-4

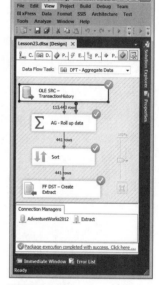

FIGURE 23-5

Please select Lesson 23 on the DVD, or online at www.wrox.com/go/ssis2012video, *to view the video that accompanies this lesson.*

24

Joining Data with the Lookup Transform

Are you looking for a way to join data from a new source into your Data Flow pipeline? The Lookup Transform in SQL Server Integration Services (SSIS) enables you to perform the equivalent of an inner and outer hash join. The only difference is that the operations occur outside the realm of the database engine.

This transform is used in many different situations, but would typically be found in an ETL process that populates a data warehouse. For example, you may want to populate a table by joining data from two separate source systems on different database platforms. The component can join only two data sets at a time, so to join three or more data sets you would need to string multiple Lookup Transforms together.

The Lookup Transform is a synchronous transform; therefore, it does not block the pipeline's flow of data. As new data enters the transform, rows that have been joined leave through one of the possible outputs. The caveat to this is that in certain caching modes, the component will initially block the package's execution for a period of time while it charges its internal caches.

Sometimes rows will not join successfully. For example, you may have a product that has no purchase history and its identifier in the product table would have no matches in the sales table. SSIS supports this by having multiple outputs on the Lookup Transform; in the simplest (default/legacy) configuration, you would have one output for matched rows and a separate output for non-matched and error rows.

CACHE MODES

The transform provides several modes of operation that allow you to trade off performance and resource usage. There is often a logical rationale for choosing a particular cache mode, which is discussed later in this lesson. To configure the Lookup Transform, drag one from the toolbox to the Data Flow design surface and double-click it to open the editor. Figure 24-1 shows the Lookup Transformation Editor where you select the cache mode and data source.

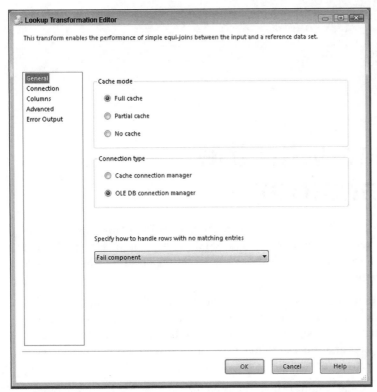

FIGURE 24-1

In *full-cache mode*, one of the tables you are joining is loaded entirely into memory, then the rows from the other table are flowed through the pipeline one buffer at a time, and the selected join operation is performed.

However, sometimes the reference table used in a lookup is too large to cache all at once in the system's memory. In these circumstances, you have two options: either you can cache some of the data or cache nothing.

For *no-cache mode*, no up-front caching is done, and each incoming row in the pipeline is compared one at a time to a specified relational table. Depending on the size of the reference data, this mode is usually the slowest, though it scales to the largest number of reference rows.

> **WARNING** *Use no-cache mode carefully because this can cause a high performance overhead on the system.*

The *partial-cache mode* gives you a middle ground between the no-cache and full-cache options. In this mode, the transform caches only the most recently used data within the memory boundaries specified. As soon as the cache grows too big, the least-used cache data is thrown away.

Try It

In this Try It, your company needs you to alter a package to show the product names with the sales of each product. Your manager tells you to create a new flat file to store the results. After this lesson, you'll know how to join data into the Data Flow pipeline using SSIS.

You can download the Lesson24a.dtsx package from the book's website at www.wrox.com.

Lesson Requirements

Make the following changes to the Lesson24a.dtsx package, which you can find at www.wrox.com:

➤   Join the data from the Production.Product table to bring in the product names with this query:

```
SELECT ProductID,Name
FROM Production.Product
```

➤   Create a new flat file and populate it with new results.

Hints

➤   Use the Lookup Transform to join Product data to your package data stream.

Step-by-Step

1.   You can either continue the work you did from Lesson 23 or open the completed Lesson24a.dtsx SSIS package from www.wrox.com.

2.   Click the Data Flow tab and delete the connecting lines between the Sort Transform and the Flat File Destination.

3.   Drag a Lookup Component into the Data Flow and rename it **LKP - Product Name**; then connect it between the Sort Transform and the Flat File Destination.

4.   Once you connect to the Flat File Destination, the Input Output Selection dialog box opens, and you should select Lookup Match Output from the Output drop-down box, as shown in Figure 24-2.

5.   Open the Lookup Transformation Editor, navigate to the Connection tab, and select the Use results of an SQL query option.

6.   In the query window, write the following select statement. Figure 24-3 shows how the editor should look at this point.

```
SELECT ProductID,Name
FROM Production.Product
```

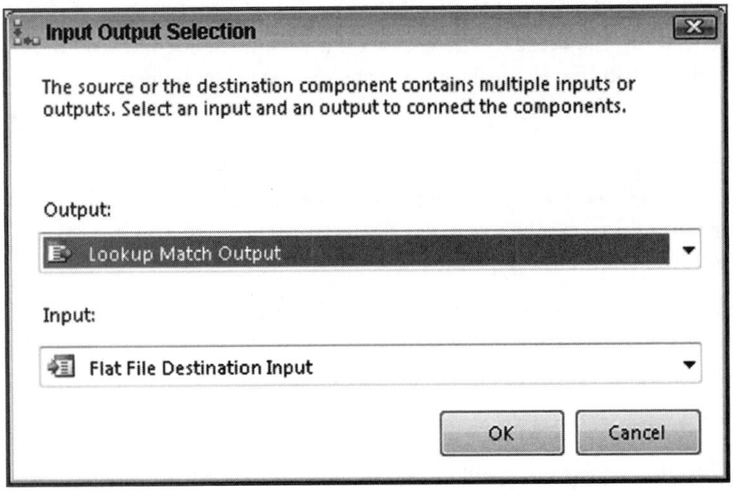

FIGURE 24-2

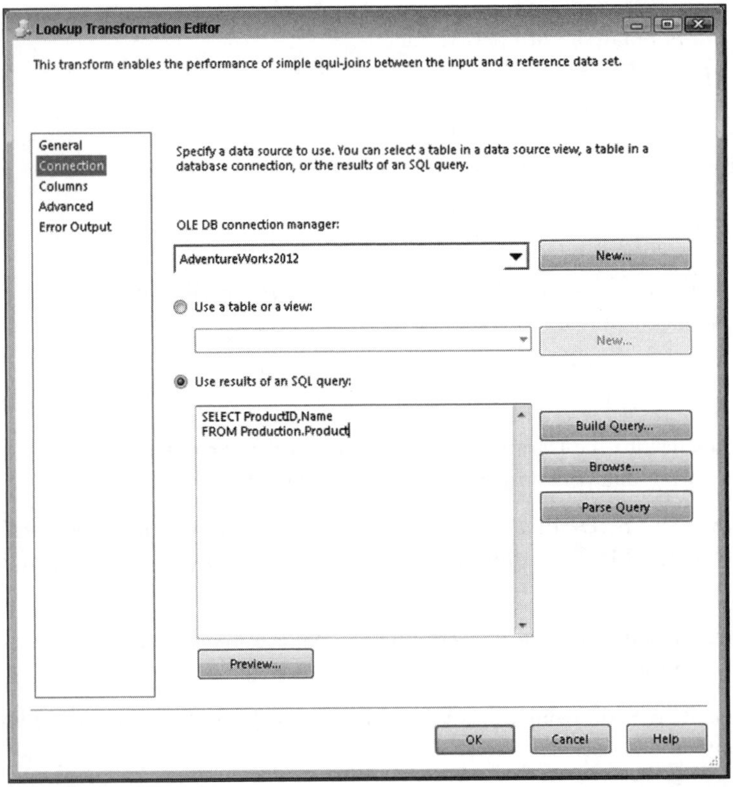

FIGURE 24-3

7. Navigate to the Columns tab and map the join columns by dragging the ProductID column from the input columns list (on the left) to the ProductID column from the lookup columns list (on the right). Check the Name column from the Available Lookup Columns list to return it in the data flow. When complete, your work should look like Figure 24-4. Then click OK.

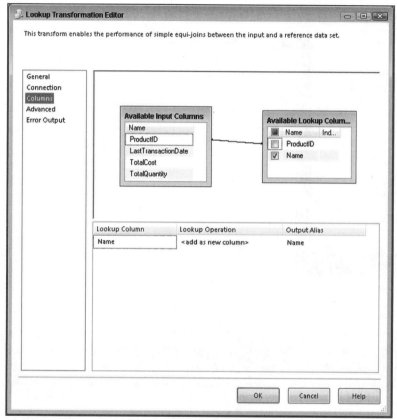

FIGURE 24-4

8. Open the Flat File Destination and click Update, which is a new feature in SSIS 2012 that enables you to easily update flat file metadata. Click OK when the Flat File Connection Manager opens to confirm the update and return back to the destination. The Name column has been added to the file connection, but still needs to be mapped to the Data Flow input. You do this by drawing the mapping from the input columns to the destination columns on the Mappings page.

9. Now execute the package. A successful run should look like Figure 24-5. The new flat file has now been created with the new column included.

FIGURE 24-5

> *Please select Lesson 24 on the DVD, or online at* www.wrox.com/go/ssis2012video, *to view the video that accompanies this lesson.*

THE CACHE CONNECTION MANAGER AND TRANSFORM

The method in the previous section of this lesson showed how the Lookup Transform could use source data for its cache only from specific OLE DB connections, and the cache could be populated by using a SQL query or table selection. An alternate way of using the Lookup Transform enables you to populate the cache using a separate pipeline in either the same or a different package. You can use source data from just about anywhere, including non–OLE DB connections.

The first method shown would reload the cache every time the transform was used. For example, if you had two pipelines in the same package that each required the same reference data set, each Lookup Transform would load its own copy of the cache separately. Using the Cache Transform, you can persist the cache to virtual memory or to permanent file storage. This means that within the same package, multiple Lookup Transforms can share the same cache, and the cache does not need to be reloaded during each iteration of a looping operation. You can load the cache to a file and share it with other packages. The cache file format is optimized for speed and can be orders of magnitude faster than reloading the reference data set from the original relational source.

The Cache Connection Manager (CCM) and Cache Transform enable you to load the Lookup cache from any source. The Cache Connection Manager is the more critical of the two—it holds a reference to the internal memory cache and can both read and write the cache to a disk-based file. In fact, the Lookup Transform uses the CCM internally as its caching mechanism.

Like other connection managers in SSIS, the CCM is instantiated in the Connection Managers pane of the package design surface. You can also create new CCMs from the Cache Transform Editor and Lookup Transform Editor. At design time, the CCM contains no data, so at run time, you need to populate it. Figure 24-6 shows the Cache Connection Manager Editor.

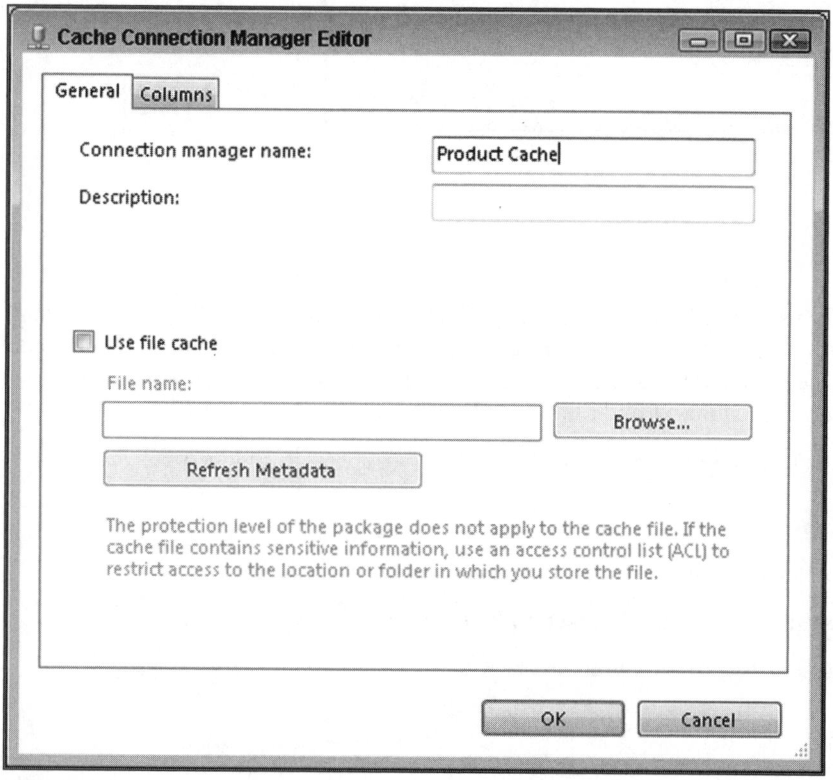

FIGURE 24-6

When you configure a CCM, it enables you to specify which columns of the input data set will be used as index fields and which columns will be used as reference fields. This is a necessary step—the CCM needs to know up front which columns you will be joining on so that it can create internal index structures to optimize the process. See Figure 24-7.

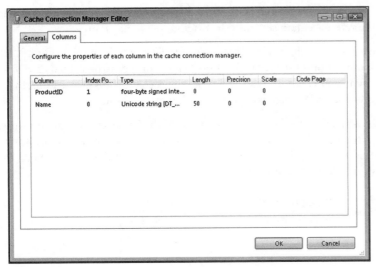

FIGURE 24-7

Try It

In this Try It, your company needs you to alter the package you worked on earlier in this lesson to show the product names using the Cache Connection Manager you just learned about. Your manager tells you to use the same flat file to store the results. After this lesson, you'll know how to use both the Cache Connection Manager and the Cache Transform.

You can download the Lesson24b.dtsx package from the book's website at www.wrox.com.

Lesson Requirements

Make the following changes to the package you created earlier in this lesson:

➤ Send the needed columns from Production.Product into a CCM.

➤ Change the source for the lookup to use the CCM.

Hints

➤ Use the Cache Transform to put the product data into the Cache Connection Manager.

➤ Use the CCM in the lookup instead of the OLE DB Connection Manager.

Step-by-Step

1. Either open the completed Lesson24b.dtsx SSIS package from www.wrox.com or alter the package you used earlier in this lesson.

2. Add a new Data Flow to the Control Flow and name it **Cache Product Table**. Then connect it to the existing Data Flow.

3. Open the new Data Flow and drag over an OLE DB Source. Then configure it as shown in Figure 24-8. Click OK.

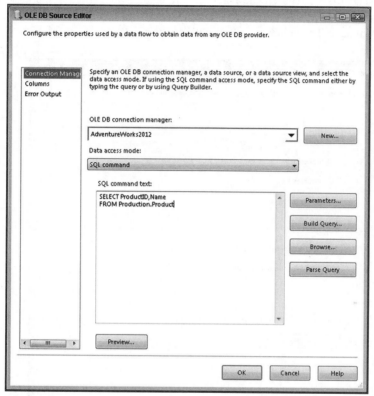

FIGURE 24-8

4. Bring a Cache Transform into the Data Flow and open the Cache Transformation Editor. Select New to create a Cache Connection Manager, which opens the Cache Connection Manager Editor.

5. On the Columns tab of the editor, change the Index Position for ProductID to 1, as shown in Figure 24-9. Then click OK.

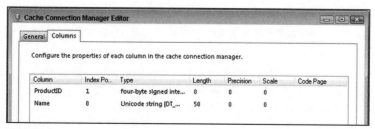

FIGURE 24-9

6. Ensure that all columns are mapped by clicking the Mappings tab in the Cache Transformation Editor. Then click OK.

7. Now enter the DFT – Aggregate Data Data Flow to change the source of the lookup transform by opening the LKP – Product Name and changing the Connection Type to Cache Connection Manager. Then click OK. You will see the results in Figure 24-10.

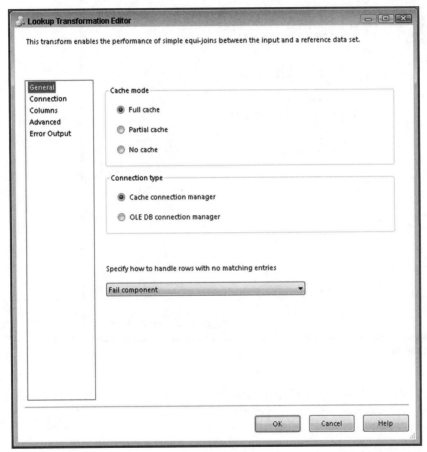

FIGURE 24-10

8. Empty the content of the flat file and then execute the package again. The results will be the same as the original package, but now the cached data can be used several times throughout the package.

Please select Lesson 24 on the DVD, or online at www.wrox.com/go/ssis2012video, *to view the video that accompanies this lesson.*

25

Auditing Data with the Row Count Transform

Often in an ETL process you may be required to create an auditing table that records how many rows were loaded. SSIS has made this easy to accomplish with the Row Count Transform.

This transform has the ability to count rows in a Data Flow and record that count for later use in conjunction with an Execute SQL Task. The count must be placed into a variable, which can then be used in the Control Flow for inserting into an audit table.

If you have used this transform in previous versions of SSIS, you will notice that it has been simplified even more in SQL Server 2012. To configure the Row Count Transform, connect it to any point in the Data Flow that you want to record the number of rows. Double-click the transform to open the Row Count Editor. In the Variable property, specify what variable (package and project parameters cannot be used here) will store the row count that the transform records.

Another valuable way to use the Row Count Transform is as a destination to send your data to. Because you don't physically have to commit stream data to a table to retrieve the count, it can act as a destination, terminating your data stream and enabling you to view the Data Flow's data with a data viewer.

TRY IT

In this Try It, your company needs you to create a package that runs only if the ErrorLog table in the AdventureWorks2012 database contains any rows. After this lesson, you'll know how to insert a row count into a variable and use it dynamically in your package.

You can find the completed Lesson25.dtsx package at www.wrox.com.

Lesson Requirements

Create a new package named Lesson25 and make the following changes, or as just noted, you can find the completed Lesson25.dtsx package at www.wrox.com:

➤ Count the rows in the ErrorLog table and place that number in a variable.

➤ Set the precedence constraint to run a Script Task if the table has at least one row.

Hints

➤ You need only one OLE DB Source in a Data Flow and one Row Count Transform that counts how many rows are in the ErrorLog table.

➤ Use a Script Task that executes only if at least one row is found in the ErrorLog table.

Step-by-Step

1. Create an SSIS package named **Lesson25** or download Lesson25.dtsx from www.wrox.com. Add a Data Flow Task to the Control Flow design surface.

2. In the Control Flow tab, add a variable named **MyRowCount**. Ensure that the variable is package-scoped and of type Int32 (Figure 25-1). If you don't know how to add a variable, select Variable from the SSIS menu and click the Add Variable button.

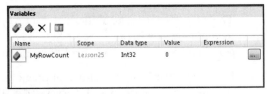

FIGURE 25-1

3. Create a connection manager that connects to the AdventureWorks2012 database. Add an OLE DB Data Source to the Data Flow design surface. Configure the source to point to your AdventureWorks2012 database's connection manager and the ErrorLog table.

4. Add a Row Count Transform to the Data Flow and connect it to the Data Source. Double-click the transform to open the Row Count Editor and select the variable named User::MyRowCount in the Variable property. Your editor should resemble Figure 25-2.

FIGURE 25-2

5. Return to the Control Flow tab and add a Script Task. This task is not really going to perform any action. Instead, it will be used to show the conditional ability to perform steps based on the value returned by the Row Count Transform.

6. Connect the Data Flow Task to the Script Task.

7. Right-click the arrow connecting the Data Flow Task and Script Task. Select the Edit menu. In the Precedence Constraint Editor, change the Evaluation Operation to Expression. Set the Expression to **@MyRowCount>0** (Figure 25-3).

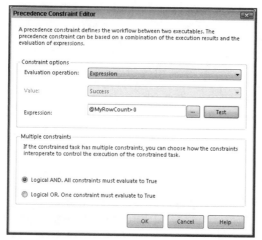

FIGURE 25-3

8.   Now execute the package. A successful run should look like Figure 25-4. The Script Task should not change to green because no rows exist in the ErrorLog table.

FIGURE 25-4

Please select Lesson 25 on the DVD, or online at www.wrox.com/go/ssis2012video, *to view the video that accompanies this lesson.*

26

Combining Multiple Inputs with the Union All Transform

The Union All Transform combines multiple inputs in the Data Flow into a single output row-set. It is very similar to the Merge Transform, but does not require the input data to be sorted. For example, in Figure 26-1, three different transforms are combined into a single output using the Union All Transform. The transformation inputs are added to the output one after the other; thus, no rows are reordered.

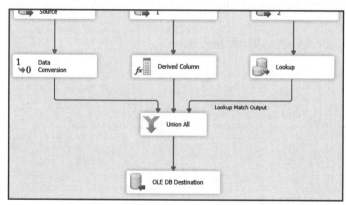

FIGURE 26-1

To configure this transform, bring the blue precedence constraints from the sources or transformations you want to combine to the Union All Transform. SSIS automatically maps the columns if they have the same name, but if you want to verify that the columns are correctly mapped, open the Union All Transformation Editor. The only time you *must* open the Union All Transformation Editor is if the column names from the different inputs do not match. During development, if upstream components get tweaked or something else changes to disrupt the column mappings of the Union All Transform, those mappings must be fixed manually.

The transform fixes minor metadata issues. For example, if you have one input that is a 20-character string and a different input that is a 50-character string, the output of this from the Union All Transform will be the longer 50-character column. Occasionally though, when you make changes above the transform, you might see red on the Union All Transform, indicating an error. In these cases, it's faster to delete the transform and re-add it than it is to spend time debugging the error.

> **NOTE** *The Union All Transform can be used as a temporary destination while you are developing to test your package. This practice allows you to test the rest of your package without landing data.*

TRY IT

In this Try It, your company needs you to create a package that has three different sources, but places the data into one flat file. After this lesson, you will know how to combine data from different sources and place that data in one Flat File Destination.

You can download the completed Lesson26.dtsx from www.wrox.com.

Lesson Requirements

Create a new package named Lesson26 and make the following changes, or download the completed Lesson26.dtsx from www.wrox.com.

Use the following tables from the AdventureWorksDW2012 database:

➤ FactInternetSales

➤ FactResellerSales

Combine these columns from each table:

➤ ProductKey

➤ SalesAmount

After the data is combined, export it to a flat file.

Hints

➤ You need two OLE DB Sources: one for FactInternetSales and one for FactResellerSales.

➤ Use a Union All Transform to combine the previously mentioned columns.

➤ Send the results of the package to a Flat File Destination.

Step-by-Step

1. Create an SSIS package named **Lesson26** or download the completed Lesson26.dtsx from www.wrox.com.

2. In the Control Flow tab, add a new Data Flow Task to the design surface and name it **DFT - Union All Sales**.

3. Create a new OLE DB Connection Manager using the AdventureWorksDW2012 database as the source. Then drag two OLE DB Sources on the designer and rename them **Reseller Sales** and **Internet Sales**.

4. In the Internet Sales Source, select SQL Command as the Data access mode and enter the following query:

```
Select ProductKey,SalesAmount
From FactInternetSales
```

5. In the Reseller Sales Source, select SQL Command as the Data access mode and enter the following query:

```
Select ProductKey, SalesAmount
From FactResellerSales
```

6. Drag a Union All Transform and connect both blue arrows from the sources to it. Verify that the columns mapped correctly by opening the Union All Transformation Editor (Figure 26-2).

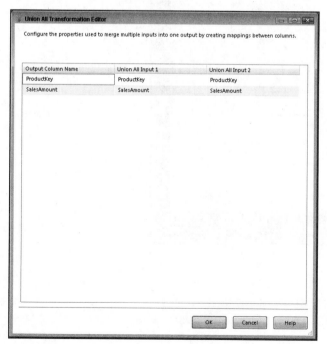

FIGURE 26-2

7. Now bring a Flat File Destination to the design surface and connect the Union All Transform to it. Name the destination **Sales Export.**

8. Open the Flat File Destination and select New to create a delimited Flat File Connection Manager.

9. Name the Flat File Connection Manager **Flat File Sales Export.** Then call the file **SalesExport. txt,** and select C:\Projects\SSISPersonalTrainer as the location for it. Also, check the Column names in the first data row option. Click OK on the connection manager. Ensure that you select the Mappings page on the destination so each column is set correctly. Click OK on the destination.

10. The package is now complete. When the package is executed, your results will look like Figure 26-3.

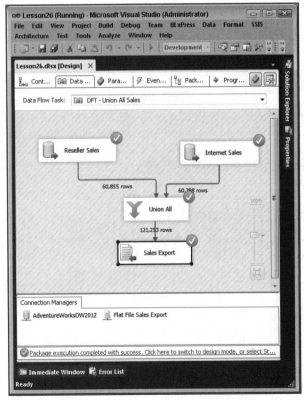

FIGURE 26-3

Please select Lesson 26 on the DVD, or online at www.wrox.com/go/ssis2012video, *to view the video that accompanies this lesson.*

27

Cleansing Data with the Script Component

Sometimes you can't accomplish your data cleansing goal in a Derived Column Transform, and you must get more advanced. Say, for example, you want to run a routine where any character data is removed from the data, or, if the data coming in is an invalid date, perhaps you want to replace it with today's date. In these examples, you can use a Script Component in the Data Flow Task. The Script Component can play one of three roles: transform, source, or destination:

- ➤ **Transform**—Generally, the focus of your Data Flow will be on using the script as a transform. In this role, you can perform advanced cleansing with the out-of-the-box components.

- ➤ **Source**—When the script is used as a source, you can apply advanced business rules to your data as it's being pulled out of the source system. (This happens sometimes with COBOL files.)

- ➤ **Destination**—When the script is used as a destination, you can use the script to write out to a non-OLE DB destination, like XML or SharePoint.

You can write your script in VB.NET or C#, but once you select a language, you can't change it. You can select the language by double-clicking the Script Component and going to the Script page of the Script Transformation Editor (shown in Figure 27-1). You can also select any variables you want to pass into the script in this page. Make sure to select the variable for ReadWrite only if the variable needs to be written to. Otherwise, the variable will be locked for the duration of the script's execution.

On the Input Columns page (Figure 27-2), select each column that you want to be passed into the script from the Data Flow and select whether you want to allow them to be accessed for writing. If you don't need the column for writing, make sure it's set to ReadOnly, because ReadWrite columns require more resources. All columns that are not checked are passed through to the next transform or destination seamlessly.

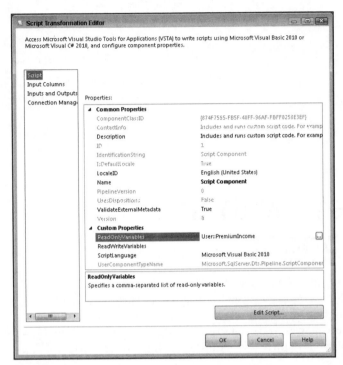

FIGURE 27-1

FIGURE 27-2

You can also add more columns that are not part of the source or a previous transform using the Inputs and Outputs page. This page enables you to add other buckets of data that you can use to direct the data down multiple paths. To do this, you must first create an additional output by clicking New Output. Then you need to set the SynchronousInputID property to the same number for each output. Set the ExclusionGroup to the same non-zero number. In the script, you can then use the DirectRowTo<outputbuffername> method to send the data to each of the paths. Because this is in the script, the data can be sent to multiple paths at the same time.

To edit the script, go to the Script page and click Edit Script. This opens the Visual Studio environment. Three subroutines are the most important to your design: PreExecute, PostExecute, and ProcessInputRow:

➤ PreExecute executes once per transform execution and is a great place to initialize objects or connections that you hope to use later.

➤ PostExecute is where you can close connections and objects or set variables.

➤ ProcessInputRow is run for every row going through the transform; from this subroutine you cannot set variables.

Accessing a row from the ProcessInputRow subroutine is simple. To do so, you must use the Row object, which contains an individual row as it is looping. For example, to read a row coming into the transform, like BRIAN KNIGHT, and translate that to a proper-cased value, like Brian Knight, use the following code, where ColumnName holds the customer name. StrConv is a string conversion function to convert a string to a new format.

```
Public Overrides Sub Input0_ProcessInputRow(ByVal Row As Input0Buffer)
    'This is the line that performs the magic to Proper Case.
    Row.ColumnName = StrConv(Row.ColumnName, VbStrConv.ProperCase)
    End Sub
```

Variables can be read from any subroutine, but you will only be able to write to them in the PostExecute subroutine. To read or write to a variable, you can use a Me.Variables statement, as shown in the following:

```
Row.YearlyIncome = Row.YearlyIncome + Me.Variables.PremiumIncome
```

Though breakpoints were allowed in the Script Task, they are not allowed in the Data Flow. Because of this, you have to use more arcane debugging techniques, like message boxes to notify you which step the engine is at in the code.

TRY IT

In this Try It, you have recently begun to receive data from an entity that has occasional issues with date data. The source application allows users to enter whatever they'd like for the birth date, so occasionally you receive invalid characters in the date or invalid dates. After completing this lesson, you'll have a better idea of how to use the Script Component to perform more complex cleansing or checking of your data.

You can download the completed Lesson27.dtsx and the Lesson27Data.txt source file from
www.wrox.com.

Lesson Requirements

In this lesson, you need to check dates of the BirthDate column from the Lesson27Data.txt source
file as each row is read into the script and send the data to one of two buckets: ValidatedData or
BadData. Additionally, if the DateFirstPurchase column is anything but a date, you need to change
the row to today's date as a default.

> **NOTE** *Normally, you would send the data in the BadData bucket to another
> business rule to cleanse it further or to an auditing table. However, the point of
> this lesson is not to write the data to a destination table, so, if you'd like, you can
> just send the data to two Union All Transforms to simulate two data streams.*

Hints

➤   The IsDate() function can determine if a column is in a date.

➤   You will want to create two buckets in the Inputs and Outputs page.

➤   Make sure the SynchronousInputID column is set to the same Script Component. Inputs and
    the ExclusionGroup property are set to 1 for each of the outputs.

Step-by-Step

1.   Create a new package called **Lesson27.dtsx** (or download the completed Lesson27.dtsx from
     www.wrox.com).

2.   Create a connection to the file that you downloaded off the Wrox website called
     Lesson27Data.txt.

3.   Create a new Flat File Connection Manager called **Extract** (creating connection managers is
     covered in Lesson 6) and point to the Lesson27Data.txt file. In the General page, check the
     Column names in the first data row box and ensure that the EmailAddress column in the Flat
     File Connection Manager is set to 100 characters in the Advanced page.

4.   Create a Data Flow Task. In the Data Flow tab, create a Flat File Source that points to the
     new connection manager that you just created in Step 3 called Extract.

5.   Drag a Script Component onto the design pane. You are immediately prompted for what
     type of script you want to use (source, transform, or destination). Select Transformation for
     the type and connect the transform to the Flat File Source.

6.   In the Script Transform Editor, select the Input Columns page and check BirthDate and
     DateFirstPurchase. Ensure that DateFirstPurchase is set to ReadWrite.

7.   Go to the Inputs and Outputs page and highlight the Output 0 Buffer and click Remove
Output, found on the bottom of the window. Then click Add Output twice. Rename the first
output you just created **BadData** and the second to **ValidatedData**. For both of the outputs,
set the SynchronousInputID to the same input buffer and set the ExclusionGroup property to
1, as shown in Figure 27-3.

FIGURE 27-3

8.   Go to the Script page, select Microsoft Visual Basic 2010 for the ScriptLanguage, and click
Edit Script. Then add the following script in the ProcessInputRow subroutine (note that the
subroutine will already exist in your code block):

```
    Public Overrides Sub Input0_ProcessInputRow(ByVal Row As
Input0Buffer)

        If IsDate(Row.DateFirstPurchase) = False Then
            Row.DateFirstPurchase = Now
        End If

        If IsDate(Row.BirthDate) = True Then
            Row.DirectRowToValidatedData()
        Else
            Row.DirectRowToBadData()

        End If
    End Sub
```

9. Ensure there is nothing underlined blue (showing bad code), then close the script and return to the designer.

10. Drag two Union All Transforms onto the design pane and connect the Script Transform to each of the Union All Transforms.

11. Execute the package, and you should see five bad rows go down the BadData path, as shown in Figure 27-4.

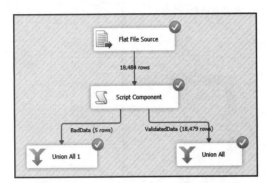

FIGURE 27-4

Please select Lesson 27 on the DVD, or online at www.wrox.com/go/ssis2012video, to view the video that accompanies this lesson.

28

Separating Data with the Conditional Split Transform

Sometimes you deal with source data that may require different treatments applied to it. For example, you want to generate a mailing list for a direct mail campaign, but you want to target only customers with children. You want to make sure to separate the customers without kids before preparing the list. You would also like anyone who has more than five kids to receive a buy-two-get-one-free coupon with the mailer.

The best way to separate data within a package to apply different types of actions is with the Conditional Split Transform. With this transform, you can send data from a single data path to multiple outputs based on conditions set in the Conditional Split Transformation Editor, shown in Figure 28-1. To open the editor, drag the transform in the design surface and double-click it.

The Conditional Split Transform uses the SSIS expression language to determine how the data pipeline should be split. For this example, all you need to know is that the Conditional Split Transform is checking to see if customers have more than five kids so they can receive the extra coupon.

> **NOTE** *If you need a reminder on how the SSIS expression language works, refer back to Lesson 21 where it is covered in more detail.*

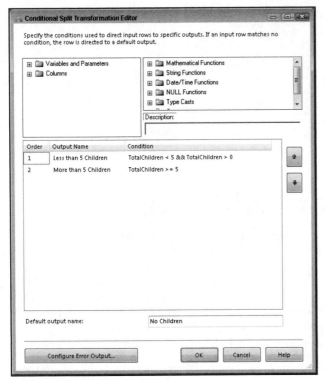

FIGURE 28-1

This check produces three possible outputs:

➤ For customers with more than five children

➤ For customers with between one and four children

➤ For customers with no children

It may look like you have only two outputs, but if you look on the bottom of the Conditional Split Transformation Editor, the Default Output Name provides an output for data that doesn't apply to the conditions declared. In the case of this package, you need only those customers with at least one child; you will see only these outputs in the final package (shown in Figure 28-2). You do not need to use the output for customers with no children.

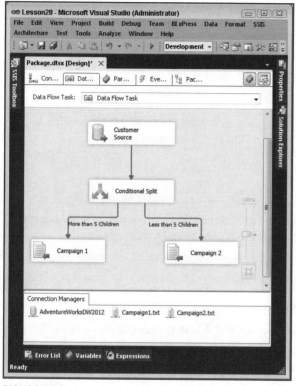

FIGURE 28-2

TRY IT

In this Try It, your company needs a list of customers for a direct mail campaign that is only going to be sent regionally. You need to create an SSIS package that generates two different mailing lists because one region is going to receive a different promotion than the other. After completing this Try It, you will know how to split data within a package based on set conditions using the Conditional Split Transform.

You can download the completed Lesson28.dtsx from www.wrox.com.

Lesson Requirements

Create a new package named Lesson28 and make the following changes. (Again, you can also find the completed Lesson28.dtsx package at www.wrox.com.)

➤ Use the following tables from the AdventureWorksDW2012 database:

  ➤ DimCustomer

  ➤ DimGeography

➤ Bring back the following columns from DimCustomer:

  ➤ Title

  ➤ FirstName

  ➤ MiddleName

  ➤ LastName

  ➤ EmailAddress

  ➤ AddressLine1

  ➤ AddressLine2

  ➤ Phone

➤ Using the GeographyKey, use any method to join the DimCustomer and DimGeography tables together and bring back the following columns from DimGeography:

  ➤ StateProvinceCode

  ➤ PostalCode

➤ Create a Conditional Split with these conditions:

  ➤ **Campaign 1**—StateProvinceCode == "FL" || StateProvinceCode == "GA"

  ➤ **Campaign 2**—StateProvinceCode == "CA" || StateProvinceCode == "WA"

➤ Send these two outputs to two separate flat files to create the regional mailing lists.

Hints

➤ In the Data Flow, you need only one OLE DB Source to bring in customer data.

➤ You need a Lookup Transform to join geography data to each customer.

➤ Use a Conditional Split Transform to separate the different state codes.

➤ You need two separate Flat File Destinations for the results.

Step-by-Step

1. Create an SSIS package named Lesson28 or download Lesson28.dtsx from www.wrox.com. Add a Data Flow Task named **DFT - Regional Mailing List** to the Control Flow design surface.

2. Create a new OLE DB Connection Manager using the AdventureWorksDW2012 database as the source. Then drag an OLE DB Source on the designer and rename it **Customer Source**.

3. In Customer Source, select AdventureWorksDW2012 as the connection manager and SQL Command as the Data access mode.

4. Enter the following query in the Data access mode window:

```
Select FirstName,
MiddleName,
LastName,
AddressLine1,
AddressLine2,
EmailAddress,
Phone,
GeographyKey
From DimCustomer
```

5. Drag a Lookup Transform on to the design pane and name it **LKP - Geography**. Open the Lookup Transformation Editor and select AdventureWorksDW2012 as the connection manager.

6. Next, select Use results of an SQL query and use the following query:

```
SELECT GeographyKey, StateProvinceCode
FROM DimGeography
```

7. Go to the Columns tab to add the StateProvinceCode to the data stream, shown in Figure 28-3.

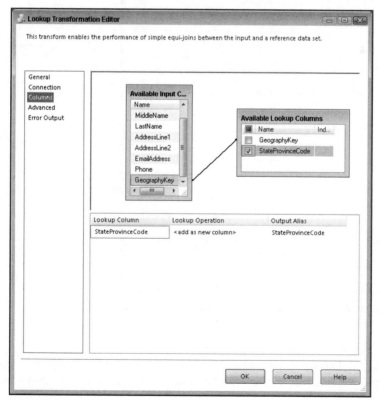

FIGURE 28-3

8. Now bring a Conditional Split Transform to the design surface and connect it to the Lookup Transform. When prompted, select Lookup Match Output for the Output of the Lookup Transform.

9. Open the Conditional Split Transformation Editor. Add a new output in the Conditional Split Transformation Editor called **Campaign1**, and then add the following condition:

```
StateProvinceCode == "FL" || StateProvinceCode == "GA"
```

10. Add a second output named **Campaign2** with the following condition:

```
StateProvinceCode == "CA" || StateProvinceCode == "WA"
```

11. Make **No Ad Campaign** the Default Output Name and click OK. After making these changes, the editor should look like Figure 28-4.

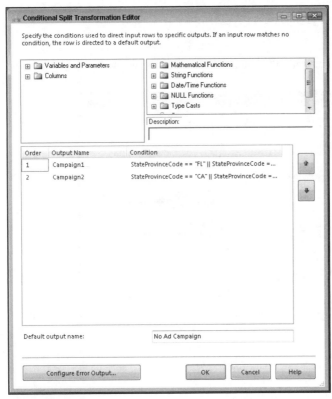

FIGURE 28-4

12. Bring two Flat File Destinations into the Data Flow and name them **Campaign1 Mailing List** and **Campaign2 Mailing List**. Create separate connection managers for them pointing to the file location of your choice.

13. The Conditional Split will have three blue output arrows. When you connect the first blue arrow to one of the two destinations, a dialog box opens asking which output you want. Connect each output to the destination that has the name associated with it. This action leaves one output unused: No Ad Campaign.

14. Open each Flat File Destination to make sure the mapping is set correctly.

15. The package is now complete. When the package is executed, your results will look like Figure 28-5.

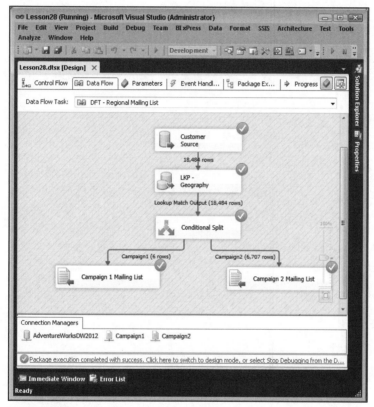

FIGURE 28-5

Please select Lesson 28 on the DVD, or online at www.wrox.com/go/ssis2012video, *to view the video that accompanies this lesson.*

29

Altering Rows with the OLE DB Command Transform

The OLE DB Command Transform is used to run a SQL statement for each row in the Data Flow. It sounds innocent enough, doesn't it? The reality is that the statement "for each row" should immediately make alarms go off in your head. This involves kicking off an update, insert, or delete statement for each row in an input stream.

To put this into perspective, imagine you are loading a product dimension table in your ETL process. Your predecessor decided it would be best to update and delete these rows using an OLE DB Command. The company you work for is a major department store, and the new spring clothing line is coming in. So, all the winter clothes are being marked down. This means you are going to get an update with a price reduction for all the winter clothes your company has in inventory at one time. Using the OLE DB Command Transform would mean that your package would be running several thousand update statements and your package would run for hours. A situation like that one is why we recommend you avoid using the OLE DB Command Transform.

> **NOTE** *So if we recommend not using the OLE DB Command Transform, what are your options? The best practice would be to insert all rows marked as updates into a staging table, and then in the Control Flow use an Execute SQL Task to update the destination table. Why is this better than using the OLE DB Command Transform? The Execute SQL Task performs this operation in bulk versus the several thousand update statements required in the OLE DB Command Transform. This method is explained in greater detail in Lesson 60, which covers loading a dimension table.*

This doesn't mean you should never use this transform, but it is important to understand its shortcomings when working with large amounts of data.

To use the OLE DB Command Transform, drag it from the Toolbox to the Data Flow design surface and double-click it. The configuration looks more complicated than it really is. From the Connection Managers tab, specify which OLE DB Connection you want to execute the SQL statement on. Figure 29-1 shows the AdventureWorks2012 database as the connection manager.

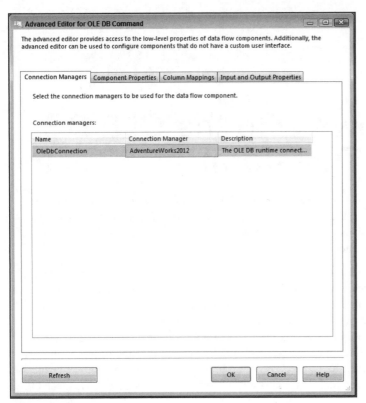

FIGURE 29-1

You set the SQL statement you plan to execute on the Component Properties tab. To enter your SQL statement, click the ellipsis next to the SqlCommand property. Remember that to tell SSIS that you are going to be using parameters in a SQL statement, you use a question mark (?).

You can also configure the amount of time before a timeout occurs in the CommandTimeout property, shown in Figure 29-2. This uses an interval of seconds where 0 denotes no timeout.

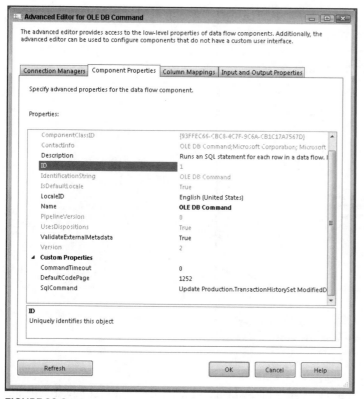

FIGURE 29-2

The Column Mappings tab in the Advanced Editor for OLE DB Command window is similar to the Mappings page in a destination editor. (Configuring destinations is discussed in more detail in Lesson 19.) It displays the input stream and destination columns, which are really the parameters indicated in the SqlCommand property. Any input column mapped to a parameter replaces the parameter with the value of that field. When you are mapping, remember that the order in which you place the parameters while writing the SQL statement is also the order in which they must be mapped. In Figure 29-3 you see how to map the following Update statement:

```
Update Production.TransactionHistory
Set ModifiedDate = ?
Where ProductID = ?
```

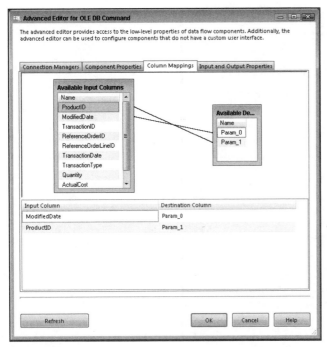

FIGURE 29-3

The last tab is the Input and Output Properties tab, which you will likely not ever have to change; it simply provides another place where you can add or remove columns that are used in the transform.

TRY IT

In this Try It, you work for a company that sells dartboard supplies. As new supplies are added to your inventory, some of the older products are being discounted. Use the flat file extract provided and update the price on all required products. After completing this lesson, you will know how to use the OLE DB Command Transform to alter data with a SQL statement inside the Data Flow.

> **NOTE** *The small package created in this example is meant only to show the capabilities of the OLE DB Command Transform. Our recommendations stated earlier in the lesson for why you might want to avoid using the OLE DB Command Transform for these sorts of situations still stand.*

You can download the completed Lesson29.dtsx and sample files for this lesson from www.wrox.com.

Lesson Requirements

Create a table in the AdventureWorks2012 database named Product_OLEDBCommand. You can find the code to create this table in the download for this lesson available at www.wrox.com.

Download the flat file named OLEDBCommandExample.txt from www.wrox.com to use as your source. Save this file to the C:\Projects\SSISPersonalTrainer directory.

Update the current flag and row end date columns in the Product_OLEDBCommand table and then create new rows in the table representing the new list price.

Hints

➤ Use the OLE DB Command Transform to update only two columns.

➤ After updating these fields, send the rest of the input stream to a regular OLE DB Destination to insert new records with the new list price.

Step-by-Step

1. Create a new package and name it **Lesson29** or download the completed Lesson29.dtsx package from www.wrox.com.

2. Drag a Data Flow Task onto your designer and name it **DFT - OLE DB Command**.

3. Create a new Flat File Connection Manager, name it **Product Price Change**, and point it to C:\Projects\SSISPersonalTrainer\OLEDBCommandExample.txt. Also, check the Column names in the first data row option. The editor should look like Figure 29-4.

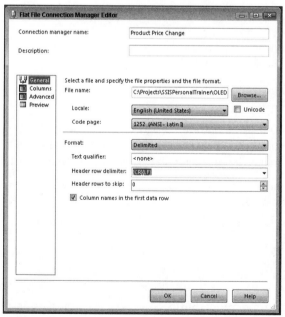

FIGURE 29-4

4. In the Data Flow, bring a new Flat File Source over and name it **Discounted Products**. Open the editor and make the connection manager the newly created Product Price Change.

5. Open Management Studio, connect to the AdventureWorks2012 database, and run the following query to create a new table called Product_OLEDBCommand (you can download the query from www.wrox.com):

```
CREATE TABLE [dbo].[Product_OLEDBCommand](
    [ProductID] [smallint] IDENTITY(1,1) NOT NULL,
    [ProductBusinessKey] int,
    [ProductName] [varchar](50) NOT NULL,
    [ListPrice] [money],
    [CurrentFlag] [smallint],
    [RowStartDate] [datetime],
    [RowEndDate] [datetime]
 CONSTRAINT [PK_Product_OLEDBCommand_ProductID] PRIMARY KEY CLUSTERED
(
        [ProductID] ASC
) ON [PRIMARY]
) ON [PRIMARY]

GO
INSERT INTO [dbo].[Product_OLEDBCommand] Select 101,
    'Professional Dartboard','49.99', '1', '1/1/2006',Null
INSERT INTO [dbo].[Product_OLEDBCommand] Select 102,
    'Professional Darts',15.99,1, '1/1/2006',Null
INSERT INTO [dbo].[Product_OLEDBCommand] Select 103,
    'Scoreboard',26.99,1, '1/1/2006',Null
INSERT INTO [dbo].[Product_OLEDBCommand] Select 104,
    'Beginner Dartboard',45.99,1, '1/1/2006',Null
INSERT INTO [dbo].[Product_OLEDBCommand] Select 105,
    'Dart Tips',1.99,1, '1/1/2006',Null
INSERT INTO [dbo].[Product_OLEDBCommand] Select 106,
    'Dart Shafts',7.99,1, '1/1/2006',Null
```

6. Next, create another connection manager, this time an OLE DB Connection Manager, using the AdventureWorks2012 database.

7. Bring an OLE DB Command Transform onto the design surface, connect it to the source called Discounted Products, and after opening the transform's editor, select AdventureWorks2012 as the connection manager on the Connection Managers tab.

8. Enter the following SQL statement in the SqlCommand property on the Component Properties tab, shown in Figure 29-5:

```
Update Product_OLEDBCommand
Set CurrentFlag = 0,
    RowEndDate = GETDATE()
Where ProductBusinessKey = ?
and RowEndDate is null
```

This statement means that for every ProductBusinessKey you have, the CurrentFlag will be set to 0, and the RowEndDate will be given today's date.

9. Next, on the Column Mappings tab you need to connect ProductBusinessKey from the Available Input Columns to Param_0 in the destination. Figure 29-6 shows there is only one parameter in this statement, so there is only one destination column.

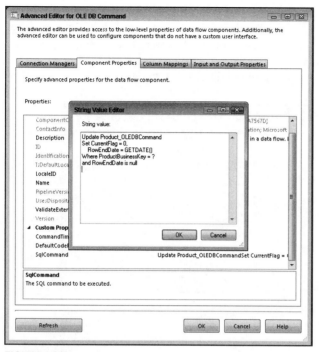

FIGURE 29-5

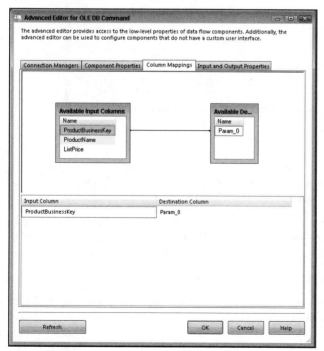

FIGURE 29-6

10. Now bring a Derived Column Transform to the Data Flow and connect the OLE DB Command to it. Open the Derived Column Transform Editor and add two new columns called **RowStartDate** and **CurrentFlag**. For the RowStartDate column, use the GETDATE() function in the Expression field, and CurrentFlag just needs a 1 in the Expression box. The Derived Column Transformation Editor should look like Figure 29-7. Click OK.

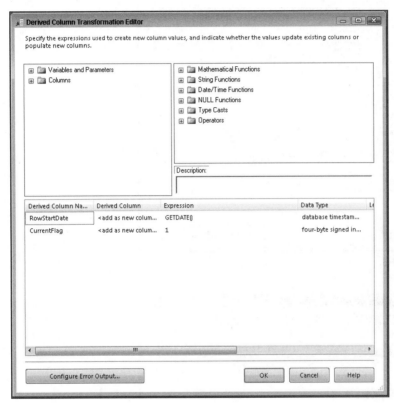

FIGURE 29-7

11. To finish this package, you need to load the new rows' results into the Product_OLEDBCommand table. Bring an OLE DB Destination onto the design surface, and from within the editor, select Product_OLEDBCommand as the destination table.

12. Go to the Mappings page of the OLE DB Destination Editor; notice how all the columns are automatically mapped except for RowEndDate, which is set in the OLE DB Command Transform. Figure 29-8 shows how the final mapped columns should look.

13. A successful run of this package should look like Figure 29-9.

14. Take a look at the table in Figure 29-10 to see the results of a completed package. Notice that the package created a new row for each product with the new price. It also closed the old row by updating the row's end date and the current flag. This is what's known as a Type 2 change in a dimension table.

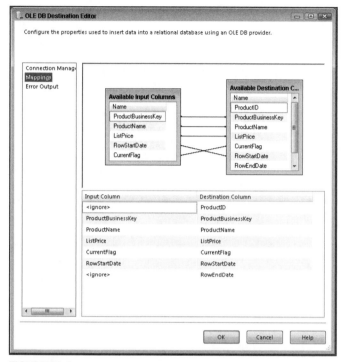

FIGURE 29-8

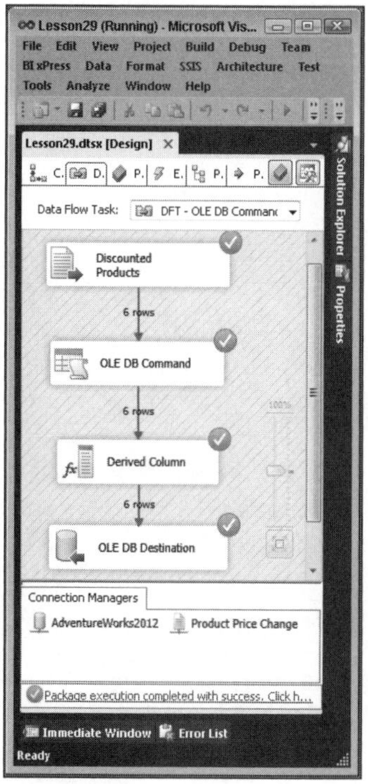

FIGURE 29-9

	ProductID	ProductBusinessKey	ProductName	ListPrice	CurrentFlag	RowStartDate	RowEndDate
1	1	101	Professional Dartboard	49.99	0	2006-01-01 00:00:00.000	2012-07-05 21:24:00.890
2	2	102	Professional Darts	15.99	0	2006-01-01 00:00:00.000	2012-07-05 21:24:00.973
3	3	103	Scoreboard	26.99	0	2006-01-01 00:00:00.000	2012-07-05 21:24:00.973
4	4	104	Beginner Dartboard	45.99	0	2006-01-01 00:00:00.000	2012-07-05 21:24:00.977
5	5	105	Dart Tips	1.99	0	2006-01-01 00:00:00.000	2012-07-05 21:24:00.980
6	6	106	Dart Shafts	7.99	0	2006-01-01 00:00:00.000	2012-07-05 21:24:00.980
7	7	101	Professional Dartboard	44.99	1	2012-07-05 21:24:01.033	NULL
8	8	102	Professional Darts	11.99	1	2012-07-05 21:24:01.033	NULL
9	9	103	Scoreboard	17.99	1	2012-07-05 21:24:01.033	NULL
10	10	104	Beginner Dartboard	38.99	1	2012-07-05 21:24:01.033	NULL
11	11	105	Dart Tips	1.09	1	2012-07-05 21:24:01.033	NULL
12	12	106	Dart Shafts	4.99	1	2012-07-05 21:24:01.033	NULL

FIGURE 29-10

NOTE *To learn more about data warehousing best practices, read Lessons 60 and 61.*

Please select Lesson 29 on the DVD, or online at www.wrox.com/go/ssis2012video, *to view the video that accompanies this lesson.*

30

Handling Bad Data with the Fuzzy Lookup

More often than not, when you are working in the real world, data is not going to be perfect like it is in the AdventureWorks2012 database. Real-world situations call for cleansing dirty data or data that has abnormalities like misspellings or truncation.

Imagine you are attempting to retrieve a foreign key from a dimension table, but, strangely, you find rows without a match. Upon investigation, you find bad data is being supplied to you. One technique might be to divert these rows without matches to a table to be dealt with later; another might be to just add the bad data regardless of misspellings and other mishaps that occur during data entry.

The Fuzzy Lookup Transform, discussed in this lesson, and the Fuzzy Grouping Transform, discussed in the next lesson, gives other alternatives to dealing with dirty data while reducing your number of unmatched rows. The Fuzzy Lookup Transform matches input records with data that has already been cleansed in a reference table. It returns the match and can also indicate the quality of the match. This way you know the likelihood of the match being correct.

> **NOTE** *A best practice tip is to use the Fuzzy Lookup Transform only after trying a regular lookup on the field first. The Fuzzy Lookup Transform is a very expensive operation that builds specialized indexes of the input stream and the reference data for comparison purposes. Therefore, it is recommended to first use a regular Lookup Transform and then divert only those rows not matching to the Fuzzy Lookup Transform.*

During the configuration of the transform, you must specify a reference table to be used for comparison. Figure 30-1 shows the reference table selection being made in the Fuzzy Lookup Transformation Editor. The transform uses this reference data and builds a token-based index (which, despite its name, is actually a table) before it begins the process of comparing entries.

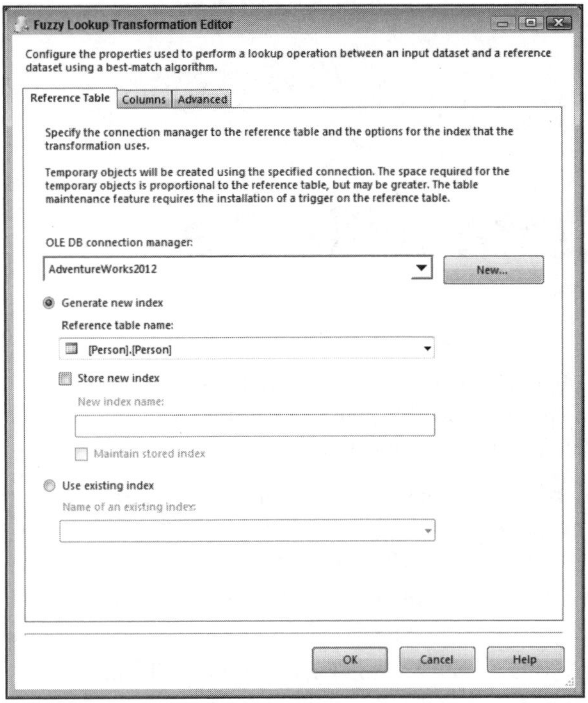

FIGURE 30-1

Using the Fuzzy Lookup Transform requires at least one field to be a string, either a DT_WSTR or DT_STR data type. On the Columns tab in the editor, you need to map at least one text field from the input to the reference table for comparison.

The Advanced tab contains the settings that control the fuzzy logic algorithms. You can set the maximum number of matches to output per incoming row. The default is set to 1, which pulls only the best record out of the reference table that meets the similarity threshold. Incrementing this setting higher than the default might generate more results that you'll have to sift through, but it might be required if you have too many closely matching strings in your data. A slider controls the similarity threshold. When you are experimenting, a good strategy is to start this setting at 0.5 and move up or down as you review the results. This setting is normally decided based on a businessperson's review of the data, not the developer's review. If a row cannot be found that's similar enough, the columns that you checked in the Columns tab will be set to NULL. The token delimiters can also be set if, for example, you don't want the comparison process to break up incoming strings with a period (.) or spaces. The default for this setting is all common delimiters. See Figure 30-2 for an example of an Advanced tab.

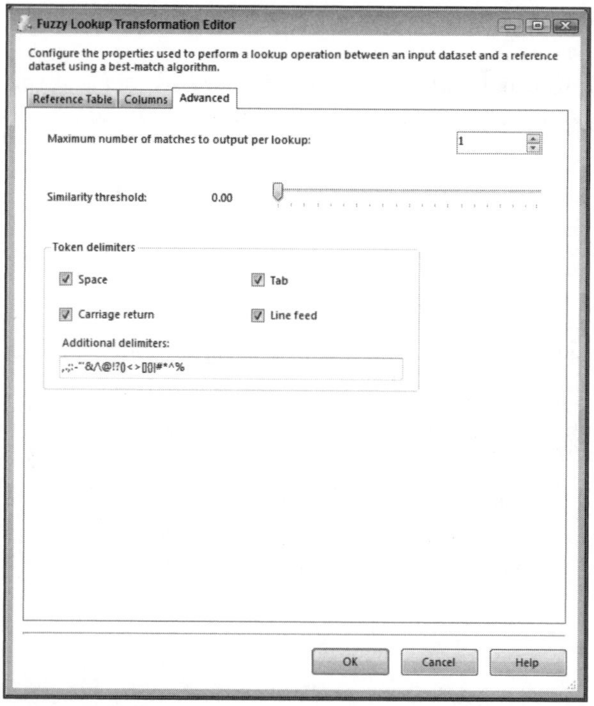

FIGURE 30-2

The transform creates several output columns that you may or may not decide are useful to store in a table. Either way, they are important to understand:

➤ **Input and Pass-Through Field Names and Values**—This column contains the name and value of the text input provided to the Fuzzy Lookup Transform or passed through during the lookup.

➤ **Reference Field Name and Value**—This column contains the name and value(s) of the matched results from the reference table.

➤ **Similarity**—This column contains a number between 0 and 1 representing similarity. Similarity is a threshold calculated by comparing one word with another; you set this when configuring the Fuzzy Lookup Transform. The closer this number is to 1, the closer the two text fields match. A similarity of 1 would indicate an exact match.

➤ **Confidence**—This column contains a number between 0 and 1 representing confidence of the match relative to the set of matched results. Confidence is different from similarity; it is not calculated by comparing just one string against another, but rather by comparing the chosen string match against all the other possible matches. Confidence gets better the more accurately your reference data represents your subject domain, and it can change based on the sample of the data coming into the ETL process.

You may not want to use each of these fields, but it is important to appreciate the value they could provide.

TRY IT

In this Try It, you use the Fuzzy Lookup Transform to attempt to correct some bad data that you receive in a flat file. After this lesson, you should have an idea of how useful the Fuzzy Lookup Transform can be in cleansing your data.

You can download the completed Lesson30.dtsx and other sample files for this lesson from `www.wrox.com`.

Lesson Requirements

Create a table in the AdventureWorks2012 database named Occupation, using the following code (which you can find as part of this lesson's download on the book's website at `www.wrox.com`):

```
CREATE TABLE [dbo].[Occupation](
    [OccupationID] [smallint] IDENTITY(1,1) NOT NULL,
    [OccupationLabel] [varchar](50) NOT NULL,
 CONSTRAINT [PK_Occupation_OccupationID] PRIMARY KEY CLUSTERED
(
    [OccupationID] ASC
) ON [PRIMARY]
) ON [PRIMARY]

GO
INSERT INTO [dbo].[Occupation] Select 'CUSTOMER SERVICE REPRESENTATIVE'
INSERT INTO [dbo].[Occupation] Select 'SHIFT LEADER'
INSERT INTO [dbo].[Occupation] Select 'ASSISTANT MANAGER'
INSERT INTO [dbo].[Occupation] Select 'STORE MANAGER'
INSERT INTO [dbo].[Occupation] Select 'DISTRICT MANAGER'
INSERT INTO [dbo].[Occupation] Select 'REGIONAL MANAGER'
```

Download the flat file named FuzzyExample.txt from `www.wrox.com` to use as your source. Save this file to the C:\Projects\SSISPersonalTrainer directory. Correct the bad data from this flat file and insert it to a new table called EmployeeRoster.

Hints

➤ Remember the best practice tip mentioned earlier in this lesson. First, attempt to use a regular Lookup and then use the Fuzzy Lookup to catch the bad data.

Step-by-Step

1. Create a new package and name it **Lesson30**, or download the completed Lesson30.dtsx package from `www.wrox.com`.

2. Drag a Data Flow Task onto your designer and name it **DFT - Fuzzy Lookup**.

3. Create a new Flat File Connection Manager (creating connection managers is discussed in Lesson 6), name it **New Employee**, and point it to C:\Projects\SSISPersonalTrainer\ FuzzyExample.txt. Check the Column names in the first data row option. The editor should look like Figure 30-3:

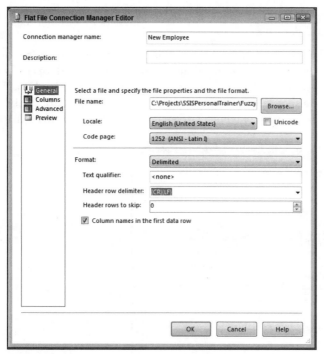

FIGURE 30-3

4. In the Data Flow, bring a new Flat File Source over and name it **New Employee Load**. Open the editor and make the connection manager the newly created New Employee.

5. On the Columns tab, change the name of the output columns to **LastName, FirstName**, and **OccupationLabel**.

6. Open Management Studio and run the following query to create a new table called Occupation (you can download the query from www.wrox.com):

```
CREATE TABLE [dbo].[Occupation](
    [OccupationID] [smallint] IDENTITY(1,1) NOT NULL,
    [OccupationLabel] [varchar](50) NOT NULL,
 CONSTRAINT [PK_Occupation_OccupationID] PRIMARY KEY CLUSTERED
(
    [OccupationID] ASC
) ON [PRIMARY]
) ON [PRIMARY]

GO
INSERT INTO [dbo].[Occupation] Select 'CUSTOMER SERVICE REPRESENTATIVE'
INSERT INTO [dbo].[Occupation] Select 'SHIFT LEADER'
INSERT INTO [dbo].[Occupation] Select 'ASSISTANT MANAGER'
INSERT INTO [dbo].[Occupation] Select 'STORE MANAGER'
INSERT INTO [dbo].[Occupation] Select 'DISTRICT MANAGER'
INSERT INTO [dbo].[Occupation] Select 'REGIONAL MANAGER'
```

7. Next, create another connection manager, this time an OLE DB Connection Manager, using the AdventureWorks2012 database.

8. Drag a Lookup Transform on the design surface and use the new [dbo].[Occupation] table to select the OccupationID based on the OccupationLabel that exists in both the source and the reference table. (Refer back to Lesson 24 if you need help with a regular Lookup.) Figure 30-4 shows what your mapping should look like. Lastly, before closing the editor, make sure to specify in the General tab that non-matching entries should redirect rows to no match output.

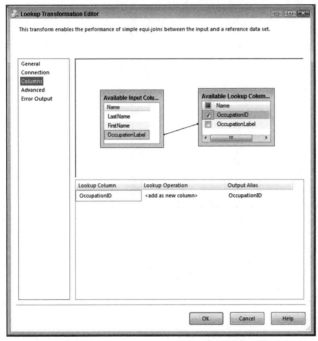

FIGURE 30-4

9. You already know from the lesson description that the source data is dirty, so now you're going to use a Fuzzy Lookup Transform to catch all the bad data the regular Lookup doesn't recognize. Drag a new Fuzzy Lookup Transform in the Data Flow and connect the blue no match output arrow from the Lookup Transform to it.

10. Open the Fuzzy Lookup and select [dbo].[Occupation] for the Reference table name property. Figure 30-5 shows the Fuzzy Lookup Transformation Editor using the Occupation table as the reference table.

11. The Columns tab should be joined by OccupationLabel as shown in Figure 30-6. It should also return the OccupationID and OccupationLabel from the reference table, which you can ensure by checking the boxes in the Available Lookup Columns box. The OccupationLabel from the reference table should replace the same column from the input stream to correct bad data. To do this, uncheck the OccupationLabel column from the Available Input Columns.

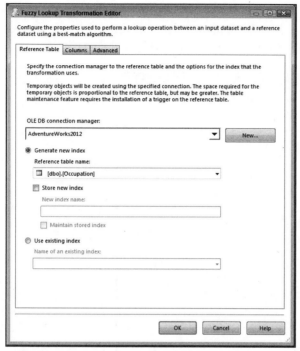

FIGURE 30-5

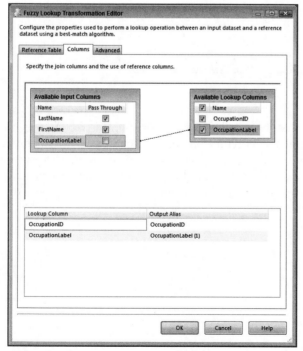

FIGURE 30-6

12. Next, in the Advanced tab, leave the Similarity threshold at the default setting and change the token delimiters to use only a period in the Additional delimiters box, as reflected in Figure 30-7. Also, modify the Similarity threshold to 0.50 and then click OK.

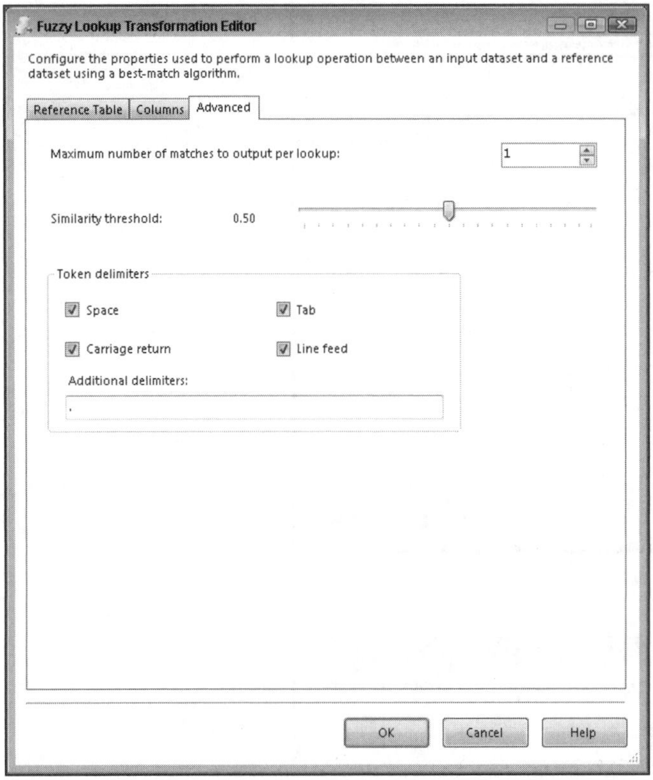

FIGURE 30-7

13. To bring together the data from both lookup transforms, drag a Union All over and connect the two lookups to it. First, connect the blue arrow from the Fuzzy Lookup Transform and then connect the blue arrow from the regular Lookup Transform. Then open the Union All Transformation Editor and delete the unneeded columns by right-clicking and selecting Delete on the columns that are not pictured in Figure 30-8. You may also need to rename the output of OccupationLabel to not include (1) in the name.

FIGURE 30-8

14. To finish off this package you need to load the results into a new table. Bring an OLE DB Destination onto the design surface, and from within the editor, select New to create a new table. Use the following code to create the EmployeeRoster table or download the code from www.wrox.com:

```
CREATE TABLE [EmployeeRoster] (
    [EmployeeID] [smallint] IDENTITY(1,1) NOT NULL,
    [LastName] varchar(50),
    [FirstName] varchar(50),
    [OccupationID] smallint,
    [OccupationLabel] varchar(50)
)
```

15. Once the mapping has been set in the destination, click OK and your package is complete. A successful run of this package should look like Figure 30-9. Compare the EmployeeRoster table to the original flat file you started with, and you will see the Fuzzy Lookup using the reference table corrected 10 rows of dirty data.

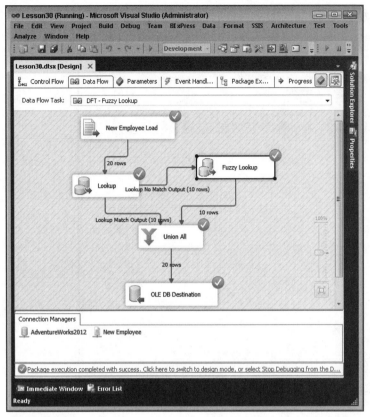

FIGURE 30-9

Please select Lesson 30 on the DVD, or online at www.wrox.com/go/ssis2012video, *to view the video that accompanies this lesson.*

31

Removing Duplicates with the Fuzzy Grouping Transform

In the previous lesson, you saw how to use the Fuzzy Lookup Transform to prevent bad data from being loaded in your dimension tables, but what if the bad data is already in your table or if you are just beginning to build your data warehouse?

In these circumstances, you can use the Fuzzy Grouping Transform to examine the contents of suspect fields and provide groupings of similar words. You can use the matching information provided by this transform to clean up the table and eliminate redundancy.

The Fuzzy Grouping Transform uses the same logic as the Fuzzy Lookup Transform, and therefore requires many of the same things. It must have a connection to an OLE DB Connection Manager to generate temporary tables that the transform uses in its algorithm. At development time, the Connection Manager tab is where you make this setting.

Also, just as was the case with the Fuzzy Lookup Transform, this transform expects an input stream with a string, either DT_WSTR or DT_STR data type. The Columns tab of the Fuzzy Grouping Transformation Editor (which you open by double-clicking the transform), shown in Figure 31-1, is where you select the string field that you want to be analyzed and grouped into logical matches. Notice in the top part of the Columns tab that you can also check Pass Through on each column, which means the data is not analyzed, but is accessible in the output stream. If you move down to the bottom part of the Columns tab, you see a table of options for each input column. You can choose the names of any of the output columns: Group Output Alias, Output Alias, and Similarity Output Alias. Often the only column you want from this group is the Group Output Alias. If you select more than one column to be analyzed, the minimum similarity evaluation is configurable at the column level.

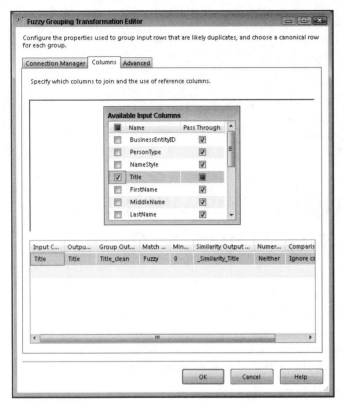

FIGURE 31-1

The Numerals option enables you to configure the numbers in the input stream when grouping text logically. This may be necessary when comparing an address field, because, more than likely, it will have leading numerals; for example, the address "834 West Elm Street" has the leading numerals "834."

Comparison flags provide the options to ignore or pay attention to case, kana type (Japanese characters), nonspacing characters, character width, symbols, and punctuation.

The Advanced tab is where you see some of the familiar configurations you saw in the Fuzzy Lookup Transform that control the logic algorithm used for finding matches. A slider controls the similarity threshold. It is recommended you start this at 0.5 to test and move the slider up or down until you get the results you are looking for. This setting is normally decided based on a business-person's review of the data, not the developer's review. The token delimiters can also be set if, for example, you don't want the comparison process to break up incoming strings with a period (.) or spaces. Figure 31-2 shows the default settings for the Advanced tab.

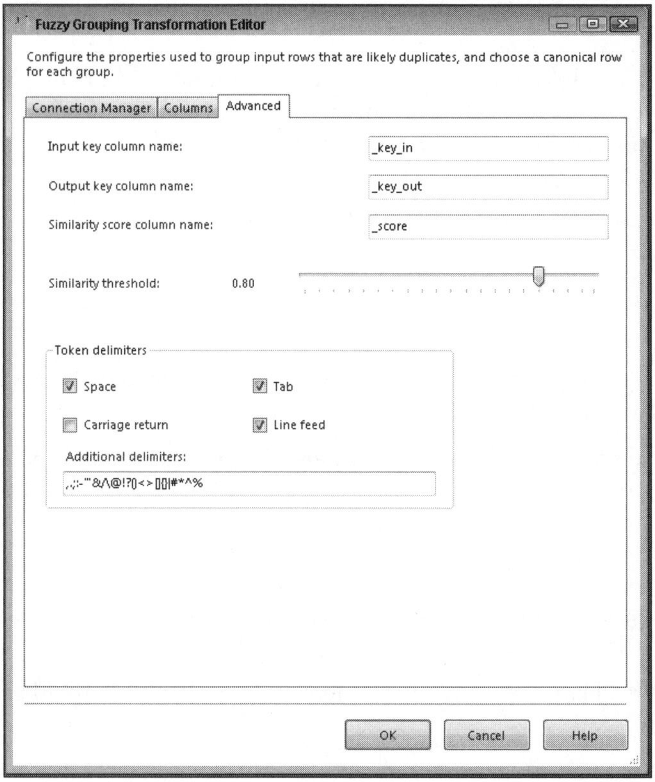

FIGURE 31-2

One feature that was not in the Fuzzy Lookup Transform is the ability to set the names of the three additional fields that are added automatically to the output of this transform. By default, these fields are named _key_in, _key_out, and _score. These new outputs that will be added to the data stream are important to understand:

➤ **_key_in**—This column uniquely identifies each row in the stream.

➤ **_key_out**—This column identifies a group of duplicate rows. Any rows that have the same _key_out value are rows that are in the same group.

➤ **_score**—This column indicates the similarity of the row with a value between 0 and 1. A similarity of 1 would be an exact match.

TRY IT

In this Try It, you create a new dimension table and populate it with occupations for your company. The import file contains several different versions of the same occupation, and you need to determine which will be the best fit. After this lesson, you will have an understanding of how to use the Fuzzy Grouping Transform to remove duplicates.

You can download the completed Lesson31.dtsx and other sample files for this lesson from www.wrox.com.

Lesson Requirements

Download the flat file named FuzzyExample.txt from www.wrox.com to use as your source. Save this file to the C:\Projects\SSISPersonalTrainer directory.

After determining which version of the occupation field is best or most similar, create a table named Occupation_FuzzyGrouping and load it.

Hints

➤ After using the Fuzzy Grouping Transform to determine the correctly spelled occupation, use a Conditional Split to bring back only the rows where _key_in == _key_out.

➤ The only column you need to load into the table is the clean version of the OccupationLabel.

Step-by-Step

1. Create a new package and name it **Lesson31** or download the completed Lesson31.dtsx package from www.wrox.com.

2. Drag a Data Flow Task onto your designer and name it **DFT - Fuzzy Grouping**.

3. Create a new Flat File Connection Manager (creating connection managers is discussed in Lesson 6), name it **Occupations,** and point it to C:\Projects\SSISPersonalTrainer\ FuzzyExample.txt. Also, check the Column names in the first data row option. The editor should look like Figure 31-3.

4. In the Data Flow, bring a new Flat File Source over and name it **Occupation Load**. Open the editor and make the connection manager the newly created Occupations.

5. On the Columns tab, select only the TITLE column to return, change the name of the output column to **OccupationLabel,** then click OK.

6. Next, create another connection manager, this time an OLE DB Connection Manager, using the AdventureWorks2012 database.

7. Bring a Fuzzy Grouping Transform in the Data Flow, connect it to your Flat File Source, and open the editor. Set the OLE DB Connection Manager to AdventureWorks2012.

8. On the Columns tab, there is only one column to bring back, so check the OccupationLabel. Figure 31-4 shows what the Columns tab should look like now.

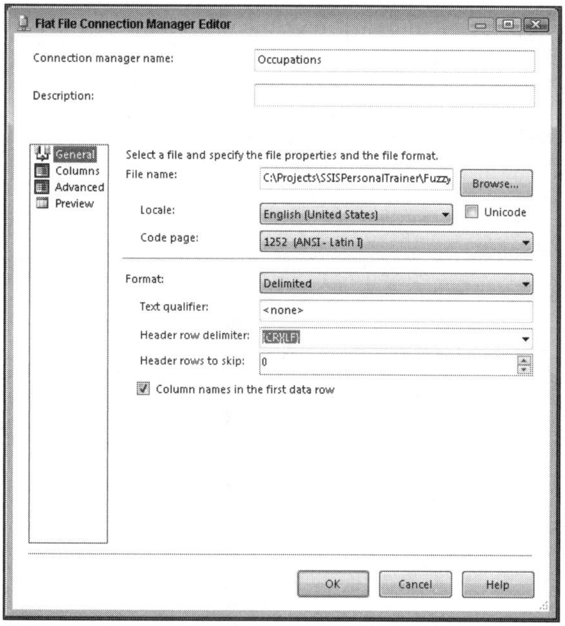

FIGURE 31-3

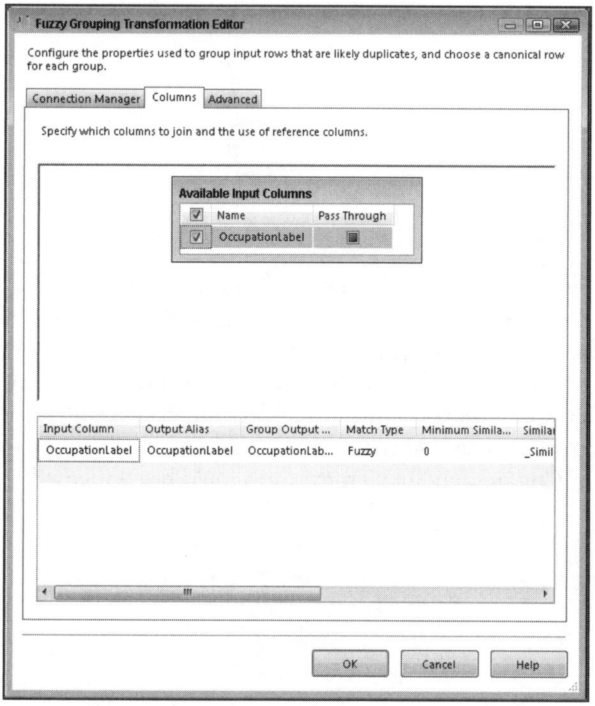

FIGURE 31-4

9. Next, in the Advanced tab, change the Similarity threshold to 0.50 and change the Token delimiters to reflect Figure 31-5. Then click OK.

FIGURE 31-5

10. If you ran this now and loaded a table, you would have 20 rows of the clean data, but you would also have several duplicate records. Remember, you are trying to create a dimension table, so to prevent duplicates in this package add a Conditional Split Transform with an Output Name of **Best Match** and a Condition of **_key_in == _key_out**. If these two values match, the grouped value is the best representative candidate for the natural key in a dimension table. All other rows are not needed, so you can name the Default Output Name **Delete**. Figure 31-6 shows how your Conditional Split Transform should be configured.

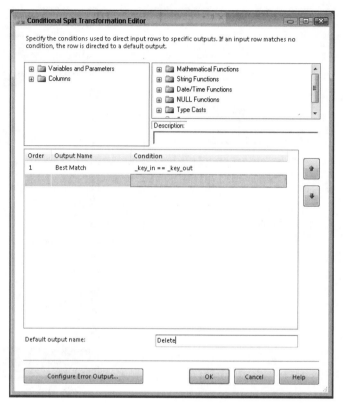

FIGURE 31-6

11. To finish off this package, you need to load the results into a new table. Bring an OLE DB Destination onto the design surface and from within the editor select New next to Name of the table or name of the view to create a new table. Use the following code to create the Occupation_FuzzyGrouping table or download the code from www.wrox.com:

```
CREATE TABLE [dbo].[Occupation_FuzzyGrouping](
    [OccupationID] [smallint] IDENTITY(1,1) NOT NULL,
    [OccupationLabel] [varchar](50) NOT NULL
    )
```

12. Remember from the beginning of this lesson that the Fuzzy Grouping Transform provides several output columns. These columns include a Group Output Alias column that you now use in the Mappings tab. Set OccupationLabel_clean to map to the OccupationLabel column in the destination. Once your Mappings tab looks like Figure 31-7, click OK.

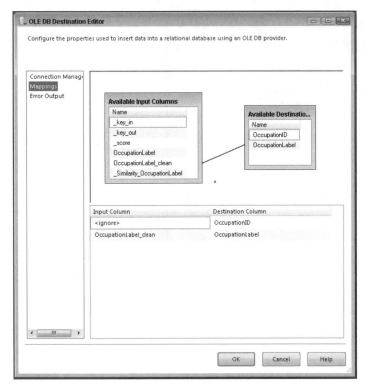

FIGURE 31-7

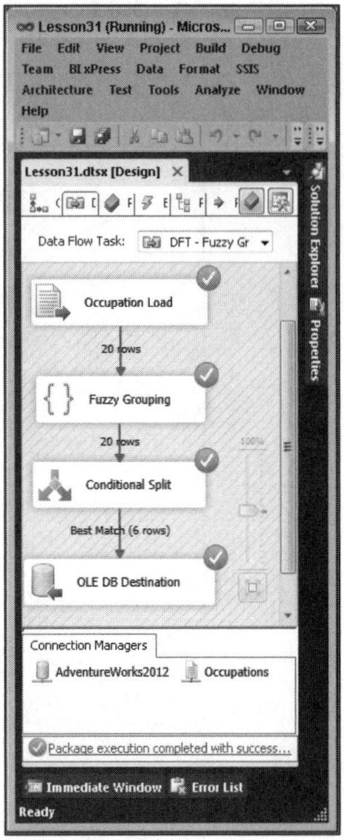

FIGURE 31-8

13. A successful run of this package should look like Figure 31-8.

14. Figure 31-9 shows the results in the Occupation_FuzzyGrouping table you just populated. If you completed Lesson 30, you might notice that you just created essentially the same table (aside from the order) that was used as a reference table in Lesson 30.

	OccupationID	OccupationLabel
1	1	CUSTOMER SERVICE REPRESENTATIVE
2	2	ASSISTANT MANAGER
3	3	REGIONAL MANAGER
4	4	STORE MANAGER
5	5	SHIFT LEADER
6	6	DISTRICT MANAGER

FIGURE 31-9

Please select Lesson 31 on the DVD, or online at www.wrox.com/go/ssis2012video, *to view the video that accompanies this lesson.*

SECTION 4
Making Packages Dynamic

32

Making a Package Dynamic with Variables

Your packages will be more flexible and more useful if they are *dynamic*. Dynamic packages in SQL Server Integration Services (SSIS) can reconfigure themselves at run time. Using variables is one of the ways you can make a package dynamic and reusable. You can use variables to set properties of components, parameters for T-SQL statements and stored procedures, in script components, in precedence constraints, and many other places. A *variable* is essentially a placeholder that has a name, data type, scope, and value. You can read and change the value of your variables within your package. Variables come in two forms: system variables and user-defined variables. *System variables* are predefined and include things like the package name and package start time. You cannot create system variables, but you can read them. *User-defined variables* are created solely by the developer.

To create a user-defined variable, simply right-click the design surface in SQL Server Data Tools (SSDT) and click Variables. This action opens the Variables window where you can create a new variable by clicking the icon in the top left. Once you create a new variable, you need to populate the fields Name, Data Type, and Value or Expression. The value can be a literal value or the result of an expression.

Scope is the context where the variable can be used. Each variable has a scope. You can set the scope to an individual component so it is available only to that object, or you can set it to the package level so it can be used anywhere in the package. For example, in Figure 32-1 the variable has a scope set to the package level. A new feature of SSIS enables you to change the scope of a variable. You can do this by selecting the Move Variable icon in the top left of the Variables dialog box and selecting a new scope.

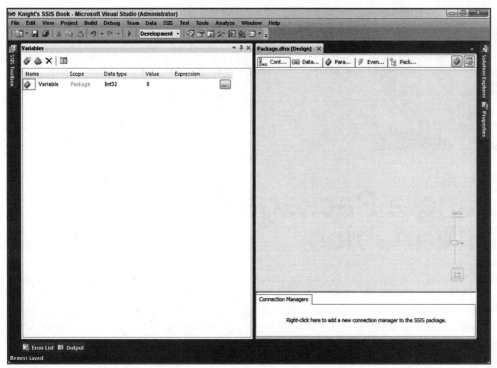

FIGURE 32-1

When you configure the data types for variables, you may notice that their names are different from Data Flow data types. In fact, you are going to find that only a subset of the data types available in the rest of the SSIS environment can be used for variables. You can use the following table to map the variable data types to standard data types found in the Data Flow:

VARIABLE DATA TYPE	SSIS DATA TYPE	DESCRIPTION
Boolean	DT_BOOL	Value either True or False
Byte	DT_UI1	1-byte unsigned integer
Char	DT_UI2	Single character
DateTime	DT_DBTIMESTAMP	Standard datetime structure
DBNull	N/A	Declarative NULL value
Decimal	DT_DECIMAL	12-byte unsigned integer with separate sign
Double	DT_R8	Double-precision, floating-point value

VARIABLE DATA TYPE	SSIS DATA TYPE	DESCRIPTION
Int16	DT_I2	2-byte signed integer
Int32	DT_I4	4-byte signed integer
Int64	DT_I8	8-byte signed integer
Object	N/A	Object reference; used to store data sets or large object structures
SByte	DT_I1	1-byte signed integer
Single	DT_R4	Single-precision, floating-point value
String	DT_WSTR	Unicode string value
UInt32	DT_UI4	4-byte unsigned integer
UInt64	DT_UI8	8-byte unsigned integer

The value of a variable can be a fixed value or the result of an expression. To create an expression for a variable, you can select a variable and press F4 to bring up the Properties window. From the Properties window, you can set EvaluateAsExpression to True and enter an expression in the Expression property. You can also type the expression directly into the Expression column of the Variables window. When you type the expression using the Variables window, SSIS automatically sets the value for the EvaluateAsExpression property. This property must be set to True for your expression to be used to set the value. To learn more about expressions and the SSIS expression language, read Lessons 34 and 35, which are dedicated to expressions.

Variable names are case-sensitive. When you use a variable in an expression, you must use the same case as the variable name. If you name a variable Test, referring to the variable as test will not work. When referring to a variable in a task or transform, as in the following tutorial, you place a question mark (?) as a placeholder for the variable name. For example, in an Execute SQL Task that is given the duty of deleting rows from the DimEmployee table in the AdventureWorksDW2012 database, the deleted rows should have an EmployeeNationalIDAlternateKey that is equal to a value in a variable named EmployeeID. To accomplish this, you would write the following query in the Execute SQL Task in the Control Flow window:

```
DELETE FROM DimEmployee
       WHERE EmployeeNationalIDAlternateKey = ?
```

Next, click the Parameters button, and on the Parameter Mappings tab assign the User::EmployeeID variable to the value for the question mark placeholder. Select User::EmployeeID in the Variable Name field, and enter "0" in the Parameter Name field. The Parameter Name field will be different for connection types other than OLE DB.

TRY IT

In this Try It, you create a flat file export of employees based on their level in the organization. The package you create should be easy to adjust based on what organization level you need. After this lesson, you will have an understanding of how to make a package dynamic using variables.

You can download the completed Lesson32.dtsx from www.wrox.com.

Lesson Requirements

Create a variable named OrgLevel to narrow down the number of employees returned based on the level in the organization. Create a flat file named OrganizationLevel.txt that contains all employees with an organization level of 2.

Hints

➤ Create a new variable that passes a value for the organization level to the OLE DB Source to return only employees with an organization level of 2.

➤ Create a flat file that has the following columns:

   ➤ NationalIDNumber

   ➤ LoginID

   ➤ OrganizationLevel

   ➤ JobTitle

   ➤ BirthDate

   ➤ MaritalStatus

   ➤ Gender

   ➤ HireDate

Step-by-Step

1. Create a new package and name it **Lesson32**, or download the completed Lesson32.dtsx package from www.wrox.com.

2. Right-click the Control Flow design surface and click Variables to open the Variables window.

3. To create a new variable, click the Add Variable icon in the top left of the Variables window. Name the variable **OrgLevel** and set the value to **2**. Figure 32-2 shows the variable with a Data Type of Int32 and a value of 2.

FIGURE 32-2

4. Drag a Data Flow Task onto your Control Flow tab and name it **DFT - Employee Export**.

5. Switch to the new Data Flow Task by clicking the Data Flow tab. Add an OLE DB Connection Manager that uses the AdventureWorks2012 database and then drag an OLE DB Source into your Data Flow.

6. Open the OLE DB Source Editor by double-clicking the OLE DB Source. In the OLE DB Source Editor OLE DB Connection Manager field, choose the connection manager you created in the previous step. Then change the data access mode to SQL Command and enter the following SQL statement:

```
SELECT NationalIDNumber
       ,LoginID
       ,OrganizationLevel
       ,JobTitle
       ,BirthDate
       ,MaritalStatus
       ,Gender
       ,HireDate
   FROM HumanResources.Employee
   WHERE OrganizationLevel=?
```

7. Next, click Parameters and set Parameter0 to use the variable created earlier: User::OrgLevel. Figure 32-3 shows the changes you have just made. Click OK twice to exit the OLE DB Source Editor.

8. Drag a new Flat File Destination from the SSIS Toolbox to the Data Flow window. Connect the OLE DB Source to the Flat File Destination Task by dragging the blue line from the source to the destination. Open the Flat File Destination Editor by double-clicking the Flat File Destination.

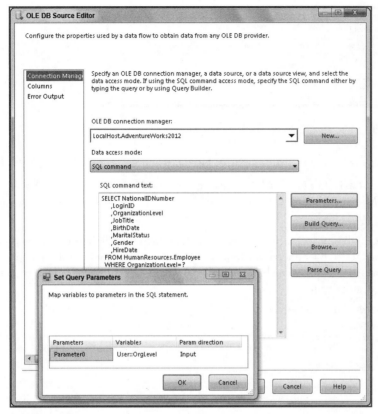

FIGURE 32-3

9. Create a new Flat File Connection Manager by choosing the New button in the Flat File Destination Editor. The Flat File Format dialog box appears. Delimited is the proper format and is the default. Click OK. Name the connection manager **Organization Level**, and set the filename to C:\Projects\SSISPersonalTrainer\OrganizationLevel.txt. You may either type the filename or click the Browse button. If the path C:\Projects\SSISPersonalTrainer\ does not already exist, you can create the folder in the File Open dialog, which appears after you click on the Browse button. The path must exist prior to running the package or you will get a failure on this step. Also, check the Column names in the first data row option.

Click OK to close the Flat File Connection Manager Editor. Select Mappings in the Flat File Destination Editor. Then Click OK to close the editor.

10. The package is now complete. It uses a variable in the WHERE clause of the SQL statement to determine which rows to load into the flat file. To export rows from a different level of the organization, you simply change the value of the OrgLevel variable. Your package is now reusable. When the package is executed, your results will look like Figure 32-4. Check your output file to ensure it contains rows with OrganizationLevel = 2.

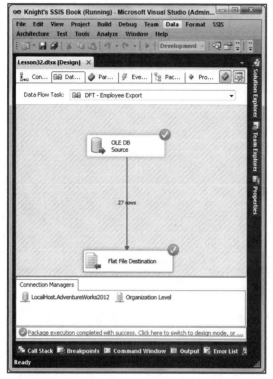

FIGURE 32-4

Please select Lesson 32 on the DVD, or online at www.wrox.com/go/ssis2012video, *to view the video that accompanies this lesson.*

33

Making a Package Dynamic with Parameters

SQL 2012 introduced a new parameter paradigm. Parameters enable you to pass in new values for a specific package execution. When your packages are deployed to the new SSIS catalog, an interface is provided to enable you to change the values of parameters prior to running the package. Parameters are very similar to variables, except parameters are easier to change and configure using the new SQL Server Management Studio interface for SSIS.

A *parameter*, like a variable, is a placeholder that has a name, data type, scope, and value. The value provided in SQL Server Data Tools is called the default or design value. You can replace this value prior to execution. Parameters also have a sensitive property and a required property. When you mark a parameter as sensitive, its value is encrypted in the database and displayed as NULL or *****. When you mark a parameter as required, you must provide the parameter value prior to execution, rather than using the design parameter.

Parameters also have a scope. Parameters can have a package scope or a project scope. A parameter with a project scope can be used in all packages within the project. Package scoped parameters can only be used within the package in which they are defined.

To create a package scoped parameter, choose the Parameters tab in the SSIS designer and create a new parameter by clicking the icon in the top left. Then populate the fields Name, Data Type, Value, Sensitive, Required, and Description. Figure 33-1 shows the completed parameter.

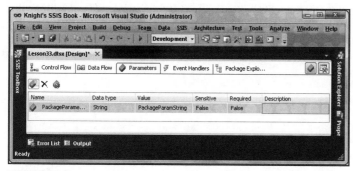

FIGURE 33-1

To create a project scoped parameter, open the Solution Explorer window and double-click the Project.params item as in Figure 33-2.

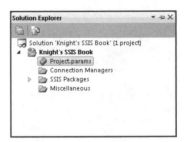

The Project.params window opens, enabling you to create and manage project scoped parameters. See Figure 33-3.

FIGURE 33-2

Using the same example as in the previous lesson, you have an Execute SQL Task that is given the duty of deleting rows from the DimEmployee table in the AdventureWorksDW2012 database. The deleted rows should have an EmployeeNationalIDAlternateKey that is equal to a value in a parameter named EmployeeID. Create a package scoped variable name EmployeeID with an integer data type and a value of 2. Write the following query in an Execute SQL Task:

```
DELETE FROM DimEmployee
    WHERE EmployeeNationalIDAlternateKey = ?
```

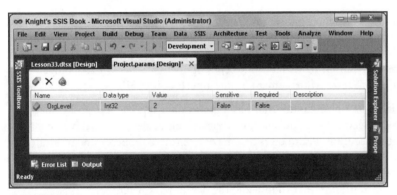

FIGURE 33-3

Next, click the Parameters button. On the Parameter Mappings tab, assign the $Package::EmployeeID variable to the value for the question mark placeholder. Select $Package::EmployeeID in the Variable Name field, and enter "0" in the Parameter Name field. The Parameter Name field value will be different for connection types other than OLE DB.

You can use parameters wherever you can use a variable. Why use a parameter instead of a variable? Parameters can be used to store and provide encrypted information for packages, like passwords. Additionally, it is much easier to provide runtime values for parameters. The greatest value of parameters is when you are running a package or using environments for configurations. You learn more about running packages from Management Studio in Lesson 57, and using parameters with environments in Lesson 54.

TRY IT

In this Try It, you recreate the extract from Lesson 32, except you use a parameter instead of a variable. You then export data from several levels in the organization without opening and changing the package. You do this by changing a project parameter.

The flat file export of employees is based on their level in the organization. After this lesson, you will have an understanding of how to make a package or all packages in a project dynamic using parameters.

This technique will become the foundation you will use for configuration of environments to deploy and move your packages safely from the development environment into the production environment.

You can download the completed Lesson33.dtsx from www.wrox.com.

Lesson Requirements

Create a project parameter named the **OrgLevel**. The export will contain the employees whose level within the organization is the same value as stored in OrgLevel parameter. Create a flat file named **OrganizationLevel.txt** that contains all employees with an organization level of 2.

Hints

➤ Create a new project parameter that passes a value for the organization level to the OLE DB Source to return only employees with an organization level of 2.

➤ Create a flat file that has the following rows:

- ➤ NationalIDNumber
- ➤ LoginID
- ➤ OrganizationLevel
- ➤ JobTitle
- ➤ BirthDate
- ➤ MaritalStatus
- ➤ Gender
- ➤ HireDate

Step-by-Step

1. Create a new package and name it **Lesson33**, or download the completed Lesson33.dtsx package from www.wrox.com.

2. Open the Project.params window at the top of the Solution Explorer window.

3. To create a new parameter, click the Add Variable icon in the top left of the Project.Params window. Name the parameter **OrgLevel** and set the value to **2**. Figure 33-4 shows the parameter with a Data Type of Int32 and a value of 2.

4. Drag a Data Flow Task onto your Control Flow canvas and name it **DFT - Employee Export**.

5. Switch to the new Data Flow Task by clicking the Data Flow tab. Add an OLE DB Connection Manager that uses the AdventureWorks2012 database, and then drag an OLE DB Source into your Data Flow.

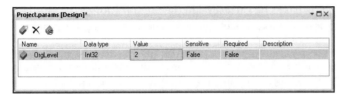

FIGURE 33-4

6. Open the OLE DB Source Editor by double-clicking the OLE DB Source. In the OLE DB Source Editor OLE DB Connection Manager field, choose the connection manager you created in the previous step. Then change the data access mode to SQL Command and enter the following SQL statement:

```
SELECT NationalIDNumber
      ,LoginID
      ,OrganizationLevel
      ,JobTitle
      ,BirthDate
      ,MaritalStatus
      ,Gender
      ,HireDate
   FROM HumanResources.Employee
   WHERE OrganizationLevel=?
```

7. Next, click Parameters item and set Parameter0 to use the project parameter you created earlier: $Project::OrgLevel. Figure 33-5 shows the changes you have just made. Click OK twice to exit the OLE DB Source Editor.

8. Drag a new Flat File Destination from the SSIS Toolbox to the Data Flow window. Connect the OLE DB Source to the Flat File Destination task by dragging the blue line from the source to the destination. Open the Flat File Destination Editor by double-clicking the Flat File Destination

9. Create a new Flat File Connection Manager by choosing the New button in the Flat File Destination Editor. The Flat File Format dialog appears. Delimited is preselected and correct. Click OK. The Flat File Connection Manager dialog will appear. Name the connection manager **Organization Level**, and set the filename to C:\Projects\SSISPersonalTrainer\ OrganizationLevel.txt. Also, check the Column names in the first data row option. The path must already exist when you run the package. However, you can create the path within Browse dialog by right-clicking in the parent folder and selecting New.

Click OK to close the Flat File Connection Manager Editor. Select Mappings in the Flat File Destination Editor. Then Click OK to close the editor.

10. The package is now complete. It uses a variable in the WHERE clause of the SQL statement to determine which rows to load into the flat file. Save and close the package. Your package is now reusable.

11. Go to the Solution Explorer window, right-click Lesson33.dtsx, and execute the package. Switch back to design mode and close Lesson33.dtsx. Now open the file C:\Projects\ SSISPersonalTrainer.OrganizationLevel.txt. You should see OrganizationLevel value of 2 in the third column. Your results will look like Figure 33-6. Close the text file.

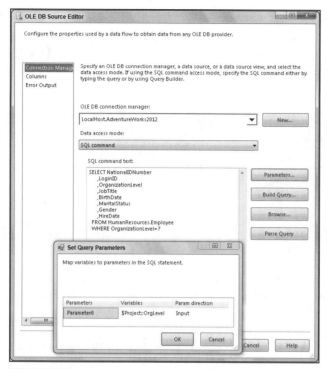

FIGURE 33-5

FIGURE 33-6

12. Go to the Project.Params window and change the value of the OrgLevel parameter to 1.

13. Go back to the Solution Explorer window, right-click Lesson33.dtsx, and execute the package. Switch back to design mode and close Lesson33.dtsx. Now open the file C:\Projects\ SSISPersonalTrainer.OrganizationLevel.txt. You should see an OrganizationLevel of 1 in the third column. Your results will look like Figure 33-7.

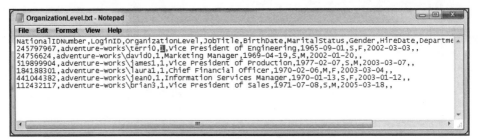

FIGURE 33-7

Please select Lesson 33 on the DVD, or online at www.wrox.com/go/ssis2012video, *to view the video that accompanies this lesson.*

34

Making a Connection Dynamic with Expressions

To expand what you can accomplish with your packages, it is essential that you learn the SQL Server Integration Services (SSIS) expression language. A common use for expressions in SSIS is creating dynamic connections. For example, this enables you to change an output file name or change the database connection while moving a package from test into production without having to reopen and edit the package. You may change any available property using an expression.

> **NOTE** *In Lesson 21 you learned about the Derived Column Transform and many of the common functions used in expressions. This lesson focuses on using expressions in connection managers, so if you want a recap on the expression language itself, refer to Lesson 21.*

To configure a connection to take advantage of expressions, select the connection manager and press F4 to open the Properties window, as shown in Figure 34-1. Find the Expression property and click the ellipsis (...). This action opens the Property Expressions Editor where you can select the connection manager property you want to define with an expression. Once you have selected the property from the drop-down box, click a second ellipsis in the Expression property to open the Expression Builder. Here you can begin building your expression for the given property you have selected.

Remember that each property has a specific data type, so you often have to cast the expression's value to the appropriate data type. Typically when dealing with connection properties, you will find they require a string value. You can convert a number to a string using the cast function DT_WSTR(<<length>>).

A common example of using expressions in connection managers is for importing a collection of flat files using the same package. You could use a Foreach Loop Container, (which is discussed in Lesson 43) to loop through a collection of flat files. You can create an expression on the connection manager to change the connection string during each iteration of the loop to the appropriate filename. To configure the Flat File Connection Manager to use expressions, you would follow the steps mentioned earlier in this lesson.

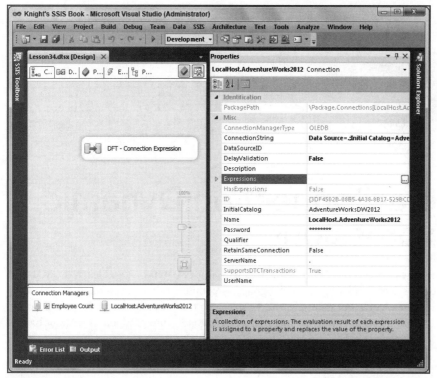

FIGURE 34-1

TRY IT

In this Try It, you create a flat file export that contains a count of employees in each department. The flat file you create should have the current date as part of the file's name. After completing this lesson, you will understand how to use expressions in a connection manager.

You can download the completed Lesson34.dtsx from www.wrox.com.

Lesson Requirements

Create a package that uses the AdventureWorksDW2012 database and the DimEmployee table to load all the departments and a count of how many employees are in each to a flat file. Name the flat file **EmployeeCount_(*Current Date*).txt,** with the current date being populated by an expression after the underscore.

The date should be in the following *mmddyyyy* format: 06022012

> **NOTE** *You must have leading zeros when month or day is only one digit.*

Hints

➤ With an OLE DB Source, show a count of all the employees grouped by their department using the DimEmployee table.

➤ Place the results in a flat file that has an expression on the Flat File Connection Manager's ConnectionString property. The filename should have the current date as part of the name.

Step-by-Step

1. Create a new package and name it **Lesson34** or download the completed Lesson34.dtsx package from www.wrox.com.

2. Drag a Data Flow Task onto your designer and name it **DFT - Connection Expression**.

3. Add an OLE DB Connection Manager that uses the AdventureWorksDW2012 database. Go to the Data Flow window and add an OLE DB Source in your Data Flow.

4. Open the OLE DB Source Editor by double-clicking the OLE DB Source. In the OLE DB Connection Manager field, select the connection manager you created in the previous step. Change the data access mode to SQL Command and enter the following SQL statement:

```
SELECT
    DepartmentName
    ,count(EmployeeNationalIDAlternateKey) EmployeeCount
FROM DimEmployee
GROUP BY DepartmentName
```

Click OK to exit the OLE DB Source Editor.

5. Drag a new Flat File Destination into your Data Flow. Then select your OLE DB Data Source to expose the blue and red arrows. Drag the green arrow from the OLE DB Source to the Flat File Destination Task.

6. Double-click the Flat File Destination Task to open it. Click the New button to create a new connection manager. Ensure Delimited is selected in the Flat File Format dialog box and click OK. The Flat File Connection Manager dialog box opens. Name the new connection manager **Employee Count**. The filename should be C:\Projects\SSISPersonalTrainer\EmployeeCount_.txt. Set the Format to Delimited and check the Column names in the first data row option. Choose Columns on the left side of the dialog box. The Column Delimiter drop-down should have Comma {,} chosen by default. Then click OK. Ensure the mapping is correct in the destination editor and then click OK again.

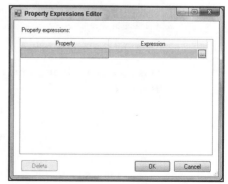

7. Click once on the connection manager named Employee Count and press F4 to bring up the Properties window. Click the Expression property once to display the ellipsis. Click the ellipsis to open the Property Expressions Editor, shown in Figure 34-2.

FIGURE 34-2

8. Click the Property drop-down box and select ConnectionString. Then click the ellipsis next to the Expression property. This opens the Expression Builder.

9. Enter the following expression, shown in Figure 34-3, which gives the desired results for a filename:

```
"C:\\Projects\\SSISPersonalTrainer\\EmployeeCount_"+
RIGHT( "0"+(DT_WSTR, 2) Month(GETDATE() ), 2 ) +
RIGHT( "0"+(DT_WSTR, 2) Day(GETDATE() ), 2 ) +
(DT_WSTR, 4) Year(GETDATE() )+".txt"
```

FIGURE 34-3

> **NOTE** *If you are copying the expression from an electronic copy of this document, you may have to redo the double quotes. Simply replace the special double quotes with plain double quotes. This is because Word and some other electronic versions of documents use special codes that the dialog editor does not understand.*

Click the Evaluate Expression button to see the resulting string.

This expression is commonly used, so take a look at some important functions that are used here:

➤ Month(GETDATE())—Returns the current month number.

➤ (DT_WSTR, 2)—Converts the month number to a string.

➤ RIGHT("0"+(DT_WSTR, 2) Month(GETDATE()), 2)—Adds a 0 to every month, but displays only the last two digits. This is so months that already have two digits like December display only 12 instead of 012, and months with one digit like January display as 01.

Also notice that each file directory contains two backslashes, but only one is displayed when the expression is evaluated. A backslash is a special character in the SSIS expression language. To include a single backslash in your string (\), you must use a double backslash (\\). To learn more about special SSIS characters, you can search for "Literals (SSIS)" on MSDN, or go to http://msdn.microsoft.com/en-us/library/ms141001.aspx.

Click OK to exit the Expression Builder and then OK again to exit the Property Expressions Editor.

10. The package is now complete and your destination filename is dynamic. Each day the package runs, it creates a new file with a different name that contains the current date. When the package is executed, your results will look like Figure 34-4.

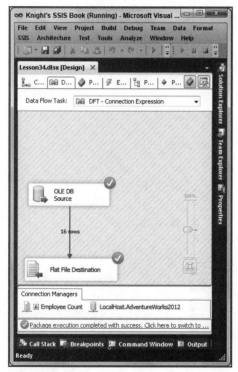

FIGURE 34-4

11. To confirm a good result, go to the C:\Projects\SSISPersonalTrainer folder. You should see the file created with the current date.

> *Please select Lesson 34 on the DVD, or online at* www.wrox.com/go/ssis2012video, *to view the video that accompanies this lesson.*

35

Making a Task Dynamic with Expressions

When you consider the many places expressions can be applied, you begin to see how highly adaptable SQL Server Integration Services (SSIS) truly is. The previous lesson discussed how you can use expressions to make connections dynamic. This lesson turns to the use of expressions in tasks. Using expressions in tasks enables an SSIS developer to alter individual properties within a task at run time. A common example is using the Send Mail Task with an expression to populate the subject line based on the results of your package.

> **NOTE** *In Lesson 21, you learned about the Derived Column Transform and many of the common functions used in expressions. This lesson focuses on using expressions in tasks, so if you want a recap on the expression language itself, refer to Lesson 21.*

You set up a task to use expressions exactly the same way you configure connections to use expressions. To configure a task to take advantage of expressions, select the desired task and press F4 to open the Properties window. Find the Expression property and click the ellipsis (...) next to it, shown in Figure 35-1. This action opens the Property Expressions Editor where you can select to which property inside the task you would like to add an expression. Once you have selected the property from the drop-down box, click the ellipsis in the Expression property to open the Expression Builder. Here you can begin building your expression for the given property you have selected.

Remember that the data type of the value for a property must match the data type of the property. You may have to cast the expression's value to the appropriate data type. Before even writing an expression, take the time to determine the data type of the property you have chosen. For example, if you have decided to make an Execute SQL Task using an expression on the SQLStatement property, then you know a string value must be returned from the expression.

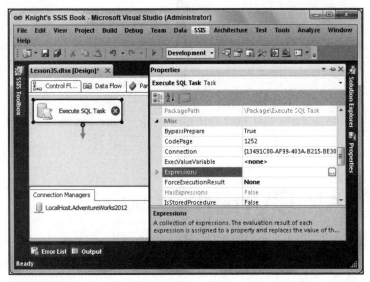

FIGURE 35-1

To gain a greater understanding of how useful expressions in tasks can be, go back to the first example from the beginning of this lesson—the Send Mail Task. You can create the value for the subject line dynamically using an expression. How do you accomplish this?

The Send Mail Task was discussed in more detail in Lesson 15. For this example, assume you have everything set up as in Lesson 15 except for the desired subject. You want the e-mail you send to contain a subject line that contains the name of the package and the package start time. Follow the steps stated earlier to open the Property Expressions Editor and select Subject from the Property drop-down box. Next, click the ellipsis in the Expression column and write the following expression in the Expression Builder that will populate the subject line:

```
"SSIS Package: "+@[System::PackageName] +" ran at " +
(DT_WSTR, 30)  @[System::StartTime]
```

Note that the quotes used in SQL should be single quotes, not the double quotes you see above. This expression is broken down like this:

➤ `"SSIS Package: "`—Simply prints the text between the quotation marks including blank spaces

➤ `@[System::PackageName]`—System variable that displays the package name, in this case Lesson 35

➤ `" ran at "`—Simply prints the text between the quotation marks including blank spaces

➤ `(DT_WSTR, 30)`—Converts the contents of the `@[System::StartTime]` to a string

➤ `@[System::StartTime]`—System variable that display the start time of the package

Click OK twice to return to the Control Flow. When you run this package now, the resulting e-mail subject line (depending on the date on which you run your package) will look something like this:

SSIS Package: Lesson 35 ran at 4/5/2012 4:59:27 PM

TRY IT

In this Try It, you create a package that deletes records from the Employee table with a NationalIDNumber = 14. No employees have this number, so no rows will actually be deleted. Both the delete statement and the NationalIDNumber will come from variables used in an expression. After completing this Try It, you will understand how to use expressions in a task.

You can download the completed Lesson35.dtsx from www.wrox.com.

Lesson Requirements

Create a package that uses the AdventureWorks2012 database for a connection manager. Then create two variables that have a scope at the package level.

➤   The first variable should have a string data type and be named **DeleteStatement** with the following as a value:

```
Delete FROM HumanResources.Employee
Where NationalIDNumber =
```

➤   The second variable should have an Int32 data type and be named **ID** with a value of 14.

Combine the two variables in an expression that evaluates the SQLStatementSource property in an Execute SQL Task.

Hints

➤   The only task you need for this lesson is an Execute SQL Task.

➤   You need two variables to create an expression that will complete the SQL statement.

Step-by-Step

1.   Create a new package and name it **Lesson35** or download the completed Lesson35.dtsx package from www.wrox.com.

2.   Add an OLE DB Connection Manager that uses the AdventureWorks2012 database. Then drag an Execute SQL Task into the Control Flow window.

3.   Next, create a package level variable named **DeleteStatement** with a string data type and the following for a value:

```
Delete FROM HumanResources.Employee
Where NationalIDNumber =
```

4.   Create a second package level variable named **ID** with an Int32 data type and a value of 14. Figure 35-2 shows the variables you just created.

FIGURE 35-2

> **NOTE** *Creating variables is covered in more detail in Lesson 32.*

5.   Click once on the Execute SQL Task and press F4 to bring up the Properties window. Click the ellipsis next to the Expressions property to open the Property Expressions Editor.

6.   Click the Property drop-down box and select SQLStatementSource. Then click the ellipsis next to the Expression property, shown in Figure 35-3.

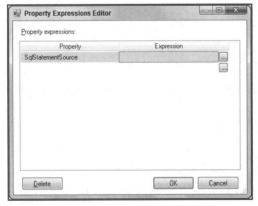

FIGURE 35-3

7.   Enter the following expression and then click the Evaluate Expression button. Your results in the Expression Builder should look like those shown in Figure 35-4.

```
@[User::DeleteStatement]+ (DT_WSTR, 10) @[User::ID]
```

With this expression you produce the following:

➤   `@[User::DeleteStatement]`—Places the value from the DeleteStatement variable you created in step 3 in the expression.

➤   `(DT_WSTR, 10)`—Converts the contents of the `@[User::ID]` variable to a string. This is necessary because this variable is an integer and the expression you are working on must be a string

➤   `@[User::ID]`—Places the integer variable you created in step 4 in the expression.

Click OK in the Expression Builder and then OK again in the Property Expressions Editor.

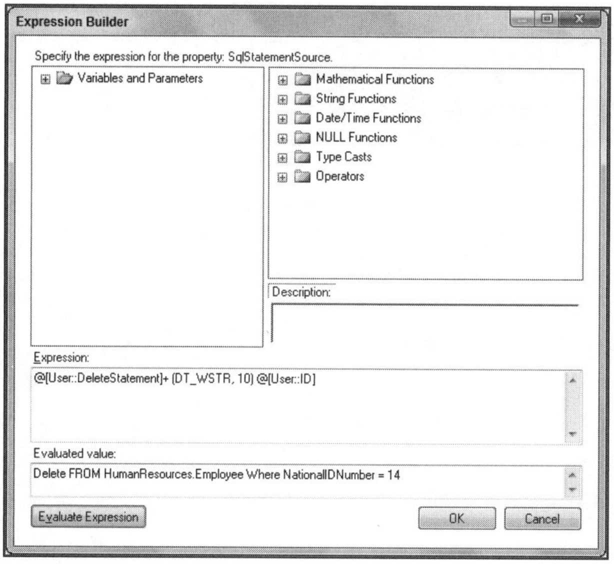

Expression Builder
Specify the expression for the property: SqlStatementSource.
Variables and Parameters
Mathematical Functions
String Functions
Date/Time Functions
NULL Functions
Type Casts
Operators
Description:
Expression:
@[User::DeleteStatement]+ (DT_WSTR, 10) @[User::ID]
Evaluated value:
Delete FROM HumanResources.Employee Where NationalIDNumber = 14
Evaluate Expression
OK
Cancel

FIGURE 35-4

8. Double-click the Execute SQL Task to open it and set the Connection to your AdventureWorks2012 Connection Manager. Then click OK.

9. The package is now complete, using an expression to make the task dynamic. When you execute the package, your results should look like Figure 35-5. Notice the small "fx" note in the top-left corner of the task. This indicates that the task has an expression associated with it.

Knight's SSIS Book (Running) - Mi...
File Edit View Project Build Debug Team
Data Format SSIS Architecture Test Tools
Analyze Window Help
Lesson35.dtsx [Design]
Execute SQL Task
Connection Managers
LocalHost.AdventureWorks2012
Package execution completed with success. Click ...
Call Stack
Breakpoints
Command Windo
Ready
Solution Explorer
Team Explorer
Properties

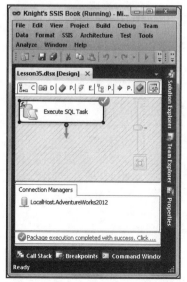

FIGURE 35-5

If you open the task now, you find that the SQLStatementSource property now reflects the value of the expression you created.

> *Please select Lesson 35 on the DVD, or online at* www.wrox.com/go/ssis2012video, *to view the video that accompanies this lesson.*

SECTION 5
Common ETL Scenarios

36

Loading Data Incrementally

Importing an entire table each time you run a package is the simplest way to work, and creating a package to do this is easy. Replacing the whole table is sometimes called a *wipe and load*. However, if the table is very large, your package may run for a long time. Instead of replacing the entire table, you can find the changes in the table and make the same changes in the destination table. This is called an *incremental load*. Generally, an incremental load runs much more quickly than a complete load. This is especially true if your source table is very large and few rows are changed each day. Incremental load packages generally handle inserts and updates from the source table. Rows that have been added to the source table will be inserted into the destination table. Rows that have been changed in the source table will be updated in the destination table. What will you do in the destination when rows are deleted from the source? You may choose to delete them in the destination, set a deleted flag to True but not delete the row, or you may choose to ignore source deletes. In a data warehouse dimension load, it is common to ignore deletes.

How will your package know which rows have been inserted, updated, or deleted in the source? Sometimes the source is audited and you will have a history table that provides the needed information. However, this is rare. Sometimes, source tables will have created and updated date columns, which indicate when rows were inserted or updated.

Absent these datetime columns, you must either keep shadow copies of the source table data, or use a Change Data Capture (CDC) technique.

> **NOTE** *Lesson 37 covers the CDC components in SSIS.*

If you want to handle deletes, it is likely that you will have to look for rows in the destination table that do not exist in the source. If a row exists in the destination, but not in the source, it must have been deleted from the source, so you would then delete it from the destination. You can do this by scanning the actual destination table, or by keeping a copy of the key values that exist in the destination table in a staging area. Using a key table in staging reduces the impact of lookups on the destination and allows the package to run more quickly.

When your package runs, it should find those rows in the source that have been inserted, updated, or deleted within a time range. It is very common for these packages to run nightly, gathering all of the changes from the prior day. As an example, the package may run every night at 2:00 a.m., looking for changes from midnight to midnight the prior day. You might store the last completed time range in a control table, and use that as the starting point for your next time range. You are going to look in the destination table for the most recent change and find all rows in the source with a modified date after that time and before midnight of the current day.

How you handle the time range is very important and is worth some thought and planning. Your package should always use a target range of time, bounded at both the beginning and the end. The package execution should begin after the target range end time.

The following example uses two patterns: the insert/update pattern and the delete pattern. A pattern is a generic example that you may use to solve other similar problems. You will work on a table called Lesson36ProductCategorySource. This lesson's Try It provides the detailed instructions. For now, try to understand each pattern. The insert/update pattern is shown in Figure 36-1. This pattern handles rows that have been inserted or updated in the source during the time range.

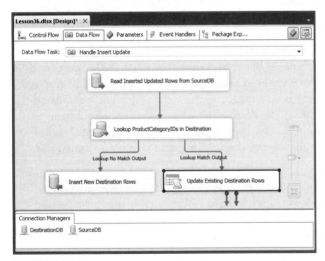

FIGURE 36-1

Select a date range and store the values in variables called StartDate and EndDate. Then read all of the rows from the source table where the ModifiedDate is within the target range. The read query looks like:

```
SELECT ProductCategoryID, Name, ModifiedDate
FROM [Production].[Lesson36ProductCategorySource]
WHERE ModifiedDate > ? and  ModifiedDate <=?
```

The two question marks will be mapped to your StartDate and EndDate variables.

The Lookup Transform uses each row that comes from the source and attempts to look up a row with the same ProductCategoryID in the destination. If the row exists in the destination, it must be updated. If the row does not exist in the destination, it must be inserted.

The output from the Lookup Transform results in two paths: one path for rows to be inserted and another path for rows to be updated.

Now take a look at the delete pattern in Figure 36-2. The delete pattern handles the rows that have been deleted from the source table. Instead of deleting the corresponding destination rows, set the Deleted Flag column value to True (T).

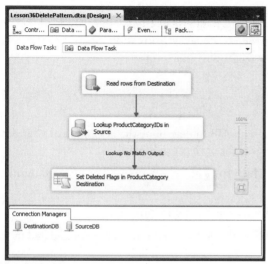

FIGURE 36-2

The Data Flow reads the DestinationDB, selecting only the key of the Lesson36ProductCategoryDestination table. For each row, look up the corresponding row in the source table. If the row does not exist in the source table, it must have been deleted. Therefore, the Lookup No Match Output will contain the rows that have been deleted from the source. These are the rows you need to update in the destination. The OLE DB Command at the bottom of the flow does this work for you.

> **NOTE** *You may find that the OLE DB Command task is slower than other destination tasks. This is because the OLE DB Command task issues a SQL statement for each row, rather than a more efficient batch operation.*

TRY IT

In this Try It, you learn how to do an incremental load. A script will create the source and destination tables using Production.ProductCategory data. The script will create both source and destination tables, then synchronize them with the same data. In the example, the initial load has been completed and you are writing the package that will handle future updates. A date range will be chosen. For rows that were inserted or updated during that range, the package will insert or update matching rows in the destination. It will also search for rows that exist in the destination, but not in the source, and mark those rows as deleted in the destination. After this lesson, you will know how to load data incrementally.

You can download the completed Lesson36.dtsx and all scripts for this lesson from `www.wrox.com`.

Lesson Requirements

You must have permissions within AdventureWorks2012 database to create tables. To load the Lesson36ProductCategorySource and Lesson36ProductCategoryDestination tables, run the Lesson36Create.sql script in SQL Server Management Studio (SSMS). Run this script before you begin the "Step-by-Step."

Hints

➤ Use the OLE DB Destination named DestinationDB to determine the beginning of your date range. The end time of the range will be midnight of the current day.

➤ Use the Lookup Transform to determine which rows have been inserted or updated during the range.

➤ Use the OLE DB Destination to insert new rows in the destination table.

➤ Use the OLE DB Command to update rows in the destination table that were updated in the source.

➤ Use the OLE DB Destination named DestinationDB to read the keys from the destination table.

➤ Use the Lookup Transform to determine which rows do not exist in the source.

➤ Use the OLE DB Command to update rows in the destination that should be marked as deleted.

Step-by-Step

1. Create a new package called **Lesson36.dtsx**.

2. Create an OLE DB Connection Manager to the AdventureWorks2012 database called **SourceDB** and another to AdventureWorks2012 called **DestinationDB**.

3. Create two variables called **StartDate** and **EndDate**. Their data type should be DateTime.

4. Drag an Execute SQL Task into the Control Flow and name it **Get Date Range**.

5. Double-click the task, set the Connection to DestinationDB, set the ResultSet property to Single row, and enter the following SQL into the SQLStatement field. The dialog box should look like Figure 36-3.

```
SELECT ISNULL( MAX(ModifiedDate),'Jan 1, 1900') as StartDate
, CONVERT(DATETIME, CONVERT(DATE, GETDATE())) as EndDate
FROM [Production].[Lesson36ProductCategoryDestination]
```

6. Click the Result Set tab on the left and map the result set. Map StartDate to User::StartDate and EndDate to User::EndDate. Click OK to exit the dialog box.

7. Drag a Data Flow Task to the Control Flow window and connect the Get Date Range SQL Task to it by dragging the green line. Name the Data Flow Task **Handle Insert Update** and then double-click the Data Flow Task to open the Data Flow window.

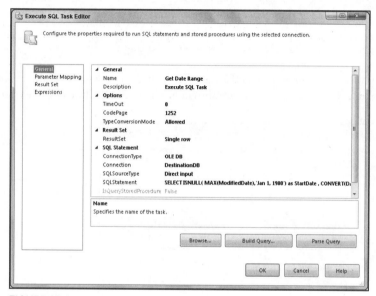

FIGURE 36-3

8. Drag an OLE DB Source into the Data Flow window and name it **Read Inserted Updated Rows from SourceDB**. Double-click it to open the editor. Choose SourceDB for the OLE DB Connection Manager and SQL Command for the Data access mode. Use the following for the SQL command text:

```
SELECT ProductCategoryID, Name, ModifiedDate
FROM [Production].[Lesson36ProductCategorySource]
WHERE ModifiedDate > ? and  ModifiedDate <=?
```

9. Click on the button named Parameters... on the right. You will create two parameters. Type 0 in the Parameters column for the first parameter. Set the Variables column value to User::StartDate and the Param direction to Input. Now create the second parameter. Type 1 in a new row in the Parameters column. Set the Variables column value to User:EndDate and the Param direction to Input.

10. Now click the Columns item on the left. Check all of the columns in the Available External Columns table and map each external column to the output column with the same name. Click OK to exit the editor.

11. Drag a Lookup Task onto the Data Flow window and connect the OLE DB Source Task to it. Name the task **Lookup ProductCategoryIDs in Destination**. Double-click the Lookup Task to open the editor. On the General window, choose the OLE DB Connection Manager, and choose Redirect rows to no match output in the Specify how to handle rows with no matching entries drop-down.

12. Click Connection on the left. Choose DestinationDB for the OLE DB Connection Manager, and select the Use results of an SQL query: radio button. Enter the following SQL into the text box:

```
SELECT ProductCategoryID
FROM   Production.Lesson36ProductCategoryDestination
```

13. Click Columns on the left. Drag ProductCategoryID from Available Input Columns to Available Lookup Columns. The results are shown in Figure 36-4. Click OK to exit this editor.

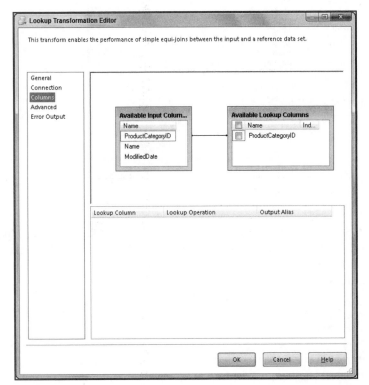

FIGURE 36-4

14. Drag an OLE DB Destination onto the Data Flow, name it **Insert New Destination Rows,** and connect it to the Lookup No Match Output of the Lookup. You can do this by dragging the blue line and selecting the no match option when the dialog box appears. Click OK to exit.

Then double-click the Destination Task to open the editor. Choose DestinationDB in the OLE DB Connection Manager, choose Table, or view - fast load in Data access mode item, and choose [Production].[Lesson36ProductCategoryDestination] in Name of the table or the view.

15. Choose Mappings and complete the mappings as shown in Figure 36-5. Click OK to close the dialog box.

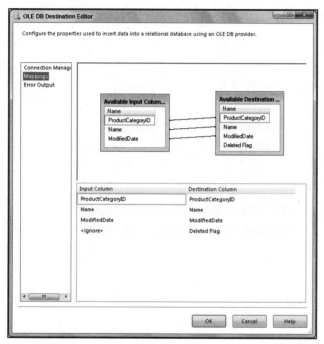

FIGURE 36-5

16. Drag an OLE DB command onto the Data Flow window and connect the Lookup Match Output to it. Name the command task **Update Existing Destination Rows**.

17. Double-click the task to open the editor. In the Connection Managers tab, choose DestinationDB for the Connection Manager.

18. In Component Properties tab, select the SqlCommand property and click the ellipsis that appears on the right-hand side. Use the following command in the String Value Editor that appears. Then click OK to exit the String Value Editor.

```
UPDATE  [Production].[Lesson36ProductCategoryDestination] SET
Name = ?,
ModifiedDate = ?,
[Deleted Flag] = 'F'
WHERE ProductCategoryID = ?
```

19. In the Column Mappings tab, set up the mappings as shown in Figure 36-6. Then click OK. Remember that Param_0 is the first question mark encountered in the SQL string, Param_1 is the next question mark, and so on.

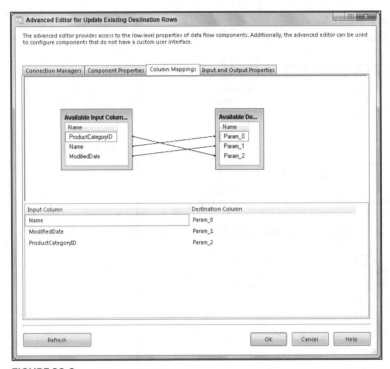

FIGURE 36-6

20. Your Data Flow Task should look like Figure 36-1, the first figure in this lesson.

21. Now you handle the deletes. Drag another Data Flow Task onto the Control Flow window and name it **Handle Deletes.** Connect the Handle Insert Update Task to the Handle Deletes Task. Double-click the task to move to the Data Flow window.

22. Drag an OLE DB Source Task onto the Data Flow window and name it **Read rows from Destination.** Double-click the task.

23. Choose Destination DB for the OLE DB Connection Manager, SQL Command for the Data access mode, and use the following SQL in the SQL command text box:

```
SELECT ProductCategoryID
FROM [Production].[Lesson36ProductCategoryDestination]
WHERE [Deleted Flag] != 'T'
```

24. Click Columns on the left. Make sure the ProductCategoryID column is checked and mapped.

25. Drag a Lookup Task onto the Data Flow, name it **Lookup ProductCategoryIDs in Source,** and connect the Read rows from Destination Task to it by dragging the blue line. Double-click the task to open the editor. In the General window, choose Redirect rows to no match output in the bottom drop-down list.

26. Choose the Connection item in the list on the left. Choose SourceDB as the source. Select the radio button titled Use the results of an SQL query:. Enter the following SQL into the text box:

```
SELECT ProductCategoryID
FROM   Production.Lesson36ProductCategorySource
```

27. Choose the Columns item from the list on the left. Drag ProductCategoryID from Available Input Columns to Available Lookup Columns. Click OK to exit the Lookup Transformation Editor.

28. Drag an OLE DB Command Task onto the Data Flow window and name it **Set Deleted Flags in ProductCategory Destination**. Drag the blue line from the Lookup Task to this task. A dialog box appears, asking whether the matching or not matching rows should be used. Select Lookup No Match Output, as shown in Figure 36-7. Click OK to exit the dialog box.

29. Double-click the Command Task to open the editor. Choose Destination DB as the Connection Manager. In the Component Properties tab, select the SqlCommand property and then click the ellipsis on the right side to open a dialog box. Use the following SQL in the dialog box. Then click OK to close the String Value Editor.

```
UPDATE  [Production].[Lesson36ProductCategoryDestination] SET
[Deleted Flag] = 'T'
WHERE ProductCategoryID = ?
```

30. In Column Mappings tab, drag ProductCategoryID from the Available Input Columns to Param_0 in the Available Destination Columns. Click OK to exit the editor.

31. Your Delete Data Flow should look like Figure 36-2 earlier in this lesson.

32. Go to the Control Flow window. It should look like Figure 36-8.

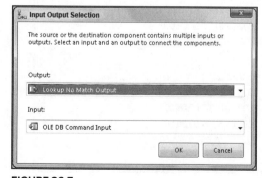

FIGURE 36-7

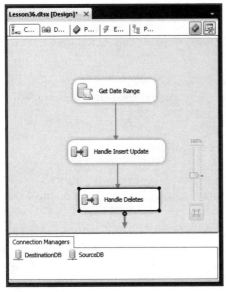

FIGURE 36-8

33. You should have already run Lesson36Create.sql while reading the lesson requirements earlier in the lesson. If you have not run it already, you can run it now. It will not hurt anything
to run this script multiple times. This script creates the tables and populates them. It shows
all rows in the source and destination tables. The result of this query is shown in Figure 36-9.
Both tables have the same data, except that the destination has the deleted flag with all values
set to F. This places your tables in a state where the initial load has been done, and the tables
are in sync.

	ProductCategoryID	Name	ModifiedDate	
1	1	Bikes	2002-06-01 00:00:00.000	
2	2	Components	2002-06-01 00:00:00.000	
3	3	Clothing	2002-06-01 00:00:00.000	
4	4	Accessories	2002-06-01 00:00:00.000	

	ProductCategoryID	Name	ModifiedDate	Deleted Flag
1	1	Bikes	2002-06-01 00:00:00.000	F
2	2	Components	2002-06-01 00:00:00.000	F
3	3	Clothing	2002-06-01 00:00:00.000	F
4	4	Accessories	2002-06-01 00:00:00.000	F

FIGURE 36-9

34. Now execute the script Lesson36MakeChanges.sql. This script simulates user actions by changing the source table. The script updates the Bikes row, adds a new row called New Category, and deletes the Accessories row. Notice that the ModifiedDate column has also been updated. No changes are made to the destination table. Then the source and destination tables will be reselected so you can see the changes, shown in Figure 36-10.

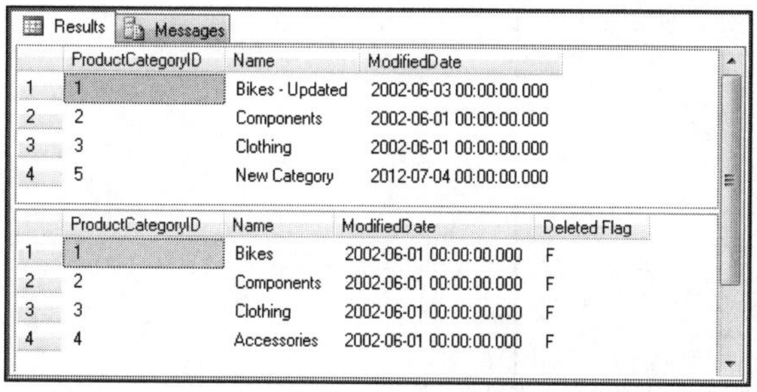

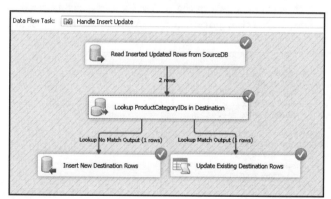

	ProductCategoryID	Name	ModifiedDate
1	1	Bikes - Updated	2002-06-03 00:00:00.000
2	2	Components	2002-06-01 00:00:00.000
3	3	Clothing	2002-06-01 00:00:00.000
4	5	New Category	2012-07-04 00:00:00.000

	ProductCategoryID	Name	ModifiedDate	Deleted Flag
1	1	Bikes	2002-06-01 00:00:00.000	F
2	2	Components	2002-06-01 00:00:00.000	F
3	3	Clothing	2002-06-01 00:00:00.000	F
4	4	Accessories	2002-06-01 00:00:00.000	F

FIGURE 36-10

35. Now save and run your package. Look at your Handle Insert Update Data Flow window. You should see two modified rows that were read from the source. These were modified during the time range you specified. One of them was a new row, and the other was an update. These results are shown in Figure 36-11.

Data Flow Task: Handle Insert Update

Read Inserted Updated Rows from SourceDB

2 rows

Lookup ProductCategoryIDs in Destination

Lookup No Match Output (1 rows)   Lookup Match Output (1 rows)

Insert New Destination Rows   Update Existing Destination Rows

FIGURE 36-11

36. Figure 36-12 shows that your Handle Deletes Data Flow read all rows from the destination. Searching for these rows in the source shows that one row was missing from the source. The Deleted Flag was set to True in the destination.

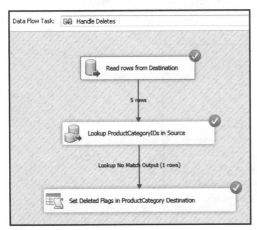

FIGURE 36-12

37. If you run the Lesson36Select.sql script, you will see the results shown in Figure 36-13. ProductCategoryID 1 has its name updated. ProductCategoryID 2 and 3 were unchanged. ProductCategoryID 4, which was deleted from the source by users, has its deleted flag set in the destination. And the new ProductCategoryID 5 was inserted into the destination. Perfect!

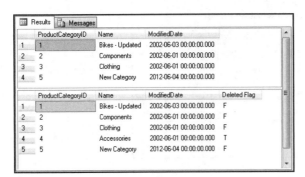

FIGURE 36-13

> *Please select Lesson 36 on the DVD, or online at* www.wrox.com/go/ssis2012video, *to view the video that accompanies this lesson.*

37

Using the CDC Components in SSIS

Lesson 36 covered loading data incrementally. That lesson covered two patterns: an insert/update pattern and a delete pattern. Those patterns also apply when using the Change Data Capture (CDC) components.

> **NOTE** *The setup of CDC within SQL Server requires sysadmin permissions. Marking a table for Change Data Capture requires db_owner permissions.*

In the prior lesson, you used a modified date to determine which rows were inserted or updated, and you used a lookup from the destination to the source to find the deleted rows. Change Data Capture components will identify which rows have been inserted, updated, and deleted. Using the patterns from the previous lesson, the CDC components will replace some of the manual reads and lookups that were used to identify the changed rows. With the insert/update pattern, CDC components will replace the Read Inserted Updated Rows from SourceDB and Lookup ProductdIDs in Destination tasks. These tasks from Lesson 36 are shown enclosed in a square box in Figure 37-1.

CDC components will replace the Read rows from Destination and Lookup ProductCategoryIDs in Source task in the delete pattern from Lesson 36, as shown in Figure 37-2.

Change Data Capture is a functionality that has been available in the SQL Server Engine since the 2008 version. Change Data Capture must be set up by an administrator on the source systems prior to use of the CDC components. CDC keeps track of insert, update, and delete activity for tables that are marked for CDC tracking. This information is made available to other applications via tables and functions. SSIS packages responsible for loading and maintaining data in data marts and data warehouses can use CDC functions as well as SSIS tasks specifically designed to consume and operate on CDC data.

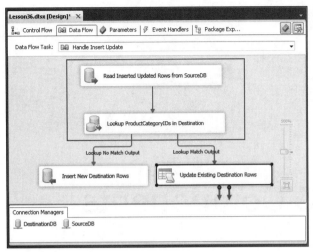

FIGURE 37-1

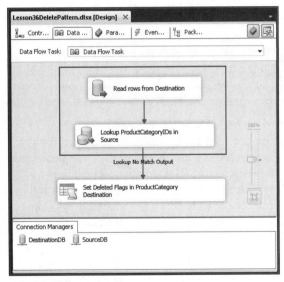

FIGURE 37-2

Three SSIS tasks are related to CDC:

➤ **CDC Control Task**—Responsible for initial loading of data and maintaining incremental load status by keeping up with the Log Serial Number (LSN) associated with changes. This task also does some error handling.

➤ **CDC Source Task**—Reads data that has been inserted, updated, or deleted within a range and provides those rows to downstream consumers in your package.

➤ **CDC Splitter Task**—Accepts the Data Flow from the CDC Source Task and splits it into three separate Data Flows: one for insertions, one for updates, and one for deletions.

Primary target consumers for CDC information are data marts and data warehouses; other possible uses include replication, data auditing, and loading. Using CDC components provides a low-impact way to determine which rows have changed. It does this by reading the SQL Server transaction log. This is especially useful when the tables do not contain any meta data columns like ModifiedDate, CreatedDate, or LastUpdatedDate. CDC tasks also simplify the use of Change Data Capture functionality within SQL Server.

When planning Change Data Capture, you must plan for two pieces of work: the initial load and the incremental load.

> The **initial load** is when the tables are loaded with data for the first time. During this one time load, all rows are copied from the source to the destination.

> The **incremental load** is when you find the rows which have changed since the last load, and update them in the destination. After the initial load, only new or changed rows are moved to the destination.

You can do the initial load in three different ways:

1. From a snapshot

2. From a quiet database (no changes being made)

3. From an in-use database

In this lesson, we take you through load scenario 3. Although this type of loading is the most complicated, it is not difficult, and load scenarios 1 and 2 are even easier.

The goal of the initial load is to add all of the rows from the source table into the destination. Imagine you do an initial load on Sunday night. Both the source and destination tables match. During the day on Monday, changes are made to the source table—rows are inserted, updated, and deleted. Monday night, you must find the inserted, updated, and deleted rows in the source, and make the appropriate changes in the destinations. This is called the incremental load. At the end of the incremental load on Monday night, the source and destination tables match again.

In the Try It section, you will do the both initial load and the incremental load. First we will look at the three SSIS tasks which you will use to do these loads. The tasks are the CDC Control Task, the CDC Source Task, and the CDC Splitter Task.

CDC CONTROL TASK

When planning the use of these components, you will probably need to maintain more than one table. Using these CDC tasks, groups of tables can be maintained together. You will create an initial load package and an incremental load package for each group. The incremental load will contain a CDC Source for each table in the group.

Which tables should be together in a group? A group of tables must load to the same destination. Tables that have primary/foreign key relationships should be in the same group to avoid referential problems in the destination. Tables with the same requirements for data recency should also be together. In general, groups that need to be updated frequently should contain a smaller number of tables than groups that are processed less frequently. For example, if a group of tables needs to be loaded once a week, placing them in a separate group can reduce system load.

There must be a way to maintain information about what data is new and what data has already been processed by prior package runs. The CDC Control Task does this by maintaining Log Sequence Number (LSN) information. The task can also persist this state information in a database. This allows for the state to be maintained across multiple packages and between multiple package runs. As you begin to create your packages, you will set up your CDC Control Task to persist state in a database and provide it to your packages in a variable.

CDC SOURCE TASK

The CDC Source Task reads the change data for a group of tables, and passes rows for a single table of your choice. In your Incremental Load Data Flow, you will have a CDC Source for each table in the group. Figure 37-3 shows a Data Flow Task with CDC Sources for Product, ProductCategory, and ProductSubcategory. These tables would be in the same group because they have primary/foreign key relationships. You will define your insert, update, and delete code for each source independently, and they will be processed in parallel.

FIGURE 37-3

The CDC Source Task is not used in the initial load. The Data Flow source and destination for the initial load will not be the CDC Source Task—you will use the OLE DB Connections for these. If you do try to use the CDC Source Task here, you will get an error.

For the CDC Source Task, you must provide the CDC Source with a capture instance. A specific CDC-enabled table may have up to two capture instances. This allows you to continue change capture during a table schema change, one instance stores the before schema change data, and the second contains the after schema change data. Since we will not change the table schema during the Try It, your table will have one capture instance. You also provide a user variable where the task will store the CDC state information. This variable must be a string data type.

You must also choose a CDC processing mode. The processing modes shown in Figure 37-4 are:

➤ **All**—Returns a row containing the new values for each change in the current range. If a row is changed several times, a row is returned for each change.

➤ **All with old values**—Returns rows for each change in the current range. Two rows are returned for each update: one with the original (old values) and one with the updated values (new values). If a row is changed multiple times, two rows are returned for each update.

➤ **Net**—Returns a single row for each change in the current range. If a row is updated multiple times, only the most recent version of the row is returned. If a row is inserted and then updated in the range, only the updated version is returned. A row that is

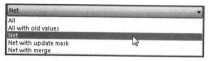

FIGURE 37-4

updated and then deleted is returned as a single delete. A single source row appears only once in the stream; the changes are split into three separate paths: insert, update, and delete.

> **NOTE** *Net is not a good choice for maintaining type 2 slowly changing dimensions, because you would not see every changed row.*

➤ **Net with update mask**—Similar to Net, but includes boolean columns that indicate which column values have changed. The added columns are named _$*<column-name>*_Changed.

➤ **Net with merge**—This is also similar to Net, except that inserts and updates are merged into a single Merge operation. This is for use with Merge or Upsert Tasks.

The CDC Source Task also includes a check box where you can request a reprocessing indicator column. When checked, your returned rows include a column indicating if this row is being reprocessed. This allows you to handle errors differently. You may choose to ignore the deletion of a nonexistent row, or the insertion of a row that returns a duplicate key error—the types of errors you might receive when reprocessing data. These values are set when your processing range overlaps the initial load or when you reprocess a range that failed in a previous run of the package. This dialog box is shown in Figure 37-5.

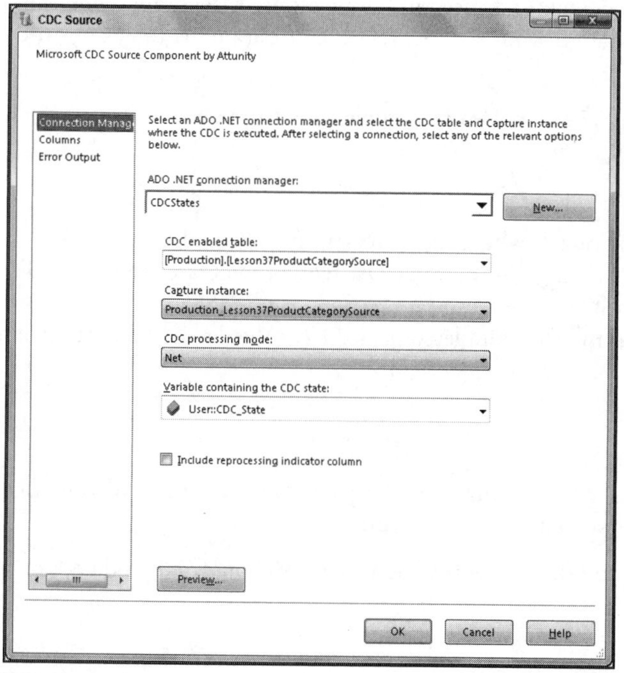

FIGURE 37-5

CDC SPLITTER TASK

The CDC Splitter Task is the other CDC-related Data Flow Task. The splitter takes the Data Flow from a CDC Source component and splits it into different data streams for insert, update, and delete. Splits are based on a column named _$operation. This column contains values from the CDC change tables maintained by SQL Server. These values are:

➤ 1—Deleted row

➤ 2—Inserted row (not available using Net with merge)

➤ 3—Updated row before values (only available with All with old values)

➤ 4—Updated row after values

➤ 5—Updated - merge row (only available with Net with merge)

Any other value is an error.

TRY IT

In this Try It, you do an initial and incremental load of a single table using the CDC components. A script creates the source and destination tables using Production.ProductCategory data. It also loads the source table. You create an initial load package and ensure the initial synchronization is completed successfully, then you create an incremental load package, make changes to the source data, and do the incremental load. The tables, data, and changes for this Try It are the same as the ones in Lesson 36, so you can easily compare the methods used in both lessons. After completing this Try It, you will understand how to keep the data in your data warehouse or data mart tables up-to-date, using the three CDC tasks in SSIS.

You can download the completed Lesson 37 examples and sample code from www.wrox.com.

Lesson Requirements

You must have sysadmin permissions on your database server to set up CDC and create tables. Additionally, SQL Server Agent must be running. To do the CDC setup and create the Lesson 37 tables, run the Lesson37Create.sql script in SQL Server Management Studio (SSMS) before you begin the Step-by-Step. Again, all scripts and the completed package for this lesson are available for download on the book's website at www.wrox.com.

Hints

➤ The CDC Control Task manages the date ranges and keeps up with the status of your CDC group. This control provides the range to the CDC Source Transform.

➤ Use the CDC Source Transform to retrieve the rows that have been inserted, updated, or deleted during the range.

➤ Use the CDC Splitter Task to generate an insert, update, and delete data stream.

➤ Use the OLE DB Destination to insert new rows in the destination table.

➤ Use the OLE DB Command to update rows in the destination table that were updated in the source.

➤ Use the OLE DB Command to update rows in the destination that should be marked as deleted.

Step-by-Step

You create the initial load package as follows:

1. Run the Lesson37Create.sql script if you have not already done so. This script inserts four rows into the [Production].[Lesson37ProductCategorySource] table. The [Production]. [Lession37ProductCategoryDestination] table will be empty.

2. Create a new package called **Lesson37InitialLoad.dtsx**.

3. Create an OLE DB Connection Manager to AdventureWorks2012 called **SourceDB** and another to AdventureWorks2012 called **DestinationDB**. Create an ADO.NET Connection Manager to AdventureWorks2012 called **CDCStates**.

4. Drag a CDC Control Task into the Control Flow window and name it **CDC Control Start**.

5. Double-click the CDC Control Start Task to open the editor. Choose CDCStates Connection Manager from the SQL Server CDC database ADO.NET connection manager drop-down. Notice that the connection manager must be ADO.NET.

6. The CDC control operation should be Mark initial load start.

7. Next to the Variable containing the CDC state box, click New. You get a prefilled dialog box to create a package variable named CDC_State. Click OK to create the package variable.

8. Check the Automatically store state in a database table box.

9. Click New next to the Table to use for storing state: box. Select Run on the dialog box that appears and a new table called CDC_States will be created. Instead of creating a new table, you may select an existing table to store states. Your completed CDC Control Task should look like Figure 37-6. Click OK.

10. Drag a Data Flow Task onto the Control Flow window and connect it to the CDC Control Start Task by dragging the green line.

11. Double-click the Data Flow Task to open the Data Flow window.

12. Drag an OLE DB Data Source onto the Data Flow window and double-click it. Use the SourceDB Connection and choose Table or view for Data access mode. Choose [Production]. [Lesson37ProductCategorySource]. Ensure that all of the columns are selected in the Columns dialog box.

13. Drag an OLE DB Destination Task onto the Data Flow window. Connect the Source Task to it by dragging the blue line.

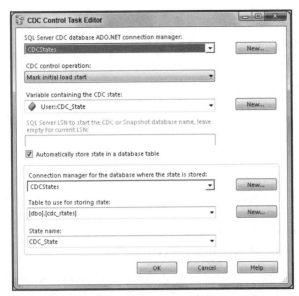

FIGURE 37-6

14. Double-click the Destination Task. Use the DestinationDB Connection and choose Table or view for Data access mode. Choose [Production].[Lesson37ProductCategoryDestination] as the table. Go to the Columns window and ensure that all the source columns are mapped correctly to the destination columns. Your completed Data Flow should look like Figure 37-7.

FIGURE 37-7

15. Go back to the Control Flow window and drag another CDC Control Task onto the Control Flow; name it **CDC Control End.** Configure it the same as CDC Control Start except the CDC Control operation should be Mark initial load end.

16. Connect the Data Flow Task to CDC Control End by dragging the green line.

17. Save and run your package. You should see that four rows were transferred. If you want, you can run Lesson37Select.sql (available in the download), and you will see that the destination table has been synchronized with the source, as in Figure 37-8.

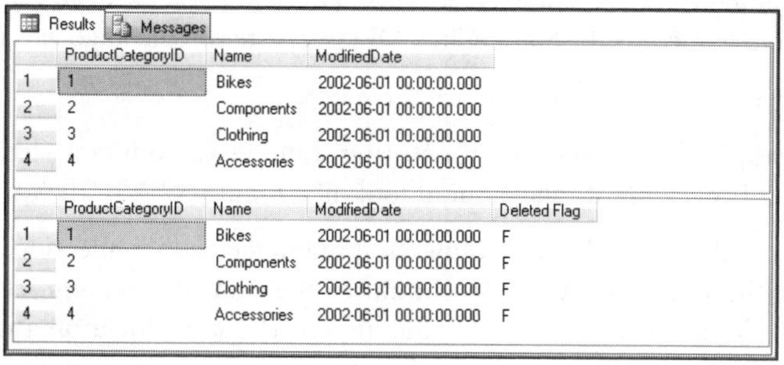

	ProductCategoryID	Name	ModifiedDate
1	1	Bikes	2002-06-01 00:00:00.000
2	2	Components	2002-06-01 00:00:00.000
3	3	Clothing	2002-06-01 00:00:00.000
4	4	Accessories	2002-06-01 00:00:00.000

	ProductCategoryID	Name	ModifiedDate	Deleted Flag
1	1	Bikes	2002-06-01 00:00:00.000	F
2	2	Components	2002-06-01 00:00:00.000	F
3	3	Clothing	2002-06-01 00:00:00.000	F
4	4	Accessories	2002-06-01 00:00:00.000	F

FIGURE 37-8

Now that the initial load is complete, you can create the incremental load package:

1. Run the Lesson37MakeChanges.sql script. This script simulates user actions by changing the source table. The script updates the Bikes row, adds a new row called New Category, and deletes the Accessories row. Notice that the ModifiedDate column has also been updated. No changes are made to the destination table. The script will show you the results of the updates as in Figure 37-9. The source table is shown at the top and the destination at the bottom.

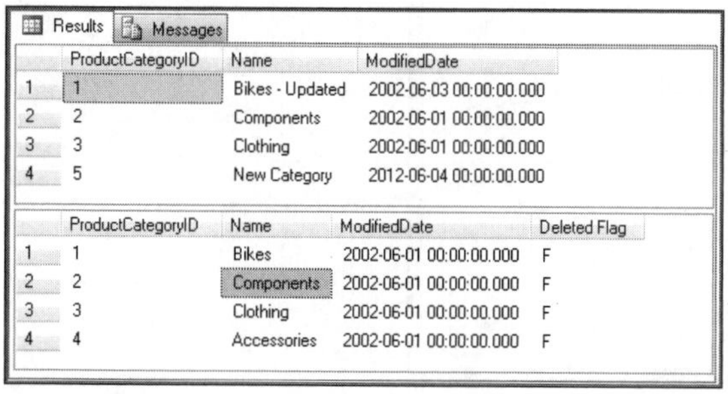

	ProductCategoryID	Name	ModifiedDate
1	1	Bikes - Updated	2002-06-03 00:00:00.000
2	2	Components	2002-06-01 00:00:00.000
3	3	Clothing	2002-06-01 00:00:00.000
4	5	New Category	2012-06-04 00:00:00.000

	ProductCategoryID	Name	ModifiedDate	Deleted Flag
1	1	Bikes	2002-06-01 00:00:00.000	F
2	2	Components	2002-06-01 00:00:00.000	F
3	3	Clothing	2002-06-01 00:00:00.000	F
4	4	Accessories	2002-06-01 00:00:00.000	F

FIGURE 37-9

2. Create a new package called **Lesson37IncrementalLoad.dtsx.**

3. Create an OLE DB Connection Manager to AdventureWorks2012 called **DestinationDB.** Create an ADO.NET Connection Manager to AdventureWorks2012 called **CDCStates.** The CDCStates connection is used for state information and to access the source data from the CDC tables.

4. Drag a CDC Control Task into the Control Flow window and name it **CDC Get Processing Range**.

5. Double-click CDC Control Start Task to open the editor. Choose CDCStates from the SQL Server CDC database ADO.NET connection manager drop-down. This is the database where the CDC tables that contain the changes exist. Notice the connection manager must be ADO.NET.

6. The CDC Control operation should be Get processing range.

7. Next to Variable containing the CDC state, click New. You will get a prefilled dialog box to create a package variable named CDC_State. Click OK to create the package variable.

8. Check the Automatically store state in a database table box.

9. Choose [dbo].[cdc_states] in the Table to use for storing state: box. Your completed CDC Control Task (**CDC Get Processing Range**) should look like Figure 37-10. Click OK.

The SQL Server CDC database ADO.NET connection manager and Connection manager for the database where the state is stored fields should be the same connection locations that were used for the initial load package. These should also be the same location and table you used in the initial load package.

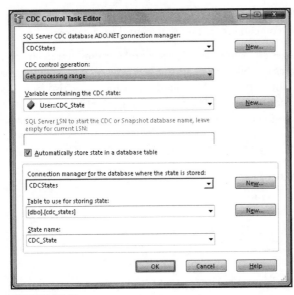

FIGURE 37-10

10. Drag a Data Flow Task onto the Control Flow window and connect the CDC Control Start Task to it by dragging the green line.

11. Double-click the Data Flow Task to open the Data Flow window.

12. Drag a CDC Source Task onto the Data Flow window and name it **CDC Source for ProductCategory**. Then double-click the task. In the CDC Source dialog that opens, choose CDCStates in the ADO.NET connection manager box, [Production]. [Lesson37ProductCategorySource] in the CDC enabled table box, NET in the CDC processing mode box, and User::CDC_State in the Variable containing the CDC state box. Your window should look the same as the one contained in Figure 37-5.

13. Drag a CDC Splitter Task onto the Data Flow and connect the CDC Source for ProductCategory Task to it by dragging the blue line.

14. Drag an OLE DB Destination Task onto the Data Flow window and name it **Insert New Destination Rows**. Connect the CDC Splitter Task to it by dragging the blue line. A dialog box appears that enables you to specify InsertOutput as the output, which will be directed to the Insert New Destination Rows Task. Figure 37-11 shows this dialog box. Click OK to exit.

FIGURE 37-11

15. Double-click the destination task. Use the DestinationDB Connection. The Data access mode should be Table or view - fast load, and choose [Production].[Lesson37ProductCategoryDestination]. Go to the Columns window and ensure that all the source columns are mapped correctly to the destination columns.

16. Drag an OLE DB Command onto the Data Flow window and connect the Lookup Match Output to it. To connect, select the CDC Splitter Task and drag its new blue line to the OLE DB Command Task. You are presented with another window; choose to map UpdateOutput to the OLE DB Command Input. Then click OK. Name the command task **Update Existing Destination Rows**.

17. Double-click the task to open the editor. In the Connection Managers tab, choose DestinationDB for the Connection Manager.

18. In Component Properties tab, select the SqlCommand property and click the ellipsis (...) that appears on the right-hand side. Use the following command in the String Value Editor that appears. Then click OK to exit the String Value Editor.

```
UPDATE  [Production].[Lesson37ProductCategoryDestination] SET
Name = ?,
ModifiedDate = ?,
[Deleted Flag] = 'F'
WHERE ProductCategoryID = ?
```

19. In the Column Mappings tab, set up the mappings as shown in Figure 37-12. Then click OK. Remember that Param_0 is the first question mark encountered in the SQL string, Param_1 is the next question mark, and so on.

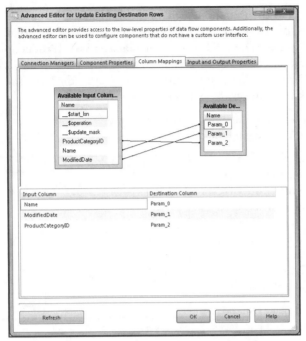

FIGURE 37-12

20.   Drag an OLE DB Command Task onto the Data Flow window and name it **Set Deleted Flags in ProductCategory Destination**. Select the CDC Splitter Task and drag the blue line from the Splitter Task to this task. This is automatically mapped to the delete output, because it is the only remaining output available.

21.   Double-click the Command Task to open the editor. Choose Destination DB as the Connection Manager. In the Component Properties tab, select the SqlCommand property and click the ellipsis (...) on the right side to open a String Value Editor dialog box. Insert the following SQL code in the dialog box. Then click OK to close the String Value Editor.

```
UPDATE  [Production].[Lesson37ProductCategoryDestination] SET
[Deleted Flag] = 'T'
WHERE ProductCategoryID = ?
```

22.   In the Column Mappings tab, drag ProductCategoryID from the Available Input Columns to Param_0 in the Available Destination Columns. Your Data Flow should look like Figure 37-13. Click OK to exit the editor.

23.   Go to the Control Flow window. Drag another CDC Control Task onto the Control Flow window and name it **CDC Mark Processed Range**. Connect it to the Data Flow Task by dragging the green line. You should configure it exactly like CDC Get Processing Range except the CDC Control operation should be Mark Processed Range. Your Control Flow should look like Figure 37-14.

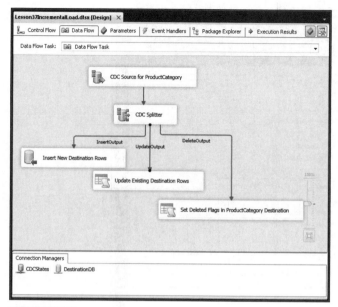

FIGURE 37-13

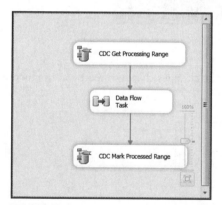

FIGURE 37-14

24.   Wait about 30 seconds, then save and run your package. Your Data Flow results should look like Figure 37-15, with one row inserted, one row updated, and one row marked for deletion. If you see no rows changed, wait another 30 seconds and retry. If you still see no rows, try re-running the Lesson37MakeChanges.sql script, then run your package again.

> **NOTE** *The reason you must wait is that a SQL Agent job waits a few seconds between log scans. You need to wait long enough for the scan to occur. The default scan interval is 5 seconds.*

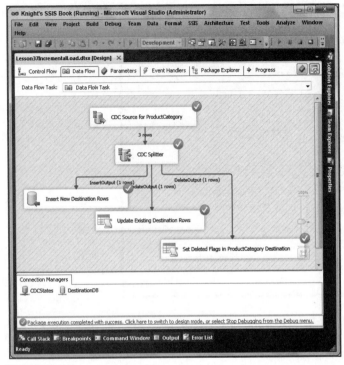

FIGURE 37-15

25. If you run Lesson37Select.sql, you will see the changes that resulted from the incremental load, as shown in Figure 37-16.

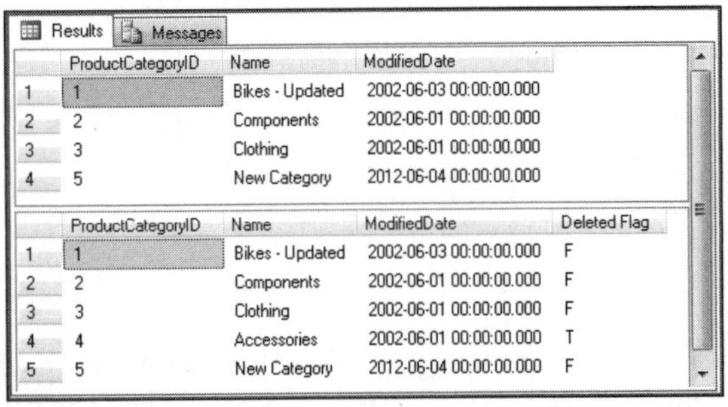

FIGURE 37-16

If you run your incremental package again, you should see a successful completion with no rows changed.

Please select Lesson 37 on the DVD, or online at www.wrox.com/go/ssis2012video, *to view the video that accompanies this lesson.*

38

Using Data Quality Services

Data Quality Services (DQS) provides some tools and services to help improve data within your organization. DQS is a very large and complex topic. This lesson includes the most basic ideas, enough to get you started with the concepts. If this is an area of interest to you, there is much more to learn about this topic. The purpose of this lesson is to prepare you with basic data quality skills, so that you will understand the data quality–related task in the next lesson.

DQS is intended to help to assist you in the following areas:

- ➤ **Completeness**—Are data values missing? If you have 25,000 customers and only 15,000 valid e-mail addresses for them, your e-mail address field is 60 percent complete.

- ➤ **Consistency**—Are data values being used consistently? If Gen Mgr and GM are alternate terms that refer to the General Manager position, are position field values used consistently? (The answer is no.) Even though you know that the values refer to the same position, you must make the values consistent. This is important because you will use this data for comparison and aggregation. Use of inconsistent values provides inaccurate results.

- ➤ **Conformity**—If special formatting is required for certain fields, do the data values match the correct formatting? You can import data from several sources that store values with the same meaning in different ways. Consider the "gender" field. One source provides values of M and F. Another system uses 1 and 2. A third system uses Male and Female. Even if the values are consistent within each system, when brought together, there is a problem. For the "gender" field to be conformed, you must choose the correct representation, and convert the input values to the conformed, approved values.

- ➤ **Validity**—Do valid data values fall within acceptable ranges? For example, the definition of an "age" field should include values between 1 and 120. Negative values do not make any sense, nor do values over 120.

- ➤ **Accuracy**—Do the values represent the true, factual value for the object? As an example, the "age" field value of 25 for me is valid, but not accurate. I am 59.

➤ **Duplication**—Are there multiple instances of the same object, for example, two rows in the customer table that represent the same object (customer)? Perhaps the single customer represented in two rows has two different names, like Bob Smith and Robert Smith. Maybe the customer is a woman who has changed her name due to marriage or divorce. Another common example that can yield duplicates is a customer who has moved, and you have a customer record for the old address and the new address. It is very common to end up with duplicate values for the same object when combining rows from multiple data sources, for instance, when two companies merge.

> **NOTE** *The definitions in the preceding list are the ones used by Microsoft to describe DQS. You will find some conflicting names and definitions to the ones I have used here. When you use names like Accuracy and Validity with other people, make sure you both agree on the use and definition of these terms.*

As you improve your data, you will make decisions about each of the areas listed previously. You can choose to replace "M" and "1" with the value "Male" in the gender field. You will define valid values for fields, and make other decisions about data quality. These decisions are contained in a store called the *Data Quality Knowledge Base (DQKB)*. During cleansing of data, the information in the DQKB is used to automate parts of the process. You can have multiple knowledge bases if you want.

Data cleansing is a process, and not a destination. It is continual and iterative. As you progress, your knowledge base will grow and improve and the manual work you have to do will decrease.

The DQS software must be installed prior to any other work. It contains two pieces: the Data Quality Server and the Data Quality Client. These are not installed by default, so you must explicitly choose these items on the Feature Selection page of the SQL Server install. The Data Quality Server must be installed on a server with the SQL engine. The Data Quality Client can be installed separately on workstations without the engine. The Client tool will be used by those working within DQS to improve the data. These are easy click-through installs.

After the SQL install, you must configure the server. You do this by running the Data Quality Server Installer. It is a program item that appears under Microsoft SQL Server 2012 ⇨ Data Quality Services.

When this runs, you must provide a database encryption key password. Save this password in a safe place; you will need it to restore this database to a different instance of SQL Server. When DQS is installed, you should see three new databases.

Use of DQS is comprised of three main steps:

➤ Knowledge Base Management

➤ Data Cleansing and Matching

➤ Administration and Monitoring

In the Knowledge Base Management phase, you create domains. An example of a domain is Gender. The Gender domain contains information about gender as a class of information, and Gender should be a string data type. You can provide a list of valid values that can be imported from a file or from the database. Valid values can also come from reference data in the cloud. You can also create rules that apply to domains. The early goal is to improve the quality of your knowledge base by ensuring that the domain information is accurate and complete.

The first screen you get during data cleansing is the Profiler tab. This tab provides information about completeness, accuracy, and other statistics regarding the incoming data. An example is shown in Figure 38-1.

Field	Domain	New		Unique		Valid in Domain		Comp
First Name	First Name	0	(0 %)	7	(100 %)	7	(100 %)	
Last Name	US - Last Name	0	(0 %)	6	(86 %)	7	(100 %)	
Gender	Gender	0	(0 %)	6	(86 %)	7	(100 %)	
Department	Department	0	(0 %)	6	(86 %)	7	(100 %)	
Department Group	Department Group	4	(57 %)	6	(86 %)	7	(100 %)	

Source Statistics

Records:	7	
Total Values:	35	
New Values:	4	(11 %)
Unique Values:	31	(89 %)
New Unique Values:	4	(11 %)
Valid in Domain Values:	35	(100 %)

FIGURE 38-1

You can also create composite domains. You can have a First Name and Last Name domains. And you can then create a composite domain called Full Name that is composed of the First Name and Last Name domains. You can supply separate, additional rules to the composite domain.

DQS enables you to define synonyms in the knowledge base. For example, you can define "M" as a synonym for "Male." DQS is not case-sensitive, but it does preserve case. One of the values in a single group of synonyms will be the surviving value, and all other values in the synonym group will be corrected to the surviving value. The synonym that survives as the corrected value is called the *leading value*. After you have defined synonyms, you can identify the leading value.

Term-based relations enable you to store abbreviations that can be used in a specific domain. The abbreviations are expanded as part of cleansing.

Domain rules can be applied to a single domain and to composite domains. Composite domain rules allow more complex conditions between the included domains to provide a corrected value. An example of a complex domain rule is shown in Figure 38-2.

The knowledge base is very powerful. It even includes a spell checker that can catch and automatically correct misspellings in the input data. Absent exact matches for valid values, it can provide suggestions and confidence levels. The more complete your knowledge base, the more accurate the cleansing will be.

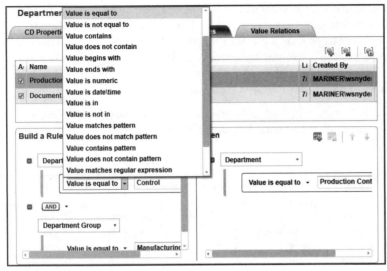

FIGURE 38-2

While cleansing data in the Data Cleansing and Matching phase, incoming data is processed using the information stored in your knowledge base. Completeness and accuracy are displayed, along with any corrections and suggestions made by the knowledge base. You can then approve or reject the values, export the output from the process, and use the output as a data source for your ETL loading of data.

In this way, data cleansing consists of both computer-assisted and interactive cleansing. The data is cleansed via knowledge base information, but interactively, you review and approve or reject, yielding the final output. In addition, you can provide a corrected value during the interactive cleansing.

The DQS cleansing processing will automatically place data in the tabs, which are described below. As you work through interactive cleansing, changes and corrections you make may cause the data to be moved into a different tab.

➤ **Correct**—An exact match was found in the knowledge base or you approved the value.

➤ **Corrected**—Values corrected by DQS with a high confidence level, or you provided a value in the Correct to column and approved.

➤ **Invalid**—Values marked in the knowledge base as invalid or that failed a domain rule or reference data, or values that were rejected by you.

➤ **New**—Valid values for which there is not enough information (not marked as invalid in the knowledge base), and values for which there is a suggestion with a low confidence.

➤ **Suggested**—DQS suggests these values. The confidence level is not high enough to be Corrected, but the confidence level is above the minimum level to provide this as a suggestion. You must review and approve/reject these values. The confidence levels for corrected and suggested can be set by the DQS administrator.

Figure 38-3 shows these tabs. In this figure, the New value for the First Name domain is selected. The value Bob is selected at the top. It is corrected to Robert and approved below. This changes the value in the output, but does not make the change in the knowledge base.

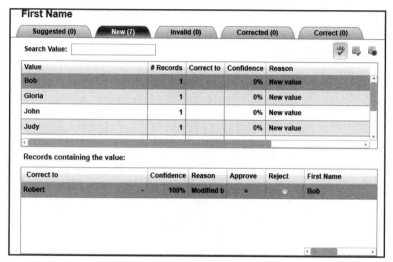

FIGURE 38-3

The Administration tab of the DQS client tool contains two buttons, Activity monitoring and Configuration. While in the Administering and Monitoring phase of DQS, you will use this tab. The configuration button leads to a location where you can set logging, confidence levels and reference data connection, and password information.

Every time someone performs a Knowledge Management task, data cleansing, or data matching, DQS logs information related to the session. Information such as session length, session type, user, and the knowledge base used are captured. Additionally, the profiler information is kept. This is the same profiler information you see when doing interactive cleansing. After you have completed this lesson, you should visit the Activity monitoring tab.

TRY IT

In this Try It, you create a knowledge base and import some valid values. You then train the knowledge base by doing some data exploration and data discovery. You then use the knowledge base in a data quality project you create to cleanse some data. After completing this Try It, you will understand how to create a knowledge base, load it with data, and use it to cleanse newly arriving data.

The spreadsheets and a completed DQS file for this lesson are available for download on the book's website at www.wrox.com.

> **WARNING** *If you are working in a version of Excel prior to Excel 2010, you will need to covert the .xlsx spreadsheets in the download to .xls spreadsheets.*

Lesson Requirements

You must have elevated permissions to complete this lesson. The minimum permission is membership in the dqs-kb-editor role.

Hints

➤   You do not need to create an SSIS project.

➤   Use the DQS Client tool.

Step-by-Step

First, you need to perform some domain management and data discovery as follows:

1.   Run the Data Quality Client. You can find it under All Programs ➪ Microsoft SQL Server 2012 ➪ Data Quality Services. You will see a Connect To Server dialog box. Type the name of the server where DQS is installed and click Connect.

2.   In the Knowledge Base Management tab, click New Knowledge Base. Use the following to complete the dialog box and click Next.

➤   **Name**—Lesson38KB

➤   **Create Knowledge Base From**—Existing Knowledge Base

➤   **Select Knowledge Base**—DQS Data

3.   The only domain you will use is US - Last Name. Delete the other domains by selecting the domain and then clicking the Delete icon. See Figure 38-4.

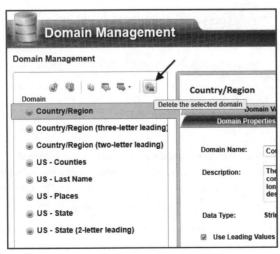

FIGURE 38-4

4.   Open Lesson38SampleData.xlsx and take a look at the data (Figure 38-5). This contains the sample data you will use to improve the knowledge base. To create a new domain, click the top-left icon in the Domain Management tab of the DQS Client (the one with the star). Create a new domain for Gender, Department, and Department Group, using the following information:

➤   **Data Type**—String

➤   **Use Leading Values**—Checked

➤   **Normalize String**—Checked

➤   **Format Output to** —None

➤   **Language**—English

➤   **Enable Speller**—Checked

➤   **Disable Syntax Error Algorithms**—Unchecked

First Name	Last Name	Gender	Department	Department Group
Wayne	Snyder	M	Resaerch and Development	R and D
Devin	Knight	Male	Shipping	Inv Mgmt
Brian	Knight	1	Design	R D
Mike	Davis	Male	QA	Quality Assurance
Debbie	Smyth	F	Human Resources	Exec Gen Admin
Christina	Raymer	2	Control	Manufacturing
Lisa	Smith	Female	Control	Quality Assurance

FIGURE 38-5

Do not create a domain for First Name right now. You will do this later, so you can see another place you can create domains.

5.   Select the Gender domain on the left, and choose the Domain Values tab. You know that Male and Female are the valid values for Gender at your company. Click the Add New Domain Value icon to the right of the Show Only New check box. The icon has a green plus sign. Type **Male** in the Value box and ensure that the green check is selected. This indicates that Male is a valid value. Do not enter anything into the Correct to box. Now add the Female Gender Value. Click Finish. When asked to publish, select No.

6.   You need to get valid values for Department and Department Group. The approved, valid values are already stored in a database. Under Recent Knowledge Base, choose Lesson38KB and click Knowledge Discovery (Figure 38-6).

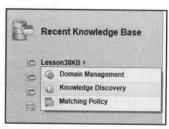

FIGURE 38-6

Use the information in the following list to import the data:

➤   **Data Source**—SQL Server

➤   **Database**—AdventureWorks2012

➤   **Table/View**—Department

➤   **Mappings**—Name (nvarchar) - Department

➤   **Mappings**—GroupName (nvarchar) - Department Group

Note that the top of this window shows the three steps to knowledge discovery: Map, Discover, and Manage Domain Values. Map is highlighted because you are in the mapping phase.

Select Next. You will see that you are now in the "discover" phase. Click Start at the top of the page. Rows from your source will be imported. Domain rules and discovery will be run on the imported rows.

7. When this is complete, the profiler tab will be populated with data, and the navigation buttons at the bottom of the page will be enabled. Click Next. Notice you are now in the third step of Knowledge Management - Manage Domain Values. The two domains you imported will be displayed in the tree on the left. You can see the new values that will be added to the domain. Click Finish, but do not publish.

8. Choose Lesson38KB ⇨ Knowledge Discovery again. Now you will use some sample data to improve the quality of your knowledge base:

> ➤ **Data Source**—Excel File

> ➤ **Excel File**—Lesson38SampleData.xlsx (in your folder)

> ➤ **Worksheet**—Sheet1$

> ➤ **Use first row as header**—Checked

> ➤ **Mappings**—Department (String) - Department

> ➤ **Mappings**—Department Group (String) - Department Group

> ➤ **Mappings**—Gender (String) - Gender

> ➤ **Mappings**—Last Name (String) - US - Last Name

Notice there is a field in the spreadsheet, First Name, that is missing from your domains. You can create a new domain right here. Click the New Domain button as shown in Figure 38-7, and create the new domain with the same attributes that you used with the other domains. After you have created the First Name domain, you can map the spreadsheet column to it. Click Next, and then click Start on the next page.

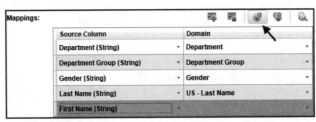

FIGURE 38-7

9. During the Knowledge Discovery process, your main focus is on new values. You must decide if these new values are valid, or if they should be mapped to existing values. You can see that the profiler shows new values in every domain except Last Name. Click Next.

10. Choose the Department domain. You will see five new values. The spell checker suggests that one value was misspelled and suggests it be mapped to Research and Development. This is the correct action, and you will not have to bother with it. Now uncheck the Show Only New check box, so you can see all of the domain values.

11. Scroll down the values until you see QA and Quality Assurance. QA is a new value. Because Quality Assurance is the valid value for the Department domain, you should correct instances of QA. To do this, select QA, then Shift-Select Quality Assurance. Right-click to get a context-sensitive menu, and choose Set as synonyms. The list will now look like Figure 38-8.

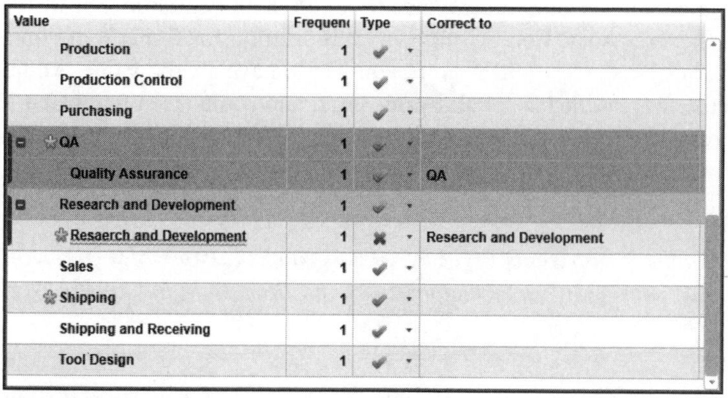

Value	Frequenc	Type	Correct to
Production	1	✔ ▾	
Production Control	1	✔ ▾	
Purchasing	1	✔ ▾	
⊟ QA	1	✔ ▾	
Quality Assurance	1	✔ ▾	QA
⊟ Research and Development	1	✔ ▾	
Resaerch and Development	1	✖ ▾	Research and Development
Sales	1	✔ ▾	
Shipping	1	✔ ▾	
Shipping and Receiving	1	✔ ▾	
Tool Design	1	✔ ▾	

FIGURE 38-8

12. Although these are now synonyms, QA is the leading value, and Quality Assurance will be changed to QA. This is backwards. Quality Assurance should be the leading value. Select Quality Assurance only, right-click, and choose Set as Leading. The correction should look like Figure 38-9.

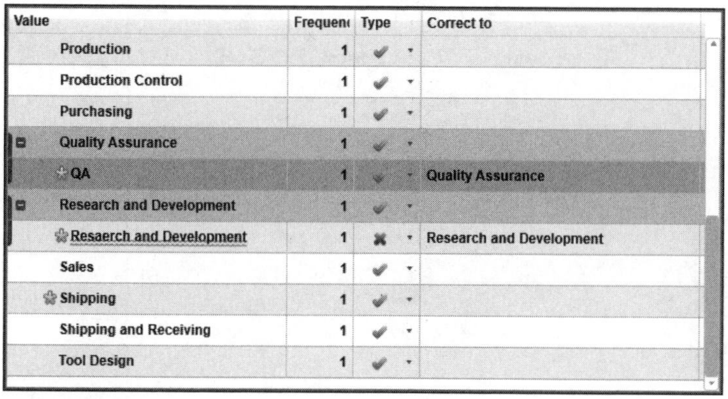

Value	Frequenc	Type	Correct to
Production	1	✔ ▾	
Production Control	1	✔ ▾	
Purchasing	1	✔ ▾	
⊟ Quality Assurance	1	✔ ▾	
QA	1	✔ ▾	Quality Assurance
⊟ Research and Development	1	✔ ▾	
Resaerch and Development	1	✖ ▾	Research and Development
Sales	1	✔ ▾	
Shipping	1	✔ ▾	
Shipping and Receiving	1	✔ ▾	
Tool Design	1	✔ ▾	

FIGURE 38-9

13. Make Shipping and Receiving the leading value, with Shipping as the synonym.

14. Make Tool Design the leading value, with Design as the synonym.

15. Scroll around and find the new value Control. This is the only new value you have not accounted for. Control could mean either Production Control or Document Control. You will fix this with a rule, but you have to go back to Domain Management, so you will come back to this one later.

16. Now choose Department Group. You see four new values. You could make these synonyms of existing valid departments. You could make Exec Gen Admin a synonym for Executive General and Administration. But you can also try a different technique that would handle a larger number of future issues. Gen is simply an abbreviation for General. If you expanded all of the three terms Exec, Gen, and Admin, you would have a valid value. Additionally, if General Manager were added as a valid value later, and someone entered Gen Manager, term expansion would automatically fix that value as well. For all of the new values for Department Group, you will use term expansion.

> **NOTE** *Now you have two items to fix when you go back: Control for Document Control or Production Control in Department and these term expansions for Department Group.*

17. Choose First Name. You are accepting all of these values as valid, so there is nothing to do.

18. Choose Gender. You know that Male and Female are the valid values. It is easy to see the use of M and F should be synonyms. Taking a look at the source spreadsheet, you find that Gender 1 is used for Brian and 2 for Christina. So you will use those synonyms as well. Fix these just as you did in the Department domain earlier. Your results should look like Figure 38-10.

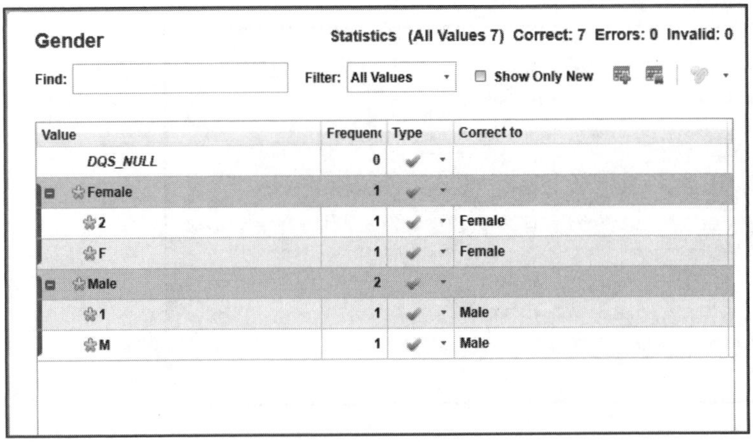

Gender		Statistics (All Values 7)	Correct: 7	Errors: 0	Invalid: 0

Value	Frequenc	Type	Correct to
DQS_NULL	0	✔ ▾	
⊟ Female	1	✔ ▾	
2	1	✔ ▾	Female
F	1	✔ ▾	Female
⊟ Male	2	✔ ▾	
1	1	✔ ▾	Male
M	1	✔ ▾	Male

FIGURE 38-10

19. Because you have no new or error values for Last Name, you do not have any work to do.

> **NOTE** *As your knowledge base improves, the amount of work you must do will decrease.*

20. Click Finish, but do not publish.

21. Click Lesson38KB ⇨ Domain Management.

22. Now create a rule to handle Control in Department. Choose the Department domain and select Domain rules. You know that when someone puts Control as the Department, it could mean either Production Control or Document Control. However, you also know that Production Control is in the Manufacturing Department Group, and Document Control is in the Quality Assurance Department Group. Create a rule that says, if the Department is Control and the Department Group is Manufacturing, the Department is Production Control. If the Department is Control and the Department Group is Quality Assurance, the Department should be Document Control. To do this, Department and Department Group must be in a composite domain.

22. Click the Create Composite Domain icon, as shown in Figure 38-11.

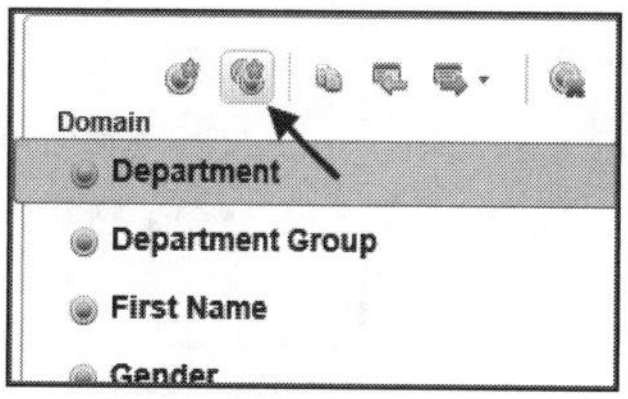

FIGURE 38-11

23. Name the composite domain **Department Group CD**. Move Department and Department Group from the Domains List to Domains in Composite Domain. Click OK.

24. Select the Department Group CD domain. In the CD Rules tab, click the Add New Domain Rule icon, with the green plus sign. Type **Production Control** as the name. In the Build a Rule section, choose Department. There is a drop down below that says "Length is equal to". Change "Length is equal to" to "Value is equal to". Then type **Control** in the text box to the right.

25. Right-click anywhere in the Build a Rule section and choose Add clause. Choose Department Group, Value is equal to, and type **Manufacturing**.

26. In the Then area, choose Department, Value is equal to, and type **Production Control**.

27. Now create a new domain rule named **Document Control**, which sets the Department to Document Control when the Department is Control and the Department Group is Quality Assurance. Your results should look like Figure 38-12.

28. Choose the Department Group domain to add all of the abbreviations. Select the Term-Based Relations tab and select the Add New Relation icon. Enter the following values in the Value and Correct to fields:

➤ R—Research

➤ D—Development

➤ Inv—Inventory

➤ **Mgmt**—Management

➤ **Exec**—Executive

➤ **Admin**—Administration

➤ **Gen**—General

Your results should look like Figure 38-13. Click Apply Changes.

FIGURE 38-12

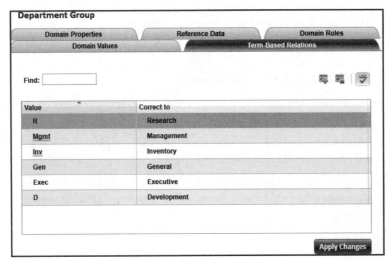

FIGURE 38-13

29. Choose Domain Values for the Department Group domain. Delete the following values, because they are not valid domain values. When these values are presented in incoming data, they will be changed into one of the valid values. You can delete the values by selecting the appropriate row and clicking the Delete icon with the red x on the top right. Delete the following:

> ➤ Exec Gen Admin

> ➤ Inv Mgmt

> ➤ R and D

30. Click Finish and publish your knowledge base.

The next steps turn to the actual data cleansing. You are going to use the knowledge base to cleanse some new data. You will import some new data, cleanse it, and then approve or reject the output values.

31. In the Data Quality Projects section, click on New Data Quality Project. Use the following information to complete the dialog, then click Next.

> ➤ **Name**—CleanSpreadsheet

> ➤ **Use Knowledge Base**—Lesson38KB

> ➤ **Select Activity**—Cleansing

32. Map the data using the following list:

> ➤ **Data Source**—Excel File

> ➤ **Excel File**—Lesson38NewData.xlsx (in your folder)

> ➤ **Worksheet**—Sheet1$

> ➤ **Use first row as header**—Checked

> ➤ **Mappings**—Department (String) - Department

> ➤ **Mappings**—Department Group (String) - Department Group

> ➤ **Mappings**—First Name (String) - First Name

> ➤ **Mappings**—Gender (String) - Gender

> ➤ **Mappings**—Last Name (String) - US - Last Name

Click View/Select Composite Domains and check Department Group CD.

33. Click Next. On the next page, click Start. The DQS cleansing will run. When it finishes, you will see the profile window populate with information and the navigation buttons will become enabled. Click Next. Choose Department Group CD. Visit each tab and check the original and corrected values. For each, choose either approve or reject. When you reject a value for a field, that column and row will have a status of Invalid. You can use these statuses to determine whether the row or column value should be placed in your data store or treated as an error. Check and approve all values for all domains. You may also type a correct value directly into the Correct to text boxes. Figure 38-14 shows this dialog. Click Next.

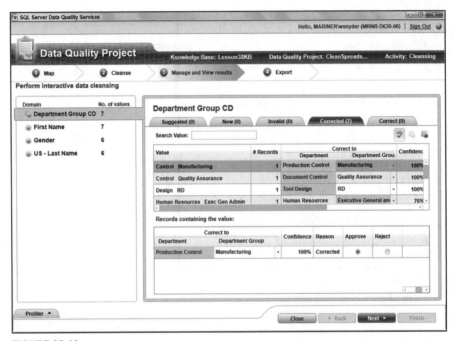

FIGURE 38-14

> **NOTE** *Pay special attention to suggested and new values.*

34. Export the data with Data and Cleansing info to an Excel file named Lesson38Output.xls.

35. The output file can now become the source for an ETL operation which loads the cleansed data into your data warehouse.

> *Please select Lesson 38 on the DVD, or online at* www.wrox.com/go/ssis2012video, *to view the video that accompanies this lesson.*

39

Using the DQS Cleansing Transform

In the previous lesson, you created a DQS knowledge base and cleansed some data, all interactively. As you improve the quality, domain coverage, and capability of your knowledge base, it will be able to correct a larger and larger percentage of values from new incoming data. As this occurs, you will benefit from automating as much of the cleansing as possible. You may want to have values that are correct or corrected with high confidence levels to move directly into the destination. Then you can review and fix only the remaining values. This capability exists with SSIS as the DQS Cleansing Transform. Additionally, you can correct and approve or reject the remaining values using the DQS Client. There is a truly intelligent cooperation between the Cleansing Task and the DQS Client.

The Cleansing Task accepts a Data Flow as input, cleanses the data using the knowledge base of your choice, adds output meta data, and passes the Data Flow forward. A commonly used Data Flow for the Cleansing Transform is shown in Figure 39-1.

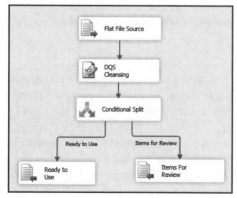

FIGURE 39-1

> **NOTE** *The DQS Client is interactive, multithreaded, and is written to run as fast as possible, because most of us are impatient. The fast run time corresponds to high memory use for the client. Because we do not sit and wait for the Cleansing Transform to run in SSIS, it was written to reduce the memory footprint (single threaded) and therefore runs for a longer period of time.*

When you double-click the DQS Cleansing Task, its editor pops up, and contains only three tabs: Connection Manager, Mapping, and Advanced.

The Connection Manager tab is where you choose the connection manager that points to your DQS server. After you choose the data quality connection manager, you can select which of the knowledge bases on that server should be used by the task. At the bottom of the window is the Configure error output check box. By default, the task will fail if there is an error, but you can choose to redirect the error rows.

In the Mapping tab, you choose which columns from the input should be cleansed and associate each of those input columns with its corresponding domain. The standard output columns for each input are Source, Output, Status, Confidence, and Reason. The default column names are supplied, but you can change these names if you want. Figure 39-2 shows the Mapping tab.

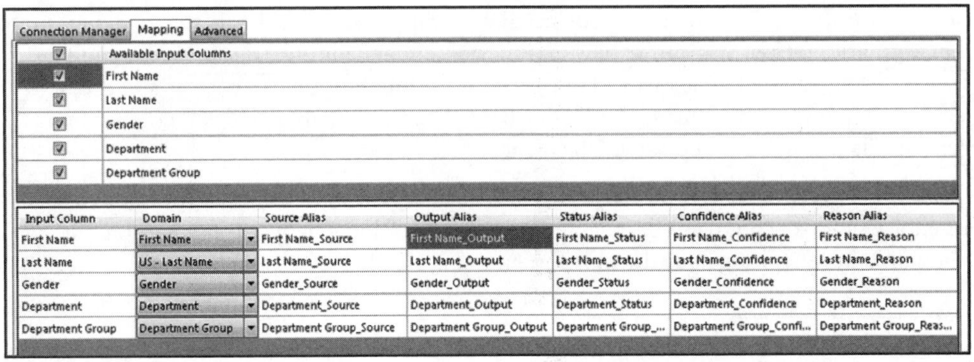

FIGURE 39-2

While each column has a status associated with it, there is also a status associated with the entire row. This enables you to use either or both statuses. The row status tells you the worst column status, which should indicate whether the data steward should trust the row or review the values in the row. For instance, if all the column statuses are Correct, the row status should be Correct. If all column statuses are Correct, except for one which is Corrected, the row status is Corrected. Though you are free to do whatever you want with these row statuses, most examples indicate Correct and Corrected as trusted values, which are sent forward without additional scrutiny. Any other row status can require individual examination, correction and approval, or rejection.

The Advanced tab shown in Figure 39-3 contains a list of additional options that you can set.

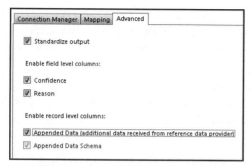

FIGURE 39-3

➤ **Standardize output**—When selected, your output will be formatted using the "Format Output To" domain properties chosen for the domain. Formatting properties for domains depend on the data type of the domain:

  ➤ **String**—Uppercase, lowercase, or capitalized

  ➤ **Date**—Format of the day, month, and year

  ➤ **Integer**—Apply a format mask

  ➤ **Decimal**—Precision and format mask

➤ **Confidence**—When chosen, this value is provided for each source column. The confidence score between 0 and 100 indicates the level of trust that the DQS Server or relevant Reference Data Source has in the accuracy of the suggested value. Higher values indicate a higher level of confidence.

➤ **Reason**—When chosen, this value is provided for each source column. This column explains the output column value. The reason "Domain Value" indicates a valid value found in the domain. "New Value" indicates the value is not marked as error or invalid in the domain, nor does it exist as a valid value. "New Value" also includes low confidence suggestions. Other examples of reasons are "Unknown," "Invalid," and "Corrected to leading value."

➤ **Appended Data**—If your domain uses a reference data source, the reference can return additional information about the domain. For instance, an address validation reference data source can provide additional longitude/latitude information.

➤ **Appended Data Schema**—Automatically selected when Appended Data is selected, this adds the schema definition you would use to interpret the information provided in the appended data column.

With the Cleansing Transform configured, you need to route the output to complete the package. You will use a Conditional Split Task to route the rows into two Data Flows: one Data Flow that will continue and be automatically added to the data warehouse, and another Data Flow that requires manual review and decisions about the data quality. Using the row status as the source, values of Correct and Corrected are routed to a "ready to use" flow. Any other value in the row status causes the rows to be routed to the "items for review" Data Flow.

Every time your package runs, a data cleansing project is created. This means the data steward can use the Client tool to interactively review the data from the SSIS cleansing in the same way that was done during knowledge discovery. You can use the DQS Client tool to open the data quality project and review, correct, approve, or reject values.

After the DQS project review is complete, you can import the new information into the knowledge base, continuously improving the knowledge base. To bring the project information into the knowledge base, open the knowledge base in the Client tool and choose Domain Management. In the Domain Values tab, choose the Import Values icon, as shown in Figure 39-4.

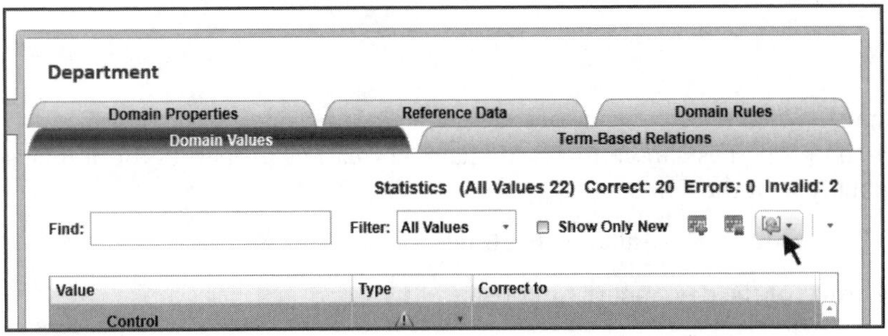

FIGURE 39-4

TRY IT

In this Try It, you create an SSIS package that uses the DQS Cleansing Transform. After the data is cleansed, you split the output into two Data Flows, one with acceptable values and another that requires further inspection. After you complete this lesson, you will be able to use SSIS to automatically clean your data.

You can download the completed Lesson39.dtsx and sample files for this lesson from www.wrox.com. You should copy these files to C:\Projects\SSISPersonalTrainer directory.

Lesson Requirements

You must have elevated permissions to complete this lesson. The minimum permission is membership in the dqs_kb_editor security role in the DQS_Main database. To create the knowledge base that will be used for cleansing, import the Lesson39KB.dqs file.

Hints

> ➤ Import Lesson39KB.dqs, which you downloaded from the www.wrox.com site to create the knowledge base.

> ➤ Use the DQS Cleansing Transform to cleanse the data.

> ➤ Use the Conditional Split Transform to partition the output and direct it to two Data Flows.

Step-by-Step

1. Run the Data Quality Services Client. You can find it under All Programs ⇨ Microsoft SQL Server 2012 ⇨ Data Quality Services. You will see a Connect To Server dialog box. Type the name of the server where DQS is installed. Click Connect.

2. In the Knowledge Base Management tab, click New Knowledge Base. Use the following to complete the dialog box and click Next.

> ➤ **Name**—Lesson39KB

> ➤ **Create Knowledge Base From**—Import from DQS file

> ➤ **Select data file**—Use Lesson39KB.dqs in your folder

3. Create a new SSIS package named **Lesson39.dtsx**. Drag a Data Flow Task onto the Control Flow tab. Double-click it to open the Data Flow tab.

4. Drag a Flat File Source onto the Data Flow tab, and double-click it to open the editor. The Flat File Source Editor window opens. Click New to create a connection manager. Name the connection manager **Lesson39SampleData**. Click Browse, navigate to your Lesson39SampleData.txt file, and select it. Click Preview and take a look at the rows to import. Notice the sample file contains some misspellings, abbreviations, and new data. Click OK to exit the Preview, and click OK again to exit the editor.

5. Drag the DQS Cleansing Transform onto the Data Flow tab, and connect the Flat File Source to it by dragging the blue line from the Flat File Source to the DQS Cleansing Transform. Then double-click it to open the editor.

6. In the Connection Manager tab, click New to create a connection manager that points to the DQS server that contains your knowledge base. Type in the name of your DQS server. Test the connection and click OK. In the Data Quality Knowledge Base tab, select Lesson39KB.

7. Choose the Mapping tab. Select all of the columns and map them to their corresponding domains. Refer back to Figure 39-2 to see what your tab should look.

8. Choose the Advanced tab. Make the following selections:

> ➤ **Standardize output**—Checked

> ➤ **Confidence**—Checked

> ➤ **Reason**—Checked

> ➤ **Appended Data**—Checked

Your tab should look like the one shown back in Figure 39-3. Click OK to exit the editor.

9. Right-click the DQS Connection Manager in the Connection Managers window and rename it to **DQS Cleansing Connection Manager**.

10. Drag a Conditional Split Transform onto the Data Flow, and connect it to the Cleansing Transform by dragging the blue line from the Cleansing Transform. Double-click the conditional split to open the editor. Make the following selections to complete the configuration:

➤ **Output Name**—Ready to Use

➤ **Condition**—[Record Status] = = "Correct" || [Record Status] = = "Corrected"

➤ **Default Output Name**—Items for Review

Your Conditional Split Transformation Editor window should look like Figure 39-5. Click OK to complete the configuration. You will now have two good Data Flows from the conditional split: Ready to Use and Items for Review.

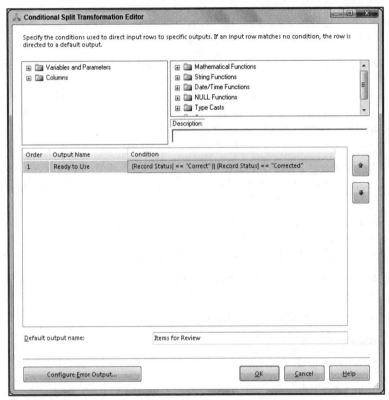

FIGURE 39-5

11. Now you will connect each of the two data flows you created in the Conditional Split Task to an output. Drag a Flat File Destination onto the Data Flow tab, and name it **Ready to Use**. Connect it to the Conditional Split by dragging the blue line from the Conditional Split to the Flat File Destination Ready to Use. An Input Output Selection dialog box appears, enabling you to choose which output from the conditional split to use. Choose Ready to Use Output. Then click OK.

12. Double-click the Ready to Use Destination to open the editor. Choose New for Flat File Connection Manager. Then choose Delimited in the Flat File Format dialog box. Click OK to exit the dialog box. The Flat File Connection Manager appears.

➤ **Connection Manager Name**—Ready to Use

➤ **File Name**—C:\Projects\SSISPersonalTrainer\Lesson39ReadytoUse.txt

➤ **Column names in the first data row**—Checked

Click OK to exit the Connection Manager Transformation Editor. You are returned to the Flat File Destination Editor. Click the Mappings tab so the columns will be configured. Click OK.

13. Create a destination for the Items for Review Data Flow. Drag a Flat File Destination onto the Data Flow tab, and name it **Items for Review**. Connect it to the Conditional Split by dragging the blue line from Conditional Split to the Flat File Destination Ready to Use. The last time you dragged a Conditional Split blue output, a dialog box allowed you to choose which of the two outputs to map. Because there is only one remaining blue output—Items for Review—no dialog box is presented. The only remaining output is used.

14. Double-click the Items for Review Destination to open the editor. Choose New for Flat File Connection Manager. Then choose Delimited in the Flat File Format dialog box. Click OK to exit the dialog box. The Flat File Connection Manager appears. Complete the configuration using the following information:

➤ **Connection Manager Name**—Ready to Use

➤ **File Name**—C:\Projects\SSISPersonalTrainer\Lesson39ReadytoUse.txt

➤ **Column names in the first data row**—Checked

Click OK to exit the Connection Manager Editor. You are returned to the Flat File Destination Editor. Click the Mappings tab so the columns will be configured. Click OK. Your Data Flow should look like Figure 39-1 earlier in this lesson.

15. Save and run the package. The completed Data Flow should look like Figure 39-6. Nine rows were read, and seven of them were correct or corrected, leaving two rows in the Items for Review file.

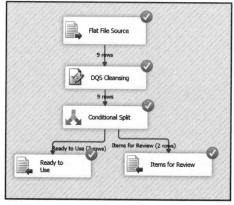

FIGURE 39-6

> **NOTE** *You can open these files in Excel and review them if you want. If you do, they are delimited files with a tab delimiter.*

16. To review the work done by this run of the Cleansing Transform, run the DQS Client application. Click Open Data Quality Project, then scroll through the Open Project list, select your SSIS package run, and select Next.

17. Here you can change, approve, and reject values just as you did in the previous lesson. Figure 39-7 shows that two new values in the First Name domain came from this cleansing exercise. Once you have completed your changes, approvals, and rejections, you can export this information to be used as input for the next cleansing activity.

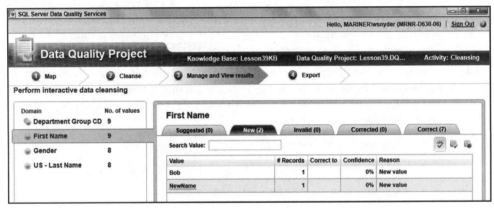

FIGURE 39-7

> *Please select Lesson 39 on the DVD, or online at* www.wrox.com/go/ssis2012video, *to view the video that accompanies this lesson.*

40

Creating a Master Package

The master package uses the Execute Package Task to run child packages. This process is covered in Lesson 46. Using a master package offers several advantages.

You must execute child packages in the proper order because some packages can depend on the success, failure, or completion of other packages. To do this, you can use the precedence constraints, invoking functions if you want (precedence constraints are covered in Lesson 9). You can use the master package to encapsulate multiple child packages for transactional consistency. Parameters and variables from the master package can be controlled globally and shared with the child packages. As you move the batch of packages from one environment to another, you can restrict your parameter and variable issues to the master package. (Environments are covered in Lesson 54 and deployment is covered in Lesson 53.) Master packages also enable you to control package parallelism, reducing processing time in the batch window. You can do this by setting the MaxConcurrentExecutables property of the parent package. The default value is –1, which means the number of logical or physical processors +2.

As you can see from the number of cross-references to other lessons you've already encountered in this lesson, when you are working on a master package, you will use many of the skills you have learned in those other lessons. However, the concept of a master package is quite simple. Think about a data warehouse example. You will have packages that load each dimension, a package to load each fact, and another package that processes each cube in Analysis Services. Part of designing a master package is an exercise is parallelism and dependency.

In the example here and in the Try It that follows later, we have two cubes, each with a single fact and two dimensions. The following bullets indicate which dimensions and facts are used by each cube:

- ➤ Sales Cube
    - ➤ Product Dim
    - ➤ Customer Dim
    - ➤ Sales Fact

➤ Customer Support Cube

    ➤ Employee Dim

    ➤ Customer Dim

    ➤ Employee Customer Calls Fact

Take a look at Figure 40-1. It contains three dimension loads, two fact loads, and two cube builds in the master package. In this master package, each item is processed, one after the other.

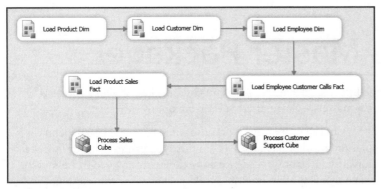

FIGURE 40-1

It does implement some required ordering, as described in the following list:

1. Load dimensions

2. Load facts

3. Process cubes

However, this design can fall short in a couple of ways.

➤ Even though the tasks contained with each child package can run in parallel, only one package will run at a time. There is no parallelism at the package level. This can mean that the entire batch will run unnecessarily long, even when hardware resources like memory, disk throughput, and processor are available.

➤ The second issue relates to unnecessary dependencies. If the Load Product Dim Task fails, neither cube will be processed. The Customer Support Cube will not be processed, even though it does not use the Product Dim.

However, a smarter design will take care of both issues.

Now take a look at Figure 40-2. It contains the same Execute Package Tasks. When the Product and Customer Dim are loaded successfully, the Product Sales Fact can be loaded. When the Product Sales Fact is loaded successfully, the Process Sales Cube can begin. Customer and Employee Dim must load prior to loading the Customer Calls Fact. Once the Customer Calls Fact loads successfully, the Process Customer Support Cube will begin. In this design, if the Product Dim load fails, the Customer Support Cube path can continue and process successfully. Parallelism is improved also, because all three dimensions can be processed in parallel.

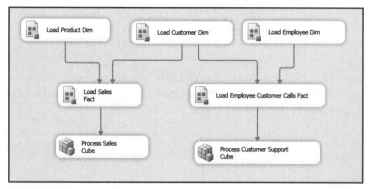

FIGURE 40-2

The way you should think about this is to allow as much as possible to complete, even when things are failing. Only put dependencies in the master package when actual data dependencies exist for the objects contained within.

TRY IT

In this Try It, you create a master package like the one mentioned earlier in this lesson. You replace the Process Cube Tasks with an Execute Package Task that does not require SQL Server Analysis Services. Each one of the packages you call from your master package does nothing but display a message box with the package name. The child packages will not complete until you OK the message boxes they present. This enables you to control when packages complete and offers you the opportunity to closely watch how this works. The purpose of this Try It is to walk you through creating a master package and to give you an easy view of parallelism and package failure results. After you complete this, you will be able to create master packages and control ordering and parallelism of the child packages.

You can download the source packages for this lesson from www.wrox.com.

Lesson Requirements

The only requirement for this lesson is that you download all of the source packages for this lesson, which are available on the book's website at www.wrox.com.

Hints

- ➤ Use only the Execute Package Task.
- ➤ Run and observe the package behavior.

➤ Limit parallelism by setting the MaxConcurrentExecutables property.

➤ Force a package failure and observe the effect of dependency constraints on the flow.

➤ As each package runs, it stops and displays a message box with the package name. You must click OK in the message box for the package to continue.

Step-by-Step

1. Create a new SSIS package called **Lesson40MasterParallel.dtsx** in a new solution. Add the following packages that you downloaded to your new solution. There is no need to re-create these packages. Each package simply displays a message box.

➤ Lesson40LoadProductDim.dtsx

➤ Lesson40LoadCustomerDim.dtsx

➤ Lesson40LoadEmployeeDim.dtsx

➤ Lesson40LoadProductSalesFact.dtsx

➤ Lesson40LoadEmployeeCustomerCallsFact.dtsx

➤ Lesson40ProcessSalesCube.dtsx

➤ Lesson40ProcessCustomerSupportCube.dtsx

2. Drag three Execute Package Tasks onto the Control Flow tab.

3. For the first Execute Package Task, on the General tab type **Load Product Dim** in the Name text box. Choose Package from the tree on the left and select Lesson40LoadProductDim.dtsx in the PackageNameFromProjectReference drop-down list.

4. For the second Execute Package Task, on the General tab, type **Load Customer Dim** in the Name text box. Choose Package from the tree on the left and select Lesson40LoadCustomerDim.dtsx in the PackageNameFromProjectReference drop-down list.

5. For the third Execute Package Task, on the General tab, type **Load Employee Dim** in the Name text box. Choose Package from the tree on the left and select Lesson40LoadEmployeeDim.dtsx in the PackageNameFromProjectReference drop-down list.

When complete, your Control Flow should look like Figure 40-3.

FIGURE 40-3

6. Drag two more Execute Package Tasks onto the Control Flow tab to represent the fact loads.

7. For the first fact Execute Package Task, on the General tab, type **Load Sales Fact** in the Name text box. Choose Package from the tree on the left and select Lesson40LoadSalesFact.dtsx in the PackageNameFromProjectReference drop-down list.

8. For the second fact Execute Package Task, on the General tab, type **Load Employee Customer Calls Fact** in the Name text box. Choose Package from the tree on the left and select Lesson40LoadEmployeeCustomerCallsFact.dtsx in the PackageNameFromProjectReference drop-down list.

9. Drag two more Execute Package Tasks onto the Control Flow tab to represent the cube processing.

10. For the first cube Execute Package Task, on the General tab, type **Process Sales Cube** in the Name text box. Choose Package from the tree on the left and select Lesson40ProcessSalesCube.dtsx in the PackageNameFromProjectReference drop-down list.

11. For the second cube Execute Package Task, on the General tab, type **Process Customer Support Cube** in the Name text box. Choose Package from the tree on the left and select Lesson40ProcessCustomerSupportCube.dtsx in the PackageNameFromProjectReference drop-down list.

12. Now set the precedence constraints:

➤ Connect Load Product Dim to Load Sales Fact

➤ Connect Load Customer Dim to Load Sales Fact

➤ Connect Load Customer Dim to Load Employee Customer Calls Fact

➤ Connect Load Employee Dim to Load Employee Customer Calls Fact

➤ Connect Load Sales Fact to Process Sales Cube

➤ Connect Load Employee Customer Calls Fact to Process Customer Support Cube

Your completed work flow should look like Figure 40-4.

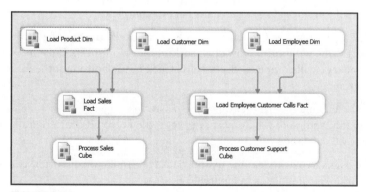

FIGURE 40-4

13. Save and run the package. You will see all of the Load Dim packages run. This is because there is no prior dependency and `MaxConcurrentExecutables` is set to –1. Three message boxes will also be up, each with the name of the task to which it belongs. When you click OK in a message box, the associated task will complete and you can follow through the execution of items in the master package. You may have to Alt+Tab to bring the message boxes to the front. You may also have to move back to your master package to see it. Your initial view should look like Figure 40-5.

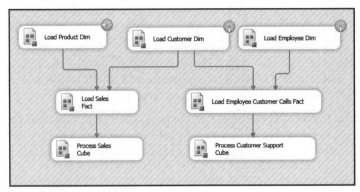

FIGURE 40-5

14. Click OK on the Load Product Dim and Load Employee Dim message boxes. Now go back to your master package. Product and Employee Dim should show a green check for successful completion, but neither of the fact loads have begun. This is because they both depend on success of the Load Customer Dim.

15. Click OK on the Load Customer Dim message box, and review the status of the master package. All load dims will be green and both load facts will be in-process.

16. Click OK on the Load Sales Fact message box. The Process Sales Cube will begin because all of its prior dependencies completed successfully. The Process Customer Support Cube is still waiting for the Load Employee Customer Calls Fact to complete.

17. Click OK on the Load Employee Customer Calls Fact message box, and the Process Customer Support Cube will begin. Now click each of the two Process Cube message boxes and the master package will complete successfully. Click at the bottom of the master package to return to design mode.

18. Next, you look at changing the parallelism of the master package. Click in a blank area of the Control Flow tab, and go to the Properties page of the Lesson40MasterParallel package. Set MaxConcurrentExecutables to 2.

19. Save and run the package. Now view the master package. Unlike the first run, you will see only two child packages running, as in Figure 40-6.

20. Now click through the message boxes. No more than two child packages will run at a time. It is very easy to change the parallelism of your entire batch in this manner. Then return to design mode by clicking at the bottom of the master package.

21. Set the MaxConcurrentExecutables property of the master package back to −1. Save the package.

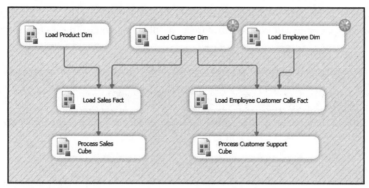

FIGURE 40-6

> **NOTE** *Because your production environment is likely to be more robust than your development environment, you may want to change parallelism. The –1 value will fire off the number of logical\physical processors +2. However, you can have multiple master packages running in parallel. If this is the case, it is a good idea to parameterize the MaxConcurrentExecutions property of the master package. This will enable you to tune parallelism quickly and easily.*

22. Next, you take a look at failure issues. In the master package, select Load Product Dim and go to the Properties window. Set the ForceExecutionResult property to Failure. This causes the Load Product Dim Task to fail.

23. Save and run the master package. All three dimension loads will begin to run. Click OK on the message boxes for all three dimension loads. Load Product Dim will show failure and the other two will show success. Your results should look like Figure 40-7.

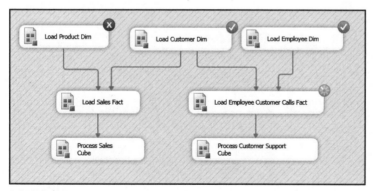

FIGURE 40-7

24. Click through all the message boxes and you're done.

Keeping and using a master package ensures that other packages are run in the correct order. A properly configured master package allows as many tasks as possible to complete, even when some packages fail.

> *Please select Lesson 40 on the DVD, or online at* www.wrox.com/go/ssis2012video, *to view the video that accompanies this lesson.*

SECTION 6
Containers

41

Using Sequence Containers to Organize a Package

Sequence Containers provide a simple and easy method for organizing the flow of a package and can help you divide a package into more manageable pieces. When you first begin exploring the Sequence Container, you may think organization is the only benefit it provides. However, to the creative developer, this container's uses go far beyond simple organization. If you know how to use it, it can also grant you the following capabilities:

➤ Grouping tasks so that you can disable a part of the package that's temporarily not needed

➤ Narrowing the scope of a variable to just the container

➤ Collapsing and expanding the container to hide the tasks within

➤ Managing the properties of multiple tasks in one step by setting the properties of the container

➤ Using one method to ensure that multiple tasks execute successfully before the next task executes

➤ Creating a transaction across a series of data-related tasks, but not on the entire package

➤ Creating event handlers on a single container so that you can send an e-mail if anything inside one container fails, and perhaps even page yourself if anything else fails (event handlers are discussed in more detail in Lesson 48)

To add a Sequence Container to a package, drag and drop the Sequence Container in the design pane just like you would any other task. To have a task as part of the container, just drag the task within the outlined box.

Once tasks have been placed inside the Sequence Container, they can be connected by precedence constraints only to other tasks within the same container. If you attempt to connect a task inside the container to one outside, you receive an error.

TRY IT

In this Try It, you explore how Sequence Containers can be used inside a package. After this lesson, you will have a better idea of the versatility that using Sequence Containers can give you when you are developing your own packages.

You can download the completed Lesson41.dtsx at www.wrox.com.

Lesson Requirements

Create a package with Sequence Containers and test different uses of the container. Just use Script Tasks to test inside the containers because Script Tasks do not require any configuration. You really are just learning more about Sequence Containers in this lesson.

Hints

➤ To do this example, you need three Sequence Containers with three Script Tasks inside each.

Step-by-Step

1. Create a new package and name it **Lesson41** or download the completed Lesson41.dtsx package from www.wrox.com.

2. Drag three Sequence Containers onto your designer and then place three Script Tasks inside each container. Connect the precedence constraints from each container to make your package look like Figure 41-1. Feel free to run this package as is because the Script Task requires no further configuration. The package will complete successfully without changing any data.

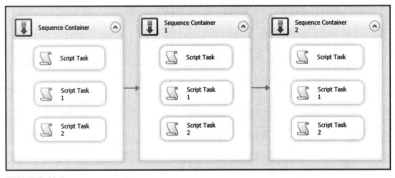

FIGURE 41-1

3. The next several steps will help you better understand the benefits and limitations of this container. First, attempt to connect the precedence constraint from any Script Task inside Sequence Container 1 to any other object in the package. You will receive the error shown in Figure 41-2 because objects inside a Sequence Container cannot be connected to any component outside the container.

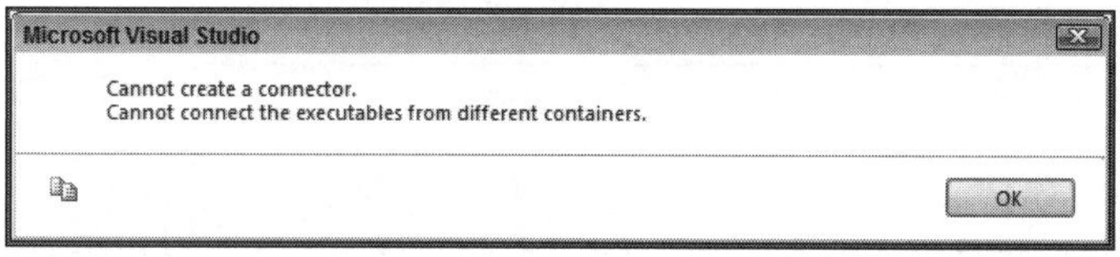

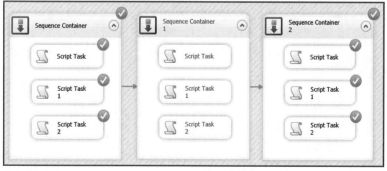

FIGURE 41-2

4. With individual tasks, you can execute a single task while excluding the rest of the package. You can also do this with entire containers. Right-click the first container and click Execute Container to execute just the tasks that are inside the container. Notice that just the first container executes while the rest of the package remains inactive. Once you're ready to go to the next step, click the stop debugging button to continue.

5. Containers also enable you to scope variables exclusive to the contents of the container. Click once on Sequence Container 2 and open the Variables window. Create a variable called **Lesson41** that has a scope set to Sequence Container 2 (creating variables is discussed in Lesson 32).

6. Next, right-click and disable Sequence Container 1 (the container in the middle) and then run the package. The results in Figure 41-3 demonstrate how Sequence Containers enable you to disable entire sections of a package with the container. Though you can't see color in this figure, the outer two containers should have green checkmarks and the middle container is gray, indicating it is disabled. Stop debugging the package.

FIGURE 41-3

7. Finally, you can collapse a container simply by clicking the arrow pointing upward next to the container name. Figure 41-4 shows all three containers collapsed. This action does not change how the package runs, but just hides the content. To expand the containers again, click the arrows that are now pointed down.

FIGURE 41-4

This should give you a basic understanding of how Sequence Containers work. These same principles can be applied to containers that are discussed in the next lessons.

> *Please select Lesson 41 on the DVD, or online at* www.wrox.com/go/ssis2012video, *to view the video that accompanies this lesson.*

42

Using For Loop Containers to Repeat Control Flow Tasks

Loops are a great tool that can be used in many programming languages. They provide a way to iterate over selected code repeatedly until it is conditionally told to stop. For example, in T-SQL a While loop is constructed so that a statement is repeated until a boolean expression evaluates as false. The For Loop Container in SSIS works much the same way.

A common reason that you might use the For Loop Container is if you have a set of Control Flow Tasks that need to be run until a condition has been met. For example, in the Try It section of this lesson, you use a For Loop Container to check to see if a table has any rows of data. If the table has no records, the loop continues to iterate until it finds that at least one row is present.

When you use a For Loop Container, you first create a variable that the container can use to store an expression value of how many times the container has completed a run. The container runs three separate expressions at run time to formulate the loop. These three expressions require only one variable because the expressions change the same variable value each time they evaluate.

To configure the For Loop Container, drag it on the design surface and double-click the top portion of the container to open the editor. Here you see the InitExpression, EvalExpression, and AssignExpression properties:

- ➤ **InitExpression**—This expression sets the initial value of the variable, so if you want the package to perform the loop a set number of times, you will likely start the variable at 1.

- ➤ **EvalExpression**—This expression tells the loop when to stop. This must be an expression that always evaluates to True or False. As soon as it evaluates to False, the loop stops.

- ➤ **AssignExpression**—This expression changes a condition each time the loop repeats. Here you tell the loop to increment or decrement the number of runs the loop has completed.

TRY IT

In this Try It, you explore how the For Loop Container uses expressions to determine how many times to run Control Flow items. The package you create continuously loops until data has been loaded in a table called ForLoop. After this lesson, you will understand how the For Loop Container is used to iterate through Control Flow Tasks a set number of times.

You can download the completed Lesson42.dtsx and the queries used in this lesson from www.wrox.com.

Lesson Requirements

Create the ForLoop table in the AdventureWorks2012 database with the following query:

```
CREATE TABLE ForLoop
    (
    ID int NOT NULL IDENTITY (1, 1),
    Name varchar(50) NULL
    )  ON [PRIMARY]
```

Create a package that runs an Execute SQL Task that checks to see if data has been loaded into the ForLoop table. Create a variable called Counter with an Int32 data type. Place the Execute SQL Task inside a For Loop Container that checks to see if new data has been loaded to the ForLoop table.

Hints

➤ After you start the package, generate an INSERT statement to insert several rows into it.

➤ Once data has been loaded to the ForLoop table, the Execute SQL Task should change the Counter variable and, therefore, complete the package.

Step-by-Step

1. Open SQL Server Management Studio and create the ForLoop table in the AdventureWorks2012 database with the following statement:

   ```
   CREATE TABLE ForLoop
       (
       ID int NOT NULL IDENTITY (1, 1),
       Name varchar(50) NULL
       )  ON [PRIMARY]
   ```

2. After this table is created, open SQL Server Data Tools (SSDT) and create a new package named **Lesson42**, or download the completed Lesson42.dtsx package from www.wrox.com.

3. Create a new OLE DB Connection Manager that uses the AdventureWorks2012 database.

4. Next, open the Variables window by right-clicking on the design surface and selecting Variables. Click the Add Variable button to add a new variable named **intCounter** with an **Int32** data type, as shown in Figure 42-1.

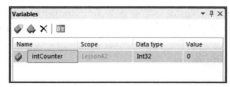

FIGURE 42-1

5. Drag an Execute SQL Task into the Control Flow and open its editor by double-clicking the task.

6. On the General tab, select AdventureWorks2012 as your connection, change the ResultSet to Single row, and type the following query into the SQLStatement property:

```
declare @RecordsInserted int

if exists(select Name
          from ForLoop )
set @RecordsInserted = 1
else

set @RecordsInserted = 0
select @RecordsInserted as RecordsInserted
```

This query checks to see if the ForLoop table has any records, and if it does, it returns the number 1. If no rows are in the table, it returns the number 0. Figure 42-2 shows the editor after these changes have been made.

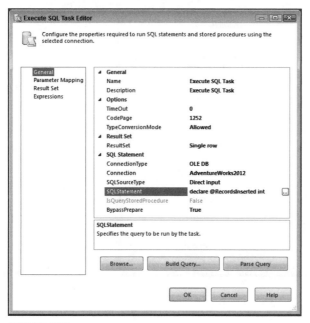

FIGURE 42-2

7. Select the Result Set tab and click Add. In the Result Name column, change the default NewResultName to **RecordsInserted** and keep the Variable Name column the default of User::intCounter. After you make these changes, the results of the Execute SQL Task will be loaded into the variable. After setting up this page, you are done with this editor, so click OK.

8. Now drag a For Loop Container in the Control Flow and place the Execute SQL Task inside the new container.

9. Open the For Loop Editor and make the following changes:

➤ **InitExpression**—@intCounter = 0

➤ **EvalExpression**—@intCounter == 0

➤ **AssignExpression**—Leave blank

> **NOTE** *Remember that variables are case-sensitive, so you must type the variable name exactly how you did when you created it.*

Once these properties have been filled, click OK. Your screen should look like Figure 42-3.

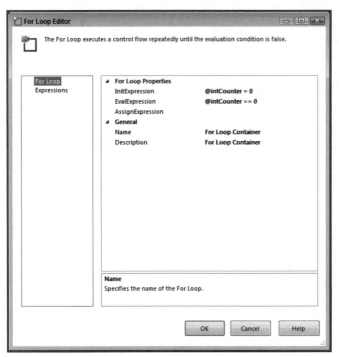

FIGURE 42-3

10. The package is now complete and ready to run. After you execute this package, you will see that because there is currently no data in the ForLoop table, the package will continue to run until new data is inserted into the table.

11. While the package is running, open SQL Server Management Studio and run the following statement to load some records in the ForLoop table:

```
INSERT INTO ForLoop
            (Name)
Select Distinct
LastName
From Person.Person
```

This should cause the package to complete because the loop you created was waiting for new records to be inserted before it could complete. Figure 42-4 shows what the completed Lesson 42 package should look like after these rows have been inserted.

FIGURE 42-4

> *Please select Lesson 42 on the DVD, or online at* www.wrox.com/go/ssis2012video, *to view the video that accompanies this lesson.*

43

Using the Foreach Loop Container to Loop Through a Collection of Objects

The Foreach Loop Container is a very powerful and very useful tool for repeating Control Flow items. It is often used when you have a collection of files to which you want to apply the same changes. If you provide the directory for a set of files, the Foreach Loop Container can apply the same Control Flow tasks to each file. You might ask yourself, how is this different from the For Loop Container? The easy answer is that the For Loop iterates through the content of the container a number of times you define or you define with an expression, whereas the Foreach Loop Container iterates through its content as many times as it takes to effect the full collection.

The configuration of the Foreach Loop Container can differ depending on which enumerator you decide to use. An *enumerator* specifies the collection of objects that the container will loop through. All tasks inside the container will be repeated for each member of a specified enumerator. The Foreach Loop Editor can significantly change depending on what you set for this option:

- ➤ **Foreach File Enumerator**—Performs an action for each file in a directory with a given file extension

- ➤ **Foreach Item Enumerator**—Loops through a list of items that are set manually in the container

- ➤ **Foreach ADO Enumerator**—Loops through a list of tables or rows in a table from an ADO recordset

- ➤ **Foreach ADO.NET Schema Rowset Enumerator**—Loops through an ADO.NET schema

➤ **Foreach From Variable Enumerator**—Loops through a SQL Server Integration Services (SSIS) variable

➤ **Foreach Nodelist Enumerator**—Loops through a node list in an XML document

➤ **Foreach SMO Enumerator**—Enumerates a list of SQL Management Objects (SMO)

To configure the Foreach Loop Container, drag it on the design surface and double-click the top portion of the container to open the editor. Click the Collection tab to choose which type of enumerator you want to use, as shown in Figure 43-1. For example, say you want to loop through a directory to load a group of flat files to a table, so you choose the Foreach File Enumerator. Then you must specify what folder directory the files are in and what kind of file extension they have. Assume the flat files are .txt files, so in the Files box *.txt is used to bring back only the text files in the directory. Last, because the flat files each have a different name, you can use the Variable Mappings tab to dynamically change a variable value for each iteration of the loop. That variable then can pass the correct file name to the Flat File Connection with an expression. Don't worry if this explanation sounds complicated because the following "Try It" section gives you a step-by-step example of how to do this exact scenario.

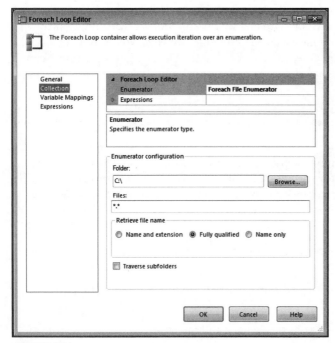

FIGURE 43-1

Another commonly used enumerator is the Foreach ADO Enumerator. This enumerator is handy for looping through a set of records and executing every task inside the container for each record in that set. For example, you want to run each task in your package for every database on a server. With the Foreach ADO Enumerator, you could loop through a table that lists all the database names on your server and dynamically change a connection manager's database name for each iteration of the loop.

TRY IT

In this Try It, you create a package that uses the most common type of enumerator, the Foreach File Enumerator, to loop through a collection of flat files and load them to a table. After this lesson, you will understand how to use the Foreach Loop Container to loop through a collection of files and load each to a table.

You can download the completed Lesson43.dtsx and the sample files used in this lesson from www.wrox.com.

Lesson Requirements

Download the four flat files named File 1.txt, File 2.txt, File 3.txt, and File 4.txt from www.wrox.com to use as your source. Save these files to the C:\Projects\SSISPersonalTrainer\Lesson 43 directory.

Create a table named ForEachLoop in the AdventureWorks2012 database to load each flat file into.

Use a Foreach Loop Container to loop through and load each file in the C:\Projects\SSISPersonalTrainer\Lesson 43 directory.

Hints

➤   Create a variable to store the location of the file that currently needs to be loaded. The loop will change the variable location after each run.

➤   Use this variable as an expression for the connection manager that points to the flat file.

Step-by-Step

1.   Create a new package and name it **Lesson43** or download the completed Lesson43.dtsx package from www.wrox.com.

2.   Drag a Data Flow Task onto your designer and name it **DFT - Load Flat Files**.

3.   Create a new Flat File Connection Manager, name it **File Extract**, and point it to File 1.txt in the following directory: C:\Projects\SSISPersonalTrainer\Lesson 43\File 1.txt. Also, check the Column names in the first data row option and go to the Columns page to ensure all the columns are defined properly; then click OK.

4.   In the Data Flow, bring a new Flat File Source over and name it **File Extract**. Open the Flat File Source Editor by double-clicking the Flat File Source and make the connection manager the newly created File Extract. Then click OK.

5. Next, create another connection manager, this time an OLE DB Connection Manager, using the AdventureWorks2012 database.

6. Bring an OLE DB Destination in the Data Flow and connect the Data Flow path from the source to it. Open the editor and set the OLE DB Connection Manager to AdventureWorks2012. Create a new table with the following SQL statement by clicking New next to the table selection drop-down box:

```
CREATE TABLE [ForEachLoop] (
    [Name] varchar(50),
    [State] varchar(50)
)
```

Ensure the columns are mapped correctly; then click OK. Your Data Flow should now look like Figure 43-2.

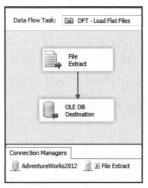

FIGURE 43-2

7. Your package is now set up to run just one file, but because you have four, you now go back to the Control Flow and drag over a Foreach Loop Container.

8. Place the Data Flow Task inside the Foreach Loop Container; then open the Foreach Loop Editor by double-clicking the top banner portion of the container. On the Collections tab, select Foreach File Enumerator from the Enumerator property drop-down box. The Foreach File Enumerator is the default when you open the editor.

9. Now, set the Folder property to the **C:\Projects\SSISPersonalTrainer\Lesson 43** directory and the Files property to ***.txt** because you want to bring back all the text files in the directory. Everything else you can leave as the default. After you make these changes, your editor should look like Figure 43-3.

10. On the Variable Mappings tab create a new variable called **strFlatFileLocation** by selecting <New Variable...> from the Variable drop-down box. Figure 43-4 shows the Add Variable dialog box.

FIGURE 43-3

FIGURE 43-4

11. This variable's value will change to the current file it is loading each time the container runs. In this specific case, after File 1.txt is completed, the container will automatically change the variable's value to the next filename. After the variable is created, click OK. The Variable Mappings tab should look like Figure 43-5. Click OK again to return to the Data Flow.

FIGURE 43-5

12. The last step is to put an expression on the File Extract Connection Manager that uses the variable you just created inside the Foreach Loop Container. Select the File Extract Connection Manager called File Extract from your list of connection managers and press F4 to bring up the Properties window. Click the ellipsis next to the Expressions property to open the Property Expressions Editor. Select ConnectionString from the Property drop-down and then click the ellipsis in the Expression box.

13. In the top left of the Expression Builder, expand the Variables and Parameters folder and drag @[User::strFlatFileLocation] down into the Expression box. If you try to click Evaluate Expression now, there will be no result. Remember that this expression will be populated at run time, so you will see nothing here yet. Your screen should look like Figure 43-6. Click OK twice to return to the Data Flow.

14. The package is now complete. A successful run will loop through and load all the files in the C:\Projects\SSISPersonalTrainer\Lesson 43 directory to the ForEachLoop table in the AdventureWorks2012 database. Figure 43-7 shows what a successful run should look like.

FIGURE 43-6

FIGURE 43-7

Please select Lesson 43 on the DVD, or online at www.wrox.com/go/ssis2012video, *to view the video that accompanies this lesson.*

SECTION 7
Configuring Packages

44

Easing Deployment with Configuration Tables

Once you have completed a set of packages, the challenge is to deploy those packages to a production environment without having to manually reconfigure them for that environment. For example, you may have to get source files from a different directory or the source databases may be on a different server than your production environment.

> **NOTE** *New project deployment options in SSIS 2012 use parameters and environments. These are covered in Lessons 33, 53, 54, and 57. This chapter and the next cover configuration tables and configuration files, which are still supported in the current release. You must decide if the packages in your project will use the new project deployment model or the package deployment model.*

Configuration tables help automate migration and reduce the risk of deployment-related errors. You can use a configuration table that contains the ConnectionString property value for each connection. Each package that uses the connection can obtain the ConnectionString from the configuration table. As part of the initial deployment to production, you create another configuration table, like the one used in development. You then copy the rows from the development configuration table to the production configuration table, changing the values for the ConnectionStrings to point to production sources and destinations. When the packages are moved to production, you can change the configuration table's server name from the development server to the production server.

This capability is not limited to connection strings. The SSIS Package Configuration option enables you to store any SSIS property for the package, connection, container, variable, or any task into a table. You will have a configuration table in the development environment that contains values for all of the properties that need to be changed for production. A similar configuration table will exist in production, but you will set values of the properties appropriately for production.

For example, say your source database server name in the development environment is TestSQL and in production it is Prod. Your configuration table in both environments would contain a row that defines the connection property of the source database connection manager. However, the values contained in the row in the development environment refer to TestSQL, and the production row refers to Prod. While the package is in development, the development configuration table is used. When the package is moved to the production server, it is configured to use the production configuration table. Once set up, this process makes deployment easier, repeatable, and less error-prone.

Here is an example where you use a configuration table to set the connection string for your source database.

First, create a project and an empty package. Add a connection manager to the package. For this example, you can use any database on any server. After you have created the connection manager, change its name to **SourceDatabase**.

To use tables for configuration, your project must use the package deployment model. Because this is not the default, you must convert your project. Right-click your project and choose Convert to Package Deployment Model. You can see how to do this in Figure 44-1.

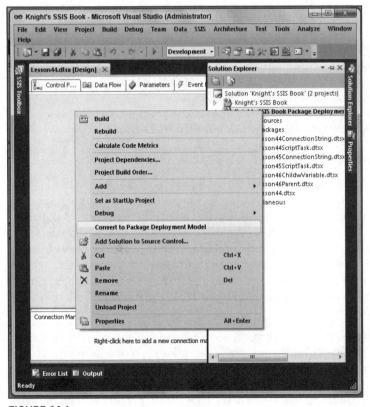

FIGURE 44-1

SSIS performs a check to ensure the packages in your project are compatible with package deployment and provides a report, as in Figure 44-2. Click OK. All of the packages within this project will be converted.

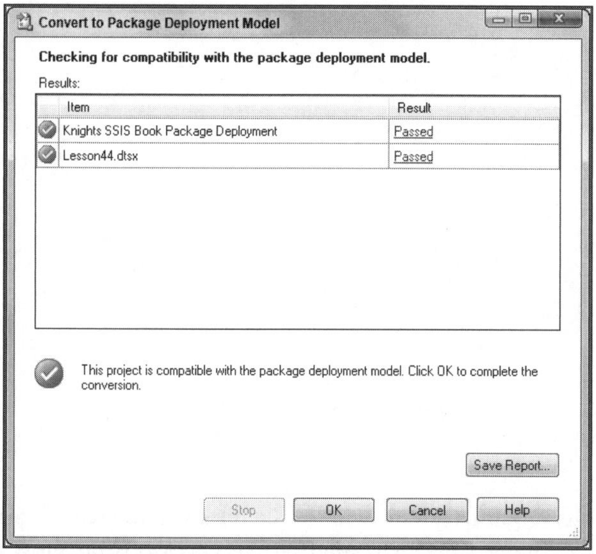

FIGURE 44-2

Create another connection manager that points to the development server where you will place the configuration table. Name this configuration manager **ConfigurationDatabase**.

> **NOTE** *It is a best practice to use a separate connection manager for the configuration database and to use this connection manager only for configuration. This is true even if the configuration table exists in a database that is also used as a source database.*

First you create the configuration table and then set the connection property for the SourceDatabase Connection Manager.

To create the configuration table for a package, right-click in the blank area of the package in the Control Flow window and choose Package Configurations, as shown in Figure 44-3.

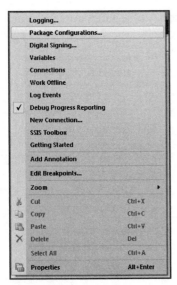

FIGURE 44-3

This action opens the Package Configurations Organizer. This window enables you to create, edit, and delete package configurations. Check the Enable package configurations check box, as shown in Figure 44-4.

FIGURE 44-4

To create the connection to the configuration table, click the Add button at the bottom of the Package Configurations Organizer. This starts the Package Configuration Wizard. The first time you add a configuration table, you see a welcome screen; you can check the option to not show this page again if you prefer. Click Next to move on.

On the next screen, select SQL Server from the Configuration Type drop-down menu. With SQL Server as the type, you can create your connection table in any SQL Server database. You can click the New button to the right of the Connection drop-down to create an OLE DB connection to a SQL Server instance. Choose the ConfigurationDatabase Connection Manager you created earlier. This connection is strictly for the package's connection to the configuration table. Data in this table contains connection strings and other configuration property values. You will store the connection string for the SourceDatabase in this table.

After you have selected the SQL connection, select the table to use. There is a default table named SSIS_Configurations. You can choose a preexisting configuration table in the database, if one exists. You can also create a new table. To create a new table, click the New button next to the Configuration Table drop-down menu. This opens the SQL query that creates the table.

Many packages may use the same configuration table. You can group collections of properties together and give them a name called a filter name. A package may request a particular set of configuration rows by using the filter name. You can choose a previously defined collection by choosing the filter from the drop-down, or you can type in a new filter name. You need to make this name broad yet descriptive. You will see this filter listed when you set up configuration rows in this table for other packages. In this example, this group of configurations contains only the connection string for your source database, which is your Enterprise Resource Planning (ERP) system. Therefore, you will create a filter called "ERPSource." Once you select the SQL Server and the table, the window should look like Figure 44-5.

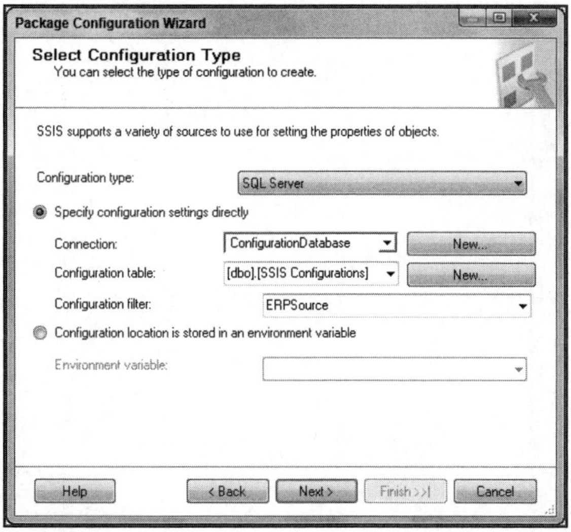

FIGURE 44-5

After you click Next, you see the list of objects in the package and the attributes for those objects. You can place a check next to each attribute you want to include for this filter in the objects list in the left pane. In the right pane, type the value that will be stored in the configuration table for the selected property. Check the ConnectionString property for the SourceDatabase connection. Then you can set the value for this property in the right pane, as in Figure 44-6.

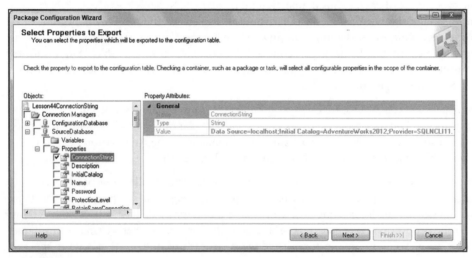

FIGURE 44-6

Now you can click Next and go to the final configuration window, where you can name the configuration. This name is used for reference in this package only. You also see the configuration type, connection name, table, filter, and the target property (Figure 44-7).

FIGURE 44-7

Click Finish to return to the Package Configurations Organizer. You can now see the new configuration listed in this window, as shown in Figure 44-8. Your configuration contains the connection string that is used to connect to the source database for your extract process. The Add, Edit, and Remove buttons at the bottom of this window enable you to alter or remove the existing configuration tables and add new ones.

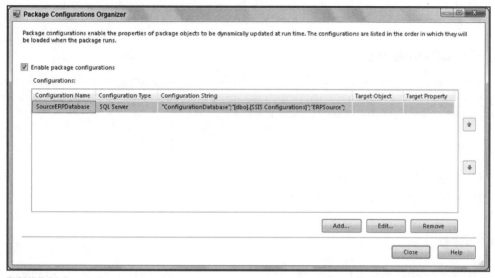

FIGURE 44-8

Once you have a configuration defined for a package, the package will use the property values from the configuration table instead of the design-time values stored in the package.

> **NOTE** *A common issue in troubleshooting occurs when you have a problem with a connection. It seems as if the data is coming from or going to the wrong place. You change the connection string in the package, but the behavior remains unchanged. You may have forgotten that the connection information in the configuration table is overriding the settings in the package. If you find yourself troubleshooting a connection, it is a good idea to disable package configurations first.*

If some properties included in the filter group do not exist in the package, they are simply ignored. For instance, if your filtered collection contains some properties for a connection named DestinationDB and that connection does not exist in your package, there is no error, and those configuration rows are not used for this package.

TRY IT

In this Try It, you learn how to create a configuration table and use the data from the configuration table. After this lesson, you should understand how configuration tables are used to pass information into a package.

The completed packages for this lesson are available for download on the book's website at www.wrox.com.

Lesson Requirements

In this lesson, you create a simple package with a Script Task that pops up a message with the configuration value instead of the value saved in the package. Then you create a configuration table and run the package to see the value in the configuration table.

Hints

- ➤ You need only a Script Task.
- ➤ The value of the string is the value used in the configuration table.

Step-by-Step

1. Create a package named **Lesson44ScriptTask**. Create a String variable named **strConfigTest** in a new package. The package must be contained in a project that has been converted to the package deployment model, described earlier in the lesson.

2. Choose String as the data type and set the value of the variable to **HardCoded**.

3. Drag a Script Task into the Control Flow and double-click it.

4. Select Microsoft Visual Basic 2010 as the script language for the task.

5. Select the variable you just created as a read-write variable in the ReadWriteVariable field.

6. Click the Edit Script button and type the following code in the Script Task where it states "Add your Code here":

   ```
   MsgBox(Dts.Variables("strConfigTest").Value)
   ```

7. Close the Script Task Editor and click OK in the Script Task.

8. Right-click in the Control Flow and select Package Configurations.

9. Check Enable Package Configurations. Click Add. Click Next in the wizard welcome screen (if it appears).

10. Set the Configuration Type as SQL Server.

11. Set the SQL Connection to AdventureWorks2012. You may have to create a new connection.

12. Select the SSIS_Configurations table (click New and create it if does not exist).

13. Set the Configuration Filter to strConfigTestVariable. Click Next.

14. Place a check in the Value attribute of the strConfigTest variable, as in Figure 44-9. (Do not provide an actual value.)

15. Click Next.

FIGURE 44-9

16. Name the configuration **Config Variable**. Click Finish.

17. Click Close in the Package Configurations Organizer.

18. Run the package and a popup appears with the text "HardCoded." Click OK to close the popup. Switch back to design mode.

19. Open SQL Server Management Studio.

20. Navigate to the SSIS_Configurations table in the AdventureWorks2012 database. Right-click the table and select Edit Top 200 Rows.

21. Change the Configured Value from HardCoded to Config Data. Press Enter.

22. Run the package again, and you should see a popup box with the text "Config Data."

FINAL DEPLOYMENT

In most cases, the connections you need will be different in each environment. For example, in development, you may have a SQL server named Dev. However, in production the server is named Prod. As you move your package from development to production, the connections will have to change. To reduce the possibility of newly introduced errors, you should be able to change the configuration from development to production without having to open, edit, and re-save your package. This is how you handle the final deployment to production.

After you have created the configuration tables in both development and production and set the values appropriately, you have one more thing to do. The connection string that points to the configuration table will need to be different in production. You can set this in several ways:

➤ Provide the connection string in SQL Agent.

➤ Provide the connection string on the command line when using DTExec or DTExecUI.

➤ Create an environment variable with the same name on both the development and production servers. The value of this variable is the connection string that points to the configuration table. Then you can create another package configuration that sets the configuration table connection string from the value obtained from the environment variable.

You can learn more about deployment and scheduling of packages in Lessons 53 and 59.

> *Please select Lesson 44 on the DVD, or online at* www.wrox.com/go/ssis2012video, *to view the video that accompanies this lesson.*

45

Easing Deployment with Configuration Files

In the previous lesson, you used tables to configure package properties. In this lesson, you learn that you can also use files to store configuration information for your packages. The goal of safe deployment with minimal changes is the same, but in this lesson, you reach your goal using files instead of tables. The SSIS Package Configuration option enables you to store values for any SSIS property for a package, connection, container, variable, or task. You can store these values in tables, as discussed in the previous lesson, or in an XML file.

Functionally, the process works the same whether the configuration uses a table or XML files. The value in the configuration file is used instead of the design value used during development of the package.

One of the advantages of an XML configuration is that deployment becomes easier. Copying the production version XML files is simpler than adding rows to a configuration table. Versioning is better also, because this method is more compatible with most source control systems.

In practice, you create a version of the configuration file for each environment. Each version contains the property settings appropriate for one environment. Then each file is copied to the same directory name on each of the servers. Once you set this up one time, all future deployments will not require any changes to the packages or the configuration files. Future deployments will be less error prone because they will not require any manual configuration-related changes.

To start, create a new package and add a connection manager. The connection manager can point to anything; here you use it to set the connection string. Name the connection manager **AdventureWorksSource**.

To use files for configuration, the project where your package resides must use the package deployment model. To convert your project to the package deployment model, right-click your project and choose Convert to Package Deployment Model. To create a configuration file for a package, right-click in the blank area of the package in the Control Flow and choose Package Configurations, as shown in Figure 45-1. This action opens the Package Configurations Organizer. In this window, you can create, edit, and delete package configuration files. First, check the Enable package configurations check box, as shown in Figure 45-2.

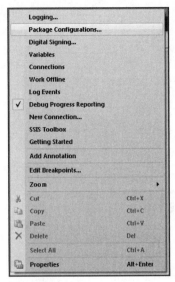

FIGURE 45-1

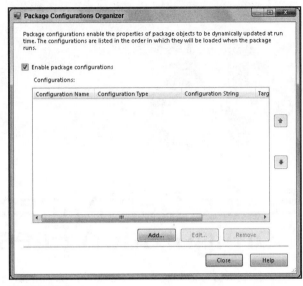

FIGURE 45-2

To create the configuration file, click the Add button at the bottom of the Package Configurations Organizer. This button starts the Package Configuration Wizard. The first time you add a configuration file you see a welcome screen. You can check the option to prevent the display of this page again if you prefer. Click Next.

Select XML Configuration File as the configuration type, and the location can be anywhere on the filesystem. You can click Browse to find a location or choose and reuse an existing configuration file. We use C:\Projects\SSISPersonalTrainer\Config\AdventureWorks2012.dtsConfig in the example. Be sure to name the configuration file something logical and descriptive about what the file contains. Once you select the type and configuration file location, the window should look like Figure 45-3.

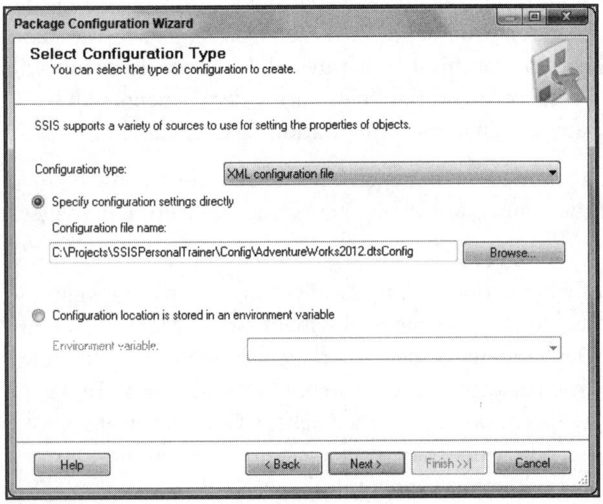

![Package Configuration Wizard dialog showing Select Configuration Type screen with XML configuration file selected and configuration file name field set to C:\Projects\SSISPersonalTrainer\Config\AdventureWorks2012.dtsConfig]

FIGURE 45-3

After you click Next, you see the list of objects in the package and the properties for those objects. Place a check next to each property you want to include in the configuration file. For example, when using the configuration file for a connection, you can select the ConnectionString attribute for the AdventureWorksSource, as in Figure 45-4. You do not have to change the connection string property at this time. You set it later using a configuration file.

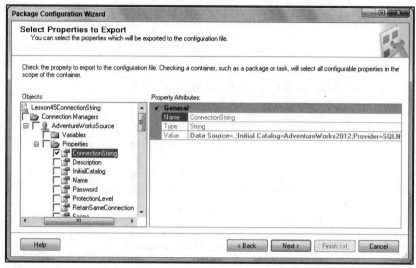

FIGURE 45-4

Click Next, and you see the final configuration window. Give the configuration a name. This name is used for reference in the package only. You also see the configuration type, filename, and properties along with the statement that a new configuration file will be created, as shown in Figure 45-5.

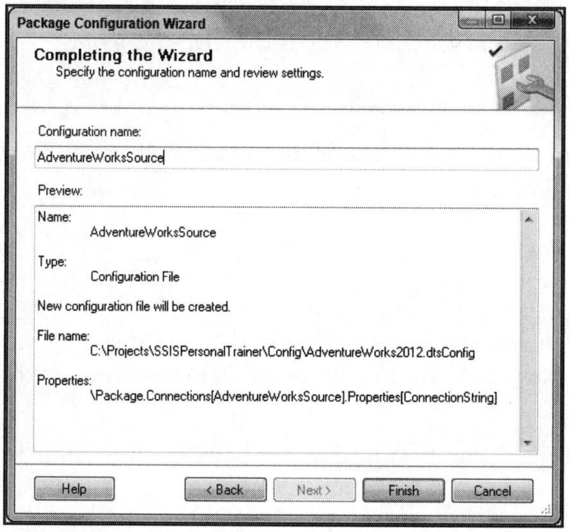

Package Configuration Wizard

Completing the Wizard
Specify the configuration name and review settings.

Configuration name:

AdventureWorksSource

Preview:

Name:
        AdventureWorksSource

Type:
        Configuration File

New configuration file will be created.

File name:
        C:\Projects\SSISPersonalTrainer\Config\AdventureWorks2012.dtsConfig

Properties:
        \Package.Connections[AdventureWorksSource].Properties[ConnectionString]

Help   < Back   Next >   Finish   Cancel

FIGURE 45-5

Click Finish to return to the Package Configurations Organizer. You now see the new configuration file listed in this window, as in Figure 45-6. Add, Edit, and Remove buttons at the bottom of this window enable you to alter or remove the existing configuration files and add new ones. You can add multiple configurations for a package. They are evaluated from the top configuration to the bottom.

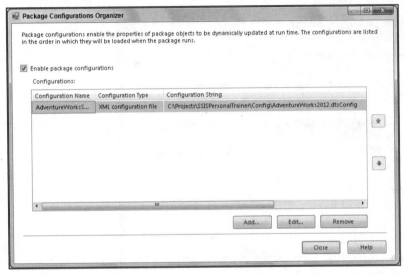

FIGURE 45-6

Once you have associated a configuration file with a package, property values from the file override any settings stored with the package.

> **NOTE** *Remember, as in the prior lesson, it is easy to forget that some properties are set from a configuration file. If you find yourself wondering why a property you just set directly in the package does not seem to work, it may have been over-ridden in the configuration file.*

Unlike how things worked in table configurations, any properties defined in an XML configuration file that do not exist in the package return an error.

TRY IT

In this Try It, you learn how to create a configuration file and show the data from the configuration file. After this lesson, you should understand how configuration files are used to pass information into a package.

The completed packages for this lesson are available for download on the book's website at www.wrox.com.

Lesson Requirements

In this example, you first create a simple package with a Script Task that pops up a message with the configuration value instead of the value saved in the package. Then you create a configuration file and run the package to see the value in the configuration file.

Hints

➤ You need only a Script Task.

➤ The value of the string is the value used in the configuration file.

Step-by-Step

1. Create a new package named **Lesson45ScriptTask**. Create a String variable named **strConfigTest** in the new package. The package must be contained in a project that has been converted to the package deployment model, described earlier in the lesson.

2. Choose String as the data type and set the value of the variable to **HardCoded**.

3. Drag a Script Task into the Control Flow and double-click it.

4. Select Microsoft Visual Basic 2010 as the script language for the task.

5. Select the variable you just created as a read-write variable in the ReadWriteVariable field.

6. Click the Edit Script button and type the following code in the Script Task where it states "Add your Code here":

```
MsgBox(Dts.Variables("strConfigTest").Value)
```

7. Close the Script Task Editor and click OK in the Script Task.

8. Right-click in the Control Flow and select Package Configurations.

9. Check the Enable package configurations check box. Click Add. Click Next in the wizard welcome screen (if it appears).

10. Leave the configuration type as XML Configuration File.

11. Set the Configuration File Name to **C:\Projects\SSISPersonalTrainer\Config\ConfigTest .dtsConfig**. Click Next.

12. Place a check in the Value attribute of the strConfigTest variable, as in Figure 45-7. (Do not change the actual value.)

13. Click Next.

14. Name the configuration **Config Variable**. Click Finish.

15. Click Close in the Package Configurations Organizer.

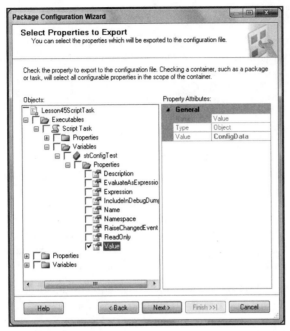

FIGURE 45-7

16. Run the package and a popup appears with the text "HardCoded." Click OK to close the popup. Switch back to design mode.

17. Navigate to the configuration file and open with a text editor.

18. Change the value from **HardCoded** to **ConfigData**. Save the file.

19. Run the package again, and you should see a popup box with the text "ConfigData."

FINAL DEPLOYMENT

It is easy to introduce bugs into your packages whenever you reopen and save them. That is why it is important and worthwhile to use deployment practices designed to allow configuration without touching the package itself. This lesson and the previous one have given you the information you need to deploy your packages safely.

Now that you have created the configuration files in both development and production and set the values appropriately, you have one more thing to do. Your configuration file has the information needed to configure the package. The XML configuration is a file that might live in a different folder on the production server than where the file existed during development. So how will the package find the configuration file after you moved it to this different location on the production server? Remember that the configuration file also has a connection string that contains the filename and directory. A package can locate the configuration file in several ways:

➤ Create a directory path that is the same on every server and place the file in that directory.

➤ Provide the connection string in SQL Agent.

➤ Provide the connection string on the command line when using DTExec or DTExecUI.

➤ Create an environment variable with the same name on both the development and production servers. The value of this variable is the connection string that points to the configuration file. Then you can create another package configuration that sets the configuration file connection string from the value obtained from the environment variable.

You can learn more about deployment and scheduling of packages in Lessons 53 and 59.

> *Please select Lesson 45 on the DVD, or online at* www.wrox.com/go/ssis2012video, *to view the video that accompanies this lesson.*

46

Configuring Child Packages

After creating many packages in your environment, you can see that some common pieces of work are done in multiple packages. You can extract these common functions and place them in separate packages that can be shared more easily. In a data warehouse environment, dimensions are processed before fact loads. In this case, you want packages to be executed in a particular order. The use of child packages can simplify both cases. A *child package* is a package executed from another package. The package that executes another package is called a *parent package*. The parent package calls the child package by using the Execute Package Task in the Control Flow.

The Execute Package Task can be placed anywhere in the Control Flow of a parent package just like any of the tasks in the Toolbox. You can use expressions and precedence constraints to decide if the Execute Package Task runs in the parent package, enabling you to control when and if the child package executes. The child package does not have to be the last task in the parent package.

When the child package completes, it reports its success or failure status to the Execute Package Task in the parent package. Other tasks can follow the Execute Package Task, linked by precedence constraints. The setting of the precedence constraint, compared to the child package status, determines whether or not the following tasks will run. This operates like any other task using a precedence constraint. When a child package fails to run, the parent package does not report the error from the child package. The message from the parent package only states "Task (*Name of the Execute Package Task*) Failed." This message is not very descriptive and does not tell you what step failed in the child package. In prior versions of SQL Server, it was common to run the child package separately from BIDS and do troubleshooting from there. New logging capabilities in SSIS 2012 allow better logging options that can be useful here. Troubleshooting a package is covered in more detail in Lesson 49.

> **NOTE** *Business Intelligence Development Studio (BIDS) was replaced by SQL Server Development Tools (SSDT) in SQL Server 2012.*

Once you begin to use the Execute Package Task, you need to think about how you will pass configuration information to the child tasks. You can choose to have each child package share the same configuration files or tables as the parent. Another way to do this is to have the parent package pass the information to the children.

CONFIGURING AN EXECUTE PACKAGE TASK

Drag in an Execute Package Task to the Control Flow and double-click it to open its editor. The first screen of the Execute Package Task Editor shows the General node with some basic properties of the task. Under the General node, you see the name and description of the Execute Package Task.

➤ The **name** is displayed on the tasks in the Control Flow.

➤ The **description** describes the purpose of the Execute Package Task.

As a best practice, always provide values for these properties.

The next node on the left pane is the Package node. The properties on this page indicate where the child package can be located and how it should run.

The first property, new to SQL 2012, is the Reference Type property. This property contains the deployment model used for the child package. You can choose between the new project deployment model (Project Reference) or the legacy package deployment model (External Reference). If you choose Project Reference, your child package can be chosen from the list of packages in the same project as the parent.

If you choose the External Reference, the Location property will be added to the window. The Location property can be either SQL Server or File System. Select SQL Server if the child package you want to execute is stored on SQL Server. If the child package is stored on the filesystem, select File System.

> **NOTE** *When referring to a folder, remember that the folder path must be valid on the server where the package will execute. As you move this package from development to production, you may need to set the location of the child packages via a configuration.*

If you select SQL Server as the Location, your next two options are Connection and Package Name. The connection will be an OLE DB Connection to the SQL Server where the package is stored. Once you have the connection set in the connection manager, you can see it in the Connection drop-down in this menu. You can also click the <New connection...> option in the drop-down menu and open the OLE DB Connection Manager Editor. This editor creates the OLE DB connection to the SQL Server in the connection manager of the package.

After you select the connection in the Execute Package Task, the package name shows all of the packages on that SQL Server. Clicking the ellipsis next to the Package Name property opens the Select Package window showing the Packages folder of the SQL Server. The Data Collector and Maintenance Plans folders on the server are listed in this window, as shown in Figure 46-1. We are only interested in the Packages folder.

As mentioned earlier in the lesson, when the child package is stored on the filesystem, you need to select File System from the Location drop-down menu. When this File System option is selected, the Package property changes to PackageNameReadOnly and that property becomes grayed out. The PackageNameReadOnly property is not needed in this situation because the name of the package will be in the file location selected in the Connection property.

The Connection drop-down now lets you select a file on the filesystem. If you do not have the connection created in the connection manager, you can select the <New connection...> option and create the file connection. Once the file connection exists in the connection manager, you can select it in the Connection drop-down menu.

FIGURE 46-1

The next property of the Execute Package Task is Password. If the child package is saved with password protection, you must provide the valid password. If the child package does not have a password, you can leave this field unchanged. Although the password property shows asterisks in the field as a default, as shown in Figure 46-2, this does not mean a password is entered into the task. Clicking the ellipsis next to the Password property opens the Password Property Editor.

FIGURE 46-2

If the package you want to execute has a password, you need to enter the password twice and click OK to save the password (Figure 46-3). Saving the password does not make any changes to the asterisks in the Password property. If you are unsure if a password is set and want to remove a password, leave both password fields blank in the Password Property Editor and click OK.

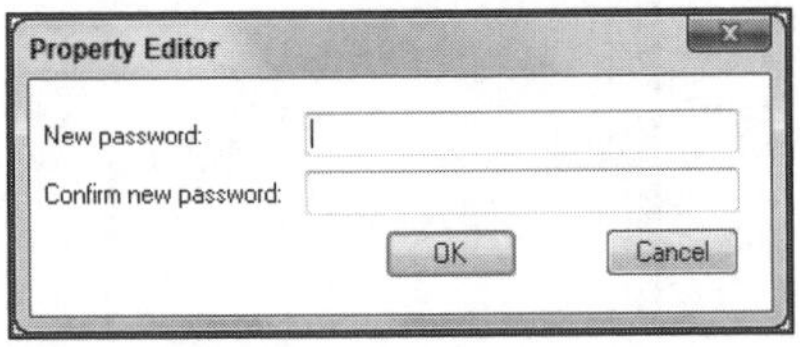

FIGURE 46-3

The next property is ExecuteOutofProcess. When this property is set to True, the child package runs in a separate process from the parent package. Running a child package in a separate process uses more memory, but it provides more flexibility. Running the child package in a separate process allows the parent package to continue when the child package fails, which is useful when you have other tasks in the parent package that you want to complete regardless of the success of the child package.

When you need the parent and child packages to fail together as one unit, you need to leave the ExecuteOutofProcess property set to False. Leave this property set to False also when you do not want to incur the additional overhead of another process.

CONFIGURING A CHILD PACKAGE

In most situations involving a parent package and child package, you are going to need to pass information from the parent package to the child package. It is very easy to pass parent parameters and parent variable values to parameters defined in the child package. (The use of parameters is discussed in Lesson 33.) Though the specific steps for configuring a child package are part of the Try It later in this lesson, the general approach is as follows.

First, you create a package to be used as a child, and include a parameter in the child package.

Now create another task that will serve as the parent task. Create a variable or parameter in the parent package. Drag an Execute Package Task onto the Control Flow window, and double-click it to open the editor. Be sure to enter a descriptive value for the Name and Description fields. Choose the Package tree item on the left. Then choose Project Reference as the ReferenceType. Set the PackageNameFromProjectReference to the name of the child package you just created.

Choose Parameter bindings from the left tree. This is where you map parent or project parameters and variables into the child parameter. Click the Add button. On the left you will see a list of all the child package parameters. On the right you will see a list of all the project and package parameters and variables in the parent. Choose the child parameter and then choose the parent value that should be passed into the child parameter. Figure 46-4 shows a parent package parameter named ParentPackageParm whose value will be passed to the child parameter named ChildPackageParm.

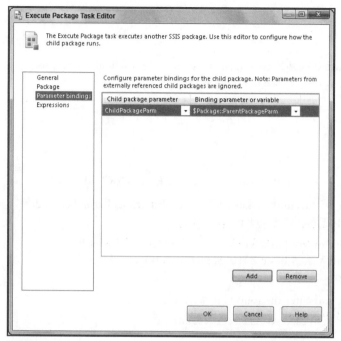

FIGURE 46-4

When using this approach, you would create a parameter in the child package for each property you want to configure. The parent would have corresponding parameters that are passed to the children.

TRY IT

In this Try It, you create a parent package and a child package. You pass a parameter from the parent to the child. After you complete this lesson, you should understand the relationship between a parent and child package and how to pass information between them.

You can download the completed parent and child packages for this lesson from www.wrox.com. The parent package is Lesson46Parent.dtsx, and the child package is Lesson46Child.dtsx.

Lesson Requirements

Your packages must live in a project that uses the project deployment model, which is the default model for SSIS 2012.

Create a child package with a parameter named **ChildPackageParm**. The child package will use a Script Task to display the value of the parameter. Create a parent package with a parameter named **ParentPackageParm**. Using an Execute Package Task, execute the child package and pass the parent parameter value to the child.

Hints

➤ You need two packages.

➤ The value of the variable should be different in each package. This will allow you to see which package provides the value you see in the message box.

➤ The Script Task code is `msgbox(DTS.Variables("ChildPackageParm").Value)`.

Step-by-Step

1. Create a package to be used as the child. Name the package **Lesson46Child.dtsx**.

2. Create a package parameter in the child package named **ChildPackageParm**. Set its data type to string and its value to ChildPackageParm.

3. Drag a Script Task onto the Control Flow window and double-click it. Set the Script Language to Microsoft Visual Basic 2010. Set ReadOnlyVariables to $Package::ChildPackageParm.

4. Click the Edit Script button and enter the following script:

   ```
   MsgBox(DTS.Variables("ChildPackageParm").Value)
   ```

5. Chose the File menu option and select Save All to save and close the Script Editor. Then click OK to close the Script Task Editor.

6. Save and run the child package. You should see a message box display "ChildPackageParm". Your child package is now working correctly.

7. Now create a package named **Lesson46Parent.dtsx**.

8. Create a package parameter in the parent package named **ParentPackageParm**. Set its data type to string and its value to ParentPackageParm.

9. Drag an Execute Package Task onto the Control Flow window, name it **Execute Child with Parameter**, and double-click it.

10. Select the Package tree item on the left. In the right pane, choose Reference Type = Project Reference, and PackageNameFromProjectReference = Lesson46Child.dtsx. Your window should look like Figure 46-5.

11. Choose Parameter bindings from the list at the left. Choose ChildPackageParm in the Child package parameter list and choose $Package::ParentPackageParm in the Binding parameters or variable list. Your window should look like Figure 46-4, shown earlier in the lesson. Click OK to close the Execute Package Task Editor.

12. Save and run the parent package.

13. The child package should run and the message box should now display ParentPackageValue instead of the original value.

FIGURE 46-5

Please select Lesson 46 on the DVD, or online at www.wrox.com/go/ssis2012video, *to view the video that accompanies this lesson.*

SECTION 8
Troubleshooting SSIS

47

Logging Package Data

Most businesses want to keep track of the packages running on their servers. The logging options in SSIS enable you to record package information at run time. This lesson shows you how to use those built-in logging options. There is a whole new logging ability built into the SSIS catalog covered in Lesson 52.

> **NOTE** *Although the logging options built into SSIS are limited, you have other ways to log information. One example is creating Execute SQL Tasks in the event handlers and passing in the system variables. However, creating and maintaining this type of logging can be time-consuming. Software is also available that creates a robust auditing framework on your packages, such as BI xPress from Pragmatic Works, Inc.*

To set up logging with the built-in SSIS logging option, right-click in the Control Flow of a package and select Logging. This action opens the Configure SSIS Logs window, as shown in Figure 47-1. To log information from the package you need to place a check next to the package name in the left pane.

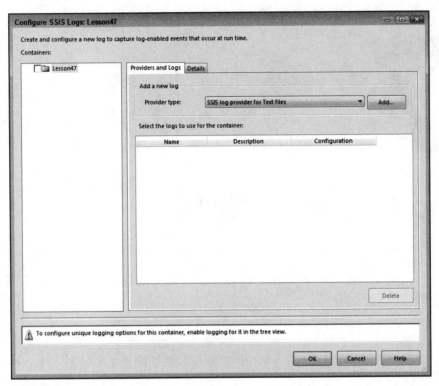

FIGURE 47-1

The drop-down menu of provider types has the available logging locations where you can save the information from the package. The options are as follows:

➤ **Windows Event Log**—The Windows Event Log option logs the data to the Windows Event Log.

➤ **Text File**—The Text File option saves the information into a plaintext file with the data comma separated.

➤ **XML File**—The XML File option saves the data in an XML File parsed into XML nodes.

➤ **SQL Server**—The SQL Server option logs the data to a table in your SQL Server. The table logged to on the server is named sysssislog. If it does not exist, this table is created automatically by SSIS when the package runs.

➤ **SQL Server Profiler**—The SQL Server Profiler option logs the data to a file as SQL that can be captured in SQL Server Profiler.

Regardless of the provider type you select, options are available as to what data you want to log and when this data is logged. You can see these options under the Details tab of the Configure SSIS Logs window, as shown in Figure 47-2.

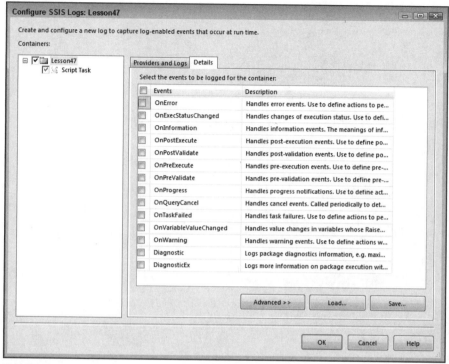

FIGURE 47-2

Under the Details tab, you select the event you want to be logged. If the event occurs during the run of the package, it logs data to the selected provider. The most commonly used events are onError, onWarning, onPreExecute, and onPostExecute.

If you select onError, if an error occurs during the execution of the package, data is stored in the selected log provider. If an error never occurs during the package execution, then no data is logged for this event. The same holds true with onWarning for warnings occurring during the package execution.

The onPreExecute event logs all the data before the package begins execution. This gives you a chance to see what the data values were before the packages performed any tasks. The onPostExecute event option logs all of the data after the package has completed execution.

The data that is saved by the SSIS logging options is shown in the Advanced window, as shown in Figure 47-3, which you bring up in the Details tab by clicking the Advanced button at the bottom of the screen. In the Advanced screen, you can select what data you want to log and on what event. You can select or unselect each item on each event. So if you want to log the computer name, but only on the onPreExecute, you can place a check under the Computer column next to the onPreExecute event only and make sure it is unchecked for the other events. This is the limit of the customization allowed by the built-in SSIS logging.

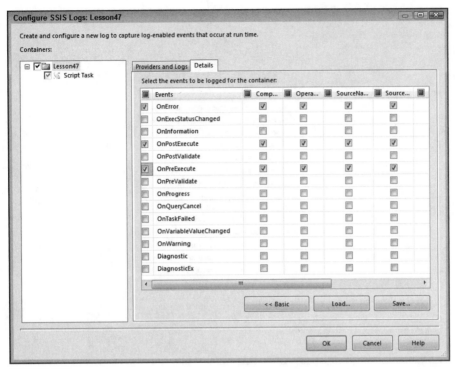

FIGURE 47-3

To create a log provider, select a provider type from the Provider Type drop-down menu on the Providers and Logs tab in the Configure SSIS Logs window, and then click the Add button. The log provider then appears in the Select the logs to use for the container pane below the drop-down menu. Place a check under the Name column to turn on the log provider. If you want to disable a log, but not remove it from this log menu, you need only remove the check in the Name column next to that log provider.

After you have created the log provider and checked the Name column to activate it, click the Configuration drop-down menu. If a connection type exists in the connection manager that is used by the selected provider, it shows in this window. If the connection does not exist, you can create it by clicking the <New connection...> option.

Next, click the Details tab to choose the events you want to log. If you want to log all events, click the check box next to the Events title at the top of the events list to select all. If you want to select just individual events, place a check next to the event you want to be logged.

After you have selected the events, click the Advanced button and uncheck any data you do not want to log so you don't have that data saved. You can also save the configuration you have selected to an XML file with the Save button that appears at the bottom of the Details tab. Later you can use this XML file in another package to select the same check boxes in this logging configuration screen automatically by clicking the Load button that also appears at the bottom of the Details tab.

TRY IT

In this Try It, you create a package with a Script Task that causes an error and logs the package information on the error, before it runs and after it completes. After this lesson, you will have an understanding of how to use SSIS logging to audit the running of your packages.

You can download the completed Lesson47.dtsx from www.wrox.com.

Lesson Requirements

Create a package with a Script Task. Edit the Script Task to open a message box pop-up with a variable that does not exist. Log the package onError, onPreExecute, and onPostExecute events.

Hints

➤ You need to turn on three event logs.

➤ Do not alter the advanced logging options.

Step-by-Step

1. Create a new package and name it **ErrorDemo**.

2. Drag a Script Task into the Control Flow.

3. Open the Script Task and set the language to Visual Basic.

4. Click Edit Script and enter the following:

   ```
   msgbox(DTS.Variables("Test").Value)
   ```

   > **WARNING** *Do not create the "Test" variable. This will cause an error you will capture in the log.*

5. Close the Script Editor and click OK in the Script Task.

6. Right-click the Control Flow and select Logging.

7. Place a check next to the package named Error Demo in the left pane.

8. Select the SSIS log provider for text files in the Provider Type drop-down menu and click Add.

9. Place a check in the Name column of the log provider.

10. Click the Configuration drop-down menu and select <New connection...>.

11. Create a connection to a text file named LogTest.txt on your local drive and select create file as the usage type. Then click OK.

12. Click the Details tab.

13. Place a check next to onError, onPreExecute, and onPostExecute.

14. Click OK.

15. Run the package by clicking the green debug arrow on the toolbar.

16. After the Script Task has a red X appear on the task, open the LogTest.txt file on your desktop.

17. You should see the error "Exception has been thrown by the target of an invocation." This is the error indicating the variable name in the Script Task is invalid.

18. You should also see the pre- and post-execute lines in the text file.

> *Please select Lesson 47 on the DVD, or online at* www.wrox.com/go/ssis2012video, *to view the video that accompanies this lesson.*

48

Using Event Handlers

Although the main tasks of SSIS packages exist in either the Control Flow or the Data Flow, the Event Handlers tab, the subject of this lesson, is another tab that is very useful when you are creating a package. *Event handlers* enable you to call tasks when events like errors or warnings occur during the execution of a package, which can be helpful in logging errors or sending notifications. The Event Handlers tab is used to call a task when an event has occurred in the package. The tasks in the event handler run only if the proper event is called in the package. Therefore, it is possible to have tasks in the event handlers of a package that don't run during the execution of the package because the proper event is not called.

Several events can occur in a package to cause an event to fire and call an event handler:

- ➤ OnError
- ➤ OnExecStatusChanged
- ➤ OnInformation
- ➤ OnPostExecute
- ➤ OnPostValidate
- ➤ OnPreExecute
- ➤ OnPreValidate
- ➤ OnProgress
- ➤ OnQueryCancel
- ➤ OnTaskFailed
- ➤ OnVariableValueChanged
- ➤ OnWarning

The most commonly used events are OnError, OnWarning, OnPreExecute, and OnPostExecute.

➤ The **OnError** event fires when an error occurs during the execution of the selected executable.

➤ The **OnWarning** event fires when a warning occurs during the execution of the selected executable.

➤ The **OnPreExecute** event fires just before the selected executable starts executing.

➤ The **OnPostExecute** event fires just after the selected executable finishes executing.

CREATING EVENT HANDLERS

When you open the Event Handlers tab for the first time, it looks similar to Figure 48-1. Notice there is a blue link in the middle. When clicked, this link creates an event handler on the package. At the top of the Event Handlers tab are two drop-down menus. The left drop-down menu contains a list of all the executables in the package. This is a list of all the tasks in the package. If no tasks have been created in the package, the only executable listed is the package.

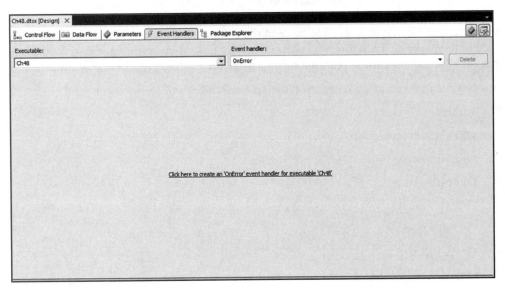

FIGURE 48-1

When you are creating an event handler, it is important to select the proper executable from the drop-down menu to ensure the tasks in the event handler execute when intended.

The second drop-down menu, on the top right of the Event Handlers tab, contains a list of all the events that can be chosen for the selected executable.

In Figure 48-2, there is a Script Task in the Control Flow of the package and a Data Flow with a source and destination. Notice the source and destination do not show in the drop-down menu of executables. Rather, the entire Data Flow is the executable. Placing an OnPostExecute Event Handler on the Data Flow means the task in the event handler will fire after the entire Data Flow finishes executing. Placing an OnError Event Handler on the Script Task means the tasks in the event handler will fire only if an error occurs on the Script Task. So, for example, if no error occurs or if an error occurs in the Data Flow (as opposed to in the Script Task), the OnError event on the Script Task will not fire.

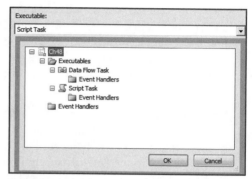

FIGURE 48-2

When you first open the Event Handlers tab and click the blue link in the middle of the tab, it creates an OnError event for the package. This causes the tasks in the event handler to execute if any errors occur during any tasks in the package. Sometimes you may want the tasks in the event handlers to fire only for a certain task in the package. To do this, first select the task in the left drop-down menu and then click the blue link in the event handler tab. This action creates an event handler for the specific tasks and executes only when the proper event occurs on the selected tasks.

COMMON USES FOR EVENT HANDLERS

Two of the most common uses for the event handlers are notification and logging. When you want to be notified via e-mail that an error has occurred, the event handlers are the right place to execute this task. Simply place a Send Mail Task in the OnError Event Handler for the package. When you want to be notified via e-mail that a package has completed, again the event handlers are the right place to execute this task. Just place a Send Mail Task in the OnPostExecute Event Handler for the package.

These Send Mail Tasks can contain information about the package. You can include any system variables in the message to tell you what occurred in the package and when.

Another useful purpose of the event handlers is logging. You can create your own custom logging framework if you are not satisfied with the built-in logging of SSIS. By creating Execute SQL Tasks in the event handlers, you can write information from the package to a database. These Execute SQL Tasks execute only when the proper event occurs, enabling you to log errors when they occur with the OnError Event Handler and log warnings when they occur with the OnWarning Event Handler.

After several event handlers have been created and these event handlers are on different executables, you might find it hard to keep track of which executable has an event handler and which does not. The Executable drop-down menu shows all of the event handlers on the package and each executable. There is also an Event Handler folder under the package and each executable. Clicking the plus sign next to this folder opens the folder and shows the event handlers in each of them.

Under the event handler is an Executables folder showing each task in the event handler. In Figure 48-3, you can see the package has three event handlers, each with an Execute SQL Task. The Data Flow and Script Task have OnError Event Handlers with Send Mail Tasks in them. You can also see this information in the Package Explorer tab.

When you click the plus sign next to any task in an event handler, you see there is another Event Handler folder. The task in the event handler can have an event handler of its own. So, you can have a Send Mail Task in the OnPostExecute Event Handler of a package and then have an Execute SQL Task in the OnError Event Handler of the Send Mail Task. If the Send Mail Task has an error, the error can then be logged with the Execute SQL Task.

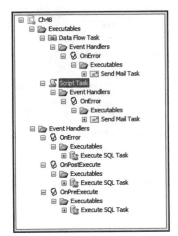

FIGURE 48-3

TRY IT

In this Try It, you create a package with an Execute SQL Task with an OnError Event Handler. The event handler is going to cause a pop-up message from a Script Task to show the error. After this lesson, you will understand how to create and use event handlers on a package.

The completed package for this lesson is available for download on the book's website at www.wrox.com.

Lesson Requirements

Create a package with an Execute SQL Task. Run it with no error, and run it with an error. The OnError Event Handler should fire when an error occurs.

Hints

➤ Create an Execute SQL Task in the Control Flow.

➤ Create an OnError Event Handler.

➤ Create a Script Task in the event handler.

Step-by-Step

1. Create a new package.

2. Drag in an Execute SQL Task.

3. Set the Connection to AdventureWorks2012.

4. Set the SQL statement to Select 1. When you are ready to cause an error, change the SQL to Select a.

5. Click the Event Handlers tab.

6.   Select the package in the Executables menu.

7.   Select the OnError Event Handler in the Event Handler menu.

8.   Click the blue link to create the OnError Event Handler.

9.   Drag a Script Task into the event handler.

10.   Double-click the Script Task.

11.   Set the Script Language to VB.

12.   Click the ReadOnlyVariables ellipsis.

13.   Place a check next to System::ErrorDescription, and then click OK.

14.   Click the Edit Script button.

15.   In the Main class under the words, Enter Code Here, type in:

```
MsgBox(Dts.Variables("ErrorDescription").Value)
```

16.   Close the Script Editor.

17.   Click OK in the Script Task Editor.

18.   Click the Control Flow tab.

19.   Click the green debug arrow on the toolbar to run the package.

20.   The Execute SQL Task should have a green check appear in the top right, and no error should occur.

21.   Click the stop debugging button on the toolbar.

22.   Change the query in the Execute SQL Task to Select a.

23.   Click the green debug arrow on the toolbar to run the package.

24.   A pop-up message appears matching Figure 48-4.

25.   Click OK in the message box and stop the debugging.

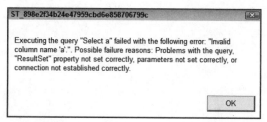

FIGURE 48-4

Please select Lesson 48 on the DVD, or online at www.wrox.com/go/ssis2012video, *to view the video that accompanies this lesson.*

Troubleshooting Errors

After creating a package with all of the tasks needed, you almost always face some necessary amount of troubleshooting. For example, a package running in your production database might suddenly stop working due to some change to the environment. You need the ability to analyze the errors from the package to determine what is going wrong and how to fix it. That's the focus of this lesson.

For example, validation errors are easy to spot in a package because the task with the error has a small red circle with a red x on it. This icon indicates that the task is not passing the validation phase of the package. In this case, the package pops up a message showing the validation error. These errors look like Figure 49-1. The error seems long, but the key message is in the third section. It states that the connection manager does not exist. This is a connection being referred to by the package that does not exist and is therefore causing this error.

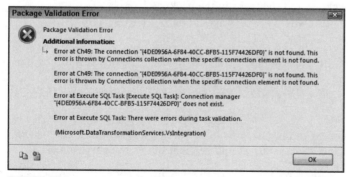

FIGURE 49-1

In cases like the one just mentioned, the error may not be caused by a problem with the package, but rather the environment. The object that is not found might need to be created, or the connection manager might be set up incorrectly. In this case, a connection is missing.

WORKING IN THE PROGRESS TAB

When you are debugging a package, errors show in the Progress tab. During troubleshooting, you spend a lot of time in the Progress tab, so it is important to get familiar with the messages and icons located there. Figure 49-2 shows a typical Progress tab with an error.

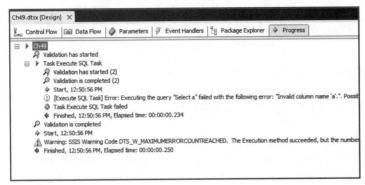

FIGURE 49-2

You need to become familiar with several icons in the Progress tab for troubleshooting purposes. They indicate key places in the flow of the package. Figure 49-3 shows a list of the icons in the Progress tab and their abbreviated meanings.

The first item listed in the Progress tab is the name of the package. There is a small blue triangle next to the package name. These blue arrows appear next to the package and the tasks in the package. This makes it easier to distinguish where the messages about a task start and stop.

▸	Start of Task or Package
⌕	Validation
➜	Start of a Task
✦	Finish of a Task
ⓘ	Error Message
⊘	Failure of a Task
⚠	Warning Message

FIGURE 49-3

There is also a minus sign next to the package name and task names. Clicking this minus sign collapses the executable next to it. If you are troubleshooting a package and you know the errors appear only in a certain task, you can collapse the other tasks to make it easier to read through the errors on the task in question.

A small magnifying glass appears next to lines to indicate validation has started and finished. *Validation* is the process of checking for the sources and destinations in the particular task.

A green arrow pointing to the right indicates the start of the task listed above the arrow. The start time of the task is listed next to the green arrow. A red arrow pointing to the left indicates the stopping point of a task. The total time the task ran is listed next to the red arrow.

Three icons indicate an error or warning has occurred in the package:

> ➤ The red exclamation point in a circle indicates an error has occurred, and the full error message is usually listed next to this icon. The icon can show several times in the Progress tab and have several different messages. The first error is usually the one that contains the meaningful information. In some cases you may even see a message referring you to the preceding error.

If the error message next to the red exclamation point is too long to read or if you need a copy of the error, you can right-click the error, click the Copy Message Text option that appears, and then paste it in an e-mail or in a text editor.

➤ The next icon after the red exclamation point is the red circle with an x in the center. The message next to this icon is usually not very useful. It does not give details of what caused the failure; it just states that the task failed. This icon is easy to spot and makes it easy to find the error messages in the Progress tab. This is especially true when the package has a lot of tasks and the Progress tab has many screens to look through.

➤ The last icon you should be familiar with is the yellow triangle with the black exclamation point in the center. This icon indicates a warning has occurred on the package. Warnings can occur on a package without stopping the package. It is normal to run a package and to have warnings occur during run time, but to still have all of the tasks in the package complete successfully.

Warnings may not cause a package to fail, but it is important to read them and decide if changes should be made to the package to prevent possible package failures in the future. One of the more common warning messages seen in Data Flows is "Truncation may occur . . .." This message does not stop a package from executing. This message indicates that a source column is set to a length that is greater than the destination column. Unless the data in the source column is actually longer than the destination, truncation will not occur, and the package will execute successfully. But that might not always be the case, and the warning is pointing out that the potential exists for a problem to occur later.

TROUBLESHOOTING STEPS

Thousands of errors can occur in a package, and the methods to correct these errors are almost always specific to the package. Too many possibilities exist to list every error message and how to fix them. However, the steps to correcting errors are the same:

1. Check the Progress tab and read all error messages.

2. Determine which tasks needs adjusting, if any; keep in mind the error could be caused by something outside of the package.

3. Stop debugging.

4. Adjust the task that caused the error.

5. Debug.

6. Repeat if more errors occur.

One of the pitfalls of troubleshooting a package is assuming the error has not changed. Once you have gone through the steps of troubleshooting and the package still fails, it is always important to return to the Progress tab and check the error message again. The error message can change; you may have fixed the first error and are now getting a new error. As you can imagine, it is even more difficult to fix a package when you are troubleshooting the wrong error.

TRY IT

In this Try It, you open the package named Lesson49.dtsx (which you can download at www.wrox.com) and troubleshoot the errors to get it working. After completing this lesson, you will have a better understanding of how to troubleshoot errors in SSIS.

Lesson Requirements

Open the package named Lesson49.dtsx. Run the package in debug mode. Look at the errors and make the necessary corrections to the package for it to run with no errors. The package should cause a pop-up box to appear with the words Adjustable Race.

Hints

➤ The Execute SQL Task has Syntax errors.

➤ The Execute SQL Task has Result Set errors.

➤ The Script Task is missing variable parameters.

➤ The Script Task has a typo in the code.

Step-by-Step

> **NOTE** *You can troubleshoot the package correctly and fix the errors in a different order than what is listed in this step-by-step walkthrough.*

1. Click the green debug arrow on the toolbar.

2. An error occurs stating the variable may have been changed.

3. Rename the variable to **strName**.

4. Debug the package again.

5. Check the Progress tab to see the invalid column name reference.

6. Change the column names in the Execute SQL Task to **Name** instead of Names.

7. Debug the package again.

8. Click the Progress tab and read the error "Exception has been thrown by the target of an invocation."

> **NOTE** *This error is not very descriptive and can have several meanings. In this case, it indicates the task is referring to an object that does not exist, the variable.*

9.   Open the Script Task Editor and select the strName variable in the ReadOnlyVariables property.

10.   Debug the package again.

11.   Notice the same error in the Progress tab.

12.   Open the Script Task and change the message box code to **MsgBox(Dts.Variables("strName").Value)**.

13.   Debug the package again.

14.   A message box should appear matching Figure 49-4.

FIGURE 49-4

Please select Lesson 49 on the DVD, or online at www.wrox.com/go/ssis2012video, *to view the video that accompanies this lesson.*

50

Using Data Viewers

The Data Flow Task moves data from sources to destinations with some transforms in between. When you are running a Data Flow in development, it might seem difficult to determine if the data is being transformed correctly. The columns might not be passed through the Data Flow at all.

You could open the destination to check on the status of the data, but this approach might not always be the best solution. Imagine a Data Flow with dozens of transforms moving thousands of rows to a destination. Opening the destination reveals that the columns are not showing the data you expected. Which transform is causing the problem? It may be hard to determine by just examining the data in the destination. This situation is where Data Viewers make tracking data changes much easier. *Data Viewers* are a development tool used to glance at the data during the Data Flow execution phase of a package. They cause a small pop-up window to show the data at certain points in a Data Flow.

Data Viewers should be removed before moving a package to production to be scheduled to run. If the Data Viewer remains on a package, the package will not stop at the point the Data Viewer is called, and the Data Viewer will load in memory and use unnecessary buffers.

> **NOTE** *It is a best practice to remove any troubleshooting items before a move to production.*

To create a Data Viewer on a Data Flow, double-click the blue or red line that connects the tasks in the Data Flow. This opens the Data Flow Path Editor, as shown in Figure 50-1. In the General node, you find the common properties of the Data Flow Path. The Metadata node shows the metadata for each column in the Data Flow at that point.

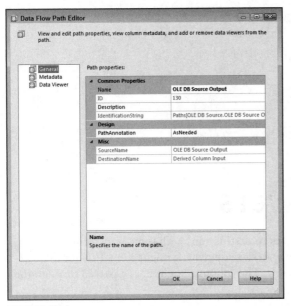

FIGURE 50-1

The last node is the Data Viewer node. Under the Data Viewer node, you can create a Data Viewer by checking the Enable data viewer check box. Below the check box, you see a list of all the columns in your Data Flow, as shown in Figure 50-2. Using the left and right arrows between the boxes enables you to add and remove columns from the Data Viewer. The double arrows remove or add all the columns. Selecting just the columns you need to see makes it much easier to find data issues.

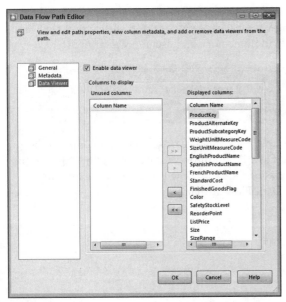

FIGURE 50-2

Once you have the desired columns selected, click OK at the bottom of the Data Flow Path Editor window. You now see a small magnifying glass symbol next to your Data Flow line, as shown in Figure 50-3. You can also take a shortcut and enable a Data Viewer on any Data Flow line by right-clicking the Data Flow line and selecting Enable Data Viewer. This selects all columns by default.

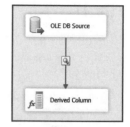

Data Viewers stop the Data Flow at about 10,000 rows unless the default buffer size property of the Data Flow has been changed. You click the small green arrow in the top left of each Data Viewer to pass in approximately the

FIGURE 50-3

next 10,000 rows. This presentation enables you to view chunks of data and is an efficient way to view lots of data as it passes through the Data Flow.

The table that appears in the Data Viewer window shows the values in each column, as shown in Figure 50-4. It shows the data in a table structure similar to Excel. You can change the size of the columns and highlight one row or multiple rows. A Copy Data button enables you to copy all of the data from the Grid View to the clipboard to be used in a text editor. A Detach button at the top of the Grid View detaches the Data Viewer from the debugging process. It allows the package to continue running without populating the rest of the data in the Data Viewer. When you click the Detach button, the last set of rows remains in the Data Viewer.

OLE DB Source Output Data Viewer at Data Flow Task

▶	Detach		Copy Data							
Pro...	ProductAlternateKey	Pro...	WeightUnitMeasure...	SizeUnitMeasure...	EnglishProductName	...F...	Stand...	Finished
1	AR-5381	NULL	NULL	NULL	Adjustable Race		NULL	False
2	BA-8327	NULL	NULL	NULL	Bearing Ball		NULL	False
3	BE-2349	NULL	NULL	NULL	BB Ball Bearing		NULL	False
4	BE-2908	NULL	NULL	NULL	Headset Ball Bearings		NULL	False
5	BL-2036	NULL	NULL	NULL	Blade		NULL	False
6	CA-5965	NULL	NULL	NULL	LL Crankarm		NULL	False
7	CA-6738	NULL	NULL	NULL	ML Crankarm		NULL	False
8	CA-7457	NULL	NULL	NULL	HL Crankarm		NULL	False
9	CB-2903	NULL	NULL	NULL	Chainring Bolts		NULL	False
10	CN-6137	NULL	NULL	NULL	Chainring Nut		NULL	False
11	CR-7833	NULL	NULL	NULL	Chainring		NULL	False
12	CR-9981	NULL	NULL	NULL	Crown Race		NULL	False
13	CS-2812	NULL	NULL	NULL	Chain Stays		NULL	False
14	DC-8732	NULL	NULL	NULL	Decal 1		NULL	False
15	DC-9824	NULL	NULL	NULL	Decal 2		NULL	False
16	DT-2377	NULL	NULL	NULL	Down Tube		NULL	False
17	EC-M092	NULL	NULL	NULL	Mountain End Caps		NULL	False
18	EC-R098	NULL	NULL	NULL	Road End Caps		NULL	False

Attached | Total rows: 0, buffers: 0 | Rows displayed = 606

FIGURE 50-4

When you are done using the Data Viewers in the Data Flow of a package, double-click the Data Flow connectors that contain Data Viewers. These are indicated by the magnifying glass shown next to the Data Flow lines. In the Data Flow Path Editor, click the Data Viewer node and uncheck the Enable data viewer check box at the top. You can also right-click the Data Flow line and click Disable Data Viewer.

TRY IT

In this Try It, you create a package with a Data Flow and create a Data Viewer on the Data Flow. After this lesson, you will understand how to use Data Viewers to assist you in developing Data Flows in SSIS. You will know how to view data between each task in a Data Flow.

You can download the completed lesson at www.wrox.com.

Lesson Requirements

Create a package with a Data Flow and create a Data Viewer after the source to see the data in the Data Viewer window.

Hints

➤   Connect to an OLE DB Source.

➤   The source can connect to a Conditional Split.

Step-by-Step

1.   Create a new package.

2.   Drag in a Data Flow Task.

3.   Double-click the Data Flow.

4.   Drag an OLE DB Source to the Data Flow.

5.   Connect the OLE DB Source to the AdventureWorks2012 database.

6.   Select the SalesOrderDetail table in the OLE DB Source.

7.   Drag in a Conditional Split.

8.   Connect the OLE DB Source to the Conditional Split Transform with the blue Data Flow line from the bottom of the OLE DB Source.

9.   Double-click the blue Data Flow.

10.   Click the Data Viewer node.

11.   Place a check in the Enable data viewer check box.

12.   Leave all of the columns selected.

13.   Click OK.

14.   Click the green debug button on the toolbar.

15. You should see a Data Viewer appear showing data.

16. Click the green continue arrow in the Data Viewer until all rows have passed through.

17. Close the Data Viewer.

18. Stop debugging the package.

Please select Lesson 50 on the DVD, or online at www.wrox.com/go/ssis2012video, *to view the video that accompanies this lesson.*

51

Using Breakpoints

When you are developing a package, many times you will need to troubleshoot issues in the package. It is helpful to know the status of data, variables, and tasks at certain points in the execution of the package. Breakpoints enable you to stop a package during execution and view the status of these items. Breakpoints, along with the Watch windows or the Locals window, also enable you to see the value of variables immediately before and after a task.

To create a breakpoint on a task, right-click the task and select Edit Breakpoints. This action opens the Set Breakpoints window, as shown in Figure 51-1. The left-hand column of this window is a set of check boxes that enable the breakpoint listed. Figure 51-1 shows the Set Breakpoints window for a For Loop Container. Notice the last breakpoint option is "Break at the beginning of every iteration of the loop." This option is available only on the For Loop and Foreach Loop Containers.

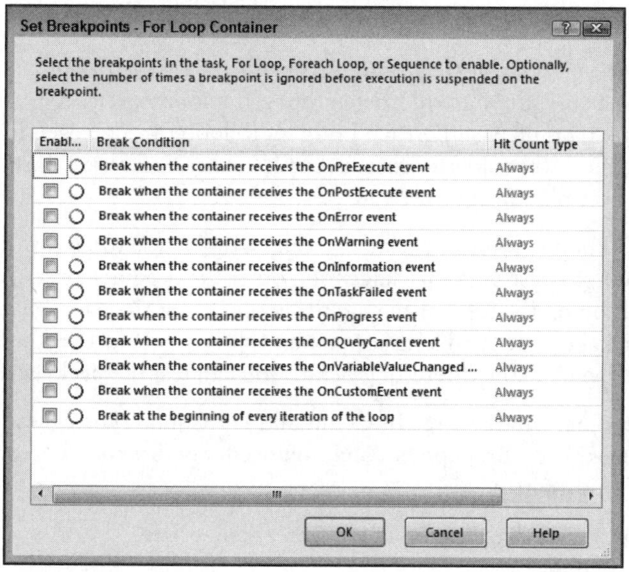

FIGURE 51-1

Each option in the Set Breakpoints window will stop the package execution at a different point during in the task:

- ➤ **OnPreExecute**—Just before the task executes
- ➤ **OnPostExecute**—Directly after the task completes
- ➤ **OnError**—When an error occurs in the task
- ➤ **OnWarning**—When a warning occurs in the task
- ➤ **OnInformation**—When the task provides information
- ➤ **OnTaskFailed**—When the task fails
- ➤ **OnProgress**—To update progress on task execution
- ➤ **OnQueryCancel**—When the task can cancel execution
- ➤ **OnVariableValueChanged**—When the value of a variable changes (the RaiseChangedEvent property of the variable must be set to true)
- ➤ **OnCustomEvent**—When the custom task-defined events occur
- ➤ **Loop Iteration**—At the beginning of each loop cycle

The most commonly used events in breakpoints are OnPreExecute, OnPostExecute, OnError, OnWarning, and Loop Iteration. By using OnPreExecute and OnPostExecute on a task, you can see the value of a variable before and after a task, which enables you to determine if the task changed the value of the variable to the expected value. The OnError and OnWarning events enable you to stop a package with a breakpoint if something goes wrong. Imagine having a package that contains two Data Flows: the first loads the data into a flat file and the second loads the data into a table. If the first Data Flow encounters a warning, you do not want the second Data Flow to load the data. An OnWarning Breakpoint on the first Data Flow can stop the package from executing the second Data Flow.

The Loop Iteration Breakpoint stops the package at the beginning of either a Foreach Loop or a For Loop. If a loop is executed ten times, the breakpoint will fire ten times. If a loop never occurs in a package, the breakpoint will never fire. If you have a Foreach Loop set to loop through each file in a folder and the breakpoint never fires, check the folder to ensure the files exist. For more information on containers like the loop tasks, see Section 6 of the book.

While a package is stopped at the breakpoint, you can click the green arrow on the toolbar to continue to the next breakpoint or through the rest of the package if no other breakpoints exist. You can also click the square blue stop button on the toolbar to stop the execution of the package at the breakpoint. Keep in mind that the package is stopped at that point and the tasks before the breakpoint have executed. This may require some manual resetting before you can test the package again.

The other properties in the Set Breakpoints window are Hit Count and Hit Count Type. These properties set the maximum number of times that a Breakpoint condition occurs before the Breakpoint stops the package. Four Hit Count Types exist:

- ➤ **Always**—The breakpoint stops the package every time the breakpoint fires.

➤ **Hit Count Equals**—The breakpoint stops the package when the breakpoint fires the number of times listed in Hit Count.

➤ **Hit Count Greater than or Equal to**—The breakpoint stops the package when the breakpoint reaches the number listed in Hit Count and every time afterwards.

➤ **Hit Count Multiple**—The breakpoint stops the package when the breakpoint reaches the number listed in Hit Count and every multiple of the Hit Count number; a Hit Count of 2 stops the package on every other breakpoint event.

Once you have decided which breakpoint to set, and close the Set Breakpoints window by clicking OK, you see a red dot on the task, as in Figure 51-2 (though note that the figure in the book doesn't show color). The red dot indicates a breakpoint exists on a task. In truth, there may be several breakpoints on a task with the red dot. You can also tell when a package is stopped at a breakpoint during debugging here. A small yellow arrow appears in the middle of the red dot on the task.

FIGURE 51-2

When a breakpoint has stopped a package from running, you can use the Watch window during debugging to see the values of the variables in the package at that time. To open a Watch window, click Debug on the toolbar and then under Windows, click Watch and Watch 1. This opens a Watch window at the bottom of Visual Studio by default. Type in the name of the variables you need to monitor to see the values of the variables. In Figure 51-3, you can see the value of some variables in the Watch window during a breakpoint and the variable types.

Watch 1		
Name	Value	Type
⊟ User::Flying	{}	String
Type	String	
Value		
⊟ User::Spaghetti	{}	String
Type	String	
Value		
⊟ User::Monster	{}	String
Type	String	
Value		

Locals   Watch 1

FIGURE 51-3

Using breakpoints and the Watch window to debug a package makes it very easy to determine what the tasks in your package are doing. You can quickly determine where the error is occurring and not occurring. In some cases, a package might be running with no error messages, but might still not be performing correctly. These types of errors would be hard to track down without breakpoints. Errors or no errors, breakpoints enable you to stop a package and examine the results up to that point. You should use breakpoints often during the development of any package.

TRY IT

In this Try It, you create a package with a For Loop to count from 1 to 10. Then you verify the value of the variable in the loop. After this lesson, you will understand how to use breakpoints to aid in the development and debugging of an SSIS package.

You can download the completed lesson at www.wrox.com.

Lesson Requirements

Create a package with a For Loop to count from 1 to 10. Use breakpoints and a Watch window to see if the loop is actually incrementing the variable value.

Hints

➤   Use an integer variable.

➤   Use a For Loop.

➤   Increment the integer variable by one for each loop.

Step-by-Step

1.   Create a blank package.

2.   Create an Integer variable named **intCounter**.

3.   Set the Value of intCounter to 1.

4.   Drag a For Loop to the Control Flow, and double-click to open the editor.

5.   Set the InitExpression of the For Loop to **@intCounter = 1**.

6.   Set the EvalExpression to **@intCounter <= 10**.

7.   Set the AssignExpression to **@intCounter = @intCounter + 1**. Now the For Loop should match Figure 51-4.

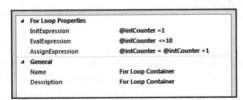

FIGURE 51-4

8.   Close the For Loop Editor by clicking OK.

9.   Right-click the For Loop and select Edit Breakpoints.

10. Place a check next to "Break at the beginning of every iteration of the loop" and click OK.

11. Click the green debug arrow on the toolbar.

12. When the package stops at the breakpoint, open a Watch window by clicking Debug on the toolbar. Then under Windows, click Watch and Watch 1.

13. Type in the name of the variable **intCounter** (it is case-sensitive).

14. The value of intCounter should be 1.

15. The red dot on the For Loop should have a yellow arrow on it, as shown in Figure 51-5, though, again, you can't see the colors in the book.

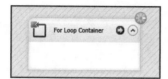

FIGURE 51-5

16. Click the green debug arrow on the toolbar to continue the package.

17. The value of intCounter in the Watch window should change to 2.

18. Continue clicking the debug arrow until the value reaches 10 and the package completes. The For Loop should have a green check appear in the top-right corner.

19. Click the blue square stop debugging button on the toolbar.

> *Please select Lesson 51 on the DVD, or online at* www.wrox.com/go/ssis2012video, *to view the video that accompanies this lesson.*

SECTION 9
Administering SSIS

52

Creating and Configuring the SSIS Catalog

One of the most significant differences between previous versions of SSIS and SQL Server 2012 is the introduction of the SSIS catalog. The catalog only applies for those who are in the project deployment model and gives you many new features for administering and configuring packages. It also enables you to run packages in T-SQL or through PowerShell.

CREATING THE CATALOG

Behind the scenes, a catalog is simply a database where your packages are stored and configured. As packages run, it stores operational information about the packages' run and any errors. Because the packages are in a database called SSISDB, much of their management can be done through T-SQL or PowerShell, that's in addition to the normal way of managing them, which is through Management Studio.

The easiest way to create the SSIS catalog (you have only one catalog per database instance) and its accompanying database is with Management Studio. In Management Studio, connect to your database engine and navigate to the Integration Services node in Object Explorer. Right-click the Integration Services Catalogs node and select Create Catalog. This opens the Create Catalog dialog box (shown in Figure 52-1) where you must type a password that will encrypt all packages. To fully utilize the package catalog, you must also have the Common Language Runtime (CLR) integration turned on by checking the Enable CLR box. Click OK to create the database and catalog.

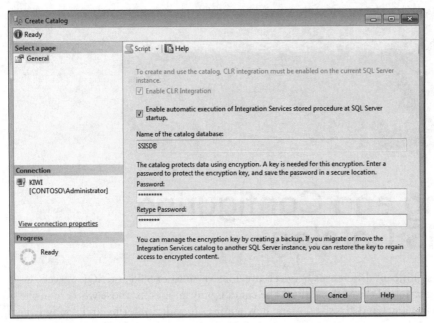

FIGURE 52-1

CONFIGURING THE CATALOG

After the catalog is created, you're then able to configure the catalog by right-clicking the SSISDB catalog and selecting Properties, which opens the Catalog Properties screen. One of the catalog's jobs is to store operational log data about your packages' execution like errors, warnings, and duration. In the Catalog Properties dialog box (Figure 52-2), you can configure how many days of that history are kept. By default, the catalog will store 365 days of history, which may be far too much for most environments.

By default, the catalog stores only basic logging. If you want to store more detailed logging for debugging, you can choose Verbose for the Server-wide Default Logging Level option, but note that this will slow down your packages and take much more space in your catalog to store the logs.

Lastly, as you deploy packages, there is a rudimentary version control system in the catalog. By default, 10 versions of your project are kept in case of a problem, but you can change that in the Catalog Properties screen with the Maximum Number of Versions per Project option.

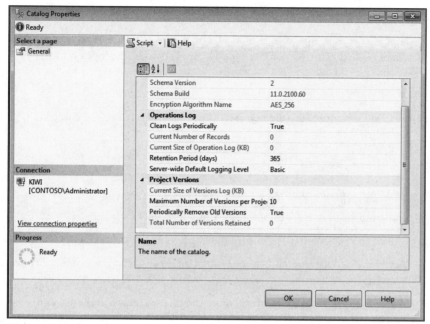

FIGURE 52-2

CREATING AND USING FOLDERS

In the catalog, folders are containers for multiple projects, much like a solution is in Visual Studio. Imagine a data warehousing project with many subject areas like HR, finance, and inventory. You could create a folder called Data Warehouse and deploy all the projects for each subject area into that central folder.

To create a new folder, right-click the catalog and select Create Folder. Name the folder and click OK. You cannot deploy an SSIS project in the project deployment model without a folder first being created. Security permissions can also be shared among any projects in a folder.

TRY IT

In this Try It, you create and configure the SSIS catalog. After this lesson, you will understand how to use the SSIS catalog and folder structure.

This lesson has no samples to download.

Lesson Requirements

Create an SSIS catalog database on your database instance. Configure the catalog to retain only 45 days of history. Also, create a folder called Data Warehouse for your projects to be deployed into.

Hints

➤ You can perform all steps within Management Studio while connected to the database engine.

Step-by-Step

1. Open SQL Server Management Studio and connect to your database engine.

2. Right-click the Integration Services Catalogs node and select New Catalog.

3. Type a password into the Password area, ensure that CLR is enabled, and click OK.

4. Right-click the newly created catalog and select Properties. This opens the Catalog Properties dialog box. Change Retention Period (days) to 30 days and click OK.

5. Right-click the catalog and select New Folder. Name the folder **Data Warehouse** and click OK.

> *Please select Lesson 52 on the DVD, or online at* www.wrox.com/go/ssis2012video, *to view the video that accompanies this lesson.*

53

Deploying Packages to the Package Catalog

In SQL Server 2005, 2008, and still in the package deployment model, you would deploy packages into SQL Server's msdb database or to the filesystem. Now, in SQL Server 2012's project deployment model, you deploy to the SSIS catalog (ssisdb database). Deploying to this model enables you to activate some of the newer features in SSIS, like environments and parameterization of packages (to name just a few). Deploying packages is simple using the Integration Services Deployment Wizard.

> **NOTE** *Because the older package deployment model is legacy, deploying packages to this model is not covered in this lesson in length.*

USING THE DEPLOYMENT WIZARD

The Deployment Wizard is the easiest way to deploy packages to the catalog. You can access the wizard through SSDT by right-clicking a project and selecting Deploy. You can also access it through Management Studio or by double-clicking an .ISPAC file. The wizard installs your packages by asking the administrator a few questions. It also creates the .ISPAC file, which is a single file that can be handed to a customer or to the DBA to install your project.

Once the wizard is open and you bypass the opening screen, you're asked which server and folder you want to deploy your project to (see Figure 53-1). (A folder is a container for a number of projects.) Click Next and Deploy to push your packages to the server. You'll also be warned if the packages are already on the server. Remember that if the packages are already there, you can overwrite them by proceeding and a version of your old project is retained on the server.

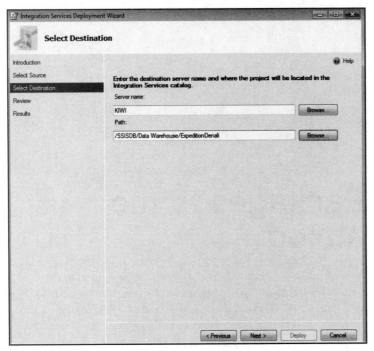

FIGURE 53-1

Another way to launch the wizard is from the .ISPAC file. You can locate your file in your project's folder under the bin\development subdirectories. An .ISPAC file is essentially a compressed file with all of your project's package and parameter files. In fact, if you were to rename the .ISPAC file to a .zip extension, you would be able to see all the files that it contains. When you double-click the .ISPAC file, the same Deployment Wizard (Figure 53-2) that was covered earlier in this lesson opens. Follow the same steps from the previous paragraph and the packages will install on your server.

You can also access this wizard in Management Studio. From Management Studio, right-click the Project folder under your folder and select Deploy Packages. One of the nice things you can do in the wizard is point to a different server and deploy your packages from QA to Production. Do this by selecting the catalog you want to import from rather than the .ISPAC file.

DEPLOYING PACKAGES IN THE PACKAGE DEPLOYMENT MODEL

In the project deployment model, you always deploy every package in the project. With the legacy package deployment model, you deploy packages individually. You can do this in Management Studio by connecting to the Integration Services service and selecting Import or you can do it in SSDT by opening the package and selecting File ➪ Save Copy As.

The final way to deploy packages in the package deployment model is with the Package Installation Wizard. You can do this by double-clicking an .SSISDeploymentManifest file from your \bin\deployment folder in your project directory. If you don't see this file, set the CreateDeploymentUtility property to True. Access this property by right-clicking the project in SSDT and selecting Properties. Then go to the Deployment tab as shown in Figure 53-3. If you don't see the CreateDeploymentUtility property, it might mean that your project is in the project deployment model. Lesson 8 shows you more about how to convert your deployment models back and forth.

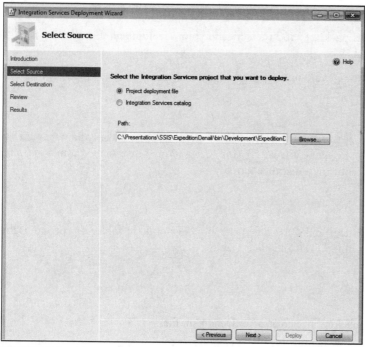

FIGURE 53-2

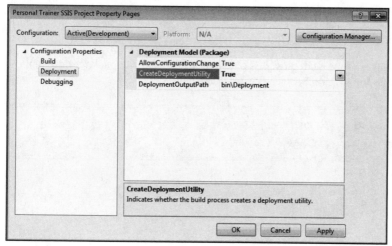

FIGURE 53-3

After the property is set, you need to build the project. You can do this under the Build menu by selecting Build <Project Name>. After this, the bin\deployment folder will be created, as well as the manifest file.

TRY IT

In this Try It, you deploy a set of packages and their files to your development server using the Integration Services Deployment Wizard.

You can download the ExpeditionDenali.zip you need for this lesson from www.wrox.com.

Lesson Requirements

Once you download and uncompress ExpeditionDenali.zip, deploy the packages and parameter files to your own server using the Deployment Wizard. If you have a named instance, you may have to point the project connection to your own instance name.

Hints

➤ You can either double-click the .ISPAC file in the \bin\development folder or you can right-click the project from within SSDT and click Deploy.

Step-by-Step

1. Open SSDT by double-clicking the ExpeditionDenali.sln file.

2. Right-click the project and select Deploy. The Deployment Wizard opens.

3. After skipping the wizard's introduction text screen, type in your database instance name for the server name (shown back in Figure 53-1) and select the folder to deploy into by clicking Browse. If one does not exist, you can also create one by clicking New.

4. Click Next and then Deploy in the Summary screen.

Congratulations; your packages are now deployed. You can confirm that the packages are deployed in Management Studio in the Integration Services node.

> *Please select Lesson 53 on the DVD, or online at* www.wrox.com/go/ssis2012video, *to view the video that accompanies this lesson.*

54

Configuring the Packages

When Microsoft was at the whiteboard trying to figure out how to make the SSIS developers and administrators' lives easier, at the top of its list was the process of how to configure a package. Before, configuring packages was clunky and, in many cases, unsecure (storing passwords of packages would have been in clear text). Microsoft spent much of the SQL Server 2012 development effort focusing on that exact thing. You can now configure packages much more easily, as long as they're in the project deployment model.

> **NOTE** *Important: This lesson is written for those who are using the project deployment model. If you are in the package deployment model, please skip this lesson.*

You can only configure packages that are deployed to the catalog. With the packages now deployed (as you learned in the previous lesson), you can find your packages in Management Studio under the Integration Services Catalogs node and SSISDB ➪ Projects. When you expand the project, you're ready to configure the packages to run in your environment. An example of when you can use this is when you have just finished development of a project and now want it to run in production by changing all the connections to point to production versus development.

CREATING ENVIRONMENTS

One really nice feature in SSIS is the ability to create environments. *Environments* are collections of properties for a customer, store, or workgroup. Imagine that your server hosts multiple customers: Customer A and Customer B. You could create an environment for each customer and then, when you go to run or schedule the package, run it under a given customer's settings with a single click.

You can create an environment under the SSIS folder in the package catalog. Start by right-clicking the Environments folder and selecting Create Environment. This opens the Create Environment dialog box. Type in the name of your first environment: **Customer A** (shown in Figure 54-1).

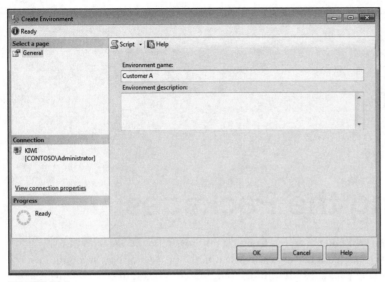

FIGURE 54-1

After the environment is created, double-click it to configure it. In the Environment Properties pane, you can secure the environment to restrict use of your properties in the Permissions tab and, more importantly, you can add additional properties in the Variables tab.

In the Variables tab, you can create a number of variables that will be grouped together for a given customer or environment (as shown in Figure 54-2). As you create each variable, you can secure it by checking the Sensitive box. These variables will eventually map to parameters in your project or packages when you go to configure the package. Notice that you can also click the Script button to create a T-SQL script to create the same variables.

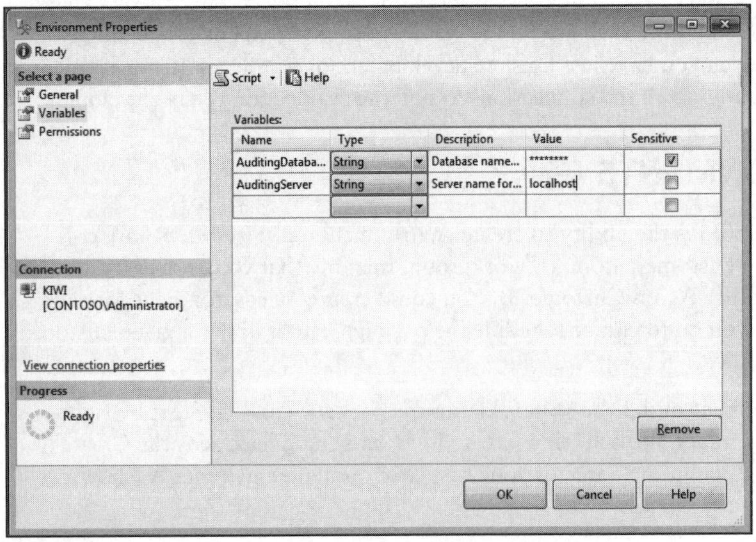

FIGURE 54-2

CONFIGURING THE PACKAGE

Before you can run the packages, you'll likely need to reconfigure them to redirect the connections to point to production instead of development. If the development of the package was done properly, there should be configuration points in your packages using parameters on each connection. This enables you, as an administrator or user of the package, to reconfigure it from Management Studio. See Section 4 of the book for a refresher on this topic if needed.

Once a project is deployed, you can reconfigure it by right-clicking the project in Management Studio (under Integration Services Catalogs ⇨ SSISDB ⇨ Folder Name) and selecting Configure. Once the Project Configuration screen opens, first allow the project to reference any environments if they exist. To do this, select the References tab and add each environment you want to have access to by clicking the Add button (shown in Figure 54-3).

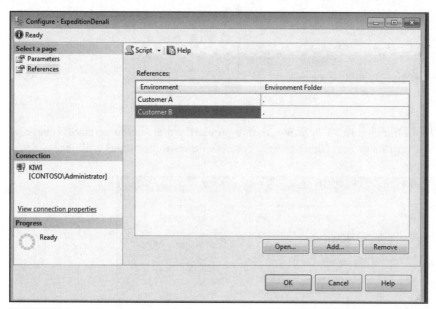

FIGURE 54-3

Back in the Parameters tab, you can see all the parameters that you can tweak across all of your packages in one screen. If you only want to see a single package's parameters, you can select the individual package in the Scope drop-down box or right-click the package and select Configure. When you find a parameter you want to change, you can click the ellipsis button next to the parameter. This opens the Set Parameter Value dialog box (shown in Figure 54-4). You can change the value to a manual value by selecting Edit value, use the default value from the package, or select Use environment variable to use the variable you created earlier. If you do this, you will now always need to specify the environment that you want to run the package under each time you schedule or run the package.

FIGURE 54-4

The final outcome looks like Figure 54-5. Values that are underlined are set to an environment. If you were to redeploy over this project, don't worry. Your configuration changes will not be lost.

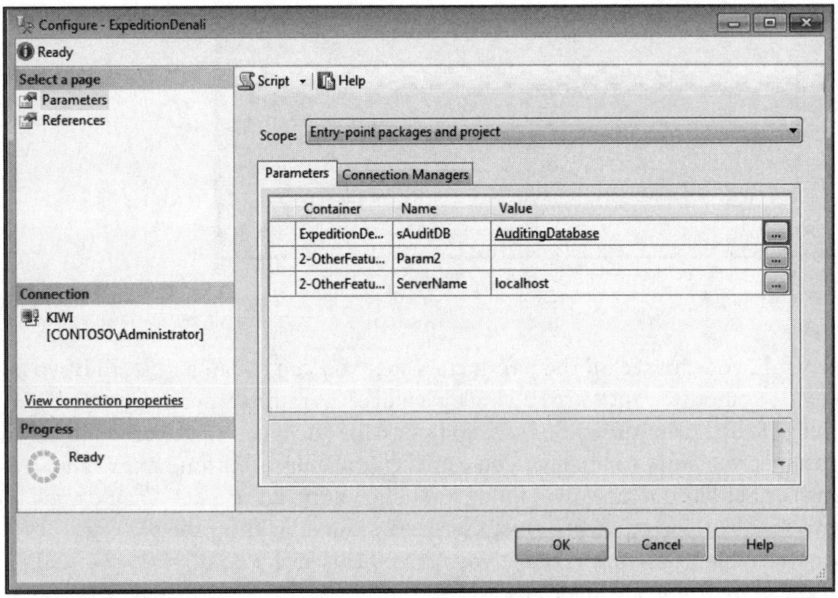

FIGURE 54-5

If there were no parameters in the project, you can also change the connection managers in the Connection Manager tab (shown in Figure 54-6). This enables you to change any connection property easily, but parameters are a better approach because it encourages reusability.

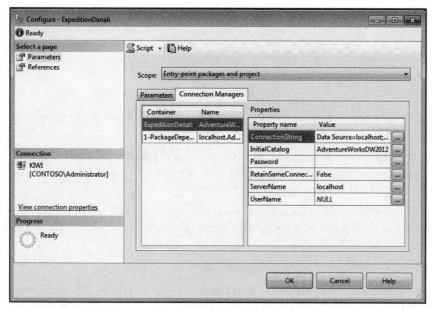

FIGURE 54-6

TRY IT

In this Try It, you learn how to configure an SSIS project and how to use environments as a container of variables. After this lesson, you should be able to configure your SSIS projects and packages to run in production.

You can download the ExpeditionDenali.zip you need for this lesson from www.wrox.com in the Lesson 53 download.

Lesson Requirements

Configure the project that you deployed in Lesson 53. If you have not deployed the project yet, download ExpeditionDenali.zip (available at www.wrox.com in the Lesson 53 download) and deploy the project. Next, create two customer environments, Customer 1 and Customer 2, then reconfigure the sAuditDB project parameter to use an environment variable for a given customer.

Hints

➤ Create two environments called Customer 1 and Customer 2 in Management Studio under the folder created in the previous lesson.

➤ Create a variable in each environment called varAuditingDB.

➤ Right-click the project to reconfigure it and set the references.

Step-by-Step

1. Open Management Studio and connect to the database instance that you deployed the project to in Lesson 53.

2. After drilling into SQL Server Integration Services catalog and your folder, right-click Environments and select New Environment. Name the environment **Customer 1** and click OK. Do the same to create an environment for Customer 2.

3. Double-click each environment and add a new variable in the Variables tab called **varAuditingDB**. The new variable should be a string with a default value of Customer1AuditDB and Customer2AuditDB (respectively).

4. Right-click the ExpeditionDenali project and select Configure.

5. Go to the References tab and add references for Customer 1 and Customer 2 by clicking Add.

6. Go back to the Parameters tab and click the ellipsis button next to the sAuditDB parameter. When the Set Parameter Value dialog box opens, select the Use Environment Variable radio box and choose the variable you created, varAuditingDB.

7. Click OK twice to exit the configuration screens.

Congratulations, your package is configured! That beats the heck out of editing an XML file, doesn't it? In a later lesson, you'll run the package with the new configuration.

> *Please select Lesson 54 on the DVD, or online at* www.wrox.com/go/ssis2012video, *to view the video that accompanies this lesson.*

55

Configuring the Service

In SQL Server 2005, 2008, and in the SQL Server 2012 package deployment model, you deploy packages into what is called the *SSIS Package Store*. The Package Store in some cases actually physically stores the package, such as the msdb database option. If you're using file system storage, the Package Store just keeps a pointer to the top-level directory and enumerates through the packages stored underneath that directory. To connect to the Package Store, the SSIS service must be running. This service is called SQL Server Integration Services, or MSDTSServer110. There is only one instance of the service per machine or per set of clustered machines.

> **NOTE** *Important: This lesson is written for those who are in the package deployment model. If you are in the project deployment model, please skip this lesson.*

Though you can run and stop packages programmatically without the SSIS service, the service makes running packages more manageable. For example, if you have the service run the package, it tracks that the package is executing and people with the proper permission can interrogate the service and find out which packages are running. Those people in the Windows Administrators group can stop all running packages. Otherwise, you can stop only packages that you have started.

The service can also aid in importing and exporting packages into the Package Store. This lesson covers other uses for the service, but one last great use for the service worth mentioning at the start is how it can enable you to create a centralized ETL server to handle the execution of your packages throughout your enterprise.

The MSDTSServer110 service is configured through an XML file that is, by default, located in the following path: C:\Program Files\Microsoft SQL Server\110\DTS\Binn\ MsDtsSrvr.ini.xml. This path will vary if you're in a cluster. If you cannot find the path, go to the HKEY_LOCAL_MACHINE\SOFTWARE\Microsoft\Microsoft SQL Server\110\SSIS\ ServiceConfigFile registry key in the Registry. The XML file should look like the following:

```xml
<?xml version="1.0" encoding="utf-8" ?>
  <DtsServiceConfiguration xmlns:xsd="http://www.w3.org/2001/XMLSchema"
xmlns:xsi="http://www.w3.org/2001/XMLSchema-instance">
  <StopExecutingPackagesOnShutdown>true</StopExecutingPackagesOnShutdown>
  <TopLevelFolders>
  <Folder xsi:type="SqlServerFolder">
  <Name>MSDB</Name>
  <ServerName>.</ServerName>
  </Folder>
  <Folder xsi:type="FileSystemFolder">
  <Name>File System</Name>
  <StorePath>..\Packages</StorePath>
  </Folder>
  </TopLevelFolders>
  </DtsServiceConfiguration>
```

There isn't really a lot to configure in this file.

This file has some interesting features. The first configuration line tells the packages how to react if the service is stopped. By default, packages that the service is running will stop if the service stops or fails over. You can reconfigure the packages to continue to run until they complete after the service is stopped by changing the StopExecutingPackagesOnShutDown property to false, as shown here:

```xml
<StopExecutingPackagesOnShutdown>false</StopExecutingPackagesOnShutdown>
```

The most important configuration sections, as shown in the following code, specify which paths and servers the MSDTSServer110 service reads from. Whenever the service starts, it reads this file to determine where the packages are stored. In the default file, there is a single entry for a SQL Server that looks like the following SqlServerFolder example:

```xml
<Folder xsi:type="SqlServerFolder">
<Name>MSDB</Name>
<ServerName>.</ServerName>
</Folder>
```

The <Name> line represents how the name will appear in Management Studio for this set of packages. The <ServerName> line represents where the connection points to. There is a problem, however: If your SQL Server is on a named instance, this file still points to the default non-named instance (.). So, if you do have a named instance, simply replace the period with your instance name.

The next section, seen in the following code, shows you where your file system packages are stored. The <StorePath> property shows the folder where all packages are enumerated from. The default path is C:\program files\microsoft sql server\110\dts\Packages, which is represented as ..\Packages in the default code that follows. This part of the statement goes one directory below the SSIS service file and then into the Packages folder.

```xml
<Folder xsi:type="FileSystemFolder">
<Name>File System</Name>
<StorePath>..\Packages</StorePath>
</Folder>
```

Everything in the Packages folder and subfolders is enumerated. You can create subdirectories under this folder, and they immediately show up in Management Studio without your having to modify the service's configuration file.

> **NOTE** *Each time you make a change to the MsDtsSrvr.ini.xml file, you must stop and start the MSDTSServer110 service.*

TRY IT

In this Try It, you learn how to configure the SSIS service to create a new grouping of packages in a new folder that is going to be monitored. After this lesson, you'll know how to configure the SSIS service if your environment is running packages in the legacy package deployment model.

This section does not require any code to be downloaded.

Lesson Requirements

Configure the SSIS service so that the Package Store contains three folders: File System, MSDB, and File System New, which points to a directory with a few packages in it or your project, like C:\Projects\Personal Trainer (if the directory exists).

Hints

➤ To achieve the goal of this lesson, modify the C:\Program Files\Microsoft SQL Server\110\ DTS\Binn\MsDtsSrvr.ini.xml file.

Step-by-Step

1. Prepare for this lesson by creating a new directory (if it doesn't already exist) called **C:\Projects\Personal Trainer**. Open the C:\Program Files\Microsoft SQL Server\110\DTS\Binn\ MsDtsSrvr.ini.xml file that you will be able to edit in Notepad or your favorite XML editor.

2. Copy and paste the FileSystemFolder node and replace it with the cloned version as follows:

   ```
   <Folder xsi:type="FileSystemFolder">
   <Name>File System New</Name>
   <StorePath>C:\projects\Personal Trainer</StorePath>
   </Folder>
   ```

3. Save the file and then stop and start the SSIS service (SQL Server Integration Services or MSDTSServer110) in the Services applet. You must have access to perform these actions.

4. Open Management Studio and connect to Integration Services to confirm the results. If you see the new File System New folder, you have successfully completed this lesson.

> *Please select Lesson 55 on the DVD, or online at* www.wrox.com/go/ssis2012video, *to view the video that accompanies this lesson.*

56

Securing SSIS Packages

Once you deploy your packages, you want to prevent those who aren't authorized from executing the packages. That's the focus of this lesson. The way you lock down your packages depends on the deployment model. In the package deployment model, the easiest security model is when you deploy to the msdb database. When you deploy your packages with the project deployment model, security is easy and more robust.

SECURING PACKAGES IN THE PACKAGE DEPLOYMENT MODEL

Before you can dive into the topic of securing the package execution, you must first understand a few things about connecting to the SSIS service, which is available to you if you choose to use the package deployment model. The only login option for connecting to the SSIS service is to use your Active Directory account. Once you connect, you see only packages that you are allowed to see. This protection is accomplished based on package roles. Package roles are available only on packages stored in the msdb database. Packages stored on the filesystem must be protected with a password and with Windows security.

You can access package roles in Management Studio by right-clicking a package that you want to protect and selecting Package Roles. The Package Roles dialog box shown in Figure 56-1 enables you to choose the msdb role to be in the writer role and reader role:

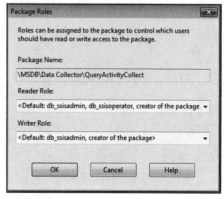

- ➤ The *writer role* can perform administration-type functions, such as overwrite a package with a new version, delete a package, manage security, and stop the package from running.

- ➤ The *reader role* can execute and view the package. The reader role can also export the package from Management Studio.

FIGURE 56-1

Package roles use database roles from the msdb database. By default, people who are in the db_dtsadmin and db_dtsoperator database roles or are the creator of the package can be a reader. The writer role is held by members of the db_dtsadmin database role or the creator of the package by default. When you select the drop-down box in the Package Roles dialog box, you can change the package role from the default one to another customized role from the msdb database.

As a quick example, you may want to customize a group of people as the only ones who can execute the accounting set of packages. Consider then how to secure a package to a role called Accounting for the writer and reader package roles. First, open Management Studio and connect to your development or local database engine instance. Then, expand System Databases ⇨ msdb ⇨ Security, right-click Roles, and select New Database Role. This opens the Database Role - New dialog box. Of course, you need the appropriate security to create a new database role.

Name the role **Accounting** and make your own login a member of the role by clicking the Add button. You can also click Browse to view a list of logins after clicking Add. Additionally, make your own user or dbo an owner of the role in the Owner property. You may have to add your login as a user to the msdb database prior to adding the role if it's not there already.

You're now ready to tie this role to a package. In Management Studio, connect to Integration Services. Right-click any package stored in the msdb database and select Package Role to secure the package. For the writer and reader roles, select the newly created Accounting role and click OK. Now, members of the Accounting role will be able to perform actions on the package, such as execute the package. If you're a member of the sysadmin role for the server, you will be able to perform all functions in SSIS, such as execute and update any package and bypass the package role.

If your packages are stored on the filesystem, you must set a package password on the package to truly secure it. You can also enforce security by protecting the directory with Windows Active Directory security on the file or folder where your packages are stored. To set a package password in SSDT, you can set the ProtectionLevel property to EncryptSensitiveWithPassword and type a password for the PackagePassword property.

To connect to a package store, the SSIS service must be started on the given server. Additionally, you must have TCP/IP port 135 open between your machine and the server. This is a common port used for DCOM, and many network administrators will not have this open by default. You also need to have the SQL Server database engine port open (generally TCP/IP port 1433) to connect to the package store in the msdb database.

SECURING PACKAGES IN THE PROJECT DEPLOYMENT MODEL

With the project deployment model, security is very similar to the packages that are in the msdb database with a few tweaks. Packages stored in the SSIS catalog use users and roles that are in the ssisdb database and are secured at the project or folder level. To secure the packages, right-click the project folder or project and select Properties. Then go to the Permissions tab (shown in Figure 56-2).

Click Browse to select the role or user for which you want to give permission to the project or folder and then select their rights. Read gives permission to see the existence of the package, Modify gives permission to update the package, and Execute gives permission to run the package.

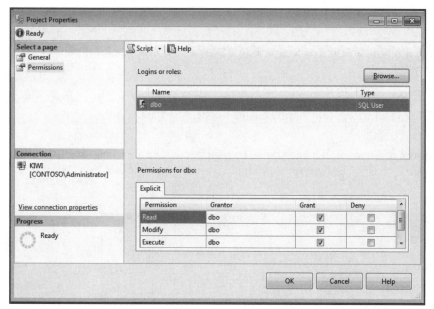

FIGURE 56-2

TRY IT

In this Try It, you make sure that only members of the HR group can execute a package of your choosing. You have just deployed a set of packages, and you now want to lock them down so that no one but the HR group can execute them. After this lesson, you'll have an understanding of how to secure your packages to allow only a given user rights to execute a package.

For this lesson, you will need the ExpeditionDenali.zip project, which is available as part of the Lesson 53 download files from the Wrox website for this book at www.wrox.com.

Lesson Requirements

To successfully complete this lesson, you want to protect your earlier deployed project (ExpeditionDenali) from executing by anyone but employees in the HR group. First, you need to create an HR role and make yourself a member of the role. Then create a package role to prevent anyone but the HR group from running the package.

Hints

➤ Connect to the database instance and create an HR database role in the ssisdb database.

➤ Connect to the database instance and set the HR role in the ExpeditionDenali project to the Execute role.

Step-by-Step

1. Open Management Studio and connect to the SQL Server database engine that has your packages installed.

2. Drill to Databases ⇨ SSISDB ⇨ Security ⇨ Roles.

3. Right-click Roles and select New Database Role to open the Database Role – New dialog box.

4. Type **HR** for the role name and make yourself a member of the role by clicking Add or by typing **dbo** as the owner. The final screen should resemble Figure 56-3. Click OK to save the role.

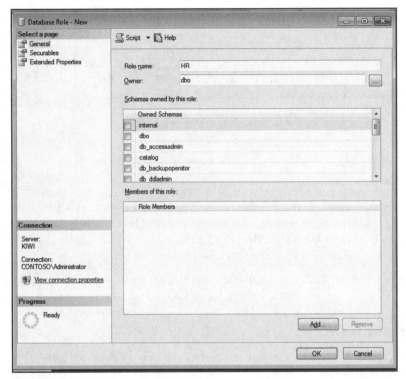

FIGURE 56-3

5. In the Object Browser in Management Studio, select Integration Services Catalogs ⇨ SSISDB, choose the folder you deployed to earlier and select the ExpeditionDenali project.

6. Right-click the ExpeditionDenali project and select Properties.

7. For the reader role for this package (remember from earlier in the lesson that the reader role can execute and view the package), select HR from the drop-down box, as shown in Figure 56-4. Your package can now be run only by the HR group.

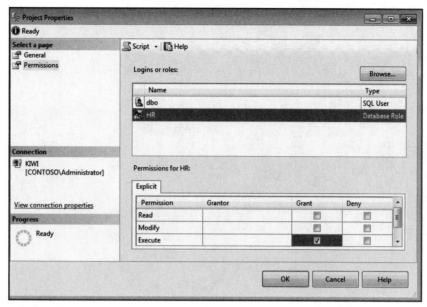

FIGURE 56-4

Please select Lesson 56 on the DVD, or online at www.wrox.com/go/ssis2012video, *to view the video that accompanies this lesson.*

57

Running SSIS Packages

When your packages are deployed, you're ready to run them. In this lesson, you see how to execute a package from a variety of places like Management Studio and from the command line. You also see some of the key differences between 32- and 64-bit machines and some of the items that may not work on a 64-bit machine.

Before you begin, there is one important caveat for packages in the package deployment model deployed to the SQL Server. Even though your package is deployed onto a server, the package uses the resources and runs from whichever machine executes it. For example, say you deploy a package to your production server and then you connect through Management Studio and execute the package from your work laptop. In this case, the package will use your laptop's resources, not the production server's resources, to run the package and will likely overwhelm your laptop. For packages in the project deployment model, this will not be the case. They would run on the server, using its resources.

One way to run a package is through Management Studio. Simply open Management Studio and connect to the Integration Services service for packages in the package deployment model or to the database instance for those stored in the project deployment model.

> **NOTE** *In case you're skipping around, Lesson 55 discusses how to connect and configure the SSIS service.*

Once connected, you can right-click any package and click Run Package (or Execute catalog packages) to execute the package.

EXECUTING PACKAGES IN THE PACKAGE DEPLOYMENT MODEL

After you click Run Package, the Execute Package Utility opens. You can also access this utility by double-clicking any package in Windows Explorer or by just running DTExecUI. The tool wraps a command-line package executor called DTExec.exe.

> **NOTE** *The Execute Package Utility tool executes packages only in 32-bit mode, so if your package requires 64-bit support, you'll need to run the package from a command line with the instructions mentioned later in this lesson.*

When you first open the Execute Package Utility (shown in Figure 57-1), you see that the package is automatically selected for you in the General page. If you enter the tool by just typing the command DTExecUI, it does not have the package name already filled out. (This lesson covers the important pages in the tool and just touches on the pages that you'll rarely use.)

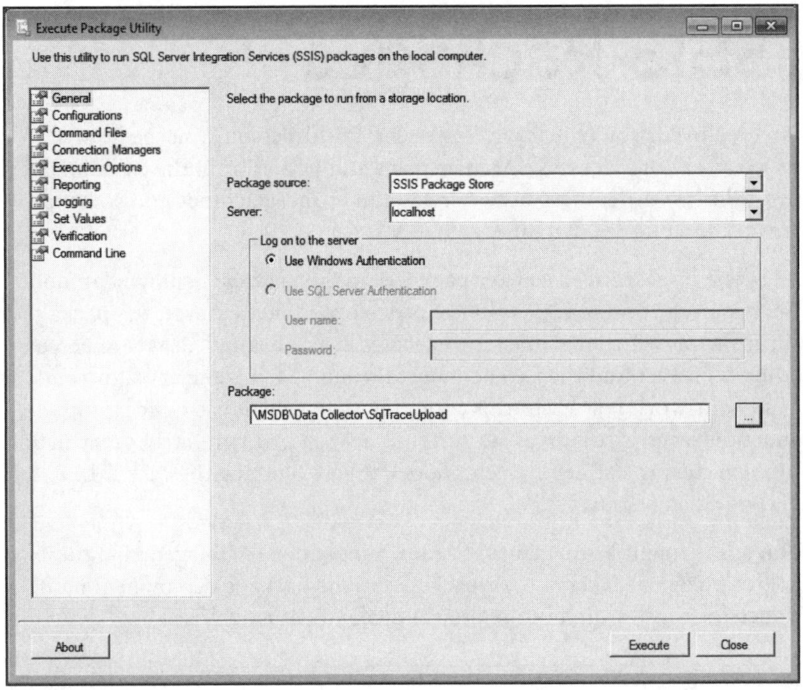

FIGURE 57-1

The next page in the Execute Package Utility is the Configurations page. In this page, you can select additional configuration files that you want to use for this execution of the package. If you do not select an additional configuration file, any configuration files that are already on the server will be used. Even though you may have configuration files already defined in the package, the existing ones will not show in the list here. This is a place where you can only add additional configuration files.

The Command Files page passes additional custom command-line switches into the DTExec.exe application.

The Connection Managers page shows the power of connection managers. This page enables you to change the connection manager settings at run time to a different setting than what the developer had originally intended by simply checking the connection you would like to change and making your changes. For example, perhaps you'd like to move the AdventureWorks2012 connection for a package to a production server instead of a QA server. Another typical example is when you don't have the same drive structure in production as they had in development and you need to move the connection manager to a different directory.

The Execution Options page is where you configure the package's execution runtime environment, such as the number of tasks that will run in parallel.

The Reporting page controls what type of detail will be shown in the console. You may decide that you'd rather show only Errors and Warnings, which would perform slightly better than the Verbose message. You can also control which columns will show in the console.

The Logging page is where you can specify additional logging providers.

Another powerful page is the Set Values page. This page enables you to override nearly any property you want by typing the property path for the property. The most common use for this is to set the value of a variable. To do this, you would use a property path that looked like \Package.Variables[VariableName].Value and then type the value for the variable in the next column. This page is also a way to work around some properties that can't be set through expressions. With those properties, you generally can access them through the property path.

In the Verification page, you can ensure that the package will run only if it's the correct build of the package.

The Command Line page is one of the most important pages in the interface. This page shows you the exact DTExec.exe command that will be executing. You can also edit the command here as well. After the command is edited how you like it, you can copy and paste it in a command prompt after the DTExec.exe command.

Keep in mind that on a 64-bit machine, you have two Program Files directories: C:\Program Files (x86) for 32-bit applications and C:\Program Files for 64-bit applications. A copy of DTExec.exe resides in each of these folders under Microsoft SQL Server\110\Dts\Binn. If you must execute a package in 32-bit mode, you can copy and paste the command from the Command Line page to a command prompt and append this command after the word DTExec.exe (once you're in the appropriate directory). For example, if you're on a 64-bit machine, packages that use Excel at the time of this writing will not work. You'll need to run those packages in 32-bit mode.

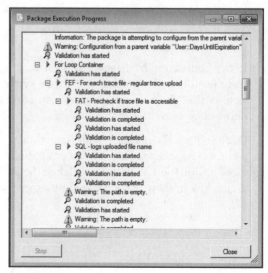

You can also execute the package by clicking the Execute button at any time from any page. After you click the Execute button, you see the Package Execution Progress window, which shows you any warnings, errors, and informational messages, as shown in Figure 57-2. You'll only see a fraction of the message in some cases, but you can hover over the message to see it in full.

FIGURE 57-2

RUNNING PACKAGES IN THE PROJECT DEPLOYMENT MODEL

Running a package in the project deployment model involves connecting to the package catalog in the database instance. Once you are connected, right-click the package under the folder and project and select Execute, which opens the Execute Package dialog box (shown in Figure 57-3). In this General tab, you can change any parameter before you run the package. If the package is using an environment, you can also select the environment you want from the Environment drop-down box.

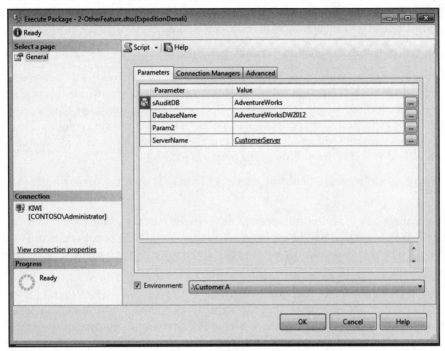

FIGURE 57-3

In the Connection Managers tab (shown in Figure 57-4), you can change connection managers for this execution. Any changes will not be kept permanently and will be rolled back after the execution. In the Advanced tab, you can also select to run the package only in 32-bit mode. Click OK once you're ready to run the package.

Once you run the package, a message similar to what is shown in Figure 57-5 appears. This is telling you that the package has run, but not telling you if it was successful. In the next lesson, you'll see more information about how to debug the packages that have run, but until then, click Yes in this dialog box to show if the package was successful.

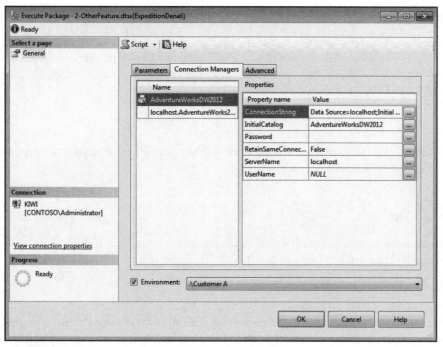

FIGURE 57-4

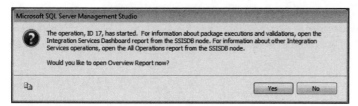

FIGURE 57-5

TRY IT

In this Try It, you learn how to execute a previously created package and change some basic properties prior to execution. You have realized that the original developer of the package left old server information in the package, and you now need to point the connection manager to a different directory to see the file without modifying the package. After this lesson, you will understand how to run a package in Management Studio and change the properties to point to a new directory.

For this lesson you will need the ExpeditionDenali.zip project, which is available as part of the Lesson 53 download files from the Wrox website for this book at www.wrox.com.

Lesson Requirements

To simulate this problem, you are going to execute the package that was deployed and configured earlier in this lesson, 2-OtherFeature.dtsx, which is in the ExpeditionDenali project. Instead of connecting to the AdventureWorks2012 database, try to change the DatabaseName parameter to point to the AdventureWorksDW2012 database.

Hints

➤ Run the package in Management Studio by right-clicking the package and selecting Execute. Go to the General page to change the parameter.

Step-by-Step

1. Open Management Studio, connect to your database instance, and drill into SSIS Catalogs ⇨ Your Folder ⇨ ExpeditionDenali ⇨ 2-OtherFeature.dtsx.

2. Right-click the package and select Execute.

3. Go to the Parameters page and change the Database parameter to AdventureWorksDW2012 by clicking the ellipsis button next to the parameter. You may also have to click Environment and select a customer's environment if you fully completed the Lesson 56 configuration.

4. Run the package by clicking OK.

> *Please select Lesson 57 on the DVD, or online at* www.wrox.com/go/ssis2012video, *to view the video that accompanies this lesson.*

58

Running Packages in T-SQL and Debugging Packages

In the project deployment model, you can run packages in T-SQL and in Windows PowerShell. Doing this is contingent on your having turned on CLR when you created the SSIS catalog. One challenge to running packages in T-SQL is that you don't receive output on whether or not execution of the package was successful. This challenge is addressed in this lesson by discussing how you can use the runtime dashboard to diagnose package failures and to see execution statistics about your packages.

RUNNING THE PACKAGE

The ability to run packages in T-SQL is a game changer for those using SSIS. In the past, when you opened Management Studio from your desktop and executed the package, the package would run on your desktop, not the server. This meant that all the files had to be placed on whatever machine was running the package, not the actual server. When you run packages in SSIS 2012, the server does the actual execution because you can use T-SQL to run the package.

Executing a package in T-SQL enables you to integrate SSIS into your stored procedure or program in a much easier way than you could before. When you run the set of stored procedures that executes the package, it runs the packages as an asynchronous process and does not wait for a success or failure response. Executing the package involves creating an execution thread using the `catalog.create_execution` stored procedure. Then, you set any parameters using the `catalog.set_execution_parameter_value` stored procedure. Finally, you execute the package with the `catalog.start_execution` stored procedure. All of these stored procedures are in the ssisdb database.

The `catalog.create_execution` stored procedure's job is to load the package and prepare it for execution. When you run the stored procedure, it returns a variable called `@execution_id`, which you will need later in the other stored procedures you use. The template for the stored procedure looks like this:

```
create_execution [ @folder_name = folder_name
     , [ @project_name = ] project_name
     , [ @package_name = ] package_name
  [  , [ @reference_id = ] reference_id ]
  [  , [ @use32bitruntime = ] use32bitruntime ]
     , [ @execution_id = ] execution_id OUTPUT
```

Most of the input variables are self-explanatory based on their names, but the one that may need a little explaining is the `@reference_id`, which refers to the folder's environment ID number and is used only if the environment is required. You can find the `@reference_id` environment parameter by querying the `catalog.environment_references` view in the ssisdb database. A completed example is shown here:

```
Declare @execution_id bigint
EXEC [SSISDB].[catalog].[create_execution]
   @package_name=N'2-OtherFeature.dtsx',
   @execution_id=@execution_id OUTPUT,
   @folder_name=N'EDW',
   @project_name=N'ExpeditionDenali',
   @use32bitruntime=False,
   @reference_id=1
```

It's critical that you capture the `@execution_id` for use in the upcoming stored procedures. The first place you'll use it is in the `catalog.set_execution_parameter_value` stored procedure. This stored procedure enables you to set optional parameters into your SSIS package:

```
EXEC [SSISDB].[catalog].[set_execution_parameter_value]
   @execution_id,
   @object_type=50,
   @parameter_name=N'LOGGING_LEVEL',
   @parameter_value=1
```

The last stored procedure to run in the batch is `catalog.start_execution`, which simply executes the package based on the `@execution_id` variable, as shown in the following code:

```
EXEC [SSISDB].[catalog].[start_execution] @execution_id
GO
```

The complete example is shown here in one batch:

```
Declare @execution_id bigint
EXEC [SSISDB].[catalog].[create_execution]
@package_name=N'2-OtherFeature.dtsx',
@execution_id=@execution_id OUTPUT,
@folder_name=N'EDW',
@project_name=N'ExpeditionDenali',
@use32bitruntime=False,
@reference_id=1

Select @execution_id
DECLARE @var0 smallint = 1
```

```
EXEC [SSISDB].[catalog].[set_execution_parameter_value]
@execution_id,
@object_type=50,
@parameter_name=N'LOGGING_LEVEL',
@parameter_value=@var0

EXEC [SSISDB].[catalog].[start_execution] @execution_id
GO
```

What's returned from this batch is simply a number that represents the execution ID. You may want this later when you want to debug if anything has gone wrong in the package. What is not returned, though, is whether or not the package was successful.

DEBUGGING WHEN SOMETHING GOES WRONG

When something goes wrong with a package execution in Management Studio or T-SQL, you won't know unless you have logging turned on or you go into the execution reports. You can access the execution reports by right-clicking the SSIS catalog folder and selecting Reports ➪ Standard Reports ➪ Integration Services Dashboard. This dashboard (shown in Figure 58-1) gives you high-level details of the package's success.

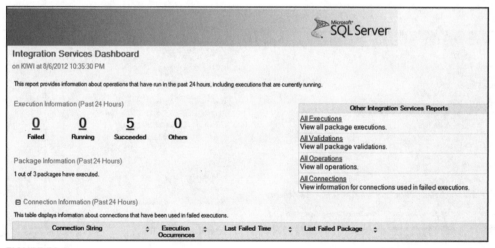

FIGURE 58-1

If you had any failures in the past 24 hours, they'd appear at a high-level in the Connection Information area at the bottom of the report. You can also click one of the numbers (such as the number 5 in Figure 58-1, which shows the successfully run packages) to see an update on the packages that have successfully run in the past 24 hours. After looking at the latest run report, you can view an overview of a given execution by clicking the Overview link in the Execution report (see Figure 58-2). The Overview report gives you the details of what happened in the package's execution (Figure 58-3).

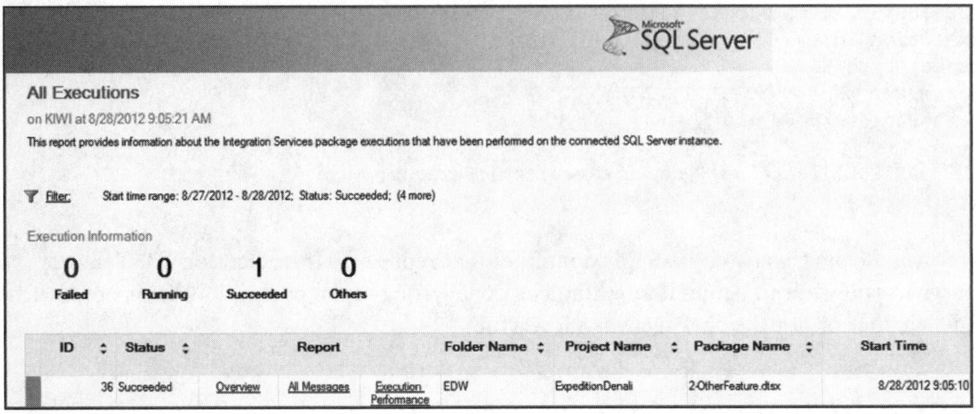

FIGURE 58-2

You can see the complete details of the execution by clicking All Messages (see Figure 58-2). Lastly, you can see the performance of the package under Execution Performance (again, see Figure 58-2), which shows you the last 10 runs of the package and the duration of the runs.

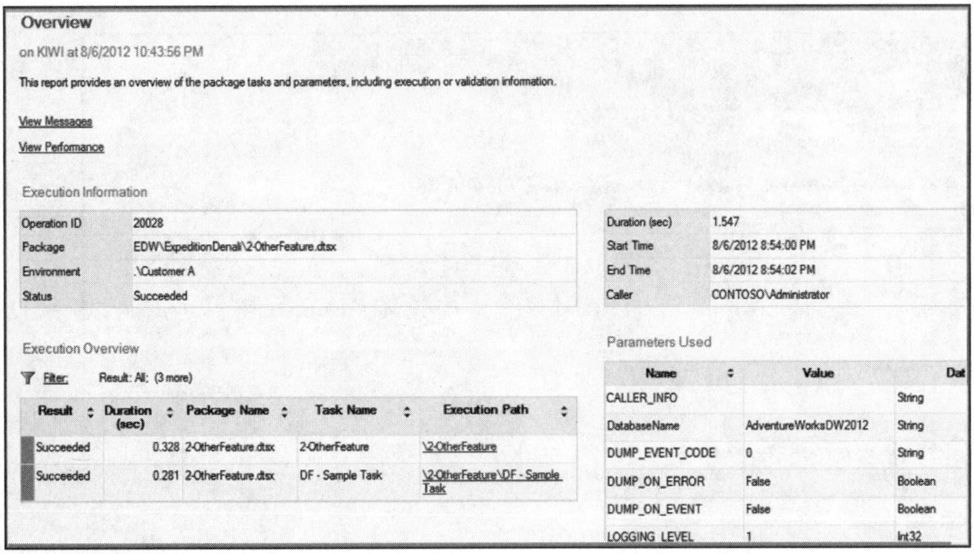

FIGURE 58-3

TRY IT

In this Try It, you learn how to execute a package of your choice through T-SQL. After this lesson, you should be able to integrate package execution into a stored procedure.

You can download the sample code for this lesson from http://www.wrox.com.

Lesson Requirements

Find a package that you've already deployed to your database in the project deployment model and try to execute it in T-SQL. The sample package used in this example is the 2-OtherFeature.dtsx package found in the ExpeditionDenali project you deployed in earlier lessons. You can also download and deploy it (as part of the Lesson 53 download) from this book's companion website at www.wrox.com.

Hints

➤ Use the create_execution and start_execution stored procedures in the catalog schema of the SSISDB database.

Step-by-Step

1. Open Management Studio and connect to your SQL Server instance.

2. Click New Query to open the query window and connect to the SSISDB database.

3. The complete query for our sample database is shown here, but yours may vary if you choose a different package to run. In that case, you'd just change the @package_name parameter. Also, if you've created environments for other folders prior to this exercise, your @reference_id may vary:

```
USE SSISDB
GO
Declare @execution_id bigint
EXEC [SSISDB].[catalog].[create_execution]
    @package_name=N'2-OtherFeature.dtsx',
    @execution_id=@execution_id OUTPUT,
    @folder_name=N'EDW',
    @project_name=N'ExpeditionDenali', @use32bitruntime=False,
    @reference_id=1
  Select @execution_id

EXEC [SSISDB].[catalog].[start_execution] @execution_id
GO
```

> *Please select Lesson 58 on the DVD, or online at* www.wrox.com/go/ssis2012video, *to view the video that accompanies this lesson.*

59

Scheduling Packages

Now that you've learned how to run packages manually, running packages through a schedule is easy. You can schedule them as a job to run automatically through SQL Server Agent or, alternatively, through a third-party scheduler. SQL Server Agent runs jobs under its own Windows account, which can pose some security issues when it comes to accessing components in your package. For example, you may have a package that uses Windows Authentication to access a database. When the package is run through SQL Server Agent, Agent will pass its credentials to the database, which may not be adequate to access the connection. To fix those issues, you can also run packages under a separate Windows account called a proxy account.

To schedule a package through SQL Server Agent, open Management Studio and expand SQL Server Agent ⇨ Jobs. Right-click Jobs and select New Job. Name the job something that you'll recognize at a later time and then go to the Steps page on the left bar and click New at the bottom. This opens the New Job Step dialog box shown in Figure 59-1. A *step* is the smallest unit of work in a job, and it can have a number of different types. For SSIS, the type of job is SQL Server Integration Services Package, so that is the type you select for your step. Next, point to the package you'd like the step to execute, as shown in Figure 59-1. Notice that you can execute packages from the SSIS catalog (for those in the project deployment model) and the msdb and filesystem (for packages in the package deployment model). The other tabs that you see look identical to what was discussed in Lesson 57 in the Package Execution Utility.

After configuration of the step, click OK and then go to the Schedule page on the left. Click New to create a new schedule, set the schedule of how often you want the package to execute, and click OK. You can also execute the job manually by right-clicking on the job under SQL Server agent and selecting Start Job at Step. To look at the job history, right-click the job and select View History.

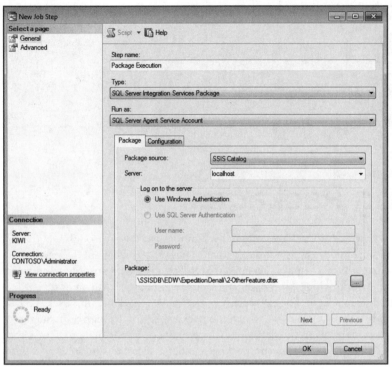

FIGURE 59-1

USING PROXY ACCOUNTS

A classic problem in SSIS is that a package may work in the design environment, but not work once scheduled. Typically, this is because you have connections that use Windows Authentication. At design time, the package uses your credentials, and when you schedule the package, it uses the SQL Server Agent service account by default. This account may not have access to a file share or database server that is necessary to successfully run the package. Proxy accounts in SQL Server enable you to circumvent this problem.

With a *proxy account*, you can assign a job to use an account other than the SQL Server Agent account with the Run as drop-down box, as shown in Figure 59-1. Creating a proxy account is a two-step process:

1. First, you must create a credential that will allow a user to use an Active Directory account that is not his own.

2. Second, you specify how that account can be used.

To first create a credential, open Management Studio, right-click Credentials under the Security tree, and select New Credential. This action opens the New Credential window (shown in Figure 59-2).

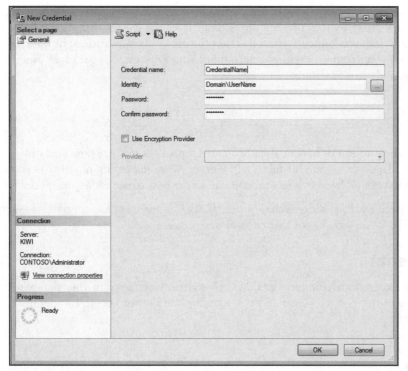

FIGURE 59-2

For this example, you create a credential called CredentialName. The credential allows users to temporarily gain administrator access. For the Identity property, type the name of an administrator account or an account with higher rights. Lastly, type the password for the Windows account and click OK.

> **NOTE** *As you can imagine, because you're typing a password here, be careful of your company's password expiry policies. Credential accounts should be treated as service accounts.*

The next step is to specify how the credential can be used. Under the SQL Server Agent tree, right-click Proxies and select New Proxy, which opens the New Proxy Account dialog box. Type a name for the Proxy name property, and the credential name you created earlier as the Credential name. Check SQL Server Integration Services Package in the "Active to the following subsystems" area to allow SSIS to use this proxy.

Optionally, you can go to the Principals page in the New Proxy Account dialog box to state which roles or accounts can use your proxy from SSIS. You can explicitly grant server roles, specific logins, or members of given msdb roles rights to your proxy. Click Add to grant rights to the proxy one at a time.

You can now click OK to save the proxy. Now if you create a new SSIS job step as was shown earlier, you can use the new proxy by selecting the proxy name from the Run as drop-down box. Any connections that use Windows Authentication then use the proxy account instead of the standard account. This enables you to connect with the account of your choosing for packages using Windows Authentication and prevent failure.

TRY IT

In this Try It, you are in the position of having already created a package and are now ready to schedule it to run nightly. To do this, you schedule a SQL Server Agent job to run nightly to execute your package. After you have completed this lesson, you will know how to schedule your packages.

For this lesson, you will need the ExpeditionDenali project, which is available as part of the Lesson 53 download files from the Wrox website for this book at www.wrox.com.

Lesson Requirements

Find a package from the ExpeditionDenali project that you've already deployed to your database and schedule the package to run nightly. Schedule a package that's in that project to run nightly at midnight.

Hints

➤ Create a new job in Management Studio under SQL Server Agent. The type of the job is SQL Server Integration Services.

Step-by-Step

1. Open Management Studio and connect to your SQL Server instance.

2. Right-click SQL Server Agent (after making sure it is started) and select New ⇨ Job.

3. In the General page, name the job **Test Job**.

4. In the Steps page, click New and name the step **Package Execution**.

5. Select SQL Server Integration Services from the Type drop-down box.

6. Change the properties in the General page in the New Job Step dialog box to point to a package from the ExpeditionDenali project you deployed earlier, as shown in Figure 59-1.

7. Click OK to return to the Steps page and go to the Schedules page.

8. Select New to create a new schedule. Name the schedule and schedule the package to run daily by changing the Frequency drop-down box to Daily, as shown in Figure 59-3.

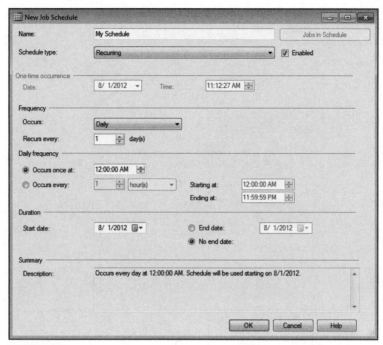

FIGURE 59-3

9. Click OK twice to save the job. Right-click the job and select Start Job at Step to begin the job execution. If a failure occurs, you can right-click the job and select View History to see the failure.

> *Please select Lesson 59 on the DVD, or online at* `www.wrox.com/go/ssis2012video`, *to view the video that accompanies this lesson.*

SECTION 10
Loading a Warehouse

60

Dimension Load

If you have a data warehouse, you've probably been thumbing through this book looking for a way to load your dimension tables. Luckily, what used to take thousands of lines of code is now done with a simple wizard in SSIS. This Slowly Changing Dimension (SCD) Wizard is a Data Flow object that takes all the complexity out of creating a load process for your dimension table.

> **NOTE** *This lesson does not cover a Step-by-Step example on how to build a data warehouse from a design perspective because that is a book in itself.*

Before we discuss the Slowly Changing Dimension Wizard, you must understand a bit of terminology. The wizard can handle three types of dimensions: Type 0, Type 1, and Type 2. Each of these types is defined on a column-by-column basis.

> ➤ A Type 0 (Fixed Attribute) dimension column does not allow you to make updates to it, such as a Social Security number. Even if the source value changes, the change is not propagated to a fixed attribute.

> ➤ A Type 1 (Changing Attribute) dimension handles updates, but does not track the history of such changes.

> ➤ A Type 2 (Historical Dimension) dimension tracks changes of a column. For example, if the price of a product changes and it's a Type 2 column, the original row is expired, and a new row with the updated data is created.

The last term you need to be familiar with is inferred members (also called late arriving dimension members). These happen when you load a fact table and the dimension data doesn't exist yet, such as if you are loading a sale record into the fact table when the product does not exist. Perhaps you get the product data from one server and the sales information from another. The server with the product data was unavailable, but the sales server was available. You, therefore, imported sales information, but were unable to update the product table. There may have been a sale for a product that you were unable to load. In that case, your fact load should create a dimension stub record in the dimension table. When the dimension record finally comes from the source, the transform updates the dimension as if it were a Type 1 dimension, even if it's classified as a Type 2.

To use the Slowly Changing Dimension Wizard, you should first create a Source and Destination Connection Manager, and then create a source component in your Data Flow. Then drag the SCD Transform onto the Data Flow window and connect it to the source. After connecting it to a source or another transform, double-click the transform to open the Slowly Changing Dimension Wizard. The first screen (Figure 60-1) specifies which destination you want to load. First, select the destination connection manager, then the destination table, and then map the source input columns to the target dimension columns. Lastly, select one key to be your business key (the primary key from the source system is sometimes called the alternate key or the business key).

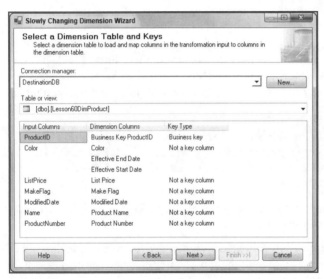

FIGURE 60-1

In the next screen (shown in Figure 60-2), assign a type to each column. These are the slowly changing dimension types discussed earlier. The SCD Wizard calls dimension Type 0 a Fixed Attribute, Type 1 a Changing Attribute, and Type 2 a Historical Attribute. This example uses List Price as Historical. All others will be Changing.

If any of those columns are set to a Historical Attribute, then in a few screens (shown in Figure 60-3) you are asked how you want to expire the row and create a new row. The top section enables you to define a column where you can set a value to Expired, Active, or whatever value you want. The bottom section sets a start date and an end date column to a date system or user variable. Don't worry—all of this can be customized later. The end date column you choose must allow nulls. Current columns will contain null and expired columns will have a non-null end date. All of this is managed by the SCD Task(s).

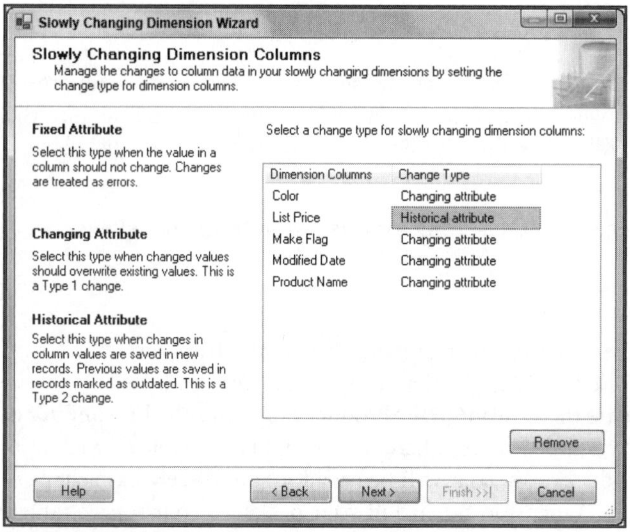

FIGURE 60-2

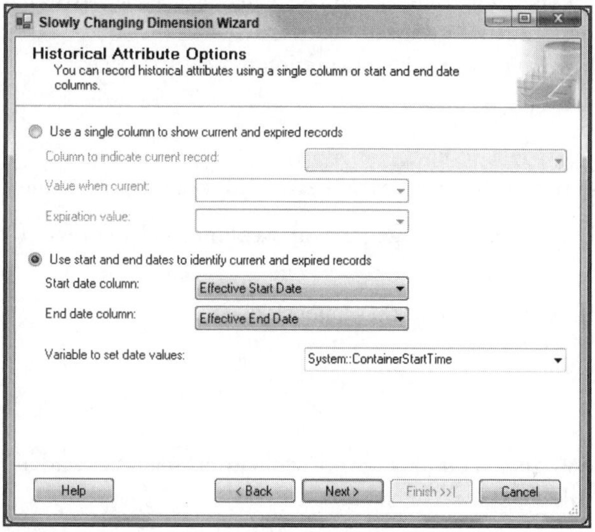

FIGURE 60-3

After you complete the wizard, the template code is created, and your dimension is ready to load. As the Data Flow Task runs, every row is checked to see if the row is a duplicate, new row, or a Type 1 or Type 2 update. Inferred members are also supported. All the code that you see can be customized, but keep in mind that if you change any code and rerun the wizard, the customization will be dropped and the template code will be recreated.

TRY IT

In this Try It, you learn how to use the Slowly Changing Dimension Wizard to load a new product dimension. You then make some changes to the source data and see the changes flow into the dimension table. After this lesson, you will understand how to load a dimension table using the Slowly Changing Dimension Wizard.

You can download the completed package and SQL scripts for this lesson from www.wrox.com.

Lesson Requirements

To complete this lesson, you must have permissions to create and drop tables from the AdventureWorks2012 and AdventureWorksDW2012 databases. To create and load the Lesson60ProductSource table and to create the Lesson60DimProduct table, run the Lesson60Create. sql script in Management Studio. (The Lesson60Create.sql creation script is available at www.wrox .com.) This script will load only four product rows, so it will be easy for you to see what is happening. You will use the Slowly Changing Dimension Wizard in your package. Your source table is Production.Lesson60ProductSource in the AdventureWorks2012 database. The destination table is Production.Lesson60DimProduct and is in AdventureWorksDW2012. The ListPrice column will be a Type 2 (Historical) dimension column. As a business requirement, you must replace null values in the Color column with the value Unknown. The Color column will be treated as a Type 1 (Changing) attribute. After you run the package, run Lesson60Update.sql to make changes to the source table. Then run the package again to propagate those changes to the destination dimension table.

Hints

➤ Use the OLE DB Source to pull data out of the Production.Lesson60ProductSource table.

➤ You can use the Derived Column Transform to change the Color column to Unknown if it is null.

➤ Use the Slowly Changing Dimension Wizard to load the dimension.

Step-by-Step

1. Create a new package called **Lesson60.dtsx**. You may also download this package and all the scripts for this lesson, which are available at www.wrox.com.

2. Create a connection manager to the AdventureWorks2012 database called **SourceDB** and another connection manager to AdventureWorksDW2012 database called **DestinationDB**.

3. Create a Data Flow Task, and in the Data Flow tab, drag an OLE DB Source over. Point the OLE DB Source to the Production.Lesson60ProductSource table in the AdventureWorks2012 database.

4. Connect a Derived Column Transform and configure it to replace the Color column with the following expression:

```
ISNULL(Color) ? "Unknown" : Color
```

5. Drag the Slowly Changing Dimension Transform from the Toolbox and connect the transform to the Derived Column Transform. Open the wizard and go to the Mappings page (shown in Figure 60-1). The Connection Manager property should be set to DestinationDB, and the table should be dbo.Lesson60DimProduct (this table is created by Lesson60Create. sql). Map all the columns by name, but the Name column from the source left side should map to Product Name in the dimension. The ProductID in the input column will map to the Business Key ProductID in the dimension column. Additionally, the Business Key ProductID should be set to the Business key. As you map columns, you may notice that spaces are added in the dimension to make them more user-friendly.

6. The next screen is the Slowly Changing Dimension screen where you assign a dimension type to each column. Set each column to a Changing Attribute except for the List Price, which should be a Historical Attribute, as shown back in Figure 60-2.

7. Click Next to go to the Fixed and Changing Attribute Options screen. You will not need to change any options on this screen, but you can take a look at what is available. On this screen, the Fail the transformation if changes are detected in a fixed attribute option tells the transform how to handle Type 0 changes. When checked, the task will fail if it detects that a fixed attribute has changed. There are no fixed attributes in the example. The second option on this screen applies to changing attributes. The option is Change all matching records, including outdated records, when changes are detected in a changing attribute. A single table may contain both Changing and Historical Attributes. Each time a Historical Attribute changes, a new version of the row is created. What should happen when a fixed attribute changes, especially when that fixed attribute is contained in all historical versions of the record? When checked, the fixed attribute change will automatically be propagated to all versions of the record.

8. Click Next to go to the Historical Attribute screen (shown back in Figure 60-3). Select the Use start and end dates to identify current and expired records option. Set the Start date column box to Effective Start Date and set the End date column box to Effective End Date. Set the Variable to set date values box to System::ContainerStartTime.

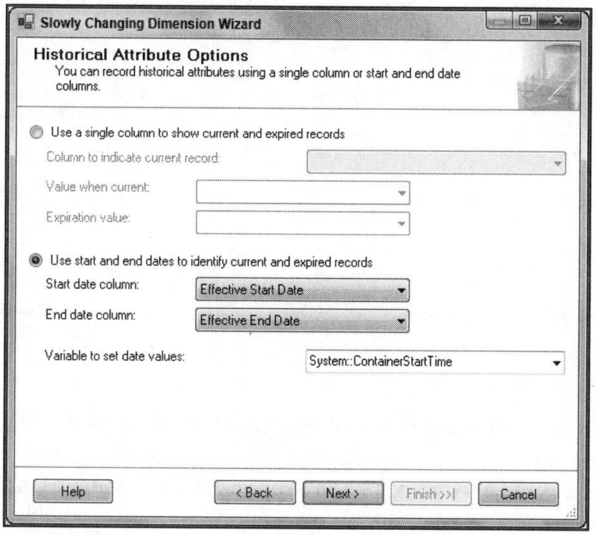

FIGURE 60-3

9. For the remainder of the screens, you can keep the default options. Click Next, and then click Finish to finish the wizard. Run the package, and the results should look like Figure 60-4.

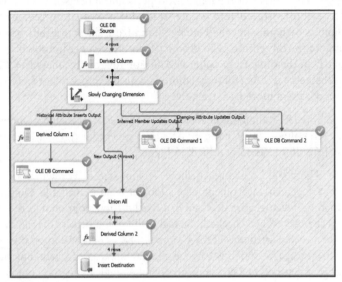

FIGURE 60-4

10. Run Lesson60Select.sql and see that the rows were copied from the source to the destination. Null colors were changed to Unknown and effective Start and End Dates were set. Figure 60-5 shows these results.

	ProductID		Name	ProductNumber	MakeFlag	Color	ListPrice	ModifiedDate
1	1		Adjustable Race	AR-5381	0	NULL	0.00	2008-03-11 10:01:36.827
2	2		Bearing Ball	BA-8327	0	NULL	0.00	2008-03-11 10:01:36.827
3	3		BB Ball Bearing	BE-2349	1	NULL	0.00	2008-03-11 10:01:36.827
4	4		Headset Ball Bearings	BE-2908	0	NULL	0.00	2008-03-11 10:01:36.827

	DWProductID	Business Key P...	Product Name	Product Number	Make Flag	Color	List Pri...	Modified Date	Effective Start Date	Effective End Date
1	1	1	Adjustable Race	AR-5381	0	Unknown	0.00	2008-03-11 10:01:36.827	2012-08-18 10:06:05.000	NULL
2	2	2	Bearing Ball	BA-8327	0	Unknown	0.00	2008-03-11 10:01:36.827	2012-08-18 10:06:05.000	NULL
3	3	3	BB Ball Bearing	BE-2349	1	Unknown	0.00	2008-03-11 10:01:36.827	2012-08-18 10:06:05.000	NULL
4	4	4	Headset Ball Bearings	BE-2908	0	Unknown	0.00	2008-03-11 10:01:36.827	2012-08-18 10:06:05.000	NULL

FIGURE 60-5

11. Run Lesson60Update.sql to make changes to the underlying data. This made a change to a Type 1 column, color was changed to Blue on ProductID = 1. A change was made to a Type 2 column, ListPrice was changed to $2.00 on ProductID = 2. ProductID = 3 was deleted and ProductID = 600 was inserted. All these changes were made to the source. The

script will show you the new source rows and the current destination dimension rows, as in Figure 60-6. The top table is the source with changes, and the bottom table is the current destination.

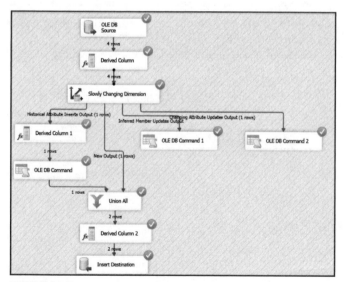

FIGURE 60-6

12. Run your package again. The results should look like Figure 60-7. Only two rows were inserted and one row was updated.

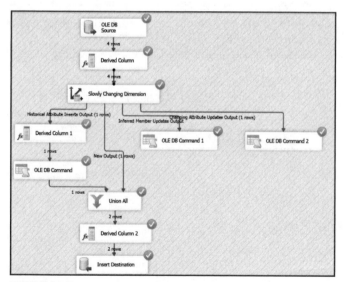

FIGURE 60-7

13. Now run Lesson60Select.sql one more time and see the results of your new package. Be sure to save your package before you exit. Figure 60-8 shows the results. You should see the Changing Attribute color has been changed to blue in place. The Historical Attribute List Price was changed for the Ball Bearing product. It changed from $0.00 to $2.00. You will see the original row with $0.00 as well as the new row. Remember the purpose of Historical Attributes is to retain the history of changes. The new product was added to the dimension. BB Ball Bearings was deleted from the source, but remains in the dimension. We chose to ignore deletions. Dimension members are rarely deleted, because there could be old historical facts that refer to them.

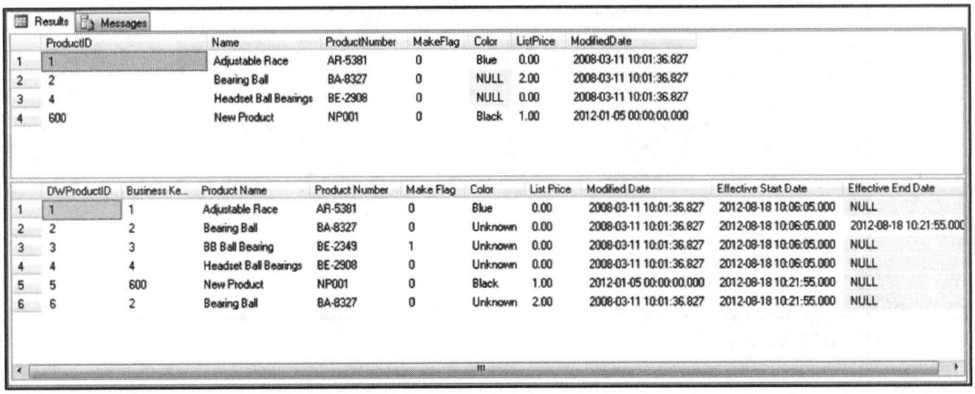

Results | Messages

	ProductID	Name	ProductNumber	MakeFlag	Color	ListPrice	ModifiedDate
1	1	Adjustable Race	AR-5381	0	Blue	0.00	2008-03-11 10:01:36.827
2	2	Bearing Ball	BA-8327	0	NULL	2.00	2008-03-11 10:01:36.827
3	4	Headset Ball Bearings	BE-2908	0	NULL	0.00	2008-03-11 10:01:36.827
4	600	New Product	NP001	0	Black	1.00	2012-01-05 00:00:00.000

	DWProductID	Business Ke...	Product Name	Product Number	Make Flag	Color	List Price	Modified Date	Effective Start Date	Effective End Date
1	1	1	Adjustable Race	AR-5381	0	Blue	0.00	2008-03-11 10:01:36.827	2012-08-18 10:06:05.000	NULL
2	2	2	Bearing Ball	BA-8327	0	Unknown	0.00	2008-03-11 10:01:36.827	2012-08-18 10:06:05.000	2012-08-18 10:21:55.000
3	3	3	BB Ball Bearing	BE-2349	1	Unknown	0.00	2008-03-11 10:01:36.827	2012-08-18 10:06:05.000	NULL
4	4	4	Headset Ball Bearings	BE-2908	0	Unknown	0.00	2008-03-11 10:01:36.827	2012-08-18 10:06:05.000	NULL
5	5	600	New Product	NP001	0	Black	1.00	2012-01-05 00:00:00.000	2012-08-18 10:21:55.000	NULL
6	6	2	Bearing Ball	BA-8327	0	Unknown	2.00	2008-03-11 10:01:36.827	2012-08-18 10:21:55.000	NULL

FIGURE 60-8

Please select Lesson 60 on the DVD, or online at `www.wrox.com/go/ssis2012video`, *to view the video that accompanies this lesson.*

61

Fact Table Load

A fact table is generally much easier to load than a dimension table. Typically, you only insert into the table and don't delete or update rows. Additionally, the components you use for a fact table load are much simpler than the Slowly Changing Dimension Transform you used in the previous lesson.

In a fact table load, the source data coming in contains the natural keys (also known as alternate or business keys) for each of the dimension attributes associated with the fact. You want to replace the business key with the key used in the dimension table. You look up the business key in the dimension table and retrieve the surrogate key (the dimension table's primary key). Then the fact is stored with its dimension keys.

You may want to add additional, derived columns to the fact table. For example, you may want to provide consumers with a Profit column in the fact table, but your source data only has Cost and SellPrice columns, which you will bring into the fact table. These two columns, Cost and SellPrice are enough to determine profit. In the Data Flow Task you would create a Derived Column Transform that applies a formula in the expression, creating the new Profit column.

Another common task is summarizing fact data. Perhaps you have a requirement for a fact that contains ProductID, Date, and SaleAmount. Your source data for this fact contains an additional column—CustomerID. You will need to add up all of the SaleAmounts for each product, for each date, and for all customers. You can do this using an Aggregate Transform. You would do a Group By ProductID and set the operation on Date to Max and SaleAmount to Sum. You could also satisfy this requirement by doing the grouping in your SQL Select statement that reads the source.

TRY IT

Now that you know the components that are involved in a fact table load, in this Try It you load one. After you complete this lesson, you'll have a better understanding of how SSIS can help you load a fact table in your own data warehouse.

To load this warehouse fact table, you'll need to retrieve the surrogate keys from the business key. You can download the completed Lesson61.dtsx and sample files for the lesson from www.wrox.com.

Lesson Requirements

Load a fact table called Lesson61FactFinance (Lesson61CreateTable.sql creates the table) in the AdventureWorksDW2012 database. The source data is a flat file called Lesson61Data.txt. As previously noted, you can download both Lesson61CreateTable.sql and Lesson61Data.txt, as well as a completed package of this lesson (Lesson61.dtsx) from the book's website at www.wrox.com.

Hints

➤ The source file is a tab-separated file with business keys and money values.

➤ Keep in mind that a fact table package is a series of surrogate key lookups. You will have a series of five Lookup Transforms, where you look up the business key in the dimension and return the surrogate key value.

➤ Use a Lookup Transform against the DimOrganization, DimScenario, DimDate, DimAccount, and DimDepartmentGroup dimension tables.

Step-by-Step

1. Run the Lesson61CreateTable.sql script to create the necessary table.

2. Create a new package in SSDT called **Lesson61.dtsx**.

3. Create a connection manager to AdventureWorksDW2012. Name it **AdventureWorksDW2012**.

> **NOTE** *Creating connection managers is first discussed in Lesson 6.*

4. Create a Flat File Connection to the Lesson61Data.txt file that you downloaded from www.wrox.com. In the General page, set the name to **Finance Extract** and select the Column names in the first data row option. In the Advanced page, set the FullDateAlternateKey column's data type to a database date. Set the OrganizationName, DepartmentGroupName, and ScenarioName columns to Unicode string. Set AccountCodeAlternateKey and ParentAccountCodeAlternateKey to four-byte signed integer. Set the Amount column to currency. Click OK to exit.

5. Create a Data Flow Task. In the task, drag a Flat File Source onto the design pane, and link it to the Flat File Connection Manager you just created.

> **NOTE** *Working with Data Flow Tasks and using sources are covered in Lessons 17 and 18, respectively.*

6. Drag a new Lookup Transform onto the Data Flow design pane and link it to the Flat File Source. Name the Lookup Transform **Organization**. In the transform, select DimOrganization as your reference table in the AdventureWorksDW2012 database in the Connection page. In the Columns page, connect OrganizationName from the source to OrganizationName on the DimOrganization table. Check OrganizationKey, as shown in Figure 61-1.

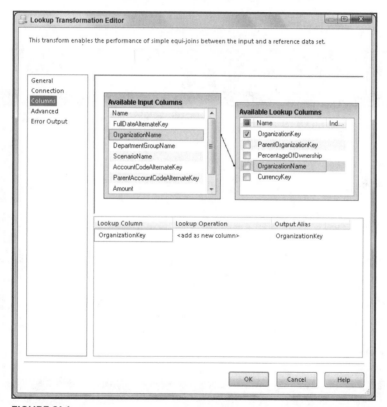

FIGURE 61-1

> **NOTE** *Lookup Transforms are covered in detail in Lesson 24.*

7. Now, repeat the same steps for the DimScenario, DimDate, DimAccount, and DimDepartmentGroup tables. For the DimScenario table, match ScenarioName columns and retrieve the ScenarioKey. For the DimDate table, match FullDateAlternateKey and retrieve DateKey. For DimDepartmentGroup, match DepartmentGroupName and retrieve DepartmentGroupKey. Finally, for DimAccount, you will look up based on two columns. Map AccountCodeAlternateKey from input to lookup and ParentAccountCodeAlternateKey from input to lookup and return AccountKey. Connect the lookup match output from each of the Lookup Transforms together in any order.

8. Connect the final Lookup Transform into a newly created OLE DB Destination. Configure the destination to load the Lesson61FactFinance table.

> **NOTE** *Loading information into destinations is discussed in Lesson 19.*

9. Save and Run the package. The final result should look like Figure 61-2.

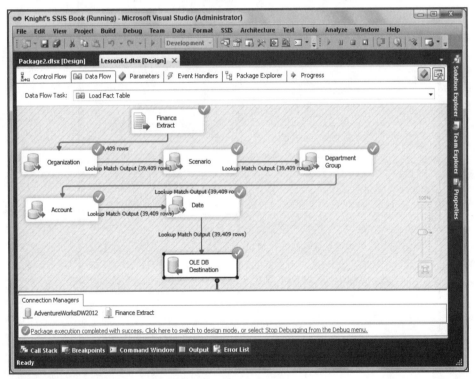

FIGURE 61-2

> *Please select Lesson 61 on the DVD, or online at* www.wrox.com/go/ssis2012video, *to view the video that accompanies this lesson.*

SECTION 11
Wrap Up and Review

62

Bringing It All Together

In the past 61 lessons, you've see most of the common SQL Server Integration Services (SSIS) components, but now it's time to think a little out of the box, or maybe just make the box bigger, and try a complete solution. In this solution, you create a package that performs a load of a few dozen files into a table and audits the fact that you did this. You also build steps in the package to prevent you from loading the same file twice.

> **NOTE** *This lesson assumes that you've gone through the rest of the book to learn the components in a more detailed fashion than will be covered in this lesson. Some of the low-level details in this lesson have intentionally been left out for that reason, but you can see those steps in this lesson's companion video.*

To work the solution in this lesson, you need to download a few files from the book's website at www.wrox.com. The files that accompany this lesson are as follows:

➤ **Lesson62Create.sql**—This is the file that creates the schema you'll be using throughout this lesson.

➤ **Lesson62Data.zip**—This contains the data that you'll be using to load.

➤ **Lesson62DataNextDay.zip**—This contains the data to simulate the next day's data.

➤ **Lesson62.dtsx**—This is a completed version of the package for this lesson.

LESSON REQUIREMENTS

The AdventureWorks, Inc., sales department wants to communicate with voters who signed a certain petition. They also want to ensure that you never load the same file twice, wasting the salesperson's time. Filenames are unique. Your requirements are as follows:

➤ Unzip Lesson62Data.zip into a new folder called C:\Projects\SSISPersonalTrainer\ Lesson62\InputFiles.

➤ Load all the files from the C:\Projects\SSISPersonalTrainer\Lesson62\InputFiles directory into the PetitionData table in the AdventureWorks2012 database.

➤ Log each time you load a file (filename), the number of rows loaded from the file, and when it was loaded (today's date in your case) into the AdventureWorks2012 database in the [Lesson62VoterLoadAudit] table.

➤ As you load the data, ensure the ZIP codes are the standard 5-digit length—ZIP +4 must be truncated.

➤ Archive the file to a new directory called C:\Projects\SSISPersonalTrainer\Lesson62\InputFiles\Archive.

➤ You should be able to rerun the package multiple times and never load the same files twice *even if the duplicate file is in the same directory.*

➤ Whether or not you've already loaded the file, you want to archive the file to an archive folder after loading it or detecting it as a duplicate file.

> **NOTE** *The files have text qualifiers (double quotes) around the columns. You need to handle this in the connection manager.*

➤ After your package successfully runs the first time, unzip Lesson62DataNextDay.zip into the C:\Projects\SSISPersonalTrainer\Lesson62\InputFiles directory to test the duplicate file requirement and rerun your package.

HINTS

To accomplish these goals:

➤ You need a Foreach Loop Container to loop over the files in the input directory, setting the FileName user variable value in each loop.

➤ Set an expression on your Flat File Connection Manager to set the connection string property to be equal to the variable that holds the filename.

➤ Load the flat file into the table by using a Data Flow Task and audit the row count with a Row Count Transform.

➤ Once loaded, audit the fact that the load occurred by using an Execute SQL Task.

➤ Lastly, place an Execute SQL Task as the first task to ensure that the same file can't be loaded twice. The query in the Execute SQL Task should look something like the following: `SELECT COUNT(*) from Lesson62VoterLoadAudit where FileName = ?`. Set the necessary property to capture the single row returned from the query into a variable. Then connect the Execute SQL Task to the Data Flow Task and set the precedence constraint to evaluate the expression to prevent the double-loading of a file. If the audit record exists, then the file has been loaded before.

STEP-BY-STEP

At this point, the step-by-step instructions aren't going to be quite as detailed as before because it's assumed that you know some of the simpler steps. If you still need more granular information, watch the video for this lesson on the accompanying DVD for very incremental steps or take a peek at the completed package. If you have any questions regarding specific tasks or transforms, please review the lessons focusing on them earlier in the book.

1. Run Lesson62Create.sql, which creates the necessary tables for this lesson.

2. Unzip Lesson62Data.zip into the C:\Projects\SSISPersonalTrainer\Lesson62\InputFiles directory. Also create a C:\Projects/SSISPersonalTrainer\Lesson62\InputFiles\Archive directory.

3. Create a new package called **Lesson62.dtsx**.

4. In the Control Flow tab, create two new variables as follows:

    ➤ **Name**—FileCount

    ➤ **Data type**—int32

    ➤ **Default Value**—0

    ➤ **Name**—RowCount

    ➤ **Data type**—int32

    ➤ **Default Value**—0

    Make sure they are scoped to the package name.

5. Create an OLE DB Connection Manager to point to the AdventureWorks2012 database.

6. Create another connection manager, this time a Flat File Connection Manager, which points to any file in the C:\Projects\SSISPersonalTrainer\Lesson62\InputFiles directory. The file is comma delimited and has a text qualifier of a double-quote.

7. Create a new Data Flow Task in the Control Flow window and name it **DF - Load Petition Data**. In the Data Flow tab, drag over a Flat File Source. Configure the Flat File Source to point to the Flat File Connection Manager you just created.

8. Add a Derived Column Transform and connect the Flat File Source to it. In the transform, add the following code to use only the first five characters for the Zip column:

    ```
    SUBSTRING([ZIP],1,5)
    ```

    Set the Derived Column drop-down box to Replace Zip column. This means that the new derived value will replace the value in the existing Zip column.

9. Drag a Row Count Transform over and connect the Derived Column Transform to it. Set the VariableName property to User::RowCount.

10. Drag an OLE DB Destination onto the design pane and connect the Row Count Transform to it. Point the destination to the Lesson62PetitionData table and set the mappings based on column names.

11. Run the package once to make sure the Data Flow works. You should have 4417 rows in the Lesson62PetitionData table. Delete the rows using the following command:

```
Delete
    FROM [AdventureWorks2012].[dbo].[Lesson62PetitionData]
```

12. Drag a Foreach Loop Container into the Control Flow tab. Drag the Data Flow Task into the container.

13. Double-click the Foreach Loop Container to open the Foreach Loop Editor. Go to the Collection page and complete it using the following information:

➤ Enumerator: Foreach File Enumerator

➤ Folder: C:\Projects\SSISPersonalTrainer\Lesson62\InputFiles

➤ Files: *.*

This is shown in Figure 62-1.

In the Variable Mappings page, select <New variable> from the Variable drop-down box and type the new string variable of **FileName**.

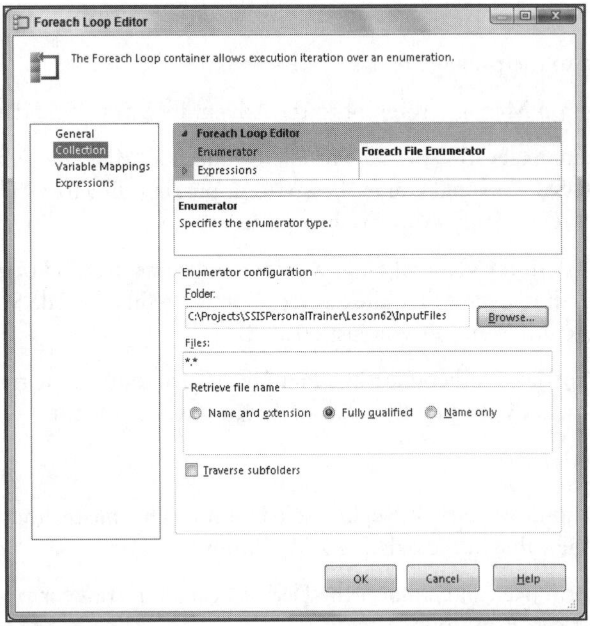

FIGURE 62-1

14.   Drag an Execute SQL Task into the Foreach Loop Container. Position it under the Data
Flow Task and connect the Data Flow Task to it. Name the new task **SQL - Audit Load**.
Set the Connection property to AdventureWorks2012 and set the SQLStatement to the fol-
lowing statement:

```
INSERT INTO Lesson62VoterLoadAudit
    (LoadFile, LoadFileDate, NumberRowsLoaded)
    VALUES (?, GETDATE(), ?)
```

15.   In the Parameter Mapping page, add two parameters, as shown in Figure 62-2.

> **NOTE** *Remember that the Parameter Name is actually the parameter number for
> the OLE DB Connection Manager. Filename is the first "?" in the SQL statement
> and has a parameter number (Name) of 0. The second "?" in the SQL statement
> is a placeholder for the RowCount variable and has a parameter number of 1.*

➤   **Name**—FileName

➤   **Data type**—Varchar

➤   **Parameter Name**—0

➤   **Name**—RowCount

➤   **Data type**—Long

➤   **Parameter Name**—1

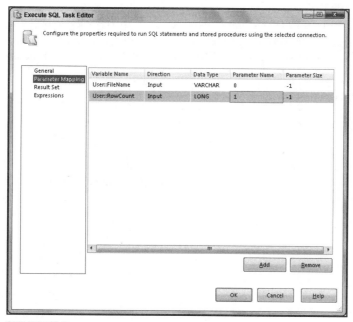

FIGURE 62-2

16. Drag an Expression Task into the For Each Loop Container. Place it at the very top of the container. Set the properties as follows:

➤ **Name**—Initialize RowCount to 0

➤ **Expression**—@[User::RowCount]=0

17. Drag another Execute SQL Task into the Foreach Loop Container, positioned between the Expression Task and the Data Flow Task. Connect the Expression Task to this Execute SQL Task. Connect this Execute SQL Task to the Data Flow Task. Name the task **Has File been Previously Loaded**. Inside the task configuration, set the connection to the AdventureWorks2012 Connection Manager and the ResultSet property to Single Row. Finally, set the SQLStatement to the following:

```
SELECT COUNT(*) From Lesson62VoterLoadAudit
WHERE LoadFile = ?
```

18. In the Parameter Mapping page, add a new parameter as follows:

➤ **Variable Name**—User::FileName

➤ **Data type**—Varchar

➤ **Parameter Name**—0

In the Result Set page, add a new result set:

➤ **ResultName**—0

➤ **Variable Name**—User::FileCount

19. Drag a File System Task into the For Each Loop Container in the Control Flow tab. Connect the last Execute SQL Task (SQL - Audit Load) to the new File System Task. Now configure the File System Task. To set the DestinationConnection property, click it and choose <New Connection> to create a connection manager. Set its Usage Type to Existing Folder, and use the folder C:\Projects\SSISPersonalTrainer\Lesson62\InputFiles\Archive. Set the properties as follows:

➤ **OverwriteDestination**—True

➤ **Operation**—Move file

➤ **SourceConnection**—Flat File Connection Manager

20. Drag a precedence constraint from the Has File been Previously Loaded Task to the SQL - Audit Load Task. Notice that the Has File been Previously Loaded Task now has two precedence constraints from it, as in Figure 62-3.

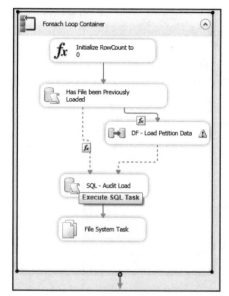

FIGURE 62-3

Now you will direct the flow between the two precedence constraints. For each file, the Has File been Previously Loaded SQL Task counts the number of rows in the audit table for that file. If no rows are in the audit for this file (@FileCount=0), you should go to DF - Load Petition Data. If the file has already been loaded (@FileCount>0), skip the load and go directly to the SQL - Audit Load Task.

21. Double-click the precedence constraint between the first Execute SQL Task and the Data Flow Task. To make sure the Data Flow Task will execute only if the file hasn't loaded yet, set the Evaluation Operator to **Expression and Constraint** and the expression to **@[User::FileCount] == 0**. Repeat the same step for the other precedence constraint coming out of the first Execute SQL Task, but this time set the Expression property to **@[User::FileCount] > 0**.

22. Next, make the Flat File Connection Manager filename dynamic by right-clicking the connection manager and choosing Properties. In the Properties window, click the ellipsis button next to the Expression property. Select the ConnectionString property from the Property drop-down box and type **@[User::FileName]** for the Expression property.

23. Finally, double-click the precedence constraint coming out of the Data Flow Task and change the Multiple Constraints property to a Logical Or. When you click OK, it will make both precedence constraints connecting into the second Execute SQL Task dotted.

24. Run the package and the final results should look like Figure 62-4. You should see the peti-tion rows in the database in Lesson62PetitionData. You should see an audit row for each file in the Lesson62VoterLoadAudit table. If you check the InputFiles folder (C:\Projects\ SSISPersonalTrainer\Lesson62\InputFiles), it should be empty, and all of the files should be copied to the archive subdirectory (C:\Projects\SSISPersonalTrainer\Lesson62\InputFiles\ Archive).

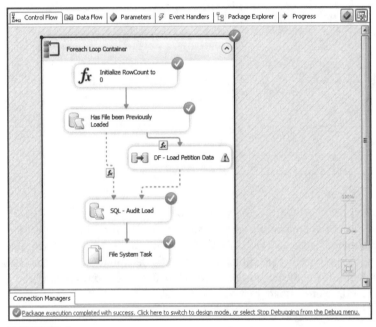

FIGURE 62-4

25. Unzip the Lesson62DataNextDay.zip file into the C:\Projects\SSI2SPersonalTrainer\Lesson62\ InputFiles folder and run it again. This time, some of the files will process and others will skip the processing. Each file is logged into the audit, even if it was previously loaded. You can confirm that some files were previously loaded by looking at the audit table. Look at all the rows for 14395con.dat. You should see two rows, the initial load of 4417 rows, and the second attempt, which loaded 0 rows.

> *Please select Lesson 62 on the DVD, or online at* www.wrox.com/go/ssis2012video, *to view the video that accompanies this lesson.*

SSIS Component Crib Notes

In this appendix, you find a list of the most commonly used tasks and transforms in SSIS with a description of when to use them. Reference these tables when you have a package to build in SSIS and you are not sure which SSIS component to use to perform the needed actions.

WHEN TO USE CONTROL FLOW TASKS

TASKS	WHEN TO USE
CDC Control Task	Use this when SQL Server's Change Data Capture provides the input data. This task manages the date and Log Serial Number (LSN) range used to identify incoming rows. LSNs are just row numbers used to identify rows in the transaction log.
Data Flow Task	Use this task when you need to pass data from a source to a destination. The source and destination can be a flat file, an OLE DB Connection, or any other connections supported in the connection manager.
Execute Package Task	Use this task when you need to call another package from within a package. The package performing the call is the parent package. The called package is the child package. You can pass information from the parent package to the child package with configurations and parameters.
Execute Process Task	Use this task to call an executable. The executable can be a batch file or an application. This task can call applications to perform functions on the files in SSIS, such as compressing a file. This task is commonly used to call third-party programs like compression or FTP tools.

TASKS	WHEN TO USE
Execute SQL Task	Use this task to perform any T-SQL operation. The SQL can be saved directly in the task, in a file, or in a variable. This task is commonly used to call stored procedures.
File System Task	Use this task to manipulate files. This task can move, rename, copy, and delete files and directories. You can also change the attributes of a file. A common use is archiving files after loading them.
FTP Task	Use this task to send or receive a file via the FTP protocol. You must have a valid FTP connection to perform this task. This task is commonly used to receive files from an FTP host for loading in a database.
Message Queue Task	Use this task to send or receive messages to a message queue. You must have a valid MSMQ connection to perform this task.
Script Task	Use this task to perform complex tasks that are not available in SSIS. This task enables you to leverage the .NET Framework to perform just about any task. Checking for the existence of a file is common use of this task. Script Tasks can be coded in VB or C#.
Send Mail Task	Use this task to send e-mail via SMTP. You must have a valid SMTP server connection to use this task. You can use this task to send notification of the package information to recipients. You can also send files via the attachments on the e-mail.
Web Service Task	Use this task to call a web service. You need a valid web service URL to perform this task.
XML Task	Use this task to perform XML functions. This task can perform common XML tasks such as Diff, used to compare two XML files and find the differences.

WHEN TO USE DATA FLOW TRANSFORMS

TRANSFORMS	WHEN TO USE
Aggregate	Use this transform to perform grouping and summing of data. This is similar to the "Group By" function in T-SQL.
Audit	Use this transform to add a column to a Data Flow with package information. You can add items like the package name and user-name as a new column in the Data Flow.

TRANSFORMS	WHEN TO USE
CDC Source	Use this transform when using Change Data Capture to load data. It reads rows from a CDC change table. Rows read are identified by the CDC Control Task.
CDC Splitter	Use this transform to divide a data stream from the CDC Source Task into streams for insert, update, and delete. This is similar to a conditional split, but works specifically with the CDC Source.
Conditional Split	Use this transform to divide data into different paths based on a boolean expression. You can use all the paths from the split or ignore some outputs.
Copy Column	Use this transform to create a new column in the Data Flow that is an exact copy of another column.
Data Conversion	Use this transform to convert data from one data type to another. For example, you can change Unicode to non-Unicode or change a string to an integer.
Derived Column	Use this transform to create or replace a column in the Data Flow with a column created by an expression. You can combine columns or use functions like getdate() to create new data.
DQS Cleansing	Use this transform to run DQS cleansing projects in batch.
Export Column	Use this transform to send a column in a Data Flow to a file. The data types can be DT_TEXT, DT_NTEXT, and DT_IMAGE.
Fuzzy Grouping	Use this transform to group data together based on a percentage match. In this transform, the data does not have to be an exact match to be grouped together. You can control the percentage of matching needed to group the data.
Fuzzy Lookup	Use this transform to find matching data in a table. The data does not have to match exactly. You can control the percentage of matching needed to group the data.
Import Column	Use this transform to import data from files into rows in a data set.
Lookup	Use this transform to compare data in a Data Flow to a table. This will find exact matches in the date and give you a match and no-match output from the transform.
Merge	Use this transform to combine two sets of data similar to a Union All. This transform requires both inputs to be sorted.
Merge Join	Use this transform to combine two sets of data similar to a left outer join. This transform requires both inputs to be sorted.

TRANSFORMS	WHEN TO USE
Multicast	Use this transform to clone the data set and send it to different locations. This transform does not alter the data.
OLE DB Command	Use this transform to send T-SQL commands to a database. You can use this to insert data into a table using the T-SQL Insert command.
Percentage Sampling	Use this transform to select a percentage of the rows in a Data Flow. The rows are randomly selected. You can set a seed to select the same rows on every execution of the transform. The unselected rows will follow a different path in the Data Flow.
Pivot	Use this transform to convert normalized data to denormalized data. This transform changes the rows into columns.
Row Count	Use this transform to write the row count in a Data Flow to a variable.
Row Sampling	Use this transform to select a number of rows in the Data Flow. The number of rows is set in the transform. The unselected rows will follow a different path in the Data Flow.
Script Component	Use this transform to perform complex transforms that are not available in SSIS. This transform enables you to leverage the .NET Framework to perform just about any transform.
Slowly Changing Dimension	Use this transform to create a dimension load for a data warehouse. This is a wizard that will walk you through the decision-making process while setting up a dimensional load.
Sort	Use this transform to order the data by a column or more than one column. This is similar to an "order by" command in T-SQL.
Term Extraction	Use this transform to find words in a Data Flow and create an output with the words listed and a score.
Term Lookup	Use this transform to compare to data in a Data Flow and determine if a word exists in the data.
Union All	Use this transform to combine two sets of data on top of each other. This is similar to the "Union" command in T-SQL.
Unpivot	Use this transform to convert denormalized data to normalized data. This transform changes the columns into rows.

Problem and Solution Crib Notes

This appendix is a result of the culmination of many student questions over years of teaching SSIS classes. After a week of training, students would typically say, "Great, but can you boil it down to a few pages of crib notes for me?" The following table shows you common problems you're going to want to solve in SSIS and a quick solution on how to solve them. These solutions are just crib notes, and you can find most of the details throughout this book or in *Professional Microsoft SQL Server 2012 Integration Services* (Wrox, 2012).

PROBLEM	QUICK SOLUTION
Loop over a list of files and load each one.	**Tasks Required:** Foreach Loop, Data Flow **Task Solution:** Configure the Foreach Loop to loop over any particular directory of files. You should configure the loop to output to a given variable. Map the given variable to a connection manager by using expressions. You can find more on this in Lesson 43.
Conditionally executing tasks.	**Solution:** Double-click the precedence constraint and set the Evaluation property to Expression and Constraint. Type the condition that you want to evaluate in the Expression box. When you are using the Expression and Constraint option, both the specified execution result and the expression condition must be satisfied for the next task to execute.

PROBLEM	QUICK SOLUTION
Pass in variables when scheduling or running a package.	**Solution:** Use the /SET command in the DTExec command line or change the Property tab in the Package Execution Utility to have the property path like \Package.Variables[User::VariableName].Properties[Value]. You can find more on this in Lesson 57.
Move and rename the file at the same time.	**Tasks Required:** File System Task **Solution:** Set the File System Task to rename the file and point to the directory you'd like to move it to. This enables you to rename and move the file in the same step. You can find more on this in Lesson 10.
Loop over an array of data in a table and perform a set of tasks for each row.	**Tasks Required:** Execute SQL Task, Foreach Loop **Solution:** Use an Execute SQL Task to load the array and send the data into an object variable. Loop over the variable in a Foreach Loop by using an ADO Enumerator. You can find more on this in Lesson 43.
Perform an incremental load of data.	**Tasks Required:** Two Execute SQL Tasks, Data Flow Task **Solution:** Have the first Execute SQL Task retrieve a date from a control table of when the target table was last loaded and place that into a variable. In the Data Flow Task, create a date range on your query using the variable. Then, update the control table using a second Execute SQL Task to specify when the table was last updated. You can find more on this in Lesson 36.
Perform a conditional update and insert.	**Components Required:** Data Flow Task, Conditional Split, Lookup Transform or Merge Join, OLE DB Command Transform **Solution:** Use the Lookup Transform or Merge Join to determine if the row exists on the destination and ignore a failed match. If the row yields blank on the key, you know the row should be inserted into target (by a Conditional Split). Otherwise, the row is a duplicate or an update. Determine if the row is an update by comparing the source value to the target value in the Conditional Split. You can perform the update using an OLE DB Command Transform or by loading the data into a staging table.

PROBLEM	QUICK SOLUTION

Create a filename with today's date.	**Expression on the ConnectionString property on the Flat File or File Connection Manager:**
	`"C:\\Projects\\MyExtract" + (DT_WSTR, 30)`
	`(DT_DBDATE)GETDATE() + ".csv"`
	Results in:
	`C:\Projects\MyExtract2009-03-20.csv`

Use a two-digit date. For example, retrieve a month in two-digit form (03 for March instead of 3).	`RIGHT("0"+(DT_WSTR,4)MONTH(Getdate()),2)` **Results in:** 03 (if the month is March)
Multiple condition if statement. In this example, the statement determines that if the ColumnName column is blank or null, it will be set to unknown. To make a Logical AND condition, use && instead of the ∥ operator.	`ISNULL(ColumnName) || TRIM(ColumnName)== "" ?` `"Unknown" : ColumnName`
Return the first five characters from a ZIP code.	**Derived Column Transform in the Data Flow:** `SUBSTRING(ZipCodePlus4,1,5)`
Remove a given character from a string (example shows how to remove dashes from a Social Security number).	**Derived Column Transform in the Data Flow:** `REPLACE(SocialSecurityNumber, "-","")`
Uppercase data.	**Derived Column Transform in the Data Flow:** `UPPER(ColumnName)`
Replace NULL with another value.	**Derived Column Transform in the Data Flow:** `ISNULL(ColumnName) ? "New Value": ColumnName`

Replace blanks with NULL values.	**Derived Column Transform in the Data Flow:**
	`TRIM(ColumnName) == "" ?`
	`(DT_STR,4,1252)NULL(DT_STR,4,1252) :`
	`ColumnName`

PROBLEM	QUICK SOLUTION

Remove any non-numeric data from a column.	**Script Transform in the Data Flow Task with the code as follows:**
	
	``
	Imports System.Text.RegularExpressions
	Public Overrides Sub
	Input0_ProcessInputRow(ByVal Row As
	Input0Buffer)
	 If Row.ColumnName_IsNull = False Or Row.
	ColumnName = "" Then
	    Dim pattern As String =
	String.Empty
	    Dim r As Regex = Nothing
	    pattern = "[^0-9]"
	  r = New Regex(pattern,
	RegexOptions.Compiled)
	 Row.ColumnName =
	Regex.Replace(Row.ColumnName, pattern, "")
	    End If
	End Sub
	``

Convert text to proper case (first letter in each word uppercase).	**Script Transform with the line of partial code as follows (note that this code should go on one line):** ``` Row.OutputName = StrConv(Row.InputName, VbStrConv.ProperCase) ```

What's on the DVD?

This appendix provides you with information on the contents of the DVD that accompanies this book. For the latest and greatest information, please refer to the ReadMe file located at the root of the DVD. Here is what you will find in this appendix:

➤ System Requirements

➤ Using the DVD

➤ What's on the DVD

➤ Troubleshooting

SYSTEM REQUIREMENTS

Make sure that your computer meets the minimum system requirements listed in this section. If your computer doesn't match up to most of these requirements, you may have a problem using the contents of the DVD.

➤ PC running Windows Vista, Windows 7, or later

➤ An Internet connection

➤ At least 512MB of RAM

➤ A DVD-ROM drive

USING THE DVD

To access the content from the DVD, follow these steps.

1. Insert the DVD into your computer's DVD-ROM drive. The license agreement appears

> **NOTE** *The interface won't launch if you have autorun disabled. In that case, start the DVD manually.*

2. Read through the license agreement, and then click the Accept button if you want to use the DVD.

The DVD interface appears. Simply select the lesson number for the video you want to view.

WHAT'S ON THE DVD

This DVD is the most exciting part of this book. With this DVD, you can listen to four geeks who love SSIS work through the lessons you've worked with throughout the book. Because we believe strongly in the value of video training, this DVD contains hours of instructional video. At the end of each lesson in the book, you will find a reference to an instructional video on the DVD that accompanies that lesson. In that video, one of us will walk you through the content and examples contained in that lesson. All you need to do is play the DVD and select the lesson you want to watch. You can also find the instructional videos available for viewing online at www.wrox.com/go/ssis2012video.

TROUBLESHOOTING

If you have difficulty installing or using any of the materials on the companion DVD, try the following solutions:

➤ **Reboot if necessary.** As with many troubleshooting situations, it may make sense to reboot your machine to reset any faults in your environment.

➤ **Turn off any anti-virus software that you may have running.** Installers sometimes mimic virus activity and can make your computer incorrectly believe that it is being infected by a virus. (Be sure to turn the anti-virus software back on later.)

➤ **Close all running programs.** The more programs you're running, the less memory you have available to other programs. Installers also typically update files and programs; if you keep other programs running, installation may not work properly.

➤ **Reference the ReadMe.** Please refer to the ReadMe file located at the root of the DVD-ROM for the latest product information at the time of publication.

CUSTOMER CARE

If you have trouble with the DVD-ROM, please call the Wiley Product Technical Support phone number at (800) 762-2974. Outside the United States, call 1(317) 572-3994. You can also contact Wiley Product Technical Support at http://support.wiley.com. John Wiley & Sons will provide technical support only for installation and other general quality control items. For technical support on the applications themselves, consult the program's vendor or author.

To place additional orders or to request information about other Wiley products, please call (877) 762-2974.

INDEX

John Wiley & Sons, Inc.
End-User License Agreement

READ THIS. You should carefully read these terms and conditions before opening the software packet(s) included with this book "Book". This is a license agreement "Agreement" between you and John Wiley & Sons, Inc. "WILEY". By opening the accompanying software packet(s), you acknowledge that you have read and accept the following terms and conditions. If you do not agree and do not want to be bound by such terms and conditions, promptly return the Book and the unopened software packet(s) to the place you obtained them for a full refund.

1. License Grant. WILEY grants to you (either an individual or entity) a nonexclusive license to use one copy of the enclosed software program(s) (collectively, the "Software") solely for your own personal or business purposes on a single computer (whether a standard computer or a workstation component of a multi-user network). The Software is in use on a computer when it is loaded into temporary memory (RAM) or installed into permanent memory (hard disk, CD-ROM, or other storage device). WILEY reserves all rights not expressly granted herein.

2. Ownership. WILEY is the owner of all right, title, and interest, including copyright, in and to the compilation of the Software recorded on the physical packet included with this Book "Software Media". Copyright to the individual programs recorded on the Software Media is owned by the author or other authorized copyright owner of each program. Ownership of the Software and all proprietary rights relating thereto remain with WILEY and its licensers.

3. Restrictions on Use and Transfer.
(a) You may only (i) make one copy of the Software for backup or archival purposes, or (ii) transfer the Software to a single hard disk, provided that you keep the original for backup or archival purposes. You may not (i) rent or lease the Software, (ii) copy or reproduce the Software through a LAN or other network system or through any computer subscriber system or bulletin-board system, or (iii) modify, adapt, or create derivative works based on the Software.
(b) You may not reverse engineer, decompile, or disassemble the Software. You may transfer the Software and user documentation on a permanent basis, provided that the transferee agrees to accept the terms and conditions of this Agreement and you retain no copies. If the Software is an update or has been updated, any transfer must include the most recent update and all prior versions.

4. Restrictions on Use of Individual Programs. You must follow the individual requirements and restrictions detailed for each individual program in the "About the CD" appendix of this Book or on the Software Media. These limitations are also contained in the individual license agreements recorded on the Software Media. These limitations may include a requirement that after using the program for a specified period of time, the user must pay a registration fee or discontinue use. By opening the Software packet(s), you agree to abide by the licenses and restrictions for these individual programs that are detailed in the "About the CD" appendix and/or on the Software Media. None of the material on this Software Media or listed in this Book may ever be redistributed, in original or modified form, for commercial purposes.

5. Limited Warranty.
(a) WILEY warrants that the Software and Software Media are free from defects in materials and workmanship under normal use for a period of sixty (60) days from the date of purchase of this Book. If WILEY receives notification within the warranty period of defects in materials or workmanship, WILEY will replace the defective Software Media.
(b) WILEY AND THE AUTHOR(S) OF THE BOOK DISCLAIM ALL OTHER WARRANTIES, EXPRESS OR IMPLIED, INCLUDING WITHOUT LIMITATION IMPLIED WARRANTIES OF MERCHANTABILITY AND FITNESS FOR A PARTICULAR PURPOSE, WITH RESPECT TO THE SOFTWARE, THE PROGRAMS, THE SOURCE CODE CONTAINED THEREIN, AND/OR THE TECHNIQUES DESCRIBED IN THIS BOOK. WILEY DOES NOT WARRANT THAT THE FUNCTIONS CONTAINED IN THE SOFTWARE WILL MEET YOUR REQUIREMENTS OR THAT THE OPERATION OF THE SOFTWARE WILL BE ERROR FREE.
(c) This limited warranty gives you specific legal rights, and you may have other rights that vary from jurisdiction to jurisdiction.

6. Remedies.
(a) WILEY's entire liability and your exclusive remedy for defects in materials and workmanship shall be limited to replacement of the Software Media, which may be returned to WILEY with a copy of your receipt at the following address: Software Media Fulfillment Department, Attn.: *<Knight's Microsoft SQL Server 2012 Integration Services 24-Hour Trainer>*, John Wiley & Sons, Inc., 10475 Crosspoint Blvd., Indianapolis, IN 46256, or call 1-800-762-2974. Please allow four to six weeks for delivery. This Limited Warranty is void if failure of the Software Media has resulted from accident, abuse, or misapplication. Any replacement Software Media will be warranted for the remainder of the original warranty period or thirty (30) days, whichever is longer.
(b) In no event shall WILEY or the author be liable for any damages whatsoever (including without limitation damages for loss of business profits, business interruption, loss of business information, or any other pecuniary loss) arising from the use of or inability to use the Book or the Software, even if WILEY has been advised of the possibility of such damages.
(c) Because some jurisdictions do not allow the exclusion or limitation of liability for consequential or incidental damages, the above limitation or exclusion may not apply to you.

7. U.S. Government Restricted Rights. Use, duplication, or disclosure of the Software for or on behalf of the United States of America, its agencies and/or instrumentalities "U.S. Government" is subject to restrictions as stated in paragraph (c)(1)(ii) of the Rights in Technical Data and Computer Software clause of DFARS 252.227-7013, or subparagraphs (c) (1) and (2) of the Commercial Computer Software - Restricted Rights clause at FAR 52.227-19, and in similar clauses in the NASA FAR supplement, as applicable.

8. General. This Agreement constitutes the entire understanding of the parties and revokes and supersedes all prior agreements, oral or written, between them and may not be modified or amended except in a writing signed by both parties hereto that specifically refers to this Agreement. This Agreement shall take precedence over any other documents that may be in conflict herewith. If any one or more provisions contained in this Agreement are held by any court or tribunal to be invalid, illegal, or otherwise unenforceable, each and every other provision shall remain in full force and effect.